SI-YU-KI

BUDDHIST RECORDS
OF
THE WESTERN WORLD

TRANSLATION FROM THE CHINESE
OF HIUTN TSIANG (A.D. 629)

SI-YU-KI

BUDDHIST RECORDS OF THE WESTERN WORLD

TRANSLATION FROM THE CHINESE
OF HIUTN TSIANG (A.D. 629)

SAMUEL BEAL

IN TWO VOLUMES
VOL. II

GYAN

Published by

GYAN

Gyan Publishing House
5, Ansari Road
Daryaganj, New Delhi-110002
Phone: 011-47034999, 9811692060
E-mail: books@gyanbooks.com

Distribution Network
gyanbooks.com
India, USA, Canada, UK, Australia, France

ISBN : 978-81-212-4545-6 (Set)
ISBN : 978-81-212-5038-2 (HB)
First Published, London, 1884

2nd Impression 2020

Printed at: Gyan Press, Delhi.

Si-Yu-Ki
Buddhist Records of the Western World Vol. II
Author: Samuel Beal

VOLUME II

CONTENTS.

BUDDHIST RECORDS OF THE WESTERN WORLD.

BOOK VI.

Contains an account of four countries, viz., (1) *Shi-lo-fu-shi-ti*; (2) *Kie-pi-lo-fa-su-tu*; (3) *Lan-mo*; (4) *Ku-shi-na-k'ie-lo.*

SHI-LO-FU-SHI-TI [ŚRÂVASTI].

THE kingdom of Śrâvastî (Shi-lo-fu-shi-ti)[1] is about 6000 li in circuit. The chief town is desert and ruined. There is no record as to its exact limits (*area*). The ruins of the walls encompassing the royal precincts[2] give a circuit

[1] The town of Śrâvastî, also called Dharmapaṭṭana (*Trikâṇḍaśêsha*, ii. 1, 13), in Uttara (Northern) Kôśala, has been identified by Cunningham with a great ruined city on the south bank of the Râptî called Sâhet Mâhet, about 58 miles north of Ayôdhyâ. As Hiuen Tsiang gives the bearing north-east, and the distance about 500 li, he evidently did not travel by the shortest route. Fa hian (chap. xx.), on the contrary, gives the distance eight *yôjanas*, and the bearing (corrected) due north, both of which are correct. For a full account of Sâhet Mâhet see Cunningham, *Arch. Survey of Ind.*, vol. i. p. 331 ff.; see also *J. R. As. S.*, vol. v. pp. 122 ff. It figures also in Brahmanical literature, in which it is said to have been founded by Śrâvasta, the son of Śrâva and grandson of Yuvanâśva. *Harivaṁśa*, 670; *Vishṇ. Pur.*, vol. iii. p. 263; Hall's *Vâsavadattâ*, Int. p. 53; *Mahâbhâr.*, iii. 12518; Pâṇini, iv. 2, 97; *Bhâgav. Pur.*, ix. 6, 21. With respect, however, to the date of Vikramâditya of Śrâvastî, Cunningham seems to be misled by the statement of Hiuen Tsiang (*ante*, p. 106) that he lived in the middle of the thousand years after Buddha, as though this meant 500 A.B., whereas it means, as stated before, in the middle of the thousand years which succeeded the 500 years after Buddha, in the middle of the "period of images," in fact. See also Burnouf, *Introd.*, pp. 20 f., 150, 209, 280; Lassen, *Ind. Alt.*, vol. iii. pp. 200 f.; Vassilief, pp. 38, 75, 188, 218.

[2] Julien translates here and elsewhere *kung shing* by *palace*, but it

of about 20 li. Though mostly in ruins, still there are a few inhabitants. Cereals grow in great abundance; the climate is soft and agreeable, the manners of the people are honest and pure. They apply themselves to learning, and love religion (*merit*). There are several hundreds of *saṅghârâmas*, mostly in ruin, with very few religious followers, who study the books of the Saṁmatîya (Ching-liang-pu) school. There are 100 Dêva temples with very many heretics. When Tathâgata was in the world, this was the capital of the country governed by Prasênajita-râja (Po-lo-si-na-chi-to-wang).[3]

Within the old precincts of the royal city are some ancient foundations; these are the remains of the palace of King Shing-kwan (Prasênajita).

From this not far to the east is a ruinous foundation, above which is built a small *stûpa;* these ruins represent the Great Hall of the Law,[4] which King Prasênajita built for Buddha.

By the side of this hall, not far from it, above the ruins a *stûpa* is built. This is where stood the *vihâra* which King Prasênajita built for Prajâpatî[5] Bhikshunî, the maternal aunt of Buddha.

should be "the royal precincts," or the portion of the city in which the royal palace stood, and which was defended by a surrounding wall. Cunningham is right therefore in his remarks on this point, p. 332, *loc. cit.*

[3] Prasênajit :—In the *Aśôka Avadâna* the following genealogy is given :—

1. Bimbisâra (cir. B.C. 540–512).
2. Ajâtaśatru, his son, 512.
3. Udayibhadra, his son, 480.
4. Muṇḍa, his son, 46.
5. Kâkavarṇin, his son, 456.
6. Sahâlin, his son.
7. Tulakuchi, his son.
8. Mahâmaṇḍala, his son, cir. 375.
9. Prasênajit, his son.
10. Nanda, his son.
11. Bindusâra, his son, 295.
12. Susîma, his son.

Little dependence, however, can be placed on this genealogy, but it may be compared with the Singhalese and Brahmanical lists, *J. As. S. Ben.*, vol. vi. p. 714; *Asiat. Res.*, vol. v. p. 286; Lassen, *Ind. Alt.*, vol. i. pp. 859, xxxviii., vol. ii. pp. 71, 222, 1207; Burnouf, *Intr.*, pp. 128, 320; Burgess, *Archæol. Surv. W. India, Rep.*, vol. v. p. 43, and *Cave Temples*, pp. 24 f. On Prasênajit, see Köppen, *Die Rel. d. Bud.*, vol. i. pp. 98, 113, 495, 507; *Vishṇ. Pur.*, vol. iv. p. 171; *Mahâbhâr.*, ii. 332, iii. 11072, xii. 5924; *Hariv.*, 709 f., 2054.

[4] The Saddharma Mahâśâlâ.

[5] Prajâpatî, formerly written, as a note tells us, *Pajapati*, with the meaning "lord of creatures;" it may be observed here that Hiuen Tsiang is the first to introduce the *Sans-*

Still east of this is a *stûpa* to record the site of the house of Sudatta[6] (Shen-shi).

By the side of the house of Sudatta is a great *stûpa*. This is the place where the Aṅgulimâlya (Yang-kiu-li-mo-lo) gave up his heresy. The Aṅgulimâlyas[7] are the unlucky caste (*the criminals*) of Srâvastî. They kill everything that lives, and maddening themselves, they murder men in the towns and country, and make chaplets for the head of their fingers. The man in question wished to kill his mother to complete the number of fingers, when the Lord of the World (Buddha), moved by pity, went to him to convert him. Beholding the Lord from far, the Aṅgulimâlya rejoicing said, "Now I shall be born in heaven; our former teacher declared that whoever injures a Buddha or kills his mother, ought to be born in the Brahmâ heaven."

Addressing his mother, he said, "Old woman! I will leave you for a time till I have killed that great Shaman." Then taking a knife, he went to attack the Lord. On this Tathâgata stepped slowly as he went, whilst the Aṅgulimâlya rushed at him without slacking his pace.

The Lord of the World addressing him said, "Why do you persevere in your evil purpose and give up the better feelings of your nature and foster the source of evil?" The Aṅgulimâlya, hearing these words, understood the wickedness of his conduct, and on that paid reverence to Buddha, and sought permission to enter the law (*i.e., the religious profession of Buddha*), and having persevered with

krit forms of proper names into the Chinese translations. Before him the Prâkṛit, or provincial, forms are used; for example, in Fa-hian, instead of Po-lo-si-na-chi-to for Prasênajita, we have Po-sz-nih, corresponding with Pasênat or Pasênadi; instead of Śrâvastî, we have She-wei for Sewet, &c. For further instances see *Fo-sho-hing-tsan-king*, p. 213, notes 1, 2.

[6] Sudatta, formerly written Su-ta, the same as Anâthapiṇḍada, "the friend of the orphan and destitute." For an account of his conversion and subsequent career, see *Fo-sho-hing-tsan-king*, p. 201, f.

[7] The Aṅgulimâlyas were a sect founded by a converted brigand, who wore round his neck a string of fingers.

diligence in his religious progress, he obtained the fruit of an Arhat.

To the south of the city 5 or 6 li is the Jêtavana.[8] This is where Anâthapiṇḍada (Ki-ku-to) (*otherwise called*) Sudatta, the chief minister of Prasênajita-râja, built for Buddha a *vihâra*. There was a *saṅghârâma* here formerly, but now all is in ruins (*desert*).

On the left and right of the eastern gate has been built a pillar about 70 feet high; on the left-hand pillar is engraved on the base a wheel;[9] on the right-hand pillar the figure of an ox is on the top. Both columns were erected by Aśôka-râja. The residences (*of the priests*) are wholly destroyed; the foundations only remain, with the exception of one solitary brick building, which stands alone in the midst of the ruins, and contains an image of Buddha.

Formerly, when Tathâgata ascended into the Trâyastriṁśas heaven to preach for the benefit of his mother, Prasênajita-râja, having heard that the king Udâyana had caused a sandal-wood figure of Buddha to be carved, also caused this image to be made.

The nobleman Sudatta was a man of "humanity" and talent. He had amassed great wealth, and was liberal in its distribution. He succoured the needy and destitute, and had compassion on the orphan and helped the aged. During his lifetime they called him Anâthapiṇḍada (Ki-ku-to—*friend of the orphan*) on account of his virtue. He, hearing of the religious merit of Buddha, conceived a

[8] Shi-to-lin, the garden of Jêta, the prince royal. For the sale of this garden to Sudatta (Shen-shi) and the circumstances attending it, see *Fo-sho-hing tsan-king*, p. 217. For a representation of the scene of the history, see *Bharhut Stûpa*, pl. lvii.

[9] Julien's translation of this passage is very confusing. He says, "On the top of the left-hand pillar is a dome (*coupole*); on the pinnacle (*faite*) of the right-hand pillar is sculptured the body of an elephant." But, in fact, the text says, "On the face (pedestal, *twan*) of the left-hand pillar is the mark (*figure*) of a wheel (the symbol of *dharma*); on the top of the right-hand pillar is the form of an ox. This is in agreement with Fa-hian's account. The only doubt is whether *twan* may not mean "the top;" in that case the wheel would be on the top of the left-hand pillar, as Fa-hian says (chap. xx.)

deep reverence for him, and vowed to build a *vihâra* for him. He therefore asked Buddha to condescend to come to receive it. The Lord of the World commanded Śâriputra (She-li-tseu) to accompany him and aid by his counsel. Considering the garden of Jêta (Shi-to-yuen), the prince, to be a proper site on account of its pleasant and upland position, they agreed to go to the prince to make known the circumstances of the case. The prince in a jeering way said, "If you can cover the ground with gold (*pieces*) I will sell it (*you can buy it*)."

Sudatta, hearing it, was rejoiced. He immediately opened his treasuries, with a view to comply with the agreement, and cover the ground. There was yet a little space not filled.[10] The prince asked him to desist, but he said, "The field of Buddha is true;[11] I must plant good seed in it." Then on the vacant spot of ground[12] he raised a *vihâra.*

The Lord of the World forthwith addressed Ânanda and said, "The ground of the garden is what Sudatta has bought; the trees are given by Jêta. Both of them, similarly minded, have acquired the utmost merit. From this time forth let the place be called the grove of Jêta (Shi-to) and the garden of Anâthapiṇḍada (Ki-ku-to).

To the north-east of the garden of Anâthapiṇḍada (Ki-ku-to) is a *stûpa.* This is the place where Tathâgata washed with water the sick Bhikshu. Formerly, when Buddha was in the world, there was a sick Bhikshu (Pi-tsu), who, cherishing his sorrow, lived apart by himself in a

[10] This incident of the broken promise is referred to by Aśvaghôsha, *Fo-sho-hing-tsan-king*, p. 217, and seems to be the subject of the Bharhut sculpture, pl. xlv. fig. 9, where "the little space not filled" is represented, and the broken promise denoted by the broken surface of the ground. It would perhaps be too bold to suggest *chitu pâdâsi-la* for the inscription, where *pâdâsi* would be the aorist form of *pradâ*, and the meaning would be "taken or caught (*la*) in breaking what he gave." The tree certainly favours this identification; and the august figure by the side of Jêta would denote the "Lord of the World," or perhaps "the magistrate" or Śâriputra.

[11] *I.e.*, the system of Buddha is founded on *truth;* alluding to the wish of Jêta to annul the agreement.

[12] *I.e.*, where there were no trees.

solitary place. The Lord of the World seeing him, inquired, "What is your affliction, living thus by yourself?" He answered, "My natural disposition being a careless one and an idle one, I had no patience to look on a man sick (*to attend on the sick*),[13] and now when I am entangled in sickness there is nobody to look on me (*attend to me*)." Tathâgata, moved with pity thereat, addressed him and said, "My son! I will look on you!" and then touching him, as he bent down, with his hand, lo! the sickness was immediately healed; then leading him forth to the outside of the door, he spread a fresh mat for him and himself, washed his body and changed his clothes for new ones.

Then Buddha addressed the Bhikshu, "From this time be diligent and exert yourself." Hearing this, he repented of his idleness, was moved by gratitude, and, filled with joy, he followed him.

To the north-west of the garden of Anâthapiṇḍada is a little *stûpa*. This is the place where Mudgalaputra (Mo-te-kia-lo-tseu) vainly exerted his spiritual power in order to lift the girdle (*sash*) of Śâriputra (She-li-tseu). Formerly, when Buddha was residing near the lake Wu-jeh-no,[14] in the midst of an assembly of men and Dêvas, only Śâriputra (She-li-tseu) was absent (*had not time to join the assembly*). Then Buddha summoned Mudgalaputra, and bade him go and command him to attend. Mudgalaputra accordingly went.

Śâriputra was at the time engaged in repairing his religious vestments. Mudgalaputra addressing him said, "The Lord, who is now dwelling beside the Anavatapta lake, has ordered me to summon you."

Śâriputra said, "Wait a minute, till I have finished repairing my garment, and then I will go with you."

[13] This differs from Julien's version; he makes the fault of the Bhikshu to consist in neglecting his own sickness; but it seems rather to have been his former indifference to the sickness of others. For an incident somewhat like that in the text, see *Sacred Books of the East*, vol. xvii. p. 241.

[14] No feverish affliction, *i.e.*, cool; *antavatapta*. See *ante*, vol. i. p. 11, note 28.

Mudgalaputra said, "If you do not come quickly, I will exert my spiritual power, and carry both you and your house to the great assembly."

Then Śâriputra, loosing his sash, threw it on the ground and said, "If you can lift this sash, then perhaps my body will move (*or*, then I will start)." Mudgalaputra exerted all his spiritual power to raise the sash, yet it moved not. Then the earth trembled in consequence. On returning by his spiritual power of locomotion to the place where Buddha was, he found Śâriputra already arrived and sitting in the assembly. Mudgalaputra sighing said, "Now then I have learned that the power of working miracles is not equal to the power of wisdom."[15]

Not far from the *stûpa* just named is a well. Tathâgata, when in the world, drew from this well for his personal use. By the side of it is a *stûpa* which was built by Aśôka-râja; in it are some *śarîras*[16] of Tathâgata; here also are spots where there are traces of walking to and fro and preaching the law. To commemorate both these circumstances, (*the king*) erected a pillar and built the *stûpa*. A mysterious sense of awe surrounds the precincts of the place; many miracles are manifested also. Sometimes heavenly music is heard, at other times divine odours are perceived. The lucky (*happy*) presages (*or*, the omens that indicate religious merit) would be difficult to recount in full.

Not far behind the *saṅghârâma* (*of Anâthapiṇḍada*) is the place where the Brahmachârins killed a courtesan, in order to lay the charge of murdering her on Buddha (*in order to slander him*). Now Tathâgata was possessed of the tenfold powers,[17] without fear,[18] perfectly wise, honoured

[15] Mudgalaputra excelled all the other disciples in miraculous power, Śâriputra excelled in wisdom. *Fo-sho-hing-tsan king*, ver. 1406.

[16] There is no mention of Śâriputra in the text, as Julien translates; the two symbols, *she li*, for *śarîra*, misled him.

[17] Buddha was called *Daśabala* (*shi-li*) on account of the ten powers he possessed, for which see Burnouf, *Lotus*, p. 781, and Hardy, *Manual of Budhism*, p. 394.

[18] Abhaya, an epithet given to every Buddha (Eitel, *Handbook*, s. v.)

by men and Dêvas,[19] reverenced by saints and sages; then the heretics consulting together said, "We must devise some evil about him, that we may slander him before the congregation." Accordingly they allured and bribed this courtesan to come, as it were, to hear Buddha preach, and then, the congregation having knowledge of the fact of her presence, they (*the heretics*) took her and secretly killed her and buried her body beside a tree, and then, pretending to be affected with resentment, they acquainted the king (*with the fact of the woman's death*). The king ordered search to be made, and the body was found in the Jêtavana. Then the heretics with a loud voice said, "This great Śramaṇa Gautama[20] is ever preaching about moral duty and about patience (*forbearance*), but now having had secret correspondence with this woman, he has killed her so as to stop her mouth; but now, in the presence of adultery and murder, what room is there for morality and continence?" The Dêvas then in the sky joined together their voices and chanted, "This is a slander of the infamous heretics."

To the east of the *saṅghârâma* 100 paces or so is a large and deep ditch; this is where Dêvadatta,[21] having plotted to kill Buddha with some poisonous medicine, fell down into hell. Dêvadatta was the son of Drônôdana-râja (Ho-wang). Having applied himself for twelve years with earnestness, he was able to recite 80,000 (*verses*) from the treasury of the law. Afterwards, prompted by covetousness, he wished to acquire the divine (*supernatural*) faculties. Associating himself with evil companions, they consulted together, and he spake thus: "I possess thirty marks (*of a Buddha*), not much less than Buddha himself; a great

[19] Devamanussapujitam.

[20] This is Buddha's gôtra name, taken from the name probably of the Purôhita of the Śâkyas. It is used in Northern books as a term of disrespect.

[21] Dêvadatta (Ti-po-ta-to) the cousin of Buddha, being the son of Drônôdana, Buddha's uncle. He is also said to be his brother-in-law, being brother to Yaśôdhara, Buddha's wife. He was tempted to aim at the first place in the Buddhist community, and when he failed in this he plotted to take the life of Buddha. (See Oldenberg, *Buddha*, p. 160.)

company of followers surround me; in what respect do I differ from Tathâgata?" Having thought thus, he forthwith tried to put a stumbling-block in the way of the disciples, but Śâriputra and Mudgalaputra, obedient to Buddha's behest, and endowed with the spiritual power of Buddha himself, preached the law exhorting the disciples to re-union. Then Dêvadatta, not giving up his evil designs, wickedly placed some poison under his nails, designing to kill Buddha when he was paying him homage. For the purpose of executing this design he came from a long distance to this spot, but the earth opening, he went down alive into hell.

To the south of this again there is a great ditch, where Kukâlî[22] the Bhikshunî slandered Tathâgata, and went down alive into hell.

To the south of the Kukâlî ditch about 800 paces is a large and deep ditch. Chanścha,[23] the daughter of a Brâhmaṇ, calumniated Tathâgata, and here went down alive into hell. Buddha was preaching, for the sake of Dêvas and men, the excellent doctrines of the law, when a female follower of the heretics, seeing from afar the Lord of the World surrounded by a great congregation who venerated and reverenced him, thought thus with herself, "I will this very day destroy the good name of this Gautama, in order that my teacher may alone enjoy a wide reputation." Then tying a piece of wood next her person, she went to the garden of Anâthapiṇḍada, and in the midst of the great congregation she cried with a loud voice and said, "This preacher of yours has had private intercourse with me, and I bear his child in my womb, the offspring of the Śâkya tribe." The heretics all believed it, but the prudent knew it was a slander. At this time, Śakra, the king of Dêvas, wishing to dissipate all doubt about the matter, took the form of a

[22] Kukâlî (Kiu-kia-li-pi-tsu) also called Kôkâlî, interpreted "bad time." She is also called Gôpâlî; she was a follower of Dêvadatta.

[23] For the history of this woman, called Chinchî (Chan-che) or Chinchîmanâ, see Hardy, *Manual of Buddhism*, p. 275; also Fa-hian, chap. xx.

white rat, and nibbled through the bandage that fastened the (*wooden*) pillow to her person. Having done so, it fell down to the ground with a great noise, which startled the assembly. Then the people, witnessing this event, were filled with increased joy; and one in the crowd picking up the wooden bolster, held it up and showed it to the woman, saying, "Is this your child, thou bad one?" Then the earth opened of itself, and she went down whole into the lowest hell of Avîchî, and received her due punishment.

These three ditches[24] are unfathomable in their depth; when the floods of summer and autumn fill all the lakes and ponds with water, these deep caverns show no signs of the water standing in them.

East of the *saṅghârâma* 60 or 70 paces is a *vihâra* about 60 feet high. There is in it a figure of Buddha looking to the east in a sitting posture. When Tathâgata was in the world in old days, he discussed here with the heretics. Farther east is a Dêva temple of equal size with the *vihâra*. When the sun is rising, the Dêva temple does not cast its shade on the *vihâra*, but when it is setting, the *vihâra* obscures the Dêva temple.

Three or four li to the east of the *vihâra* "which covers with its shadow" is a *stûpa*. This is where Śâriputra discussed with the heretics. When Sudatta first bought the garden of the Prince Jêta for the purpose of building a *vihâra* for Buddha, then Śâriputra accompanied the nobleman to inspect and assist the plan. On this occasion six masters of the heretics sought to deprive him of his spiritual power. Śâriputra, as occasion offered, brought them to reason and subdued them. There is a *vihâra* by the side, in front of which is built a *stûpa*; this is where Tathâgata defeated the heretics and acceded to the request of Viśâkhâ.[25]

[24] These gulfs or ditches have all been identified by Cunningham. See *Arch. Survey*, vol. i. p. 342.

[25] That is, accepted her offer to build a *vihâra*. For the history of Viśâkhâ, see Hardy, *Man. of Budh.*, p. 220 seq.

On the south of the *stûpa* erected on the spot where Buddha acceded to Viśâkhâ's request is the place where Virûḍhaka-râja,[26] having raised an army to destroy the family of the Śâkyas, on seeing Buddha dispersed his soldiers. After King Virûḍhaka had succeeded to the throne, stirred up to hatred by his former disgrace, he equipped an army and moved forward with a great force. The summer heat being ended and everything arranged, he commanded an advance. At this time a Bhikshu, having heard of it, told Buddha; on this the Lord of the World was sitting beneath a withered tree; Virûḍhaka-râja, seeing him thus seated, some way off alighted from his chariot and paid him reverence, then as he stood up he said, "There are plenty of green and umbrageous trees; why do you not sit beneath one of these, instead of under this withered one with dried leaves, where you walk and sit?" The Lord said, "My honourable tribe is like branches and leaves; these being about to perish, what shade can there be for one belonging to it?" The king said, "The Lord of the World by his honourable regard for his family is able to turn my chariot." Then looking at him with emotion, he disbanded his army and returned to his country.

By the side of this place is a *stûpa;* this is the spot where the Śâkya maidens were slaughtered. Virûḍhaka-râja having destroyed the Śâkyas, in celebration of his victory, took 500 of the Śâkya maidens for his harem. The girls, filled with hatred and rage, said they would never obey the king, and reviled the king and his household. The king, hearing of it, was filled with rage, and ordered them all to be slaughtered. Then the officers, obedient to the king's orders, cut off their hands and feet, and cast them into a ditch. Then all the Śâkya maidens, nursing their grief, invoked Buddha. The Lord

[26] Virûḍhaka was the son of Prasênajit by a servant-woman of the Śâkyas. He had asked a wife of them, and they deceived him. See *infra*.

by his sacred power of insight having beheld their pain and agony, bade a Bhikshu take his garment and go to preach the most profound doctrine to the Śâkya girls, viz., on the bonds of the five desires, the misery of transmigration in the evil ways, the pain of separation between loved ones, and the long period (*distance*) of birth and death. Then the Śâkya maidens, having heard the instructions of Buddha, put away the defilement of sense, removed all pollutions, and obtained the purity of the eyes of the law; then they died and were all born in heaven. Then Śakra, king of Dêvas, taking the form of a Brâhmaṇ, collected their bones and burnt them. Men of succeeding years have kept this record.

By the side of the *stûpa* commemorating the slaughter of the Śâkyas, and not far from it, is a great lake which has dried up. This is where Virûḍhaka-râja went down bodily into hell. The world-honoured one having seen the Śâkya maidens, went back to the Jêtavana, and there told the Bhikshus, "Now is King Virûḍhaka's end come; after seven days' interval a fire will come forth to burn up the king." The king hearing the prediction, was very frightened and alarmed. On the seventh day he was rejoiced that no harm had come, and in order to gratify himself he ordered the women of his palace to go to the lake, and there he sported with them on its shores, strolling here and there with music and drinking. Still, however, he feared lest fire should burst out. Suddenly, whilst he was on the pure waters of the lake, the waves divided, and flames burst forth and consumed the little boat in which he was, and the king himself went down bodily into the lowest hell, there to suffer torments.

To the north-west of the *saṅghârâma* 3 or 4 li, we come to the forest of *Obtaining-Sight* (Âptanêtravana?) where are vestiges of Tathâgata, who walked here for exercise, and the place where various holy persons have engaged in profound meditation. In all these places they have erected posts with inscriptions or else *stûpas*.

Formerly there was in this country a band of 500 robbers, who roamed about through the towns and villages and pillaged the border of the country. Prasênajita-râja having seized them all, caused their eyes to be put out and abandoned them in the midst of a dark forest. The robbers, racked with pain, sought compassion as they invoked Buddha. At this time Tathâgata was in the *vihâra* of the Jêtavana, and hearing their piteous cries (*i.e., by his spiritual power*), he was moved to compassion, and caused a soft wind to blow gently from the Snowy Mountains, and bring with it some medicinal (*leaves?*) which filled up the cavity of their eye-sockets. They immediately recovered their sight, and lo! the Lord of the World was standing before them. Arriving at the heart of wisdom, they rejoiced and worshipped. Fixing their walking-staves in the ground, they departed. This was how they took root and grew.

To the north-west of the capital 16 li or so, there is an old town. In the Bhadra-kalpa when men lived to 20,000 years, this was the town in which Kâśyapa Buddha was born. To the south of the town there is a *stûpa*. This is the place where he first met his father after arriving at enlightenment.

To the north of the town is a *stûpa*, which contains relics of the entire body[27] of Kâśyapa Buddha. Both these were built by Aśôka-râja. From this point going south-east 500 li or so, we come to the country of Kie-pi-lo-fa-sse-ti (Kapilavastu).

KIE-PI-LO-FA-SU-TU [KAPILAVASTU].

This country[28] is about 4000 li in circuit. There are

[27] The expression used here is the same as that employed by Fa-hian when speaking of the great Kâśyapa (chap. xxxiii.), whose "entire body" is preserved in the Cock's-foot Mountain near Buddha Gayâ.

[28] This is the country of Buddha's birth. The story of his ancestors' occupation of this district will be found in Sp. Hardy, *Man. of Budh.*, chap. vi., and elsewhere. Speaking generally, the country of Kapilavastu is the tract of land lying be-

some ten desert[29] cities in this country, wholly desolate and ruined. The capital is overthrown and in ruins. Its circuit cannot be accurately measured. The royal precincts[30] within the city measure some 14 or 15 li round. They were all built of brick. The foundation walls are still strong and high. It has been long deserted. The peopled villages[31] are few and waste.

There is no supreme ruler; each of the towns appoints its own ruler. The ground is rich and fertile, and is cultivated according to the regular season. The climate is uniform, the manners of the people soft and obliging. There are 1000 or more ruined *saṅghârâmas* remaining; by the side of the royal precincts there is still a *saṅgâhrâma* with about 3000 (*read* 30) followers in it, who study the Little Vehicle of the Saṁmatîya school.

There are a couple of Dêva temples, in which various sectaries worship (*live*). Within the royal precincts are some ruined foundation walls; these are the remains of the proper[32] palace of Śuddhôdana-râja; above is built a *vihâra* in which is a statue of the king. Not far from this is a ruined foundation, which represents the sleeping

tween the Ghâgrâ river and the Gaṇḍakâ, from Faîzâbâd to the confluence of these rivers. The direct measurement gives a circuit of 550 miles, which would represent upwards of 600 miles by road. Hiuen Tsiang estimates the circuit at 4000 li. The capital of the country, called by the same name, has been identified by Mr. Carlleyle, with a site called Bhuila, in the north-western part of the Basti district, about 25 miles north-east from Faîzâbâd. It is plain that if this is so, the distance from Śrâvastî given by Hiuen Tsiang is much in excess of the actual distance. See *Arch. Survey of India*, vol. xii. p. 83.

[29] The expressions used in the text are very marked; the pilgrim says "desert cities ten in number are waste and desolate to the highest degree."

[30] Here we have again the expression *kung shing* to denote the fortified part of the town, within which was the palace and its surroundings. This is in agreement with Mr. Carlleyle's remark in *Archæolog. Survey of India*, vol. xii. p. 144.

[31] Or, the inhabited suburbs or streets.

[32] It may be either "the proper," *i.e.*, private, or "the principal" palace (*ching*). From Mr. Carlleyle's remarks we may perhaps conclude that this palace was situated in the southern portion of the enclosed precinct. The *vihâra* had evidently been built after the palace was in ruins. The statue of the king seems to have been there in Hiuen Tsiang's time.

palace of Mahâmâyâ,[33] the queen. Above this they have erected a *vihâra* in which is a figure of the queen.

By the side of this is a *vihâra;*[34] this is where Bôdhisattva descended spiritually into the womb of his mother. There is a representation of this scene[35] drawn in the *vihâra.* The Mahâsthavira school say that Bôdhisattva was conceived on the 30th night of the month *U-ta-lo-'an-sha-cha* (Uttarâshâḍha). This is the 15th day of the 5th month (*with us*). The other schools fix the event on the 23d day of the same month. This would be the 8th day of the 5th month (*with us*).

To the north-east of the palace of the spiritual conception is a *stûpa;* this is the place where Asita the Ṛishi prognosticated the fortune (*took the horoscope or signs of*) the royal prince.[36] On the day when the Bôdhisattva was born there was a gathering (*a succession*) of lucky indications. Then Śuddhôdana-râja summoned all the soothsayers, and addressing them said, "With respect to this child, what are the fortunate and what the evil (*signs*)? As it is right, so do you clearly answer me." In reply they said, "According to the record of the former saints the signs are especially fortunate. If he remains in secular life he will be a Chakravartin monarch; if he leaves his home he will become a Buddha."[37]

[33] Mr. Carlleyle excavated a site which he thinks represents this "bed-chamber." If we may judge from the size of the building (71 feet square), it would represent the palace of the king and the chamber of the queen. The fact of its being built of "very large ancient bricks" certainly favours the identification of the place with the inner city described by Hiuen Tsiang.

[34] Mr. Carlleyle places this *vihâra* about 50 feet W.N.W. from the bed-chamber ruins, the *stûpa* of Asita being situated to the north-east of it.

[35] This representative scene is one of the best known of the Buddhist sculptures. See *Tree and Serpent Worship*, pl. xxxiii.; *Stûpa of Bharhut*, pl. xxviii.; *Lalita Vistara* (Foucaux), pl. v.

[36] The horoscope cast by Asita the soothsayer is another well-known incident in the Buddhist legend *Fo-sho-hing-tsan-king*, vv. 70 ff. For an interesting representation of it see Mrs. Speirs' *Life in Ancient India*, p. 248, also Burgess, *Cave Temples* (Ajaṇṭâ), p. 308. The *stûpa* of Asita is supposed by Mr. Carlleyle to be the solid brick structure he found about 400 feet N.N.E.½N. from the bed-chamber of Mâyâ. This may be so; but the horoscope was actually cast within the palace.

[37] Arrive at complete, equal, perfect,

At this time the Ṛĭshi Asita, coming from afar, stood before the door,[38] and requested to see the king. The king, overjoyed, went forth to meet and reverence him, and requested him to be seated on a precious chair; then addressing him he said, "It is not without an object that the Great Ṛĭshi has condescended to visit me this day." The Ṛĭshi said, "I was quietly resting (*or*, observing the summer rest) in the palace of the Dêvas, when I suddenly saw the multitude of the Dêvas dancing together for joy.[39] I forthwith asked why they rejoiced in this extravagant way, on which they said, 'Great Ṛĭshi, you should know that to-day is born in Jambudvîpa, of Mâyâ, the first queen of Śuddhôdana-râja of the Śâkya line, a royal son, who shall attain the complete enlightenment of *sambôdhi*, and become all-wise.'[40] Hearing this, I have come accordingly to behold the child; alas! that my age should prevent me awaiting the holy fruit."[41]

At the south gate of the city is a *stûpa*. This is where the royal prince, when contending with the Śâkya princes, cast the elephant away.[42] The royal prince having contended in the public competition (*of arts and athletic exercises*), was left entirely alone (*without compeer*) among them all, (*or*, in every exercise). And now the

wisdom. "To leave his home" means, if he becomes a hermit or ascetic. The signs on the child's body are alluded to in ver. 45 of the *Buddha-charita* (*Fo-sho-hing-tsan-king*), and the exact words of the prediction in the following verse, 46.

[38] From this it is plain that the site on which the *stûpa* was afterwards built was originally a part of the palace.

[39] *Shau mo tsuh to*, moving their hands and feet. Such a scene among the Dêvas will be found in *Tree and Serpent Worship*, pl. lxxiii. fig. 2.

[40] Julien remarks in a note that this phrase *yeh tsai chi* (Sambuddhasa) corresponds to the name given to the prince, viz., Sarvârthasiddha, but this signifies "possessed of every excellency" (*yih tsai yau i*).

[41] That is, either seeing him arrived at the holy fruit of a Buddhha, or myself arriving at the holy fruit of an Arhat by his teaching.

[42] The spot should be just inside the southern gate of the city, not necessarily the royal city or the palace precincts, but the entire city. The story as it is generally received is that the elephant when it fell blocked the gate entrance, and that Nanda pulled it off the road and left it on one side. The prince then flung the elephant across the moat. It must, therefore, have been within the moat.

Mahârâja Śuddhôdana, after receiving congratulations (*or*, congratulating him), was about to go back to the city.[43]

At this time the coachman was leading out the elephant and just about to leave the city. Dêvadatta, confident as ever in his brute strength, was just entering the gate from without; forthwith he asked the coachman, "Who is going to ride on this gaily caparisoned elephant?" He said, "The royal prince is just about to return, therefore I am going to meet him." Dêvadatta, in an excited manner, pulled the elephant down, and struck his forehead and kicked his belly, and left him lying senseless, blocking the way so that no one could pass. As they could not move him out of the way, the passers-by were stopped on their route. Nanda coming afterwards, asked, "Who has killed the elephant?" They said, "It was Dêvadatta." Forthwith he (*Nanda*) drew it on one side of the road. The prince-royal then coming, again asked, "Who had done the foul deed of killing the elephant?" They replied, "Dêvadatta killed it and blocked up the gate with it, and Nanda drew it on one side to clear the road." The royal prince then lifted the elephant on high and threw it across the city moat; the elephant falling on the ground caused a deep and wide ditch; the people since then have commonly called it "the fallen-elephant ditch."[44]

By the side of this is a *vihâra* in which is a figure of the royal prince. By the side of this again is a *vihâra*; this was the sleeping apartment of the queen and the prince; in it is a likeness of Yaśôdharâ and (*the child*)

[43] Julien makes this return refer to the prince. But there is no mention made of him, but of the king.

[44] That is, the "Hastigarta." There is a circular tank about 340 feet to the south of the ditch of Bhuila which is still called the "Hâthi Kund" or "Hâthi Gadhe." General Cunningham is perfectly convinced that this is the spot indicated in the text (*Arch. Surv.*, vol. xii. Introd.) But, of course, the whole matter is legendary. The *vihâras* by the side of this ditch, and said to be built on the site of the palace of the prince and his wife, would indicate that his palace was outside the walls; how, then, are we to explain the story of his flight from the palace?

Râhula. By the side of the queen's chamber is a *vihâra* with a figure of a pupil receiving his lessons; this indicates the old foundation of the school-house of the royal prince.

At the south-east angle of the city is a *vihâra* in which is the figure of the royal prince riding a white and high-prancing horse;[45] this was the place where he left the city. Outside each of the four gates of the city there is a *vihâra* in which there are respectively figures of an old man, a diseased man, a dead man, and a Śramaṇ.[46] It was in these places the royal prince, on going his rounds, beheld the various indications, on which he received an increase of (*religious*) feeling, and deeper disgust at the world and its pleasures; and, filled with this conviction, he ordered his coachman to return and go home again.

To the south of the city going 50 li or so, we come to an old town where there is a *stûpa*. This is the place where Krakuchchhanda Buddha was born, during the Bhadra-kalpa when men lived to 60,000 years.[47]

To the south of the city, not far, there is a *stûpa*; this is the place where, having arrived at complete enlightenment, he met his father.

To the south-east of the city is a *stûpa* where are that Tathâgata's relics (*of his bequeathed body*); before it is erected a stone pillar about 30 feet high, on the top of which is carved a lion.[48] By its side (*or*, on its side) is a

[45] Julien gives "a white elephant."

[46] That is, the sights which met the prince's gaze when he left the city on his excursion. These predictive signs are well known. They are found also in the History of Barlaam and Joasaph (Bodhisat), to which I called attention in the year 1869, *Buddhist Pilgrims*, p. 86, n. Mr. Carlleyle notices four mounds outside the citadel of Bhuila corresponding with the sites of these *vihâras*.

[47] Krakuchchhanda was the first of the five Buddhas of the Bhadra-kalpa. The fabled birthplace of this Buddha must be sought about a *yôjana* (8 miles) to the south-west of Kapilavastu, and not, as Mr. Carlleyle indicates, at Nagra, 7½ miles to the north-west of that place. Fa-hian visited this place after leaving Śrâvastî, then went north about 8 miles, then east 8 miles to Kapilavastu. *Ind. Ant.*, vol. xi. p. 293.

[48] Mr. Carlleyle, when at Nagra, thought he had discovered the pedestal on which this pillar stood; the pillar was gone, and the natives denied all knowledge of it or its history. Their ignorance is not to

record relating the circumstances of his *Nirvâṇa*. It was erected by Aśôka-râja.

To the north-east of the town of Krakuchchhanda Buddha, going about 30 li, we come to an old capital (*or*, great city) in which there is a *stûpa*. This is to commemorate the spot where, in the Bhadra-kalpa when men lived to the age of 40,000 years, Kanakamuni Buddha was born.[49]

To the north-east of the city, not far, is a *stûpa;* it was here, having arrived at complete enlightenment, he met his father.

Farther north there is a *stûpa* containing the relics of his bequeathed body; in front of it is a stone pillar with a lion on the top, and about 20 feet high; on this is inscribed a record of the events connected with his *Nirvâṇa;* this was built by Aśôka-raja.

To the north-east of the city about 40 li is a *stûpa*. This is the spot where the prince sat in the shade of a tree to watch the ploughing festival. Here he engaged in profound meditation and reached the condition of "absence of desire."[50] The king seeing the prince in the shade of the tree and engrossed in quiet contemplation, and observing that whilst the sun's rays shed their bright light around him, yet the shadow of the tree did not move,

be wondered at, considering they lived 16 or 18 miles from the site named by Hiuen Tsiang.

[49] Kanakamuni, a mythological person, the second of the five Buddhas of the Bhadra-kalpa. His birthplace is identified by Mr. Carlleyle with a village called Kanakpur, about a *yôjana* to the west of Kapilavastu. As this distance and bearing agree with Fa-hian's account, and nearly so with that of Hiuen Tsiang, it may be correct.

[50] This incident is recorded in all the Lives of Buddha. See *Fo-sho-hing-tsan-king*, vv. 330 ff. The figure of the prince lost in meditation under the Jambu tree will be found in *Tree and Serpent Worship*, pl. xxv. fig. 1, where the leaves or flowers of the tree are bent down to cover the young prince, from the top of whose head the light of profound meditation proceeds, whilst the figures searching throughout the garden, and looking in at the three palaces of the prince, denote the perplexity of his attendants and father, as to his whereabouts. See the particulars in the *Romantic Legend of Buddha*.

his heart, recognising the spiritual character of the prince, was deeply reverent.

To the north-west of the capital there are several hundreds and thousands of *stûpas*, indicating the spot where the members of the Śâkya tribe were slaughtered. Virûḍhaka-râja having subdued the Śâkyas, and captured the members of their tribe to the number of 9990 myriads of people, then ordered them to be slaughtered.[51] They piled their bodies like straw, and their blood was collected in lakes. The Dêvas moved the hearts of men to collect their bones and bury them.

To the south-west of the place of massacre are four little *stûpas*. This is the place where the four Śâkyas withstood an army. When first Prasênajita became king, he sought an alliance by marriage with the Śâkya race. The Śâkyas despised him as not of their family, and so deceived him by giving him as a wife a child of a servant, whom they largely endowed. Prasênajita-râja established her as his principal queen, and she brought forth in due time a son, who was called Virûḍhaka-râja. And now Virûḍhaka was desirous to go to the family of his maternal uncles to pursue his studies under their direction. Having come to the south part of the city, he there saw a new preaching-hall, and there he stopped his chariot. The Śákyas hearing of it, forthwith drove him away, saying, "How dare you, base-born fellow! occupy this abode, an abode built by the Sâkyas, in appearance (*or*, intended for) an abode of Buddha?"

After Virûḍhaka had succeeded to the throne he longed to revenge his former insult; he therefore raised an army

[51] The enmity of Virûḍhaka (Pi-lu-tse-kia) was owing to the insult the Śâkyas had paid his father in wedding him to a slave, and also to the epithet "base born" they applied to him (see *ante*, vol. i. p. 128). His father, Prasênajita, was not a kinsman of the Śâkyas (as Mr. Carlleyle states, p. 173), but an alien. The position the Śâkyas held as "a holy family" is a peculiarity not yet thoroughly understood. The site of the slaughter has been identified with a place called Bhatâ or Badhâ, about 8 miles to the north-west of Bhuila.

and occupied this place with his troops, who took possession of the fields. Four men of the Śâkyas who were engaged in ploughing between the watercourses[52] immediately opposed the progress of the soldiers, and having scattered them, entered the town. Their clansmen, considering that their tribe was one in which there had been a long succession of universal monarchs, and that the honourable children of such righteous kings[53] had dared to act cruelly and impetuously, and without patience to kill and slay, and so had brought disgrace on their family, drove them away from their home.

The four men, having been banished, went to the north among the Snowy Mountains; one became king of the country of Bamyân, one of Udyâna, one of Himatala, one of Śâmbi (Kauśâmbî?). They have transmitted their kingly authority from generation to generation without any interruption.[54]

To the south of the city 3 or 4 li is a grove of Nyagrôdha trees in which is a *stûpa* built by Aśôka-râja. This is the place where Śâkya Tathâgata, having returned to his country after his enlightenment, met his father and preached the law.[55] Śuddhôdana-râja, knowing that Tathâgata had defeated Mâra and was engaged in travelling about, leading people to the truth and converting them, was moved by a strong desire to see him, and considered how he could pay him the reverence due to him. He therefore sent a messenger to invite Tathâgata, saying, "Formerly you promised, when you had completed your purpose to become a Buddha, to return to your native place. These are your words still unperformed; now then

[52] *Hün man*, the rills dividing fields.

[53] This is a difficult passage, and the translation doubtful, but it is less obscure than that in the French. The idea is that Śâkya children, descended from holy kings, ought not to have resisted even an invader.

[54] This story of the banishment of the Śâkya youths is met with in the Southern records (*Mahâvaṁśa*). See Max Müller, *Hist. Anc. Sansk. Lit.*, p. 285. The story of the king of Udyâna and the Nâga girl occurs above, Book iii., vol. i. p. 129.

[55] For this part of Buddha's history see *Fo-sho-hing-tsan-king*, varga 19.

is the time for you to condescend to visit me." The messenger having come to the place where Buddha was, expressed to him the king's desire (*mind*). Tathâgata in reply said, "After seven days I will return to my native place." The messenger returning, acquainted the king with the news, on which Śuddhôdana-râja ordered his subjects to prepare the way by watering and sweeping it, and to adorn the road with incense and flowers; and then, accompanied by his officers of state, he proceeded 40 li beyond the city, and there drew up his chariot to await his arrival. Then Tathâgata with a great multitude advanced; the eight Vajrapâṇis surrounded him as an escort, the four heavenly kings went before him; divine Śakra, with a multitude of Dêvas belonging to the world of desires (Kâma-lôka), took their place on the left hand; Brahmâ-râja with Dêvas of Rûpa-lôka accompanied him on the right. The Bhikshu priests walked in order behind, Buddha by himself, as the full moon among the stars, stood in the midst; his supreme spiritual presence shook the three worlds, the brightness of his person exceeded that of the seven lights;[56] and thus traversing the air he approached his native country.[57] The king and ministers having reverenced him, again returned to the kingdom, and they located themselves in this Nyagrôdha grove.

By the side of the *saṅghârâma*, and not far from it, is a *stûpa;* this is the spot where Tathâgata sat beneath a great tree with his face to the east and received from his aunt a golden-tissued *kashâya* garment.[58] A little farther on is another *stûpa;* this is the place where Tathâgata converted eight king's sons and 500 Śâkyas.

Within the eastern gate of the city, on the left of the road, is a *stûpa;* this is where the Prince Siddârtha practised (*athletic sports and competitive*) arts.

[56] Sun, moon, and five planets.

[57] The exaggeration found in the visit of Buddha to his native country is common to all the records.

[58] This is the garment supposed to be kept by the great Kâśyapa in the Cock's-foot Mountain for Maitrêya. Buddha's aunt was Mahâprajâpatî, who was at the head of the female disciples.

Outside the gate is the temple of Îśvara-dêva. In the temple is a figure of the Dêva made of stone, which has the appearance of rising in a bent position.[59] This is the temple which the royal prince when an infant (*in swaddling clothes*) entered. King Śuddhôdana was returning from the Lumbinî (Lavaṇî—La-fa-ni) garden,[60] after having gone to meet the prince. Passing by this temple the king said, "This temple is noted for its many spiritual exhibitions (*miracles*). The Śâkya children[61] who here seek divine protection always obtain what they ask; we must take the royal prince to this place and offer up our worship." At this time the nurse (*foster-mother*), carrying the child in her arms, entered the temple; then the stone image raised itself and saluted the prince. When the prince left, the image again seated itself.

Outside the south gate of the city, on the left of the road, is a *stûpa;* it was here the royal prince contended with the Śâkyas in athletic sports (*arts*) and pierced with his arrows the iron targets.[62]

From this 30 li south-east is a small *stûpa.*[63] Here there is a fountain, the waters of which are as clear as a mirror. Here it was, during the athletic contest, that the

[59] This is, as it seems, the meaning of the passage, literally, "the appearance of rising, bendingly," *i.e.*, rising and bending. This rendering, which differs so widely from Julien's, is confirmed by the scene found in *Tree and Serpent Worship*, pl. lxix. (upper disc), where the large figure "rising bendingly" is that of Îśvara, and the cloth with the feet marked on it represents the infant Buddha. Suddhôdana and Mâyâ (or Prajâpatî) are also represented.

[60] This garden was Buddha's birthplace. The name Lumbinî is said to have been derived from that of the wife of Suprabuddha; his daughter was Mâyâ, the mother of Buddha. The Chinese equivalent in the text, La-fa-ni, may possibly be connected with the Sanskrit *lâvaṇa*, saline; but Lavaṇî is a feminine personal name

[61] In the plate referred to above, there are none but women present (except Śuddhôdana), as if they were praying for their children.

[62] The account of the contest with the Śâkya princes will be found in the *Romantic Legend of Buddha.* See also Fa-hian, p. 86, n. 3. The spot is identified by Mr. Carlleyle; *Report*, p. 187.

[63] Fa-hian places this *stûpa* at the same distance and in the same direction. It has been identified with a spot called Sur-kuiâ, a corruption of Śara-kûpa (arrow well), about 4½ miles due south of the former *stûpa* (*Arch. Survey*, vol. xii. p. 188). The bearing does not, however, correspond with that given by the Chinese pilgrims. The story of the arrow is given in the *Lalita Vistara*, p. 149.

arrow of the prince, after penetrating the targets, fell and buried itself up to the feather in the ground, causing a clear spring of water to flow forth. Common tradition has called this the *arrow fountain* (*Sarakûpa*); persons who are sick by drinking the water of this spring are mostly restored to health; and so people coming from a distance taking back with them some of the mud (*moist earth*) of this place, and applying it to the part where they suffer pain, mostly recover from their ailments.

To the north-east of the *arrow well* about 80 or 90 li, we come to the Lumbinî (Lavaṇî) garden. Here is the bathing tank of the Śâkyas, the water of which is bright and clear as a mirror, and the surface covered with a mixture of flowers.

To the north of this 24 or 25 paces there is an *Aśôka-flower* tree,[64] which is now decayed; this is the place where Bôdhisattva was born on the eighth day of the second half of the month called Vaiśâkha, which corresopnds with us to the eighth day of the third month. The school of the Sthâviras (Shang-tso-pu) say it was on the fifteenth day of the second half of the same month, corresponding to the fifteenth day of the third month with us. East from this is a *stûpa* built by Aśôka-râja, on the spot where the two dragons bathed the body of the prince.[65] When Bôdhisattva was born, he walked without assistance in the direction of the four quarters, seven paces in each direction, and said, "I am the only lord in heaven and earth; from this time forth my births are finished." Where his feet had trod there sprang up great lotus flowers. Moreover, two dragons sprang forth, and, fixed in the air, poured down the one a cold and the other a warm water stream from his mouth, to wash the prince.

To the east of this *stûpa* are two fountains of pure

[64] *Wu-yu-shu.* It is curious that it should be so frequently stated that the child was born under a *sal* tree (Carlleyle, *op. cit.*, p. 200, and elsewhere); S. Hardy, *Man. Bud.*, p. 167.

[65] For all these events the ordinary Lives of Buddha may be consulted. I have been unable to follow Mr. Carlleyle in his various identifications of the spots named in the text.

water, by the side of which have been built two *stûpas*. This is the place where two dragons appeared from the earth. When Bôdhisattva was born, the attendants and household relations hastened in every direction to find water for the use of the child. At this time two springs gurgled forth from the earth just before the queen, the one cold, the other warm, using which they bathed him.

To the south of this is a *stûpa*. This is the spot where Śakra, the lord of Dêvas, received Bôdhisattva in his arms. When Bôdhisattva was born, then Śakra, the king of Dêvas, took him and wrapped him in an exquisite and divine robe.

Close to this there are four *stûpas* to denote the place where the four heavenly kings received Bôdhisattva in their arms. When Bôdhisattva was born from the right side of his mother, the four kings wrapped him in a golden-coloured cotton vestment, and placing him on a golden slab (*bench*) and bringing him to his mother, they said, "The queen may rejoice indeed at having given birth to such a fortunate child!" If the Dêvas rejoiced at the event, how much more should men!

By the side of these *stûpas* and not far from them is a great stone pillar, on the top of which is the figure of a horse, which was built by Aśôka-raja. Afterwards, by the contrivance of a wicked dragon, it was broken off in the middle and fell to the ground. By the side of it is a little river which flows to the south-east. The people of the place call it the *river of oil*.[66] This is the stream which the Dêvas caused to appear as a pure and glistening pool for the queen, when she had brought forth her child, to wash and purify herself in. Now it is changed and become a river, the stream of which is still unctuous.

From this going east 300 li or so, across a wild and deserted jungle, we arrive at the kingdom of Lan-mo (Râmagrâma).

[66] It is plain from this that "the river of oil" was close to the spot where the child was born, and flowed through the garden.

LAN-MO [RÂMAGRÂMA].

The kingdom of Lan-mo[67] has been waste and desolate for many years. There is no account of its extent. The towns are decayed and the inhabitants few.

To the south-east of the old capital (*town*) there is a brick *stûpa*, in height less than 100 feet. Formerly, after the *Nirvâṇa* of Tathâgata, a previous king of this country having got a share of the *śarîras* of his body, returned home with them, and to honour these relics he built (*this stûpa*). Miraculous signs are here displayed, and a divine light from time to time shines around.

By the side of the *stûpa* is a clear lake (*tank*). A dragon at certain periods[68] comes forth and walks here, and changing his form and snake-like exterior, marches round the *stûpa*, turning to the right to pay it honour. The wild elephants come in herds, gather flowers, and scatter them here. Impelled by a mysterious power, they have continued to offer this service from the first till now. In former days, when Aśôka-râja, dividing the relics, built *stûpas*, having opened the *stûpas* built by the kings of the seven countries, he proceeded to travel to this country, and put his hand to the work (*viz., of opening this stûpa*);[69] the dragon, apprehending the desecration of the place, changed himself into the form of a Brâhmaṇ, and going in front, he bowed down before the elephant[70]

[67] The Chinese equivalents give us simply Râma, but that is the name of the country. Râmagrâma would be the old capital. There can be no doubt as to the restoration; the *Mahâwaṅśo* refers to the relic tower of Râmagâmo (Turnour's *Mahâw.*, pp. 184, 185), which is described by Hiuen Tsiang and Fa-hian. The site has not been satisfactorily determined. See Cunningham, *Anc. Geog.*, pp. 420 f.

[68] Or it may be translated "every day."

[69] This translation differs entirely from Julien's; the story, however, of Aśôka's dividing the relics which the seven kings had acquired after the cremation is well known. (See *Fo-sho-hing-tsan-king*, vers. 2297, 2298).

[70] It is possible that *siang* (elephant) in this passage is a misprint for *t'how* (head): it would then be, "knocking his head (*k'how t'how*) before the king, he said," &c.; but as there is allusion to a carriage or conveyance in the next sentence, the reading may be correct.

and said, "Mahârâja! your feelings are well affected to the law of Buddha, and you have largely planted (*good seed*) in the field of religious merit. I venture to ask you to detain your carriage awhile and condescend to visit my dwelling." The king replied, "And where is your dwelling? is it near at hand?" The Brâhman said, "I am the Nâga king of this lake. As I have heard that the great king desires to build a superior field of merit,[71] I have ventured to ask you to visit my abode." The king, receiving this invitation, immediately entered the dragon precinct, and sitting there for some time, the Nâga advanced towards him and said, "Because of my evil *karma* I have received this Nâga body; by religious service to these *śarîras* of Buddha I desire to atone for and efface my guilt. Oh, that the king would himself go and inspect (the *stûpa*, or, the *relics*) with a view to worship. Aśôka-râja having seen (*the character of the place*), was filled with fear, and said, "All these appliances for worship are unlike anything seen amongst men." The Nâga said, "If it be so, would that the king would not attempt to destroy the *stûpa*!" The king, seeing that he could not measure his power with that of the Nâga, did not attempt to open the *stûpa* (*to take out the relics*). At the spot where the dragon came out of the lake is an inscription to the above effect.[72]

Not far from the neighbourhood of this *stûpa* is a *saṅghârâma*, with a very few priests attached to it. Their conduct is respectful and scrupulously correct; and one Śrâmaṇera manages the whole business of the society. When any priests come from distant regions, they entertain them with the greatest courtesy and liberality; during three days they keep them in their society, and offer them the four necessary things.[73]

The old tradition is this: Formerly there were some Bhikshus who agreed[74] to come together from a distance,

[71] *I.e.*, to obtain a superior merit by building *stûpas*.

[72] For a similar account, see Fa-hian, chap. xxiii.

[73] Food, drink, clothing, medicine.

[74] So I translate *tung chi*, "were of the same mind." Julien renders

and to travel to worship this *stûpa*. They saw when they had arrived a herd of elephants, coming and departing together. Some of them brought on their tusks shrubs (*leaves and branches*), others with their trunks sprinkled water, some of them brought different flowers, and all offered worship (*as they stood*) to the *stûpa*. When the Bhikshus saw this, they were moved with joy and deeply affected. Then one of them giving up his full orders[75] (*ordination*), vowed to remain here and offer his services continually (*to the stûpa*), and expressing his thoughts to the others, he said, "I indeed, considering these remarkable signs of abounding merit, count as nothing my own excessive labours during many years amongst the priests.[76] This *stûpa* having some relics of Buddha, by the mysterious power of its sacred character draws together the herd of elephants, who water the earth around the bequeathed body (*of the saint*). It would be pleasant to finish the rest of my years in this place, and to obtain with the elephants the end (*at which they aim*)." They all replied, "This is an excellent design; as for ourselves, we are stained by our heavy (*sins*); our wisdom is not equal to the formation of such a design; but according to your opportunity look well to your own welfare, and cease not your efforts in this excellent purpose."

Having departed from the rest, he again repeated his earnest vow, and with joy devoted himself to a solitary life during the rest of his days.

it, "their brethren," as the equivalent of "those of the same mind," and he makes these invite (*siang chaou*) the other. It may be so, but there were evidently no brethren at the *stûpa*, as the narrative shows. This old tradition is also related by Fa-hian (chap. xxiii.)

[75] This is undoubtedly the meaning of the passage. He was a Bhikshu, *i.e.*, fully ordained; but now he gives up the privilege of that position, and undertakes the duties of a Śrâmaṇêra, to water and sweep the courts of the *stûpa*.

[76] This appears to me to be the meaning of the passage: The Bhikshu was led by witnessing the devotion of the elephants to count his own conduct as trifling compared with theirs. He therefore casts in his lot with them. M. Julien takes a different view of the meaning of the original.

On this he constructed for himself a leafy *paṇṇasâlâ*,[77] led the rivulets so as to form a pool, and at their proper seasons gathered flowers, and watered and swept and garnished the *stûpa*. Thus during a succession of years he persevered without change of purpose or plan.

The kings of the neighbouring countries, hearing the history, greatly honoured him; gave up their wealth and treasure, and together founded the *saṅghârâma*. Then they requested (*the Śrâmaṇêra*) to take charge of the affairs of the congregation; and from that time till now there has been no interruption in the original appointment, and a Śrâmaṇêra has ever held the chief office in the convent.

Eastward from this convent, in the midst of a great forest, after going about 100 li, we come to a great *stûpa* built by Aśôka-râja. This is the place where the prince-royal, after having passed from the city, put off his precious robes, loosed his necklace, and ordered his coachman[78] to return home. The prince-royal in the middle of the night traversing the city, at early dawn arrived at this place,[79] and then, heart and body bent on accomplishing his destiny, he said, "Here have I come out of the prison stocks. Here have I shaken off my chains." This is the place where he left for the last time his harnessed horse,[80] and taking the *maṇi* gem[81] from his crown, he commanded his coachman, saying, "Take this gem, and, returning, say to my father the king, now I am going away, not in inconsiderate disobedience, but to banish lust, and to destroy the power of impermanence, and to stop all the leaks of existence."

[77] *Pansala* is a Sinhalese word for "leafy hut," *i.e.*, a residence made out of boughs of trees.

[78] His coachman, or equerry, was called Chaṇḍaka. For an account of his dismissal see *Fo-sho-hing-tsan-king*, varga 6.

[79] The place appears to be "Manêya," about 34 miles E.S.E. of Bhuila.

[80] It is true that *keä* means "a chariot;" but it also means "a horse saddled for service;" and as all the evidence, both of the books and sculptures, is in favour of the prince sending back his "horse," I have used this translation. But it may also be translated "chariot," as the answer of Chaṇḍaka seems to require.

[81] *Mo-ni*, generally called the *chûḍâmaṇi*.

Then Chaṇḍaka (Chen-tc-kia) replied, "What heart can I have to go back thus, with a horse without a rider?" The prince having persuaded him with gentle words, his mind was opened and he returned.

To the east of the *stûpa* where Chaṇḍaka returned is a Jambu tree with leaves and branches fallen off but the trunk still upright. By the side of this is a little *stûpa*. This is the place where the prince exchanged his precious[82] robe for one made of deerskin. The prince had cut off his hair and exchanged his lower garments, and although he had got rid of his collar of precious stones, yet there was one divine garment (*still on his person*). "This robe," he said, "is greatly in excess (*of my wants*); how shall I change it away?" At this time a Śuddhâvâsa-dêva[83] transformed himself into a hunter with robes of deerskin, and holding his bow and carrying his quiver. The prince, raising his garment, addressed him thus: "I am desirous to exchange garments with you. Oh, that you would assent." The hunter said "Good!" The prince, loosing his upper garment, gave it to the hunter. The hunter having received it, resumed his Deva body, and holding the garment he had obtained, rose into the air and departed.

By the side of the *stûpa* commemorating this event, and not far from it, is a *stûpa* built by Aśôka-râja. This is the spot where the prince had his head shaved. The prince taking a knife (*sword*) from the hands of Chaṇḍaka, himself cut off his locks. Śakra, king of Dêvas, took the hair to his heavenly palace to offer it worship. At this time a Śuddhâvâsa-dêva, transforming himself into a barber, and holding his razor in his hand, advanced towards the prince. The latter hereupon addressed him, "Can you shave off the hair? Will you favour me by so doing to

[82] His robe ornamented with various gems. I find nothing about "a hunter" in the text, although it was with a hunter the exchange was made.

[83] A Dêva of the "pure abodes;" a Dôva of the five highest Rûpa-brahma heavens. See Childers' *Pāli Dict.* sub voc. *Sattalôka*.

me?" The transformed Dêva being so directed, accordingly shaved his head.

The time when the prince left the city and became a recluse is not quite fixed. Some say that Bôdhisattva was then nineteen years of age; others say he was twenty-nine, and that it was on the eighth day of the second half of the month Vaiśâkha, which corresponds to our fifteenth day of the third month.

To the south-east of the head-shaving *stûpa*, in the middle of a desert, going 180 or 190 li, we come to a Nyagrôdha grove in which there is a *stûpa* about 30 feet high. Formerly, when Tathâgata had died and his remains had been divided, the Brâhmaṇs who had obtained none, came to the place of cremation, and taking the remnant of coals and cinders to their native country, built this *stûpa* over them,[84] and offered their religious services to it. Since then wonderful signs have occurred in this place; sick persons who pray and worship here are mostly cured.

By the side of the ashes *stûpa* is an old *saṅghârâma*, where there are traces of the four former Buddhas, who walked and sat there.

On the right hand and left of this convent there are several hundred *stûpas*, among which is one large one built by Aśôka-râja; although it is mostly in ruins, yet its height is still about 100 feet.

From this going north-east through a great forest, along a dangerous and difficult road, where wild oxen and herds of elephants and robbers and hunters cause incessant trouble to travellers, after leaving the forest we come to the kingdom of Kiu-shi-na-k'ie-lo (Kuśinagara).

KIU-SHI-NA-K'IE-LO [KUŚINAGARA].

The capital[85] of this country is in ruins, and its towns

[84] This is the "Ashes Dâgoba," referred to *Fo-sho-hing-tsan-king*, v. 2284.

[85] Kuśinagara, Kuśinagarî, Kuśanagara, Kuśigrâmaka, or Kuśinârâ, the scene of Buddha's death

and villages waste and desolate. The brick foundation walls[86] of the old capital are about 10 li in circuit. There are few inhabitants, and the avenues of the town are deserted and waste. At the north-east angle of the city gate[87] is a *stûpa* which was built by Aśôka-râja. This is the old house of Chunda (Chun-t'o);[88] in the middle of it is a well which was dug at the time when he was about to make his offering (*to Buddha*). Although it has overflown for years and months, the water is still pure and sweet.

To the north-west of the city 3 or 4 li, crossing the Ajitavatî ('O-shi-to-fa-ti)[89] river, on the western bank, not far, we come to a grove of śâla trees. The *śâla* tree is like the *Huh* tree, with a greenish white bark and leaves very glistening and smooth. In this wood are four trees of an unusual height, which indicate the place where Tathâgata died.[90]

There is (*here*) a great brick *vihâra*, in which is a figure of the *Nirvâṇa* of Tathâgata. He is lying with his head to the north as if asleep. By the side of this *vihâra* is a *stûpa* built by Aśôka-râja; although in a ruinous state, yet it is some 200 feet in height. Before it is a stone

and burial, has been identified by Wilson and Cunningham with the present village of Kasia, 35 miles to the east of Gôrakhpûr. It stood close to the Hiraṇyavatî river (*Fo-sho-hing-tsan-king*, v. 2200); this must be the same as the Little Gaṇdakî river, or one of its feeders. The channel of this river, however, has undergone frequent changes. See *J. R. As. S.*, vol. v. pp. 123 f.; Burnouf, *Introd.* (2d ed.), pp. 75, 347; Lassen, *Ind. Alt.* (2d ed.), vol. i. pp. 171, 662; *Lalita Vistara*, pp. 416 f., 419 ff.

[86] Cunningham speaks of the *bricks* of which the *stûpas* were built (*Arch. Survey*, vol. i. p. 77).

[87] Aśvaghôsha speaks of the *Lung-siang* gate, which must have led towards the river (*Fo-sho-hing-tsan-king*, v. 2200).

[88] Chunda was a householder who invited Buddha to his house and there gave him his last repast (*Fo-sho-hing-tsan-king*, v. 1947). For an account of Chunda's offering, according to the later school of Buddhism, see as above, Note iii., pp. 365 ff.

[89] In Chinsse Wu-shing, "invincible." This is the same as the Shi-laï-na-fa-ti or Hiranyavatî river, in Chinese Yeu-kin-ho, "the river that has gold."

[90] The record generally speaks of *two* sâla trees (*Shorea robusta*) (*Fo-sho-hing-tsan-king*, v. 1950), and they are represented in the sculpture of the *Nirvâṇa* in Cave xxvi. at Ajaṇṭâ (Burgess, *Cave Temples*, pl. l.).

pillar to record the *Nirvâṇa* of Tathâgata; although there is an inscription on it, yet there is no date as to year or month.

According to the general tradition, Tathâgata was eighty years old when, on the 15th day of the second half of the month Vaiśâkha, he entered *Nirvâṇa*. This corresponds to the 15th day of the 3d month with us. But the Sarvâstivâdins say that he died on the 8th day of the second half of the month Kârtika, which is the same as the 8th day of the 9th month with us. The different schools calculate variously from the death of Buddha. Some say it is 1200 years and more since then. Others say, 1300 and more. Others say, 1500 and more. Others say that 900 years have passed, but not 1000 since the *Nirvâṇa*.[91]

By the side of the *vihâra*, and not far from it, is a *stûpa*. This denotes the place where Bôdhisattva, when practising a religious life, was born as the king of a flock of pheasants (*chi*—S. *kapiñjala*), and caused a fire to be put out. Formerly there was in this place a great and shady forest, where beasts and birds congregated and built their nests or dwelt in caves. Suddenly a fierce wind burst from every quarter, and a violent conflagration spread on every side. At this time there was a pheasant who, moved by pity and tenderness, hastened to plunge itself in a stream of pure water, and then flying up in the air, shook the drops from its feathers (*on the flames*). Whereupon Śakra, king of Dêvas, coming down, said (*to the bird*), "Why are you so foolish as to tire yourself, thus fluttering your wings? A great fire is raging, it is burning down the forest trees and the desert grass; what can such a tiny creature as you do to put it out?" The bird said, "And who are you?" He replied, "I am Śakra, king of

[91] The various dates here recorded would correspond with 552 B.C., 652 B.C., 852 B.C., and a date between 252 B.C. and 352 B.C. By this last Hiuen Tsiang probably means to place the *Nirvâṇa*, a hundred years before Aśôka, *i.e.*, about 325 B.C., which is the date he employs elsewhere. The Southern date is 543 B.C., but the most recent researches place it between 477 and 482 B.C. This is generally accepted.

Dêvas." The bird answered, "Now Śakra, king of Dêvas, has great power of religious merit, and every wish he has he can gratify; to deliver from this calamity and avert the evil would be as easy as opening and shutting his hand. There can be no propriety in permitting this calamity to last.[92] But the fire is burning fiercely on every side, there is no time for words." And so saying he flew away again, and ascending up, sprinkled the water from his wings. Then the king of the Dêvas took the water in the hollow of his hand[93] and poured it out on the forest and extinguished the fire; the smoke was cleared away and the living creatures saved. Therefore this *stûpa* is still called "the extinguishing-fire *stûpa*."

By the side of this, not far off, is a *stûpa*. On this spot Bôdhisattva, when practising a religious life, being at that time a deer, saved (*or*, rescued)[94] living creatures. In very remote times this was a great forest; a fire burst out in the wild grass that grew in it. The birds[95] and beasts were sorely distressed. Before them was the barrier of a swiftly flowing river. Behind them the calamity of the raging fire which barred their escape. There was no help for it but to plunge into the water, and there drowned, they perished. This deer, moved by pity, placed his body across the stream, which lashed his sides and broke his bones, whilst he strove with all his strength to rescue the drowning creatures. A worn-out hare coming to the bank, the deer with patience bearing his pain and fatigue, got him safely across, but his strength being now worn out, he was engulfed in the water and died. The Dêvas collecting his bones raised this *stûpa*.

[92] This may be otherwise translated: "if my request is without effect, with whom lies the fault?"

[93] Taking a handful of water.

[94] There is an error in the text, *sha* (killed) for *kew* (delivered). Julien translates the passage "took the form of a deer, and sacrificed his life." The former part, "took the form of a deer," cannot be correct, the original is *wei luh*, being a deer; with regard to the second part, "sacrificed his life," the original is *sha săng*, which is literally "to kill living animals for food." I have preferred to consider *shă* a mistake for *kew*, to deliver.

[95] It is difficult to understand why the *birds* should be afraid of the river.

To the west of this place, not far off, is a *stûpa.* This is where Subhadra[96] (Shen-hien) died (*entered Nirvâṇa*). Subhadra was originally a Brâhmaṇ teacher. He was 120 years of age; being so old, he had acquired in consequence much wisdom. Hearing that Buddha was about to die, he came to the two[97] (*sâlâ*) trees, and asked Ânanda, saying, "The Lord is about to die; pray let me ask him respecting some doubts I have, which still hamper me." Ânanda replied, "The Lord is about to die; pray do not trouble him." He said, "I hear that Buddha is difficult to meet in the world, and that the true law is difficult to hear. I have some grave doubts; there is no ground for fear." On being invited, Subhadra at once entered, and first asked Buddha, "There are many different persons who call themselves masters, each having a different system of doctrine, and pretending therewith to guide the people. Is Gautama (Kiu-ta-mo)[98] able to fathom their doctrine?" Buddha said, "I know their doctrine thoroughly;" and then for Subhadra's sake he preached the law.

Subhadra having heard (*the sermon*), his mind, pure and faithful, found deliverance, and he asked to be received into the church as a fully ordained disciple. Then Tathâgata addressed him saying, "Are you able to do so? Unbelievers and other sectaries who prepare themselves for a pure mode of life[99] ought to pass a four years' novitiate, to exhibit their conduct and test their disposition; if their characters and words be unexcep-

[96] For the circumstances attending the conversion of Subhadra (Su-po-t'o-lo), see *Fo-sho-hing-tsan-king*, varga 26, p. 290. In Chinese his name is Shen-hien, "the very virtuous."

[97] Here the two trees are referred to. The four which existed in Hiuen Tsiang's time were probably of a later date, and had been planted two at the head and two at the feet where Buddha died.

[98] The expression "Gautama" is used by Subhadra because he was a Brâhman unbeliever.

[99] This does not, as it appears, refer to the life of a Śramaṇa, but to the preparation of a Brahmachâra; the previous discipline of the Brâhman (*Fan-hing* . . .). The "unbelievers," in Chinese *Wai-tao*, translated Tîrthikas, in the *Mahâvyutpatti.*

tionable, then such persons may enter my profession; but in your case, whilst living amongst men, you have observed their discipline. There should be no difficulty, then, to prevent your full ordination?"

Subhadra said, "The Lord is very pitiful and very gracious, without any partiality. Is he then willing to forego in my case the four years of the threefold preparatory discipline?"[100]

Buddha said, "As I before stated, this has been done whilst living among men."

Then Subhadra, leaving his home immediately, took full orders as a priest. Then applying himself with all diligence, he vigorously disciplined both body and mind, and so being freed from all doubt, in the middle of the night (*of Buddha's Nirvâṇa*), not long after (*the interview*), he obtained the fruit, and became an Arhat without any imperfection. Being thus perfected in purity, he could not bear to await Buddha's death (*great Nirvâṇa*), but in the midst of the congregation, entering the *samâdhi* of "fire-limit" (*Agni-dhâtu*), and after displaying his spiritual capabilities, he first entered *Nirvâṇa*. He was thus the very last convert of Tathâgata, and the first to enter *Nirvâṇa*. This is the same as the hare who was last saved in the story that has just been told.

Beside (*the stûpa of*) Subhadra's *Nirvâṇa* is a *stûpa;* this is the place where the Vajrapâṇi (Chi-kin-kang)[101]

[100] The whole of this passage is obscure; the reference seems to be to a four years' preparatory course of discipline practised by the *S'ikshyamâṇa* (pupil); for the threefold character of their discipline, see *Fo-koue-ki*, p. 182. This previous course of discipline Buddha is willing to remit in the case of Subhadra, because he had already practised it "in the world," that is, in his own religious training.

[101] This incident is also referred to by Fa-hian (Beal, *Buddhist Pilgrims*, p. 95). There is some difficulty in the matter, because the Mallas, who were present at the *Nirvâṇa*, are called *lih sse*, and they did "sink prostrate on the earth" (*Fo-sho-hing-tsan-king*, ver. 2195). But the text seems to refer to some superhuman being, for the Vajrapâṇi is called "holding-diamond-mace-spiritual-secret-vestige-mighty-lord;" this phrase is explained by Eitel (*Handbook*, sub voc. *Vadjrapâṇi*) to refer to Indra, a sort of demon king, with 500 Yaksha followers. In the great picture of the *Nirvâṇa* brought from Japan by Mr. Borlase, and exhibited for a time at Bethnal Green, there is such a figure lying on the ground.

fell fainting on the earth. The great merciful Lord of the World, having, according to the condition of the persons concerned, finished his work of converting the world, entered on the joy of the *Nirvâṇa* between the two *śâla* trees; with his head to the north, he there lay asleep. The Mallas, with their diamond maces and divine though secret characteristics,[102] seeing Buddha about to die, were deeply affected with pity, and cried, "Tathâgata is leaving us and entering the great *Nirvâṇa;* thus are we without any refuge or protection to defend us; the poisonous arrow has deeply penetrated our vitals, and the fire of sorrow burns us up without remedy!" Then letting go their diamond clubs, they fell prostrate on the earth, and so remained for a long time. Then rising again, and deeply affected with compassion and love, they thus spake together, "Who shall now provide us a boat to cross over the great sea of birth and death? Who shall light a lamp to guide us through the long night of ignorance?"

By the side where the diamond (*mace-holders*) fell to the earth is a *stûpa.* This is the place where for seven days after Buddha had died they offered religious offerings. When Tathâgata was about to die, a brilliant light shone everywhere; men and Dêvas were assembled, and together showed their sorrow as they spake thus one to the other, "Now the great Buddha, Lord of the World, is about to die, the happiness of men is gone, the world has no reliance." Then Tathâgata, reposing on his right side upon the lion-bed, addressed the great congregation thus, "Say not Tathâgata has gone for ever (*perished*), because he dies; the body of the law[103] endures for ever! unchangeable is this! Put away all

[102] I have retained this translation, notwithstanding Dr. Eitel's explanation, as it is literally correct, and in agreement with Aśvaghôsha. Moreover, from the subsequent exclamations, it is plain that the persons who spoke were mortals, and disciples of Buddha, and they offered their services after his death for seven days.

[103] The *Dharmakâya,* the spiritual presence of Buddha in his words.

idleness, and without delay seek for emancipation (*from the world*)."

Then the Bhikshus sobbing and sighing with piteous grief, Aniruddha[104] bade the Bhikshus cease. "Grieve not thus," he said, "lest the Dêvas should deride." Then all the Mallas (Mo-la) having offered their offerings, desired to raise the golden coffin, and bring it to the place of cremation. Then Aniruddha addressed them all, and bade them stop, for the Dêvas desired to offer their worship during seven days.

Then the Dêvas (*the heavenly host*), holding exquisite divine flowers, discoursed through space the praises of his sacred qualities, each in full sincerity of heart offering his sacrifice of worship.

By the side of the place where the coffin was detained is a *stûpa;* this is where the queen Mahâmâyâ[105] wept for Buddha.

Tathâgata having departed, and his body being laid in the coffin, then Aniruddha, ascending to the heavenly mansions, addressed the queen Mâyâ and said, "The supremely holy Lord of Religion has now died!"

Mâyâ having heard of it, suppressed her sobs, and with the body of Dêvas came to the two *sâla* trees. Seeing the *saṅghâṭî* robe, and the *pâtra*, and the religious staff, she embraced them as she recognised each, and then ceased awhile to act,[106] till once again with loud accents she cried, "The happiness of men and gods is done! The world's eyes put out! All things are desert, without a guide!"

[104] Aniruddha ('O-ni-liu-t'o). There is some difficulty in knowing whether Aniruddha (cousin of Buddha, being a son of Amṛitôdana), or Anuruddha is referred to in the text; in the one case, Burnouf (*Lotus*, p. 294) states that Anuruddha was the personal attendant on Buddha at the time of his death; but, on the other hand, Aśvaghôsha (*Fo-sho*, ver. 2123) derives the name of this person from *a* + *niruddha* not-stopped, in agreement with the Tibetan *ma hgags-pa*, celui qui n'a pas été arrêté (*Lotus*, p. 293); *As. Res.* vol. xx. p. 440). Conf. Eitel, *Handbook*, sub voc.

[105] In the picture alluded to above (n. 97) there is a representation of Anuruddha or Aniruddha conducting Mahâmâyâ from heaven to the scene of the *Nirvâṇa*.

[106] That is, she fainted.

Then by the holy power of Tathâgata the golden coffin of itself opened; spreading abroad a glorious light, with hands conjoined, and sitting upright, he saluted his loving mother (*and said*), "You have come down from far; you who live so religiously need not be sad!"

Ânanda, suppressing his grief, inquired and said, "What shall I say hereafter when they question me?" In answer he rejoined, "(Say this), when Buddha had already died, his loving mother Mâyâ, from the heavenly courts descending, came to the twin *śâla* trees. Then Buddha, bent on teaching the irreverent among[107] men, from out his golden coffin, with hands conjoined, for her sake, preached the law."

To the north of the city, after crossing the river,[108] and going 300 paces or so, there is a *stûpa*. This is the place where they burnt the body of Tathâgata. The earth is now of a blackish yellow, from a mixture of earth and charcoal. Whoever with true faith seeks here, and prays, is sure to find some relics of Tathâgata.

When Tathâgata died, men and Dêvas, moved with love, prepared a coffin made of the seven precious substances, and in a thousand napkins swathed his body; they spread both flowers and scents, they placed both canopies and coverings over it; then the host of Mallas raised the bier and forward marched, with others following and leading on. Passing the golden river (Kin-ho) to the north, they filled the coffin up with scented oil, and piled high up the odorous wood and kindled it. Then, after all was burnt, there were two napkins left—one that lay next the body, the other from the outside covering. Then they divided the *śarîras* for the world's sake, the hair and nails alone remained untouched by fire. By the side of the place of cremation is a *stûpa*; here Tathâgata,

[107] That is, those who have no reverence for parents. This incident, which is a late invention, would recommend itself to Hiuen Tsiang as in agreement with the customs of his country, where the highest reverence of parents is inculcated.

[108] The Ajitavatî or Hiraṇyavatî.

for Kâśyapa's sake, revealed his feet. When Tathâgata was in his golden coffin, and the oil poured on it and the wood piled up, the fire would not enkindle. When all the beholders were filled with fear and doubt, Aniruddha spoke, "We must await Kâśyapa."

At this time Kâśyapa, with 500 followers from out the forest, came to Kuśinagara, and asked Ânanda saying, "Can I behold Tathâgata's body?" Ânanda said, "Swathed in a thousand napkins, enclosed within a heavy coffin, with scented wood piled up, we are about to burn it."

At this time Buddha caused his feet to come from out the coffin. Above (*or*, on) the wheel sign[109] lo! there were different coloured marks. Addressing Ânanda then, he said, "And what are these?" Answering he said, "When first he died the tears of men and gods, moved by pity, falling upon his feet, left these marks.[110]

Then Kâśyapa worshipped and walked round the coffin uttering his praises. Then the scented wood caught fire of its own accord, and burnt the whole with a great conflagration.

When Tathâgata died he appeared three times from his coffin: first, when he put out his arm and asked Ânanada, "(Have you) prepared the way?"[111] secondly, when he sat up and preached the law for his mother's sake; and thirdly, when he showed his feet to the great Kâśyapa.

By the side of the place where he showed his feet is a *stûpa* built by Aśôka-râja. This is the place where the eight kings shared the relics. In front is built a stone pillar on which is written an account of this event.

When Buddha died, and after his cremation, the kings of the eight countries with their troops (*four kinds of*

[109] *Lun siang*; see *ante*, vol. i. p. 94.

[110] In the *Vinaya* it is stated that these marks were made by the tears of a woman who wept at his feet. See *Abstract of Four Lectures*, pp. 69, 82.

[111] This is the literal translation; but it probably refers to Kâśyapa, as Julien explains (n. 1, p. 346); or the word *che* may be equal to "the chief," alluding to Kâśyapa; the sentence would then be, "has the chief arrived?"

troops) sent a right-minded Brâhmaṇ (Drôna)[112] to address the Mallas of Kuśinagara, saying, "The guide of men and gods has died in this country; we have come from far to request a share of his relics." The Mallas said, "Tathâgata has condescended to come to this land; the guide of the world is dead! the loving father of all that lives has gone! We ought to adore the relics of Buddha; your journey here has been in vain, you will not gain your end." Then the great kings having sought humbly for them and failed, sent a second message saying, "As you will not accede to our request, our troops are near." Then the Brâhmaṇ addressing them said, "Reflect how the Lord, the great merciful, prepared religious merit by practising patience; through successive ages his renown will last. Your desire now to try force is not right. Divide then the relics into eight portions, so that all may worship them. Why resort to arms?"[113] The Mallas, obedient to these words, divided the relics into eight parts.

Then Śakra the king of gods said, "The Dêvas also should have a share; dispute not their right."

Anavatapta[114] the Nâga also, and Muchilinda (Wen-lin), and Êlâpatra (I-lo-po-ta-lo) also, deliberated and said, "We ought not to be left without a bequest; if we seek it by force it will not be well for you!" The Brâhmaṇ said, "Dispute not so!" Then he divided the relics into three portions, one for the Dêvas, one for the Nâgas, and one remnant for the eight kingdoms among men. This addition of Dêvas and Nâgas in sharing the relics was a source of great sorrow to the kings of men.[115]

112 This name is given in the *Fo-sho-hing-tsan-king*, v. 2231. The phrase *chi sing* means "right minded," or "impartial;" it may possibly be a proper name (Ṛiju-bhâva), as Julien supposes.

113 The argument of the Brâhman is given in full by Aśvaghôsha, *Fo-sho-hing-tsan-king*, pp. 328, 329.

114 In Tibetan Ma-dros-pa, the king of the Nâgas (snakes) of the lake of the same name. See *Asiat. Res.*, vol. xx. p. 448.

115 Julien's translation can hardly be correct; "the eight kings having obtained a double portion, the gods, the Nâgas, and the kings of men grieved much on that account." The eight kings did not, in fact, obtain a double portion. The translation

To the south-west of the relic-dividing *stûpa*, going 200 li or so, we come to a great village; here lived a Brâhmaṇ of eminent wealth and celebrity, deeply learned in all pure literature, versed in the five *Vidyâs*,[116] acquainted with the three treasures (*piṭakas*). By the side of his home he had built a priest's house, and had used all his wealth to adorn it with magnificence. If by chance any priests in their travels stopped on their way, he asked them to halt, and used all his means to entertain them. They might stop one night, or even throughout seven days.

After this, Śaśâṅka-râja having destroyed the religion of Buddha, the members of the priesthood were dispersed, and for many years driven away. The Brâhmaṇ nevertheless retained for them, through all, an undying regard. As he was walking he chanced to see a Śramaṇa, with thick eyebrows and shaven head, holding his staff, coming along. The Brâhmaṇ hurried up to him, and meeting him asked, "Whence come you?" and besought him to enter the priest's abode and receive his charity. In the morning he gave him some rice-milk (*rice balls with milk*). The Śramaṇa having taken a mouthful, thereupon returned it (*i.e., the rest*) to his alms-bowl with a great sigh. The Brâhmaṇ who supplied the food prostrating himself said, "Eminent sir! (*bhadanta*), is there any reason why you should not remain with me one night? is not the food agreeable?" The Śramaṇa graciously answering said, "I pity the feeble merit possessed by the world, but let me finish my meal and I will speak to you further." After finishing his food he gathered up his robes as if to go. The Brâhmaṇ said, "Your reverence agreed to speak with me, why then are you silent?" The Śramaṇa said, "I have not forgotten; but to talk with you is irksome; and the circumstance is likely to create doubt, but yet I will tell you in

is evidently *chung fen*, "the additional division," *tin lung*, "among Dêvas and Nâgas," *jin wang mo puh pi*, "the kings of men were much grieved." That is, the relics were carried away from the world, and this caused the sorrow.

[116] See *ante*, vol. i. p. 78.

brief. When I sighed, it was not on account of your offering of rice; for during many hundreds of years I have not tasted such food. When Tathagâta was living in the world I was a follower of his when he dwelt in the Vêṇuvana-vihâra, near Râjagṛiha (Ho-lo-she-ki-li-hi);[117] there it was, stooping down, I washed his *pâtra* in the pure stream of the river—there I filled his pitcher—there I gave him water for cleansing his mouth; but alas! the milk you now offer is not like the sweet water of old! It is because the religious merit of Dêvas and men has diminished that this is the case!" The Brâhmaṇ then said, "Is it possible that you yourself have ever seen Buddha?" The Śramaṇa replied, "Have you never heard of Râhula, Buddha's own son? I am he! Because I desire to protect the true law I have not yet entered *Nirvâṇa.*"

Having spoken thus he suddenly disappeared. Then the Brâhmaṇ swept and watered the chamber he had used, and placed there a figure of him, which he reverenced as though he were present.

Going 500 li through the great forest we come to the kingdom of P'o-lo-ni-sse (Bânâras).

[117] In Chinese, Wang-she-ch'ing.

END OF BOOK VI.

BOOK VII.

Includes the following countries, (1) *P'o-lo-ni-sse*; (2) *Chen-chu*; (3) *Fei-she-li*; (4) *Fo-li-shi*; (5) *Ni-po-lo*.

P'O-LO-NI-SSE (VÂRÂNASÎ[1] OR BÂNÂRAS).

THIS country is about 4000 li in circuit. The capital borders (*on its western side*) the Ganges river. It is about 18 or 19 li in length and 5 or 6 li in breadth; its inner gates are like a small-toothed comb;[2] it is densely populated. The families are very rich, and in the dwellings are objects of rare value. The disposition of the people is soft and humane, and they are earnestly given to study. They are mostly unbelievers, a few reverence the law of Buddha. The climate is soft, the crops abundant, the trees (*fruit trees*) flourishing, and the underwood thick in every place. There are about thirty *saṅghârâmas* and 3000 priests. They study the Little Vehicle according to the Sammatîya school (Ching-liang-pu). There are a hundred or so Dêva temples with about 10,000 sectaries. They honour principally Mahêśvara (Ta-tseu-tsaï). Some cut their hair off, others tie their hair in a knot, and go

[1] This is the restoration of the Chinese equivalents. A note in the original gives the sound of *ni* as $=n(iu)+(he)\breve{a}$, *i.e.*, *nă*; the restoration, therefore, is Vârâṇâsî, the Sanskrit form of the name of Bânâras. It was so called because it lies between the two streams Varaṇâ and Asi or Asî, affluents of the Ganges. See Sherring, *Sacred City of the Hindus*.

[2] Julien gives here, "the villages are very close together;" but, as noticed before (p. 73, n. 13), the Chinese symbols *leu yen* mean "the inner gates" of a city, and the expression *tsch pi* means "like a tooth comb." I conclude it means that the inner gates of the city consisted of closely joined, and perhaps sharpened, iron or other bars.

naked, without clothes (Nirgranthas); they cover their bodies with ashes (Paśupatas), and by the practice of all sorts of austerities they seek to escape from birth [3] and death.

In the capital there are twenty Dêva temples, the towers and halls of which are of sculptured stone and carved wood. The foliage of trees combine to shade (*the sites*), whilst pure streams of water encircle them. The statue of the Dêva Mahêśvara, made of *teou-shih* (*native copper*), is somewhat less than 100 feet high. Its appearance is grave and majestic, and appears as though really living.

To the north-east of the capital, on the western side of the river Varaṇâ, is a *stûpa* [4] built by Aśôka-râja (Wu-yau). It is about 100 feet high; in front of it is a stone pillar; it is bright and shining as a mirror; its surface is glistening and smooth as ice, and on it can be constantly seen the figure of Buddha as a shadow.

To the north-east of the river Varaṇâ about 10 li or so, we come to the *saṅghârâma* of *Lu-ye* (*stag desert*).[5] Its precincts are divided into eight portions (*sections*),[6] connected by a surrounding wall. The storeyed towers with projecting eaves and the balconies are of very superior work. There are fifteen hundred priests in this convent who study the Little Vehicle according to the Saṁmatîya school. In the great enclosure is a *vihâra* about 200 feet high; above the roof is a golden-covered figure of the Âmra (*'An-mo-lo*—mango) fruit. The foundations of the building are of stone, and the stairs also, but the towers and niches

[3] Not "life and death," but "birth and death;" *i.e.*, to arrive at a condition of uninterrupted life.

[4] Julien here gives *Pó-lo-ni-sse* by mistake, it should be *Pó-lo-ni* (read *na*), referring to the Varaṇâ or Baraṇâ (see Dr. Fitzedward Hall's remarks in the Introduction to Sherring's *Sacred City of the Hindus;* also Cunningham, *Anc. Geog.*, p. 436 n.)

[5] The same as Mṛigadâva, generally called *Lu-yuen*, "the deer garden." This is the spot where Buddha preached his first sermon to the five mendicants. For an account of his march to Bânâras and the sermon he preached see *Fo-sho-hing-tsan-king*, varga 15, p. 168.

[6] Probably meaning that the enclosure was an octagon, as the great tower of Dhamek was (*Arch. Survey*, vol. i. p. 111).

are of brick. The niches are arranged on the four sides in a hundred successive lines, and in each niche is a golden figure of Buddha. In the middle of the *vihâra* is a figure of Buddha made of *teou-shih* (*native copper*). It is the size of life, and he is represented as turning the wheel of the law (*preaching*).[7]

To the south-west of the *vihâra* is a stone *stûpa* built by Aśôka-râja. Although the foundations have given way, there are still 100 feet or more of the wall remaining. In front of the building is a stone pillar about 70 feet high. The stone is altogether as bright as jade. It is glistening, and sparkles like light; and all those who pray fervently before it see from time to time, according to their petitions, figures with good or bad signs. It was here that Tathâgata (*ju-lai*), having arrived at enlightenment, began to turn the wheel of the law (*to preach*).

By the side of this building and not far from it is a *stûpa*. This is the spot where Âjñâta Kauṇḍinya ('O-jo-kio-ch'in-ju) and the rest, seeing Bôdhisattva giving up his austerities, no longer kept his company, but coming to this place, gave themselves up to meditation.[8]

By the side of this is a *stûpa* where five hundred Pratyêka Buddhas entered at the same time into *Nirvâṇa*. There are, moreover, three *stûpas* where there are traces of the sitting and walking of the three former Buddhas.

By the side of this last place is a *stûpa*. This is the spot where Maitrêya Bôdhisattva received assurance of his becoming a Buddha. In old days, when Tathâgata was living in Râjagṛiha (Wang-she), on the Gṛidhrakûṭa

[7] The wheel is the symbol of "preaching," or of *dharma*. The scene of Buddha's teaching near Bânâras is the district called Sâr-nâth, which, according to Cunningham, is a contraction of Sâraṅganâtha, *lord of deer*. Buddha himself was once the "king of deer," and this may be the origin of the name. For an account of the excavations made on this spot see *Arch. Survey*, vol. i. p. 107 ff.

[8] The five ascetics who had accompanied the Bôdhisattva to Uravilva, and fasted with him for six years, when they saw him receive the rice milk of Nandâ, supposing he had given up the object of his religious life, left him, and came to the deer park at Bânâras.

mountain,[9] he spoke thus to the Bhikshus: "In future years, when this country of Jambudvîpa shall be at peace and rest, and the age of men shall amount to 80,000 years, there shall be a Brâhmaṇ called Maitrêya (*Sse-che*). His body shall be of the colour of pure gold, bright and glistening and pure. Leaving his home, he will become a perfect Buddha, and preach the threefold[10] law for the benefit of all creatures. Those who shall be saved are those who live, in whom the roots of merit have been planted through my bequeathed law.[11] These all conceiving in their minds a profound respect for the three precious objects of worship, whether they be already professed disciples or not, whether they be obedient to the precepts or not, will all be led by the converting power (*of his preaching*) to acquire the fruit (*of Bôdhi*) and final deliverance. Whilst declaring the threefold law for the conversion of those who have been influenced by my bequeathed law, by this means also hereafter others will be converted."[12]

At this time Maitrêya Bôdhisattva (Meï-ta-li-ye-pu-sa) hearing this declaration of Buddha, rose from his seat and addressed Buddha thus: "May I indeed become that lord called Maitrêya." Then Tathâgata spoke thus: "Be it so! you shall obtain this fruit (*condition*), and as I have just

[9] The "Peak of the Vulture," near Râjagṛha.

[10] Julien translates this by "three great assemblies." It is true *hwuy* means "an assembly," but in this passage *san hwuy* refers to the law "thrice repeated." Hence it is said to be "a triple twelve-part trustworthy knowledge of the four truths" (Oldenberg, *Buddha*, p. 129 and note. Compare also the phrase *tikutiko chakamo* in the Bharhut sculptures, pl. xxviii., the meaning of which has escaped General Cunningham. Mr. B. Nanjio, also, in his *Catalogue of the Buddhist Tripiṭaka*, pp. 9, 10, has not noticed that the Chinese symbol *hwui* corresponds with the Sanskrit *kûta*, and so has translated the phrase as though it referred to "an assembly."

[11] That is, those who shall be saved by the preaching of Maitrêya are those in whose hearts my bequeathed law shall have worked the necessary preparation.

[12] The same influence, *i.e.*, of Maitrêya's teaching, will act as a "good friend" for their subsequent conversion. The expression "*shen yau*," "illustrious friend," refers to the guidance of *Bôdhi*, or wisdom. There is some difficulty in understanding how this assurance could have been given to Maitrêya whilst Buddha was on the Gṛidhrakûṭa mountain, and yet that the spot should be at Bânâras, unless, indeed, it was repeated there.

explained, such shall be the power (*influence*) of your teaching."

To the west of this place there is a *stûpa*. This is the spot where Śâkya Bôdhisattva (Shih-kia-pu-sa) received an assurance (*of becoming a Buddha*). In the midst of the Bhadra-kalpa when men's years amounted to 20,000, Kâśyapa Buddha (Kia-she-po-fo) appeared in the world and moved the wheel of the excellent law (*i.e., preached the law*), opened out and changed the unclosed mind (*of men*), and declared this prediction to Prabhâpâla Bôdhisattva (Hu-ming-pu-sa).[13] "This Bôdhisattva in future ages, when the years of men shall have dwindled to 100 years, shall obtain the condition of a Buddha and be called Śâkya Muni."

Not far to the south of this spot are traces where the four Buddhas of a bygone age walked for exercise. The length (*of the promenade*) is about fifty paces and the height of the steps (*stepping spots*) about seven feet. It is composed of blue stones piled together. Above it is a figure of Tathâgata in the attitude of walking. It is of a singular dignity and beauty. From the flesh-knot on the top of the head there flows wonderfully a braid of hair. Spiritual signs are plainly manifested and divine prodigies wrought with power (*fineness, éclat*).

Within the precincts of the enclosure (*of the saṅghârâma*)[14] there are many sacred vestiges, with *vihâras* and *stûpas* several hundred in number. We have only named two or three of these, as it would be difficult to enter into details.

To the west of the *saṅghârâma* enclosure is a clear lake of water about 200 paces in circuit; here Tathâgata occasionally bathed himself. To the west of this is a great

[13] Julien translates "and received *from* Prabhâpâla Bôdhisattva the prediction following." But this would destroy the connection of the sentence; it is Kâśyapa Buddha who declares *to* Prabhâpâla that he (Prabhâpâla) shall become a Buddha. See *Wong Pûh* (*J. R. As. S.*, vol. xx. p. 139), §§ 4, 5.

[14] Or of the "deer park," the modern Sârnâth.

tank about 180 paces round; here Tathâgata used to wash his begging-dish.

To the north of this is a lake about 150 paces round. Here Tathâgata used to wash his robes. In each of these pools is a dragon who dwells within it. The water is deep and its taste sweet; it is pure and resplendent in appearance, and neither increases nor decreases. When men of a bad character bathe here, the crocodiles (*kin-pi-lo,—kumbhîras*) come forth and kill many of them; but in case of the reverential who wash here, they need fear nothing.

By the side of the pool where Tathâgata washed his garments is a great square stone, on which are yet to be seen the trace-marks of his *kashâya* (*kia-sha*) robe. The bright lines of the tissue are of a minute and distinct character, as if carved on the stone. The faithful and pure frequently come to make their offerings here; but when the heretics and men of evil mind speak lightly of or insult the stone, the dragon-king inhabiting the pool causes the winds to rise and rain to fall.

By the side of the lake, and not far off, is a *stûpa*. This is where Bôdhisattva, during his preparatory life, was born as a king of elephants, provided with six tusks (*chhadanta*).[15] A hunter, desirous to obtain the tusks, put on a robe in colour like that of a religious ascetic, and taking his bow, awaited the arrival of his prey. The elephant king, from respect to the *kashâya* robe, immediately broke off his tusks and gave them to the hunter.

By the side of this spot, and not far from it, is a *stûpa*. It was here Bôdhisattva, in his preparatory career, grieved to see that there was little politeness (*reverence*) amongst men, took the form of a bird, and joining himself to the

[15] Chhadanta, which seems to mean six-tusked, according to Siamese legend, is the name of an elephant living in a golden palace on the shores of the Himalayan lake Chatthan, attended by eighty thousand ordinary elephants.—Alabaster, *Wheel of the Law*, p. 305; conf. Sp. Hardy, *Eastern Monachism*, p. 178; *Manual of Budhism*, p. 17; *Mahawanso* (Turnour's trans.), pp. 22, 134; Upham, *Sac. and Hist. Books*, vol. iii. p. 269; Burgess, *Reports, Arch. Sur. W. Ind.*, vol. iv. pp. 45, 46; Cunningham, *Bharhut Stûpa*, pp. 62, 63; Beal, *Rom. Leg. Bud.*, p. 367.

company of a monkey and a white elephant, he asked them in this place, "Which of you saw first this Nyagrôdha (*Ni-ku-liu*) tree?" Each having answered according to circumstances, he placed them according to their age.[16] The good effects of this conduct spread itself little by little on every side; men were able to distinguish the high from the low, and the religious and lay people followed their example.

Not far from this, in a great forest, is a *stûpa.* It was here that Dêvadatta and Bôdhisattva, in years gone by, were kings of deer and settled a certain matter. Formerly in this place, in the midst of a great forest, there were two herds of deer, each 500 in number. At this time the king of the country wandered about hunting through the plains and morasses. Bôdhisattva, king of deer, approaching him, said, "Mahârâja! you set fire to the spaces enclosed as your hunting-ground, and shoot your arrows and kill all my followers. Before the sun rises they lie about corrupting and unfit for food. Pray let us each day offer you one deer for food, which the king will then have fresh and good, and we shall prolong our life a little day by day." The king was pleased at the proposition, and turned his chariot and went back home. So on each day a deer from the respective flocks was killed.

Now among the herd of Dêvadatta there was a doe big with young, and when her turn came to die she said to her lord, "Although I am ready to die, yet it is not my child's turn."

The king of the deer (*i.e.*, Dêvadatta) was angry, and said, "Who is there but values life?"

The deer answered with a sigh, "But, O king, it is not humane to kill that which is unborn."[17]

She then told her extremity to Bôdhisattva, the king of deer. He replied, "Sad indeed; the heart of the loving

[16] Here I follow Julien's translation, but there is probably an error in the text.

[17] This may be translated otherwise: "Our king is not humane in putting to death without reprieve;" or, "Our king is not humane; I die without reprieve."

mother grieves (*is moved*) for that which is not yet alive (*has no body*). I to-day will take your place and die."

Going to the royal gate (*i.e., the palace*), the people who travelled along the road passed the news along and said in a loud voice, "That great king of the deer is going now towards the town." The people of the capital, the magistrates, and others, hastened to see.

The king hearing of it, was unwilling to believe the news; but when the gate-keeper assured him of the truth, then the king believed it. Then, addressing the deer-king he said, "Why have you come here?"

The deer-(*king*) replied, "There is a female in the herd big with young, whose turn it was to die; but my heart could not bear to think that the young, not yet born, should perish so. I have therefore come in her place."

The king, hearing it, sighed and said, "I have indeed the body of a man, but am as a deer. You have the body of a deer, but are as a man." Then for pity's sake he released the deer, and no longer required a daily sacrifice. Then he gave up that forest for the use of the deer, and so it was called "the forest given to the deer,"[18] and hence its name, the "deer-plain" (*or*, wild).

Leaving this place, and going 2 or 3 li to the south-west of the *saṅghârâma*, there is a *stûpa* about 300 feet high. The foundations are broad and the building high, and adorned with all sorts of carved work and with precious substances. There are no successive stages (*to this building*) with niches; and although there is a standing pole erected above the cupola (*fau poh*[19]), yet it has no encircling bells.[20] By the side of it is a little *stûpa*. This

[18] Commonly called the Mṛīgadâva. This is the site referred to before,—the present Sârnâth or Sâraṅganâtha.

[19] Julien translates this "a sort of vase belonging to a religious person, inverted;" but I take *fau poh* to mean the cupola of a *stûpa*, in agreement with the account given above, p. 47 and n. 163.

[20] *Lun-to*, circular bells, or encircling bells, referring to the circular plates with bells generally attached to the surmounting pole of a *stûpa*. Julien translates, "it is not crowned with a cupola in form like a bell." This seems to be impossible, as it is before stated that the *stûpa* was surmounted by a pole.

the spot where Âjñâta Kauṇḍinya and the other men, five in number, declined to rise to salute Buddha.[21] When first Sarvârthasiddha (Sa-p'o-ho-la-t'a-si-to[22]) left the city to sojourn in the mountains and to hide in the valleys, forgetful of self and mindful of religion, then Śuddhôdana-râja (Tsing-fan) commanded three persons of his own tribe and household, and two of his maternal uncles, saying, "My son Sarvârthasiddha has left his home to practise wisdom; alone he wanders through mountains and plains and lives apart in the forests. I order you, therefore, to follow him and find out where he dwells. You within (*the family*), his uncles, and you without (*the family*), ministers and people, exert yourselves diligently to find out where he has gone to live." The five men, after receiving the order, went together, casting along the outposts of the country. And now, during their earnest search, the thought of leaving their homes occurred to them also,[23] and so they thus spake one to the other: "Is it by painful discipline or by joyful means we attain to supreme wisdom?" Two of them said, "By rest and by pleasant discipline wisdom is obtained." Three of them said, "It is by painful discipline." Whilst they yet contended without agreeing, two to three, the prince had already entered on the painful discipline of the unbelievers, considering this to be the true way to overcome sorrow; and so, like them, he took only a few grains of rice and millet to support his body.

The two men seeing him thus, said, "This discipline of the prince is opposed to the true way (*of escape*); intel-

[21] For an account of this incident see the *Fo-sho-hing-tsan-king*, p. 172, vv. 1222, 1223. For the origin of Âjñâta Kauṇḍinya's ('O-jo-kiao-ch'in-ju) name see *op. cit.* v. 1268.

[22] This was the name given to Bôdhisattva by his parents. It is explained to mean "one by whom all objects are effected" (Monier Williams, *Sans. Dict.*, sub voc. *Sarva*). In Chinese it is translated into "Yih-tsai-i-shing," which seems to signify "one who is perfected in all ways," or "the completely perfect."

[23] Such appears to be the force of the passage, as though the five men by their long search for the prince had become accustomed to a solitary life, and so were unwilling to return home.

ligence is obtained by agreeable methods, but now he is practising severe discipline, he cannot be our companion." So they departed far off and lived in seclusion under the idea that they would (*in their own way*) attain the fruit (*of enlightenment*). The prince having practised austerities for six years [24] without obtaining *Bôdhi*, desired to give up his rigorous discipline, as being contrary to the truth; he then prepared himself to receive the rice-milk (*offered by the girl*), with a view, by this method, to obtain enlightenment.[25] Then the three men (*who advocated penance*) hearing thereof, sighed and said, "His merit was just ripening, and now it is all dissipated! For six years enduring penance, and now in a day to lose all his merit!" On this they went together to seek for and consult with the two men. Having met them, they sat down and entered on an excited conversation. Then they spake together thus: "In old days we saw the Prince Sarvârthasiddha leave the royal palace for the desert valleys: he put off his jewels and robes, and assumed the skin doublet (*of the hunter*), and then, with all his might and determined will, gave himself to austerities to seek after the deep mysterious law and its perfect fruit. And now, having given all up, he has received the rice-milk of the young shepherd-girl, and ruined his purpose. We know now he can do nothing."

The two men replied, "How is it, my masters, ye have seen this so late, that this man acts as a madman? When he lived in his palace he was reverenced and

[24] The period of mortification is lengthened to seven years in the Southern accounts, or rather that Mâra pursued the Bôdhisattva for seven years up to the last vain attack he made upon him. See Oldenberg, *Buddha*, p. 420, Eng. trans. It is probable that the seven years' torture said to have been undergone by St. George, and the legend generally, is borrowed from the story of Bôdhisâttva.

[25] Julien has translated this passage as if it were spoken by "the two men" who were opposed to severe mortification as a method of religious discipline. But this necessitates the prediction that he would receive enlightenment after receiving the rice-milk, "Mais quand il aura reçu une bouillie de riz au lait, il obtiendra l'intelligence" (p. 365). This is highly improbable, and I have therefore translated it as in the text.

powerful; but he was not able to rest in quiet, and so went wandering far off through mountains and woods, giving up the estate of a *Chakravartin* monarch to lead the life of an abject and outcast. What need we think about him more; the mention of his name but adds sorrow to sorrow."

And now Bôdhisattva, having bathed in the Nairañjanâ river, seated himself under the *Bôdhi* tree and perfected himself in supreme wisdom, and was named "The lord of dêvas and men." Then reflecting in silence, he thought who was worthy (*fit*) to be instructed in the way of deliverance—"The son of Râma, Udra by name (Yo-t'eu-lan), he is fit to receive the excellent law, as he has reached the *Samâdhi*, which admits of no active thought."[26]

Then the Dêvas in space raised their voices and said, "Udra-Râmaputra has been dead for seven days." Then Tathâgata sighing (*said*) with regret, "Why did we not meet? ready as he was to hear the excellent law and thereby to obtain quick conversion!"

Again he gave himself to consideration, and cast about through the world to seek (*for some one to whom he might first preach*). There is (*he thought*) Ârâḍa Kâlâma (*'O-lan-kia-lan*), who has reached the ecstatic point "of having nothing to obtain;"[27] he is fit to receive the highest reason. Then again the Dêvas said, "He has been dead for five[28] days."

Again Tathâgata sighed, in knowledge of his incompleted merit. Once more considering who was worthy to receive his instruction, he remembered that in the "deer park" there were the five men,[29] who might first receive the converting doctrine. Then Tathâgata, rising from the *Bôdhi* tree, went forward with measured step[30] and digni-

[26] *Naivasañjñâ samâdhi* (Jul.) The theory of Udra-Râmaputra (*Yeu-tau-lan-tseu*) with respect to final deliverance is explained in the twelfth varga of the *Fo-sho-hing-tsan-king*. His system appears to have been a refinement on that of Kapila.

[27] *Akiñchavyâyatana*—(Julien).

[28] In the *Lalita Vistara* the number of days is *three*. In the *Buddha-charita* there is no period named.

[29] That is, the Mṛigadâva (Sârnâth), at Bânâras.

[30] "Step by step, like the king of beasts (the lion), did he advance

fied mien to the "deer-park garden," shining with glory; his (*circle of*) hair[31] reflecting its brilliant colours, and his body like gold. Gracefully he advanced to teach those five men. They, on their parts, seeing him afar off, said one to another,[32] "Here comes that Sarvârthasiddha; for years and months he has sought for the sacred fruit, and has not obtained it, and now his mind is relaxed, and so he comes to seek us as disciples (*or,* to seek our company); let us remain silent, and not rise to meet him or pay him respect."

Tathâgata gradually approaching, his sacred appearance affecting all creatures, the five men, forgetting their vow, rose and saluted him, and then attached themselves to him with respect. Tathâgata gradually instructed them in the excellent principles (*of his religion*), and when the double[33] season of rest was finished, they had obtained the fruit (*of Bôdhi*).

To the east of the "deer forest" 2 or 3 li, we come to a *stûpa* by the side of which is a dry pool about 80 paces in circuit, one name of which is "saving life,"[34] another name is "ardent master." The old traditions explain it thus: Many hundred years ago there was a solitary sage (*a sorrowful or obscure master*) who built by the side of this pool a hut to live in, away from the world. He practised the arts of magic, and by the extremest exercise of his spiritual power he could change broken fragments of bricks into

watchfully through the grove of wisdom."—*Fo-sho-hing-tsan-king,* v. 1199.

[31] That is, the circle of hair between his eyes (the *urṇa*).

[32] According to the *Buddha-charita,* vv. 1220, 1221, the five men were named Kauṇḍinya, Daśabâla-Kâśyapa, Vâśpa, Aśvajit, Bhadrika. The *Lalita Vistara* gives Mahânâmâ instead of Daśabâla. For the incident named in the text see *Buddha-charita,* loc. cit.

[33] That is, the season of rain, during which the disciples retired into fixed homes. But this ordinance was not yet introduced into the Buddhist system; it seems to have been a custom, however, among religious communities before Buddha's time, for in the *Vinaya* complaint is made to Buddha that *his* disciples continued to wander through the country when the seeds were first growing, contrary to the ordinary rule.

[34] There is no expression for "pool," as in the French translation.

precious stones, and could also metamorphose both men and animals into other shapes, but he was not yet able to ride upon the winds and the clouds, and to follow the Ṛĭshis in mounting upwards. By inspecting figures and names that had come down from of old, he further sought into the secret arts of the Ṛĭshis. From these he learned the following: "The spirit-Ṛĭshis are they who possess the art of lengthening life.[35] If you wish to acquire this knowledge, first of all you must fix your mind on this—viz., to build up an altar enclosure 10 feet round; then command an 'ardent master' (*a hero*), faithful and brave, and with clear intent, to hold in his hand a long sword and take his seat at the corner of the altar, to cover his breath, and remain silent from evening till dawn.[36] He who seeks to be a Ṛĭshi must sit in the middle of the altar, and, grasping a long knife, must repeat the magic formulæ and keep watch (*seeing and hearing*). At morning light, attaining the condition of a Ṛĭshi, the sharp knife he holds will change into a sword of diamond (*a gem-sword*), and he will mount into the air and march through space, and rule over the band of Ṛĭshis. Waving the sword he holds, everything he wishes will be accomplished, and he will know neither decay nor old age, nor disease nor death."[37] The man having thus obtained the method (*of becoming a Ṛĭshi*), went in search of such an "ardent master." Diligently he searched for many years, but as yet he found not the object of his desires. At length, in a certain town

[35] The magic art of lengthening life, or of a long life. The "elixir of life" and the art of transmuting metals had been sought after in the East long before the Arabs introduced the study of alchemy into Europe. The philosopher's stone is the *tan sha* of the Chinese, *i.e.*, the red bisulphuret of mercury, or cinnabar. See an article on *Tauism* in the *Trans. of the China Branch of the R.A.S.*, part v. 1855, by Dr. Edkins, p. 86.

[36] We may compare with this the ceremonies observed anciently on conferring the dignity of knighthood, especially the vigil before the altar. (Ingulphus, quoted by Mr. Thoms in his *Book of the Court*, p. 138.)

[37] The account of this magic gem-sword may be compared with the "great brand, Excalibur," of King Arthur—

"But 'ere he dipt the surface, rose an arm
Clothed in white samite, mystic, wonderful,
And caught him by the hilt, and brandished him
Three times. . . ."—*Tennyson*.

he encountered a man piteously wailing as he went along the way. The solitary master seeing his marks (*the marks on his person*),[38] was rejoiced at heart, and forthwith approaching him, he inquired, "Why do you go thus lamenting, and why are you so distressed?" He said, "I was a poor and needy man, and had to labour hard to support myself. A certain master seeing this, and knowing me to be entirely trustworthy, used me (*engaged me for his work*) during five years, promising to pay me well for my pains. On this I patiently wrought in spite of weariness and difficulties. Just as the five years were done, one morning for some little fault I was cruelly whipped and driven away without a farthing. For this cause I am sad at heart and afflicted. Oh, who will pity me?"

The solitary master ordered him to accompany him, and coming to his cabin (*wood hut*), by his magic power he caused to appear some choice food, and ordered him to enter the pool and wash. Then he clothed him in new garments, and giving him 500 gold pieces, he dismissed him, saying, "When this is done, come and ask for more without fear."[39] After this he frequently bestowed on him more gifts, and in secret did him other good, so that his heart was filled with gratitude. Then the "ardent master" was ready to lay down his life in return for all the kindness he had received. Knowing this, the other said to him, "I am in need of an enthusiastic person.[40] During a succession of years I sought for one, till I was fortunate enough to meet with you, possessed of rare beauty and a becoming presence, different from others.[41] Now, therefore, I pray you, during one night (*to watch*) without speaking a word."

The champion said, "I am ready to die for you, much

[38] *Siang*, the marks indicating his noble character.

[39] *Wu-wai* may also mean "seek it not elsewhere." Julien translates it "do not despise me."

[40] "A brave champion"—Julien.

[41] So I translate the passage, but it may be "your beauty (or figure) corresponds to the ideal portrait I had formed of it." So Julien translates; but *fi yau ta* would more naturally be rendered "unlike that of any other."

more to sit with my breath covered."[42] Whereupon he constructed an altar and undertook the rules for becoming a Ṛishi, according to the prescribed form. Sitting down, he awaited the night. At the approach of night each attended to his particular duties. The "solitary master" recited his magic prayers; the champion held his sharp sword in his hand. About dawn suddenly he uttered a short cry, and at the same time fire descended from heaven, and flames and smoke arose on every side like clouds. The "solitary master" at once drew the champion into the lake,[43] and having saved him from his danger, he said, "I bound you to silence; why then did you cry out?"

The champion said, "After receiving your orders, towards the middle of the night, darkly, as in a dream, the scene changed, and I saw rise before me all my past history. My master[44] in his own person came to me, and in consolatory words addressed me; overcome with gratitude, I yet restrained myself and spoke not. Then that other man came before me; towering with rage, he slew me, and I received my ghostly body[45] (*I wandered as a shade or shadowy body*). I beheld myself dead, and I sighed with pain, but yet I vowed through endless ages not to speak, in gratitude to you. Next I saw myself destined to be born in a great Brâhmaṇ's house in Southern India, and I felt my time come to be conceived and to be brought forth. Though all along enduring anguish, yet from gratitude to you no sound escaped me.

[42] From this it seems that the portion relating to "holding the breath" is omitted in the previous sentence.

[43] That is, to escape the fire.

[44] That is, "my lord or master, whom I now serve"—the solitary master or Ṛishi. It cannot be my old master, the one who treated him so cruelly (as Julien construes it), for he comes on the scene in the next sentence. The symbols *sih sse* are not to be taken with *chu*, as though it were "my old master;" but with *kin*, as I have translated it, "there arose before me the former events of my life."

[45] This ghostly body or shade (*chung yin shan*) corresponds with the εἴδωλον of the Greeks—

Ψυχὴ καὶ εἴδωλον, ἀτὰρ
φρένες οὐκ ἔνι πάμπαν.

—*Iliad*, xxiii. 104.

After a while I entered on my studies, took the cap (*of manhood*), and I married; my parents dead, I had a child. Each day I thought of all your kindness, and endured in silence, uttering no word. My household connections and clan relatives all seeing this, were filled with shame. For more than sixty years and five I lived. At length my wife addressed me, 'You must speak; if not, I slay your son!' And then I thought, 'I can beget no other child, for I am old and feeble; this is my only tender son.' It was to stop my wife from killing him I raised the cry."

The "solitary master" said, "All was my fault; 'twas the fascination of the devil."[46] The champion, moved with gratitude, and sad because the thing had failed, fretted himself and died. Because he escaped the calamity of fire, the lake is called "Saving the Life," and because he died overpowered by gratitude, it has its other name, "The Champion's Lake."

To the west of this lake there is a *stûpa* of "the three animals." In this place, when Bôdhisattva was practising his preparatory life, he burnt his own body. At the beginning of the kalpa in this forest wild, there lived a fox, a hare, and a monkey, three creatures of different kinds but mutually affectionate. At this time Śakra, king of Dêvas, wishing to examine into the case of those practising the life of a Bôdhisattva, descended spiritually in shape as an old man. He addressed the three animals thus: "My children, two or three,[47] are you at ease and without fear?" They said, "We lie upon (*tread on*) the rich herbage, wander through the bosky brakes, and though of different kinds we are agreed together, and are at rest and joyful." The old man said, "Hearing that you, my chil-

[46] Of Mâra: it is plain that this weird story, taken in connection with the dream, the inability to move or speak, and the actual reference of it all to Mâra, is but an account of "the enthusiastic hero's" suffering from "nightmare."

[47] There appears to be an error in the text, as though *san* (three) had been repeated, but the middle stroke of the first symbol erased. But as the same symbols are used in the next sentence, the meaning may be simply, "My children."

dren, two or three, were peaceful at heart and living in sweet accord, though I am old, yet have I come from far alone, forgetting my infirmities, to visit you; but now I am pressed with hunger, what have you to offer me to eat?" They said, "Wait here awhile, and we will go ourselves in search of food." On this, with one mind and with single purpose, they searched through the different ways for food. The fox having skirted a river, drew out from thence a fresh carp fish. The monkey in the forest gathered fruits and flowers of different kinds. Then they came together to the appointed place and approached the old man. Only the hare came empty, after running to and fro both right and left. The old man spake to him and said, "As it seems to me, you are not of one mind with the fox and monkey; each of those can minister to me heartily, but the hare alone comes empty, and gives me nought to eat; the truth of what I say can easily be known." The hare, hearing these words and moved by their power, addressed the fox and monkey thus, "Heap up a great pile of wood for burning, then I will give (*do*) something." The fox and monkey did accordingly; running here and there, they gathered grass and wood; they piled it up, and when it was thoroughly alight the hare spake thus: "Good sir! I am a small and feeble thing; it is difficult for me to obtain you food, but my poor body may perhaps provide a meal." On this he cast himself upon the fire, and forthwith died. Then the old man reassumed his body as King Śakra, collected all the bones, and after dolorous sighs addressed the fox and monkey thus: "He only could have done it (*or*, unprecedented event). I am deeply touched; and lest his memory should perish, I will place him in the moon's disc to dwell." Therefore through after ages all have said, "The hare is in the moon." After this event men built a *stûpa* on the spot.[48]

[48] The preceding story is known as *The Hare Jâtaka*. It is given in Rhys Davids' *Buddhism*; it is found also in the Chinese Jâtaka-book; see also Fausböll, *Five Jâtakas*, p. 58.

Leaving this country and going down the Ganges eastward 300 li or so, we come to the country of Chen-chu.

THE KINGDOM OF CHEN-CHU[40] [GHÂZIPUR].

This kingdom is about 2000 li in circuit; its capital, which borders on the Ganges river, is about 10 li in circuit. The people are wealthy and prosperous; the towns and villages are close together. The soil is rich and fertile, and the land is regularly cultivated. The climate is soft and temperate, and the manners of the people are pure and honest. The disposition of the men is naturally fierce and excitable; they are believers both in heretical and true doctrine. There are some ten *saṅghârâmas* with less than 1000 followers, who all study the doctrines of the Little Vehicle. There are twenty Dêva temples, occupied by sectaries of different persuasions.

In a *saṅghârâma* to the north-west of the capital is a *stûpa* built by Aśôka-râja. The Indian tradition[50] says this *stûpa* contains a peck of the relics of Tathâgata. Formerly, when the Lord of the World dwelt in this place,[51] during seven days he preached the excellent law for the sake of an assembly of the Dêvas.

Beside this place are traces where the three Buddhas of the past age walked and where they sat.

Close by is an image of Maitrêya Bôdhisattva: although of small dimensions, its spiritual presence is great, and its divine power is exhibited from time to time in a mysterious manner.

Going east from the chief city about 200 li, we come to a *saṅghârâma* called 'O-pi-t'o-kie-la-na ("Ears not

[49] Chen-chu, meaning "lord of conflict or battle," is the translation of Garjanapati, and has been identified by Cunningham with Ghâzipur, a town on the Ganges just 50 miles east of Bânâras. The original Hindu name of the place was Garjapur.

[50] Or the work called *In-tu-ki*, *i.e.*, the Records of India.

[51] Julien translates "in this convent," but the original names only "the place." It would be natural to suppose that Aśôka built the *stûpa*, and the *saṅghârâma* was erected subsequently.

pierced"—Aviddhakarṇa[52]). The circuit (*encircling wall*) is not great, but the ornamental work of the building is very artistic. The lakes reflect the surrounding flowers, and the eaves of the towers and pavilions (*or*, the tower-pavilions) touch one another in a continuous line. The priests are grave and decorous, and all their duties are properly attended to. The tradition states: Formerly there were two or three Śramaṇas, passionately fond of learning, who lived in the country of Tu-ho-lo[53] (Tukharâ), to the north of the Snowy Mountains, and were of one mind. Each day during the intervals of worship and reciting the scriptures, they talked together in this way: "The excellent principles of religion are dark and mysterious, not to be fathomed in careless talk. The sacred relics (*traces*) shine with their own peculiar splendour; let us go together from place to place, and tell our faithful (*believing*[54]) friends what sacred relics we ourselves have seen."

On this the two or three associates, taking their religious staves,[55] went forth to travel together. Arrived in India, at whatever convent gates they called, they were treated with disdain as belonging to a frontier country, and no one would take them in. They were exposed to

[52] The distance and bearing from Ghâzipur given in the text would indicate Baliya as the site of this convent. There is a village called Bikapur, about one mile east of Baliya, which Cunningham thinks may be a corruption of Aviddhakarṇapura. It may be the same *vihâra* as that called "Desert" by Fa-hian (cap. xxxiv.) But we can hardly accept Cunningham's restoration of *Kwang ye* (which simply means "wilderness" or "desert") to Vṛihadâraṇya or Bṛihadâraṇya, which he thinks may have been corrupted into Biddhkarn.

[53] See vol. i. p. 37. For further remarks on the country Tu-ho-lo and the Tokhari people see a pamphlet by G. de Vasconcellos-Abreu on the probable origin of the Toukhari (*De l'Origine probable des Toukhares*), Louvain, 1883. This writer combats the opinion of Baron Richtofen and others that the Yue-chi and the Tokhari are identical. This is in agreement with vol. i. p. 57, n. 121, of the present work.

[54] "Our non-heretical friends or relatives," or it may be simply "our attached friends."

[55] There are two such foreign pilgrims with their staves sculptured at Amarâvati. *Tree and Serpent Worship*, pl. lxxxii. fig. 1. Mr. Fergusson suggests they may be Scythians; probably they are these Tokhari people. If this be so, their position beneath the palm-tree indicates the misery they endured, as described in the text; and the grouping may be compared with the "Judæa capta" medal.

the winds and the rains without, and within they suffered from hunger; their withered bodies and pallid faces showed their misery. At this time the king of the country in his wandering through the suburbs of the city saw these strange priests. Surprised, he asked them, "What region, mendicant masters, come you from? and why are you here with your unpierced ears[56] and your soiled garments?" The Śramaṇas replied, "We are men of the Tu-ho-lo country. Having received with respect the bequeathed doctrine,[57] with high resolve we have spurned the common pursuits of life, and following the same plan, we have come to see and adore the sacred relics. But alas! for our little merit, all alike have cast us out; the Śramaṇs of India deign not to give us shelter, and we would return to our own land, but we have not yet completed the round of our pilgrimage. Therefore, with much fatigue and troubled in heart, we follow on our way till we have finished our aim."

The king hearing these words, was much affected with pity, and forthwith erected on this fortunate (*excellent*) site a *saṅghârâma*, and wrote on a linen scroll the following decree: "It is by the divine favour of the three precious ones (*Buddha, Dharma, Saṅgha*) that I am sole ruler of the world and the most honoured among men. Having acquired sovereignty over men, this charge has been laid on me by Buddha, to protect and cherish all who wear the garments of religion (*soiled or dyed garments*). I have built this *saṅghârâma* for the special entertainment of strangers. Let no priest with pierced ears ever dwell in this convent of mine." Because of this circumstance the place received its name.

Going south-east from the convent of 'O-pi-t'o-kie-la-na about 100 li, and passing to the south of the Ganges, we come to the town Mo-ho-sa-lo (Mahâsâra),[58] the in-

[56] Hence the name, *Aviddhakarṇa*.

[57] That is, the bequest or testamentary doctrine of Buddha's religion.

[58] The town of Mahâsâra, has been identified by M. V. de St. Martin with Masâr, a village six miles to the west of Ârâ (Arrah).

habitants of which are all Brâhmaṇs, and do not respect the law of Buddha. Seeing the Śramaṇ, they first inquired as to his studies, and ascertaining his profound knowledge, they then treated him with respect.

On the north side of the Ganges[59] there is a temple of (Na-lo-yen) Nârâyaṇa-dêva.[60] Its balconies and storied towers are wonderfully sculptured and ornamented. The images of the Dêvas are wrought of stone with the highest art of man. Miraculous signs, difficult to explain, are manifested here.

Going east from this temple 30 li or so, there is a *stûpa* built by Aśôka-râja. The greater part (*a great half*) is buried in the earth. Before it is a stone pillar about 20 feet high, on the top of which is the figure of a lion. There is an inscription cut in it (*i.e., the pillar*) respecting the defeat of the evil spirits. Formerly in this place there was some desert[61] demons, who, relying on their great strength and (*spiritual*) capabilities, fed on the flesh and blood of men. They made havoc of men and did the utmost mischief. Tathâgata, in pity to living creatures, who were deprived of their natural term of days, by his spiritual power converted the demons, and led them, from reverence to him (*kwai i*[62]), to accept the command against murder. The demons, receiving his instruction respectfully, saluted him (*by the pradakshiṇa*). Moreover, they brought a stone, requesting Buddha to sit down, desiring to hear the excellent law (*from his mouth*), that they might learn how to conquer their thoughts and hold themselves in check. From that time the disciples of the unbelievers have all endeavoured to remove the stone which the demons placed for a seat; but though 10,000

[59] According to Cunningham, the pilgrim must have crossed the Ganges above Revelganj, which is nearly due north of Masâr exactly 16 miles. This point, near the confluence of the Ganges and Ghâgrâ, is deemed especially holy.

[60] That is, of Vishṇu.

[61] The expression used for "desert" (*kwang ye*) is the same as that found in Fa-hian, referred to above, n. 49.

[62] The Chinese phrase *kwai i* corresponds with the Sanskrit *śaraṇa*, "to take refuge in." Hence General Cunningham traces the name of this district Sâran to the incident recorded in the text.

of them strove to do so, they would be unable to turn it. Leafy woods and clear lakes surround the foundation on the right and left, and men who approach the neighbourhood are unable to restrain a feeling of awe.

Not far from the spot where the demons were subdued there are many *saṅghârâmas*, mostly in ruins, but there are still some priests, who all reverence the doctrine of the Great Vehicle.

Going south-east from this 100 li or so, we come to a ruined *stûpa*, but still several tens of feet high. Formerly, after the *Nirvâṇa* of Tathâgata, the great kings of the eight countries[63] divided his relics. The Brâhmaṇ who meted out their several portions, smearing the inside of his pitcher with honey,[64] after allotting them their shares, took the pitcher and returned to his country. He then scraped the remaining relics from the vessel, and raised over them a *stûpa*, and in honour to the vessel (*pitcher*) he placed it also within the *stûpa*, and hence the name (*of Drôṇa stûpa*) was given it.[65] Afterwards Aśôka-râja, opening (*the stûpa*), took the relics and the pitcher, and in place of the old[66] one built a great *stûpa*. To this

[63] See above, pp. 40, 41.

[64] This translation is somewhat forced. Literally the passage runs thus — "honey - smearing - pitcher - within."

[65] The Drôṇa *stûpa* (called the Kumbhân *stûpa* by Turnour, *J. A. S. B.*, vol. vii. p. 1013) is said to have been built by Ajâtaśatru (*Aśôkâvadâna*, translated by Burnouf, *Introd.*, p. 372). It may have stood near a village called Degwâra. It is named the "golden pitcher *stûpa*" by Aśvaghôsha, *Fo-sho*, v. 2283 (compare Spence Hardy, *Manual of Budhism*, p. 351). The Brâhmaṇ himself is sometimes called Drôṇa, or Drôha, or Dauna. Drôṇa corresponds with the Chinese *p'ing*, a pitcher or vase. Julien, in a note (p. 383, n. 1), seems to imply that Drôṇa is simply a measure of capacity, and so he restores *p'ing* to *karka*. But it also means a vessel or vase; probably in this case the Brâhmaṇ's pitcher. Compare *Fo-sho*, v. 1408; see also Cunningham, *Anc. Geog. of India*, p. 442.

[66] Julien translates, "then he reconstructed the monuments and enlarged it;" but in the original, as in all cases when speaking of Aśôka's building, it is implied that he destroyed the old erection, and in its place he built "a great *stûpa*." It would be gratifying if we could ascertain the character of the pre-Aśôka monuments. They are said by Cunningham to have been "mere mounds of earth," the sepulchral monuments of the early kings of the country even before the rise of Buddhism.—*Anc. Geog. of India*, p. 449.

day, on festival occasions (*fast-days*), it emits a great light.

Going north-east from this, and crossing the Ganges, after travelling 140 or 150 li, we come to the country of Fei-she-li (Vaiśâlî).

FEI-SHE-LI (VAIŚÂLÎ).

This kingdom[67] is about 5000 li in circuit.[68] The soil is rich and fertile; flowers and fruits are produced in abundance. The *âmra* fruit (*mango*) and the *môcha* (*banana*) are very plentiful and much prized. The climate is agreeable and temperate. The manners of the people are pure and honest. They love religion and highly esteem learning. Both heretics and believers are found living together. There are several hundred *saṅghârâmas*, which are mostly dilapidated. The three or five[69] which still remain have but few priests in them. There are several tens of Dêva temples, occupied by sectaries of different kinds. The followers of the Nirgranthas are very numerous.

The capital city of Vaiśâlî (*or*, called Vaiśâlî) is to a great extent in ruins. Its old foundations are from 60 to 70 li in circuit. The royal precincts are about 4 or 5 li round: there are a few people living in it. North-west

[67] The pilgrim must have crossed the Gaṇḍak river, not the Ganges. This river flows within 12 miles of Degwâra, the probable site of the Drôṇa *stûpa*. Vaiśâlî, therefore, is to the east of the Gaṇḍak, and is placed by Cunningham on the site of the present village of Besârh, where there is an old ruined fort still called Râja-Bisal-ka-garh, or the fort of the Râja Visala. It is exactly 23 miles north-north-east from Degwâra. Vaiśâlî was probably the chief town, or the first in importance, of the people called Vṛijjis or Vajjis. These people were a northern race who had taken possession of this part of India (viz., from the foot of the mountains to the Ganges on the south, and from the Gaṇḍak on the west to the Mahânadî on the east) from an early period; how early we cannot say, but as early as the redaction of the Buddhist books at least.

[68] This is much in excess of the actual measurement, even if the country of Vṛijji be included. But for these calculations of area or circuit the pilgrim had no data except the ordinary statements of the people, which would be certainly exaggerated.

[69] Julien proposes to substitute *four* for *five*. I have kept to the original, which is in accordance with Oriental idiom.

of the royal city (*precincts*) 5 or 6 li, is a *saṅghârâma* with a few disciples. They study the teaching of the Little Vehicle, according to the Saṁmatîya school.

By the side of it is a *stûpa*. It was here Tathâgata delivered the *Vimalakîrttî Sûtra* (*Pi-mo-lo-kie-king*), and the son of a householder, Ratnâkara,[70] and others offered precious parasols (*to Buddha*).[71] To the east of this is a *stûpa*. It was here Śâriputra and others obtained perfect exemption (*became Arhats*).

To the south-east of this last spot is a *stûpa*; this was built by a king of Vaiśâlî. After the *Nirvâṇa* of Buddha, a former king of this country obtained a portion of the relics of his body, and to honour them as highly as possible raised (*this building*).[72]

The records of India state: In this *stûpa* there was at first a quantity of relics equal to a "*hoh*" (ten pecks). Aśôka-râja opening it, took away nine-tenths of the whole, leaving only one-tenth behind. Afterwards there was a king of the country who wished again to open the *stûpa*, but at the moment when he began to do so, the earth trembled, and he dared not proceed to open (*the stûpa*).

To the north-west is a *stûpa* built by Aśôka-râja; by the side of it is a stone pillar about 50 or 60 feet high, with the figure of a lion[73] on the top. To the south of

[70] So Julien restores *p'ao-tsi*, treasure heap. It is sometimes restored to Ratnakûṭa (B. Nanjio, *Catalogue*, p. 10 ss.); but, as before stated, the Chinese symbol for *kûṭa* is *kwui*, not *tsi*. Ratnâkara is perhaps the same as Yaśada.

[71] Yaśada is generally represented with a parasol over his head. Much of the later Buddhist legend appears to have been borrowed or adopted from the history of Yaśada. Pl. lxiii. fig. 3, *Tree and Serpent Worship*, probably relates to him.

[72] The Lichhavis of Vaiśâlî obtained a share of the relics of Buddha, and raised over them a *stûpa*. (See Varga 28 of the *Fo-sho-hing-tsan-king*). The scene found at Sâñchi (pl. xxviii. fig. 1, *Tree and Serpent Worship*) probably refers to this *stûpa* and its consecration. The appearance of the men shows they were a Northern race; their hair and flowing hair-bands and musical instruments agree with the account given of the people of Kuché (vol. i. p. 19, *ante*). It is stated both in the Pâli and Northern Buddhist books that the Lichhavis were distinguished for their bright coloured and variegated dresses and equipages. All the evidence seems to point to these people being a branch of the Yue-chi.

[73] The Lichhavis were called "lions." See *Fo-sho*, v. 1906. It would seem that the four animals

the stone pillar is a tank. This was dug by a band of monkeys (Markaṭahrada) for Buddha's use. When he was in the world of old, Tathâgata once and again dwelt here. Not far to the south of this tank is a *stûpa;* it was here the monkeys, taking the alms-bowl of Tathâgata, climbed a tree and gathered him some honey.

Not far to the south is a *stûpa;* this is the place where the monkeys offered the honey [74] to Buddha. At the north-west angle of the lake there is still a figure of a monkey.

To the north-east of the *saṅghârâma* 3 or 4 li is a *stûpa;* this is the old site of the house of Vimalakîrttî (Pi-mo-lo-ki); [75] various spiritual signs (*manifestations*) are exhibited here.

Not far from this is a spirit-dwelling [76] (*a chapel?*), its shape like a pile of bricks. Tradition says [77] this stone-pile is where the householder Vimalakîrttî preached the law when he was sick.

Not far from this is a *stûpa;* this is the site of the old residence of Ratnâkara (P'ao tsi).[78]

Not far from this is a *stûpa;* this is the old house of the lady Âmra.[79] It was here the aunt of Buddha and other Bhikshunîs obtained *Nirvâṇa.*

named in vol. i. pp. 11, 12, are typical of the four regions respectively; the "lion" would therefore typify Northern nations.

[74] This scene is also found at Sanchi (pl. xxvi. fig. 2, *Tree and Serpent Worship*). It is on the same pillar as the consecration scene alluded to above. The pillar was evidently the work or gift of the Vaiśâlî people.

[75] Vimalakîrttî is explained by the Chinese equivalents *wu kau ching, i.e.*, undefiled reputation. He was a householder (chang-ché) of Vaiśâlî and a convert to Buddhism. There is little said about him in the books; but he is supposed to have visited China (Eitel, *Handbook*, sub voc.)

[76] This was probably one of the Vajjian shrines, Chetiyâni or Yakkha-chetiyâni, of which we read in the *Book of the Great Decease*, and elsewhere. (Compare *Sac. Bks. of the East*, vol. xi. p. 4.)

[77] Julien translates—"Tradition has preserved for it the name of 'piled-up stone' (Aśmakûṭa?)." But there is no symbol for "name;" it is simply "tradition says." Julien has omitted the title of "householder" (*chang-ché*).

[78] There is some difficulty in restoring *P'ao tsi.* Julien, in the passage before us, restores it to Ratnâkara, but in note 1 (same page) he restores the same symbols to Ratnakûṭa.

[79] For an account of the lady Âmra, see *Fo-sho-hing-tsan-king*, varga 22. Julien restores the expression to "daughter of the Âmra" (Âmradârikâ). It may be so; but

To the north of the *sanghârâma* 3 or 4 li is a *stûpa;* this indicates the place where Tathâgata stopped when about to advance to Kuśinagara to die, whilst men and Kinnaras followed him.[80] From this not far to the north-west is a *stûpa;* here Buddha for the very last time gazed upon the city of Vaiśâlî.[81] Not far to the south of this is a *vihâra,* before which is built a *stûpa;* this is the site of the garden of the Âmra-girl,[82] which she gave in charity to Buddha.

By the side of this garden is a *stûpa;* this is the place where Tathâgata announced his death.[83] When Buddha formerly dwelt in this place, he told Ânanda as follows:—"Those who obtain the four spiritual faculties are able to extend their lives to a kalpa. What is the term of years of Tathâgata then?" Thrice he asked this question, and Ânanda answered not, through the fascination of Mâra. Then Ânanda rising from his seat, gave himself up to silent thought in a wood. At this time Mâra coming to Buddha,[84] asked him, saying, "Tathâgata has for a long time dwelt in the world teaching and converting. Those whom he has saved from the circling streams (*of transmi-*

"the lady Âmra" appears more natural. She is called the "Mango girl" in the Southern records (*Sac. Books of the East,* vol. xi. p. 33), and the Chinese would bear this translation. She was a courtesan, and otherwise called Ambapâli. For an account of her birth and history, see *Manual of Budhism,* p. 327 *ss.*

[80] The Kinnaras are said to be the horse-faced musicians of Kuvêra (Eitel, *sub voc.*); but the Chinese symbols describe them as "something different from men." They may be seen figured in the sculpture at Sanchi, pl. xxvi. fig. 1, where they are coming to the place where Buddha stopped (figured by the oblong stone); this is another sculpture of the Vaiśâlî pillar, and illustrates the notice in the text.

[81] The incident connected with Buddha's last look at Vaiśâlî is narrated, *Fa-hian,* cap. xxv.; *Sac. Books of the East,* vol. xi. p. 64, and vol. xix. p. 283.

[82] Or, the lady Âmra; for an account of the gift of the garden, see *Fo-sho* as above.

[83] For an account of this incident compare *Fa-hian,* cap. xxv.; *Sac. Books of the East,* vol. xi. p. 41, and vol. xix. p. 267.

[84] This interview of Mâra (called Piśuna, the wicked one, in the Chinese version, *S. B. E.,* vol. xix. p. 267) is again found among the Sâñchi sculptures on the Vaiśâlî pillar, pl. xxvi. fig. 1, lower scene. Mâra is known by the escort of women, his daughters; he is here standing in front of the tree which symbolises Buddha's presence. His appearance and escort here are the same as in pl. xxx. fig. 1, upper part; he is there represented above the scene of rejoicing among the Dêvas of the Trayastrimśas heaven around

gration) are as numerous as the dust or the sands. This surely is the time to partake of the joy of *Nirvâṇa.*" Tathâgata taking some grains of dust on his nail, asked Mâra, saying, "Are the grains of dust on my nail equal to the dust of the whole earth or not?" He answered, "The dust of the earth is much greater." Buddha said, "Those who are saved are as the grains of earth on my nail; those not saved like the grains of the whole earth; but after three months I shall die." Mâra hearing it, was rejoiced and departed.

Meantime Ânanda in the wood suddenly had a strange dream, and coming to Buddha he told it to him, saying, "I was in the wood, when I beheld in my dream a large tree, whose branches and leaves in their luxuriance cast a grateful shade beneath, when suddenly a mighty wind arose which destroyed and scattered the tree and its branches without leaving a mark behind. Oh, forbid it that the lord is going to die! My heart is sad and worn, therefore I have come to ask you if it be so or not?"

Buddha answered Ânanda, "I asked you before, and

the head-turban of Buddha after the great renunciation; he is fitly placed above that heaven as being the "lord of the world of desire," and therefore always described as occupying the upper mansion of this tier of heavens. His distress and rage are indicative of his condition of mind in knowledge of Bôdhisattva's renunciation. If the four identifications on this pillar are correct, we may conclude that the people of Vaiśâlî were a Northern people allied to the Yue-chi, which illustrates the observation of Csoma Körösi, "that Tibetan writers derive their first king about 250 B.C. from the Litsabyis or Lichhavis" (*Manual of Budhism*, p. 236, note). The Śâkya family of Buddha is also said to belong to this tribe. *Mémoire* by V. de St. Martin, p. 367, note. The symbols used by the Chinese for the Yue-chi and for the Vrĭjjis are the same. Unless we are to suppose a much earlier incursion of these people into India than is generally allowed, the date of the Southern books of Buddhism (the book of the *Great Decease* and others), which contain accounts respecting the character, habits, and dress of the Lichhavis (which correspond with the Northern accounts), must be brought down considerably later than the assumed date of the redaction of the Pâli canon. But, on the other hand, if it be true that the incursion of these people took place when Pâṭaliputra was strengthened as a fortified outpost to repel their advance, *i.e.*, about the time of Buddha, then we must allow an early advance on their part into India. We know they were regarded as intruders, for Ajâtaśatru, king of Magadha, was desirous to attack and root out "these Vajjians," and it was he also who strengthened the city of Pâṭaliputra. The question deserves consideration.

Mâra so fascinated you that you did not then ask me to remain in the world. Mâra-râja has urged me to die soon, and I have covenanted to do so, and fixed the time. This is the meaning of your dream."[85]

Not far from this spot is a *stûpa*. This is the spot where the thousand sons beheld their father and their mother.[86] Formerly there was a Rĭshi who lived a secret life amid the crags and valleys. In the second month of spring he had been bathing himself in a pure stream of water. A roe-deer which came to drink there just after, conceived and brought forth a female child, very beautiful beyond human measure, but she had the feet of a deer. The Rĭshi having seen it, adopted and cherished it (*as his child*). As time went on, on one occasion he ordered her to go and seek some fire. In so doing she came to the hut of another Rĭshi; but wherever her feet trod there she left the impression of a lotus-flower on the ground. The other Rĭshi having seen this, was very much surprised, and bade her walk round his hut and he would give her some fire. Having done so and got the fire, she returned. At this time Fan-yu-wang (Brahmadatta-râja[87]) going out on a short excursion, saw the lotus-flower traces, and followed them to seek (*the cause*). Admiring her strange and wonderful appearance, he took her back in his carriage. The soothsayers casting her fortune said, "She will bear a thousand sons." Hearing this, the other women did nothing but scheme against her. Her time having been accomplished, she brought forth a lotus-flower of a thousand leaves, and on each leaf was seated a boy. The other women slandered her on its account, and saying it was "an unlucky omen," threw (*the lotus*) into the Ganges, and it was carried away by the current.

[85] For a full account of this incident, see, as before, *The Sacred Books of the East*, vols. xi. and xix.

[86] Compare *Fa-hian*, p. 97 (Beal's edition). Julien has no notice of "the father" of the children: perhaps it is an error in my text.

[87] If *yu* be taken in the sense of "given," Brahmadatta may be the right restoration. Julien proposes Brahmânadita doubtfully.

The king of Ujiyana (U-shi-yen), down the stream going out for an excursion, observed a yellow-cloud-covered box floating on the water and coming towards him. He took it and opened it, and there saw a thousand boys; being well nourished, when they came to perfect stature, they were of great strength. Relying on these, he extended his kingdom in every direction, and encouraged by the victories of his troops, he was on the point of extending his conquests to this country (*i.e.*, Vaiśâlî). Brahmadatta-râja hearing of it, was much alarmed; fearing his army was not able to contend successfully with the invaders, he was at a loss what to do. At this time the deer-footed girl, knowing in her heart that these were her sons, addressed the king thus: "Now that these youthful warriors are approaching the frontier, from the highest to the lowest there is an absence of courage (*heart*). Your feeble wife by her thought is able to conquer those redoubtable champions." The king not yet believing her, remained overwhelmed with fear. Then the deer-girl, mounting the city wall, waited the arrival of the warriors. The thousand youths having surrounded the city with their soldiers, the deer-girl said to them, "Do not be rebellious! I am your mother; you are my sons." The thousand youths replied, "What extravagant words are these!" The deer-girl then pressing both her breasts, a thousand jets of milk flowed out therefrom, and by divine direction fell into their mouths. Then they laid aside their armour, broke their ranks, and returned to their tribe and family. The two countries mutually rejoiced, and the people rested in peace.

Not far from this spot is a *stûpa*. This is where Tathâgata walked for exercise, and left the traces thereof. In teaching (*or*, pointing to the traces) he addressed the congregation thus: "In ancient days, in this place, I returned to my family[88] on seeing my mother. If you would

[88] Fa-hian calls this place the spot where Buddha "laid aside his bow and his club."

know then, those thousand youths are the same as the thousand Buddhas of this Bhadra-kalpa."

To the east of the spot where Buddha explained this birth (*jâtaka*) is a ruined foundation above which is built a *stûpa*. A bright light is from time to time reflected here. Those who ask (*pray*) in worship obtain their requests. The ruins of the turretted preaching-hall, where Buddha uttered the *Samantamukha*[89] *dhâraṇi* and other *sûtras*, are still visible.

By the side of the preaching-hall, and not far from it, is a *stûpa* which contains the relics of the half body of Ânanda.[90]

No far from this are several *stûpas*—the exact number has not yet been determined. Here a thousand Pratyêka Buddhas (To-kio) attained *Nirvâṇa*. Both within and without the city of Vaiśâlî, and all round it, the sacred vestiges are so numerous that it would be difficult to recount them all. At every step commanding sites and old foundations are seen, which the succession of seasons and lapse of years have entirely destroyed. The forests are uprooted; the shallow lakes are dried up and stinking; nought but offensive remnants of decay can be recorded.

Going north-west of the chief city 50 or 60 li, we come to a great *stûpa*. This is where the Lichhavas (Li-ch'e-p'o) took leave of Buddha.[91] Tathâgata having left the city of Vaiśâlî on his way to Kuśinagara, all the Lichhavas, hearing that Buddha was about to die, accompanied him wailing and lamenting. The Lord of the World having observed their fond affection, and as words were useless to calm them, immediately by his spiritual power caused to appear a great river with steep sides and deep, the waves of which flowed on impetuously. Then the Lichhavas were abruptly stopped on their way, moved with grief

[89] *Pu-men-t'o-lo-ni-king;* this is a section of the *Saddharma puṇḍarika Sûtra*, but we cannot suppose that any portion of this work is as old as the time of Buddha.

[90] For an account of the division of Ânanda's body consult *Fa-hian*, cap. xxvi.

[91] For this event see *Fa-hian*, cap. xxiv.

as they were. Then Tathâgata left them his *pâtra* as a token of remembrance.

Two hundred li to the north-west of the city of Vaiśâlî, or a little less, is an old and long-deserted city, with but few inhabitants. In it is a *stûpa.* This is the place where Buddha dwelt when, in old days, for the sake of an assembly of Bôdhisattvas, men, and Dêvas, he recited an explanatory *jâtaka* of himself when as a Bôdhisattva he was a *Chakravartin* monarch of this city and called Mahâdêva (Ta-tien). He was possessed of the seven treasures,[92] and his rule extended over the world (*the four empires*). Observing the marks of decay in himself,[93] and concluding in his mind about the impermanency of his body, he took a high resolve (*being secretly affected by his reflections*), left his throne, gave up his country, and, becoming a hermit, assumed the dark robes and gave himself to study.

Going south-east from the city 14 or 15 li, we come to a great *stûpa.* It was here the convocation of the seven hundred sages and saints was held.[94] One hundred and ten years after the *Nirvâṇa* of Buddha there were in Vaiśâlî some Bhikshus who broke the laws of Buddha and perverted the rules of discipline. At this time Yaśada (Ye-she-t'o) Âyushmat[95] was stopping in the country of Kôsala (Kiao-so-lo); Sambôgha (San-pu-kia) Âyushmat was dwelling in the country of Mathurâ; Rêvata (Li-po-to) Âyushmat was stopping in the country of Han-jo (Kanyâkubja?[96]); Sâla[97] (Sha-lo) Âyushmat was stopping in the country of Vaiśâlî; Pujasumira (Fu-she-su-mi-lo=Kujjasôbhita?) Âyushmat

[92] That is, the seven treasures of a holy-wheel king, or Chakravartin. For an account of these treasures see Sénart, *La Legende du Buddha*, pp. 20 ff.

[93] These marks of decay were the first white hairs that appeared on his head. On seeing these he resigned the throne to his son and became an ascetic. He is called Makhâdêwa by Spence Hardy, *Manual of Budhism*, pp. 129, 130.

[94] This is generally called "the second Buddhist convocation." For an account of it see Oldenberg, *Vinayapiṭakam*, vol. i.; *Abstract of Four Lectures*, p. 83, *ss.*, &c.

[95] So the Chinese *Chang-lo* may be rendered.

[96] Julien restores this doubtfully as Hañjna.

[97] Julien has omitted all mention of Sâla.

was stopping in the country of Sha-lo-li-fo (Salarîbhu ?): all these were great Arhats, possessed of independent power, faithful to the three *piṭakas*, possessed of the three enlightenments (*vidyâs*), of great renown, knowing all that should be known, all of them disciples of Ânanda.

At this time Yaśada sent a message to summon the sages and saints to a convocation at the city of Vaiśâlî. There was only wanting one to make up the 700, when Fu-she-su-mi-lo by the use of his divine sight saw the saints and sages assembled and deliberating about religious matters. By his miraculous power he appeared in the assembly. Then Sambôgha in the midst of the assembly, baring his right breast and prostrating himself, (*arose*) and exclaimed with a loud voice, "Let the congregation be silent, respectfully thoughtful! In former days the great and holy King of the Law, after an illustrious career, entered *Nirvâṇa*. Although years and months have elapsed since then, his words and teaching still survive. But now the Bhikshus of Vaiśâlî have become negligent and pervert the commandments. There are ten points in which they disobey the words of the Buddha (*the ten-power-daśabâla*). Now then, learned sirs, you know well the points of error; you are well acquainted with the teaching of the highly virtuous (*bhadanta*) Ânanda: in deep affection to Buddha let us again declare his holy will."

Then the whole congregation were deeply affected; they summoned to the assembly the Bhikshus, and, according to the *Vinaya*, they charged them with transgression, bound afresh the rules that had been broken, and vindicated the holy law.

Going south 80 or 90 li from this place, we come to the *saṅghârâma* called Śvêtapura (Shi-fei-to-pu-lo); its massive towers, with their rounded shapes and double storeys, rise in the air. The priests are calm and respectful, and all study the Great Vehicle. By the side of this building are traces where the four past Buddhas sat and walked.

By the side of these is a *stûpa* built by Aśôka-râja. It

was here, when Buddha was alive, that, on going southwards to the Magadha country, he turned northwards to look at Vaiśâlî, and left there, on the road where he stopped to breathe, traces of his visit.

Going south-east from the Śvêtapura *saṅghârâma* 30 li or so, on either (south and north) side of the Ganges river there is a *stûpa;* this is the spot where the venerable Ânanda divided his body between the two kingdoms. Ânanda was on his father's side cousin of Tathâgata. He was a disciple (*śaiksha*[98]) well acquainted with the doctrine (*collectanea*), thoroughly instructed in ordinary matters (*men and things*), and of masculine understanding. After Buddha's departure from the world he succeeded the great Kâśyapa in the guardianship of the true law, and became the guide and teacher of men devoted to religion (*men not yet Arhats*). He was dwelling in the Magadha country in a wood; as he was walking to and fro he saw a Śrâmaṇêra (*novice*) repeating in a bungling way a *sûtra* of Buddha, perverting and mistaking the sentences and words. Ânanda having heard him, his feelings were moved towards him, and, full of pity, he approached the place where he was; he desired to point out his mistakes and direct him in the right way. The Śrâmaṇêra, smiling, said, "Your reverence is of great age; your interpretation of the words is a mistaken one. My teacher is a man of much enlightenment; his years (*springs and autumns*) are in their full maturity. I have received from him personally the true method of interpreting (*the work in question*); there can be no mistake." Ânanda remained silent, and then went away, and with a sigh he said, "Although my years are many, yet for men's sake I was wishful to remain longer in the world, to hand down and defend the true law. But now men (*all creatures*) are stained with sin, and it is exceedingly difficult to instruct them. To stay longer would be useless: I will die soon." On this, going from Magadha, he went towards the city of Vaiśâlî,

[98] In Chinese, *To-wan*. He was the son of Śuklôdana-râja.

and was now in the middle of the Ganges in a boat, crossing the river. At this time the king of Magadha, hearing of Ânanda's departure, his feelings were deeply affected towards him, and so, preparing his chariot, he hastened after him with his followers (*soldiers*) to ask him to return. And now his host of warriors, myriads in number, were on the southern bank of the river, when the king of Vaiśâlî, hearing of Ânanda's approach, was moved by a sorrowful affection, and, equipping his host, he also went with all speed to meet him. His myriads of soldiers were assembled on the opposite bank of the river (*the north side*), and the two armies faced each other, with their banners and accoutrements shining in the sun. Ânanda, fearing lest there should be a conflict and a mutual slaughter, raised himself from the boat into mid-air, and there displayed his spiritual capabilities, and forthwith attained *Nirvâṇa*. He seemed as though encompassed by fire, and his bones fell in two parts, one on the south side, the other on the north side of the river. Thus the two kings each took a part, and whilst the soldiers raised their piteous cry, they all returned home and built *stûpas* over the relics and paid them religious worship.

Going north-east from this 500 li or so, we arrive at the country of Fo-li-shi (Vṛïjji).[99]

Fo-li-shi (Vṛïjji).[100]

This kingdom is about 4000 li in circuit. From east to west it is broad, and narrow from north to south. The soil is rich and fertile; fruits and flowers are abundant.

[99] Northern people call this San-fa-shi-Samvaji. It is in Northern India.—*Ch. Ed.*

[100] The country of the Vṛïjjis or Samvṛïjjis, *i.e.*, united Vṛïjjis, was that of the confederated eight tribes of the people called the Vṛïjjis or Vajjis, one of which, viz., that of the Lichhavis, dwelt at Vaiśâlî. They were republicans, and, if we may rely on the inferences found in note 80 *ante*, they were a confederation of Northern tribes who had at an early date taken possession of this part of India. They were driven back by Ajâtaśatru, king of Magadha. Compare Cunningham, *Anc. Geog.*, p. 449. *Sacred Books of the East*, xi. 2 ss.

The climate is rather cold; the mên are quick and hasty in disposition. Most of the people are heretics; a few believe in the law of Buddha. There are about ten *saṅghârâmas;* the disciples (*priests*) are less than 1000. They study assiduously both the Great and Little Vehicles. There are several tens of Dêva temples, with a great number of unbelievers. The capital of the country is called Chen-shu-na.[101] It is mostly in ruins. In the old royal precinct (*citadel or inner city*) there are yet some 3000 houses; it may be called either a village or a town.

To the north-east of the great river is a *saṅghârâma.* The priests are few, but they are studious and of a pure and dignified character.

From this going west along the side of the river, we find a *stûpa* about 30 feet high. To the south of it is a stretch of deep water. The great merciful Lord of the World converted here some fishermen. In days long past, when Buddha was living, there were 500 fishermen who joined in partnership to fish for and catch the finny tribes, whereupon they entangled in the river stream a great fish with eighteen heads; each head had two eyes. The fishermen desired to kill it, but Tathâgata being then in the country of Vaiśâlî, with his divine sight saw what was going on, and raising within him a compassionate heart, he used this opportunity as a means for converting and directing (*men*). Accordingly, in order to open their minds, he said to the great congregation, "In the Vṛĭjji country there is a great fish; I wish to guide it (*into the right way*), in order to enlighten the fishermen; you therefore should embrace this opportunity."

[101] Julien restores this to Chañśuṇa. V. de St. Martin connects the name with Janaka and Janakapura, the capital of Mithila (*Mémoire*, p. 368). Compare Cunningham, *Anc. Geog.*, p. 445. The interesting account the last writer gives of the old mounds or *stûpas* (arranged as a cross) at the old town of Navandgarh in this territory (p. 449 *op. cit.*), and the respect which the Vajjians observed towards them, reminds us of the record of Herodotos respecting the veneration of the Skythians for the tombs (mounds) of their ancestors (*Melpomene*, 133).

On this the great congregation surrounding him, by their spiritual power passed through the air and came to the river-side. He sat down as usual, and forthwith addressed the fishermen: "Kill not that fish. By my spiritual power I will open the way for the exercise of expedients, and cause this great fish to know its former kind of life; and in order to this I will cause it to speak in human language and truly to exhibit human affections (*feelings*)." Then Tathâgata, knowing it beforehand, asked (*the fish*), "In your former existence, what crime did you commit that in the circle of migration you have been born in this evil way and with this hideous body?" The fish said, "Formerly, by the merit I had gained, I was born in a noble family as the Brâhmaṇ Kapitha (Kie-pi-tha). Relying on this family origin, I insulted other persons; relying on my extensive knowledge, I despised all books and rules, and with a supercilious heart I reviled the Buddhas with opprobrious words, and ridiculed the priests by comparing them to every kind of brute beast, as the ass, or the mule, or the elephant, or the horse, and every unsightly form. In return for all this I received this monstrous body of mine. Thanks, however, to some virtuous remnants during former lives, I am born during the time of a Buddha's appearance in the world, and permitted to see his sacred form, and myself to receive his sacred instruction and to confess and repent of my former misdeeds."

On this Tathâgata, according to the circumstance, instructed and converted him by wisely opening his understanding. The fish having received the law, expired, and by the power of this merit was born in heaven. On this he considered his body, and reflected by what circumstances he was thus born. So, knowing his former life and recollecting the circumstances of his conversion, he was moved with gratitude to Buddha, and, with all the Dêvas, with bended form he bowed before him and worshipped, and then having circumambulated him, he withdrew, and, standing apart, offered precious flowers and unguents in religious service. The Lord of the World having directed the fishermen to consider this, and on their account preached the law, they were all forthwith enlightened and offered him profound respect. Repenting of their faults, they destroyed their nets, burnt their boats, and having taken refuge in the law, they assumed the religious habit, and by means of the excellent doctrine they heard came out of the reach of worldly influences and obtained the holy fruit (*of Arhats*).

Going north-east from this spot about 100 li, we come to an old city, on the west of which is a *stûpa* built by Aśôka-râja, in height about 100 feet. Here Buddha, when living in the world, preached the law for six months and converted the Dêvas. Going north 140 or 150 paces is a little *stûpa;* here Buddha, for the sake of the Bhikshus, established some rules of discipline. West of this not far is a *stûpa* containing hair and nail relics. Tathâgata formerly residing in this place, men from all the neighbouring towns and villages flocked together and burnt incense, and scattered flowers, and lighted lamps and torches in his honour.

Going north-west from this 1400 or 1500 li, crossing some mountains and entering a valley, we come to the country of Ni-po-lo (Nêpâla).

NI-PO-LO (NÊPÂL).

This country is about 4000 li in circuit, and is situated among the Snowy Mountains. The capital city is about 20 li round. Mountains and valleys are joined together in an unbroken succession. It is adapted for the growth of cereals, and abounds with flowers and fruits. It produces red copper, the *Yak* and the *Mingming* bird (*jîvañjîva*). In commerce they use coins made of red copper. The climate is icy cold; the manners of the people are false and perfidious. Their temperament is hard and fierce, with little regard to truth or honour. They are unlearned but skilful in the arts; their appearance is ungainly and revolting. There are believers and heretics mixed together. The *saṅghârâmas* and Dêva temples are closely joined. There are about 2000 priests, who study both the Great and Little Vehicle. The number of heretics and sectaries of different sorts is uncertain. The king is a Kshattriya, and belongs to the family of the Licchavas. His mind is well-informed, and he is pureand dignified in character. He has a sincere faith in the law of Buddha.

Lately there was a king called Aṁśuvarman[102] (An-chu-fa-mo), who was distinguished for his learning and ingenuity. He himself had composed a work on "sounds" (*Śabdavidyâ*); he esteemed learning and respected virtue, and his reputation was spread everywhere.

To the south-east of the capital is a little stream and a lake. If we fling fire into it, flames immediately arise; other things take fire if thrown in it, and change their character.

From this going back[103] to Vaiśâlî, and crossing the Ganges to the south, we arrive at the country of Mo-kie-t'o (Magadha).

END OF BOOK VII.

[102] In Chinese, Kwang-cheu: the only Aṁśuvarman in the lists of Nepâl dynasties is placed by Prinsep immediately after Śivadêva, whose date he adjusted tentatively to A.D. 470. In Wright's lists Śivadêva is omitted, and Aṁśuvarman stands at the head of the Thâkuri dynasty. In an inscription of Śivadêva, Aṁśuvarman is spoken of as a very powerful feudal chieftain, who probably ruled at first in the name of Śivadêva, but afterwards assumed the supreme power; and in other inscriptions dated Saṁ. 39 and 45, he is styled king, and the traditional account says he married the daughter of his predecessor and began a new dynasty; but it makes him contemporary with Vikramâditya of Ujjani (? cir. 540 to 580 A.D., Max Müller, *India*, p. 289). From Hiuen Tsiang's allusion we should be inclined to place Aṁśuvarman's reign about A.D. 580–600. His sister Bhôgadêvî was married to a Prince Sûrasêna, and by him was the mother of Bhôgavarman and Bhâgyadêvî. Aṁśuvarman was probably succeeded by Jishṇugupta, of whom we have an inscription dated Saṁ. 48. If these dates refer to the Śrî Harsha era, then Aṁśuvarman ruled about A.D. 644–652—at the close of the lifetime of Hiuen Tsiang—which is rather late. See Wright's *History of Nepâl*, p. 130 f.; Prinsep's *Ind. Ant.*, vol. ii., *U. T.*, p. 269; *Ind. Ant.*, vol. ix. pp. 169–172.

[103] But the pilgrim does not appear himself to have gone into Nepâl. He went to the capital of the Vṛîjjis, and there speaks from report. His return therefore must be calculated from this place.

BOOK VIII.

Contains the First Part of the Account of the Country of Magadha (Mo-kie-t'o).

THE country of Magadha (Mo-kie-t'o)[1] is about 5000 li in circuit. The walled cities have but few inhabitants, but the towns[2] are thickly populated. The soil is rich and fertile and the grain cultivation abundant. There is an unusual sort of rice grown here, the grains of which are large and scented and of an exquisite taste. It is specially remarkable for its shining colour. It is commonly called "the rice for the use of the great."[3] As the ground is low and damp, the inhabited towns are built on the high uplands. After the first month of summer and before the second month of autumn, the level country is flooded, and communication can be kept up by boats. The manners of the people are simple and honest. The temperature is pleasantly hot; they esteem very much the pursuit of learning and profoundly respect the religion of Buddha. There are some fifty *saṅghârâmas*, with about 10,000 priests, of whom the greater number study the teaching of the Great Vehicle. There are ten Dêva temples, occupied by sectaries of different persuasions, who are very numerous.

To the south of the river Ganges there is an old city about 70 li round. Although it has been long deserted, its foundation walls still survive. Formerly, when men's

[1] Or, it may mean the chief city or capital.

[2] *Yih*, the towns; Julien gives *villages*.

[3] This appears to be the rice called *Mahâśâli* and *Sugandhikâ* (Julien).

lives were incalculably long, it was called Kusumapura (K'u-su-mo-pu-lo),[4] so called because the palace of the king had many flowers. Afterwards, when men's age reached several thousands of years, then its name was changed to Pâṭaliputra[5] (Po-ch'a-li-tsu-ch'ing).

At the beginning there was a Brâhmaṇ of high talent and singular learning. Many thousands flocked to him to receive instruction. One day all the students went out on a tour of observation; one of them betrayed a feeling of unquiet and distress. His fellow-students addressed him and said, "What troubles you, friend?" He said, "I am in my full maturity (*beauty*) with perfect strength, and yet I go on wandering about here like a lonely shadow till years and months have passed, and my duties (*manly duties*)[6] not performed. Thinking of this, my words are sad and my heart is afflicted."

On this his companions in sport replied, "We must seek then for your good a bride and her friends." Then they supposed two persons to represent the father and mother of the bridegroom, and two persons the father and mother of the bride,[7] and as they were sitting under a *Paṭali* (*Po-ch'a-li*) tree, they called it the tree of the son-in-law.[8] Then they gathered seasonable fruits and pure

[4] Explained in a note to mean Hiang-hu-kong-sh'ing,—the city, or royal precinct, of the scented flower (*kusuma*).

[5] The text seems to refer the foundation of this city to a remote period, and in this respect is in agreement with Diodoros, who says (lib. ii. cap. 39) that this city ἐπιφανεστάτη καὶ μεγίστη was founded by Herakles. The Buddhist accounts speak of it as a village, Pâṭaligâma, which was being strengthened and enlarged by Ajâtaśatru, contemporary of Buddha, for the purpose of repelling the advance of the Vṛijjis. See *Sac. Books of the East*, vol. xi. pp. 16, 17; Bigandet, *Life of Gaudama*, p. 257; *Fo-sho-hing-tsan-king*, p. 249, n. 3; Cunningham, *Anc. Geog. of India*, p. 453.

[6] So it seems, from the story following, the passage must be understood. Julien confines the meaning to his "studies" not yet completed. But there would be no point in the pretended marriage, if that were his regret.

[7] This is the natural translation of the passage, and makes good sense without the alteration proposed by Julien.

[8] That is, they made the tree the father-in-law of the student; in other words, he was to marry the daughter of the tree, a *Pâṭali* flower (*Bignonia suaveolens*). I can find no authority for Julien's statement that the word son-in-law corresponds to *Pâṭali*; this statement is also repeated by Eitel, *Handbook*, sub voc. *Pâṭala*.

water, and followed all the nuptial customs, and requested a time to be fixed. Then the father[9] of the supposed bride, gathering a twig with flowers on it, gave it to the student and said, "This is your excellent partner; be graciously pleased to accept her." The student's heart was rejoiced as he took her to himself. And now, as the sun was setting, they proposed to return home; but the young student, affected by love, preferred to remain.

Then the other said, "All this was fun; pray come back with us; there are wild beasts in this forest; we are afraid they will kill you." But the student preferred to remain walking up and down by the side of the tree.

After sunset a strange light lit up the plain, the sound of pipes and lutes with their soft music (*was heard*), and the ground was covered with a sumptuous carpet. Suddenly an old man of gentle mien was seen coming, supporting himself by his staff, and there was also an old mother leading a young maiden. They were accompanied by a procession along the way, dressed in holiday attire and attended with music. The old man then pointed to the maiden and said, "This is your worship's wife (*lady*)." Seven days then passed in carousing and music, when the companions of the student, in doubt whether he had been destroyed by wild beasts, went forth and came to the place. They found him alone in the shade of the tree, sitting as if facing a superior guest. They asked him to return with them, but he respectfully declined.

After this he entered of his own accord the city, to pay respect to his relatives, and told them of this adventure from beginning to end. Having heard it with wonder, he returned with all his relatives and friends to the middle of the forest, and there they saw the flowering tree become a great mansion; servants of all kinds were hurrying to and fro on every side, and the old man came forward and received them with politeness, and entertained them with all kinds of dainties served up amidst the sound of music.

[9] We must suppose him to represent the tree, the real father.

After the usual compliments, the guests returned to the city and told to all, far and near, what had happened.

After the year was accomplished the wife gave birth to a son, when the husband said to his spouse, "I wish now to return, but yet I cannot bear to be separated from you (*your bridal residence*); but if I rest here I fear the exposure to wind and weather."

The wife having heard this, told her father. The old man then addressed the student and said, "Whilst living contented and happy why must you go back? I will build you a house; let there be no thought of desertion." On this his servants applied themselves to the work, and in less than a day it was finished.

When the old capital of Kusumapura[10] was changed, this town was chosen, and from the circumstance of the genii building the mansion of the youth the name henceforth of the country was Pâṭaliputra pura (the city of the son of the Pâṭali tree).

To the north of the old palace of the king is a stone pillar several tens of feet high; this is the place where Aśôka (Wu-yau) râja made "a hell." In the hundredth year after the *Nirvâṇa* of Tathâgata, there was a king called Aśôka ('O-shu-kia), who was the great-grandson of Bimbisâra-râjâ.[11] He changed his capital from Râjagṛiha to Pâṭali (pura), and built an outside rampart to surround the old city. Since then many generations have

[10] From this it would appear that Kusumapura was not on the same site as Pâṭaliputra. Râjagṛiha was the capital in the time of Ajâtaśatru, and it was he who strengthened Pâṭaliputra. In the next clause it is said that Aśôka changed his capital from Râjagṛiha to Pâṭaliputra. He is described as the great-grandson of Bimbasâra, and therefore the grandson of Ajâtaśatru. The *Vâyu Purâṇa* states that Kusumapura *or* Pâṭaliputra was founded by Râja Udayâśva, the grandson of Ajâtaśatru; but the *Mahâwanso* makes Udaya the son of the king. See Cunningham, *Anc. Geog.*, p. 453.

[11] Hiuen Tsiang uses in this passage the phonetic equivalents for Aśôka, *'O-shu-kia*; on this Dr. Oldenberg founds an argument that the king referred to is not Dharmâśôka, but Kâlâśôka (*Vinaya Piṭakam*, vol. i., Introd., p. xxxiii. n.) But a note in the text states that *'O-shu-kia* is the Sanskrit form of *Wu-yau*; the latter in the Chinese form, signifying "sorrowless." For Bimbisara, see p. 102, n. 41.

passed, and now there only remain the old foundation walls (*of the city*). The *saṅghârâmas*, Dêva temples, and *stûpas* which lie in ruins may be counted by hundreds. There are only two or three remaining (*entire*). To the north of the old palace,[12] and bordering on the Ganges river, there is a little town which contains about 1000 houses.

At first when Aśôka (Wu-yau) râja ascended the throne, he exercised a most cruel tyranny; he constituted a hell for the purpose of torturing living creatures. He surrounded it with high walls with lofty towers. He placed there specially vast furnaces of molten metal, sharp scythes, and every kind of instrument of torture like those in the infernal regions. He selected an impious man[13] whom he appointed lord of the hell. At first every criminal in the empire, whatever his fault, was consigned to this place of calamity and outrage; afterwards all those who passed by the place were seized and destroyed. All who came to the place were killed without any chance of self-defence.

At this time a Śramaṇa, just entered the religious order, was passing through the suburbs begging food, when he came to hell-gate. The impious keeper of the place laid hold upon him to destroy him. The Śramaṇa, filled with fear, asked for a respite to perform an act of worship and confession. Just then he saw a man bound with cords enter the prison. In a moment they cut off his hands and feet, and pounded his body in a mortar, till all the members of his body were mashed up together in confusion.

The Śramaṇa having witnessed this, deeply moved with pity, arrived at the conviction of the impermanence (*anitya*) of all earthly things, and reached the fruit of "exemption from learning" (*Arhatship*). Then the infernal

[12] This may refer to Kusumapura, the "flowery palace" city, or to the palace in the old town of Pâṭaliputra.

[13] There seems to be only *one* man; Julien has "un troupe de scélérats." The story of this place of torment is found also in *Fa-hian*, cap. xxxii.

lictor said, "Now you must die." The Śramaṇa having become an Arhat, was freed in heart from the power of birth and death, and so, though cast into a boiling caldron, it was to him as a cool lake, and on its surface there appeared a lotus flower, whereon he took his seat. The infernal lictor, terrified thereat, hastened to send a messenger to the king to tell him of the circumstance. The king having himself come and beheld the sight, raised his voice in loud praise of the miracle.

The keeper, addressing the king, said, "Mahârâja, you too must die." "And why so?" said the king. "Because of your former decree with respect to the infliction of death, that all who came to the walls of the hell should be killed; it was not said that the king might enter and escape death."

The king said, "The decree was indeed established, and cannot be altered. But when the law was made, were *you* excepted? You have long destroyed life. I will put an end to it." Then ordering the attendants, they seized the lictor and cast him into a boiling caldron. After his death the king departed, and levelled the walls, filled up the ditches, and put an end to the infliction of such horrible punishments.

To the south of the earth-prison (*the hell*), and not far off, is a *stûpa*. Its foundation walls are sunk, and it is in a leaning, ruinous condition. There remains, however, the crowning jewel of the cupola.[14] This is made of carved stone, and has a surrounding balustrade.[15] This was the

[14] *Shai pao*, the distinctive or strong ornament. It seems to refer to "the *tee* (*htî*)," as it is called; the ornamental enclosure above the cupola would represent the region of the heaven of the thirty-three Dêvas.

[15] So the dome of Sañchi is surmounted as restored by Mr. Fergusson, *Tree and Serpent Worship*, pl. ii. (see also the remarks of the same writer, *op. cit.* p. 100, 1st ed.) The enclosed space or box on the summit of the *stûpa* is not, however, a simulated relic-box, but represents the first heaven, or the Trayastriṁśas heaven of Śakra and the thirty-two Dêvas. The Dêvas, therefore, are constantly represented in the sculptures as surrounding this enclosure and offering their gifts, in token of the relics of Buddha (his hair, golden bowl, &c.), taken there for worship. The Tee or Htî is the cone of metal circles, raised above this enclosed space, representing the lands (*khêttas*, or *kshêtras*) above the Trayastriṁśas heaven.

first (*or*, one) of the 84,000 (*stûpas*). Aśôka-râja erected it by the power (*merit*) of man[16] in the middle of his royal precinct (*or* palace). It contains a *ching* (measure) of relics of Tathâgata. Spiritual indications constantly manifest themselves, and a divine light is shed round it from time to time.

After King Aśôka had destroyed the hell, he met Upagupta,[17] a great Arhat, who, by the use of (*proper*) means,[18] allured him in a right way according as the opportunity (*or*, springs of action, *i.e.*, his power or capacity to believe) led, and converted him. The king addressed the Arhat and said, "Thanks to my acquired merit in former births, I have got (*by promise*) my kingly authority, but in consequence of my faults I did not, by meeting Buddha, obtain conversion. Now, then, I desire in all the greater degree to honour the bequeathed remains of his body by building *stûpas*."

The Arhat said, "My earnest desire is that the great king by his merits may be able to employ the invisible powers (*the spirits*) as agents in fulfilling his vow to protect the three precious ones." And then, because of the opportune occasion, he entered largely on the narrative of his offering the ball of earth, and on that account of Buddha's prediction, as the origin of his desire to build.[19]

The king having heard this, was overpowered, and he summoned the spirits to assemble, and commanded them, saying, "By the gracious disposal and spiritual efficacy of the guiding power of the King of the Law I have become, as the result of my good actions in former states of life, the highest amongst them. (*I wish now*) with especial care

[16] Or it may probably be "by his religious merit as a man."

[17] For some remarks on Upagupta (Kin-hu), see vol. i. p. 182, n. 48.

[18] *Upâya*, expedients or skilful use of means.

[19] The offering of the ball of earth refers to the circumstance related by Fa-hian at the opening of chap. xxxii. Julien has overlooked this, and refers the offering to the charity of Aśôka in giving Jambudvîpa to the priests. But it is plain that no prediction of Buddha hinged on this. Kanishka is said also to have been converted by the relation of a prediction referring to him made by Buddha, and explained by a shepherd boy.

to prepare a means of paying religious worship to the bequeathed body of Tathâgata. Do you, then, spirits and genii, by your combined strength and agreement of purpose, raise *stûpas* for the relics of Buddha throughout the whole of Jambudvîpa, to the very last house of all[20] (*i.e.*, to the extremity of the land). The mind (*or* purpose) is mine, the merit of completing it shall be yours. The advantage to be derived from this excellent act of religion I wish not to be confined to one person only; let each of you, then, raise a building in readiness (*for completion*), and then come and receive my further commands."

Having received these instructions, the genii commenced their meritorious work in the several quarters where they were; and having finished the task (*so far*), they came together to ask for further directions. Aśôkarâja (Wu-yau-wang) having opened the *stûpas* of the eight countries where they were built, divided the relics, and having delivered them to the genii, he addressed the Arhat[21] and said, "My desire is that the relics should be deposited in every place at the same moment exactly: although ardently desirous of this, my mind has not yet been able to perfect a plan for accomplishing it."[22]

The Arhat addressed the king and said, "Command the genii to go each to his appointed place and regard the sun.[23] When the sun becomes obscured and its shape as if a hand covered it, then is the time: drop the relics into the *stûpas*." The king having received these instructions, gave orders accordingly to the genii to expect the appointed day.

Meantime the king, Aśôka, watching the sun's disc,

[20] The text is difficult. Julien translates it "dans chaque ville possédant un *keou-tchi* (un kôti de souvarnas)." This may be correct, but the phrase *mwan keou chi* seems to me to refer to the full tale of inhabited places—everywhere.

[21] That is, Upagupta.

[22] Such appears to be the meaning of the passage. Julien translates it, "my desire is not yet accomplished." His desire was to find out a plan or method for depositing the relics at the same instant.

[23] Or it may be, "await an appointed day."

waited for the sign; then at noon (*or* the day) the Arhat, by his spiritual power, stretched forth his hand and concealed the sun. At the places where the *stûpas* had been built for completion, all (*the genii*[24]) observing this event, at the same moment concluded the meritorious undertaking.

By the side of the *stûpa*, and not far from it, in a *vihâra*, is a great stone on which Tathâgata walked. There is still the impression of both his feet on it, about eighteen inches long and six inches broad; both the right and left impress have the circle-sign,[25] and the ten toes are all fringed with figures of flowers (*or* flower scrolls) and forms of fishes, which glisten brightly in the light (*morning light*). In old time Tathâgata, being about to attain *Nirvâṇa*, was going northward to Kuśinagara, when turning round to the south and looking back at Magadha, he stood upon this stone and said to Ânanda, "Now for the very last time I leave this foot-impression, being about to attain *Nirvâṇa*, and looking at Magadha. A hundred years hence there shall be a King Aśôka;[26] he shall build here his capital and establish his court; he shall protect the three religious treasures and command the genii."

When Aśôka (Wu-yau) had ascended the throne, he changed his capital and built this town; he enclosed the stone with the impression; and as it was near the royal precinct, he paid it constant personal worship. Afterwards the kings of the neighbourhood wished to carry it off to

[24] So it must signify, not the inhabitants of the several places, but the genii who were awaiting the signal.

[25] The circle-sign is the *chakra;* this is the principal mark on the sole of Buddha's feet; see Alabaster's *Wheel of the Law*, p. 286 and *plate*. Julien translates the passage as if the *chakra* were visible on the right and left of the feet, instead of on the right and left imprint of the feet.

[26] It is plain that this prediction concerning Wu-yau-wang, supposed by Oldenberg always to refer to Dharmâśôka (see above, *note* 11), relates to O-chu-kia or Kâlâśôka, for it was he, the grandson of Ajâtaśatru, who established his capital at Pâṭaliputra; so also in the next sentence. Hiuen Tsiang probably translated all the records relating to Aśôka as though referring to the same person, using either 'O-shu-kia or 'O-yu, or Wu-yau, indifferently.

their own country; but although the stone is not large, they could not move it at all.

Lately **Śaśâṅka-râja**, when he was overthrowing and destroying the law of Buddha, forthwith came to the place where that stone is, for the purpose of destroying the sacred marks. Having broken it into pieces, it came whole again, and the ornamental figures as before; then he flung it into the river Ganges, but it came back to its old place.

By the side of the stone is a *stûpa*, which marks the place where the four past Buddhas walked and sat down, the traces of which still remain.

By the side of the *vihâra* which contains the traces of Buddha, and not far from it, is a great stone pillar about thirty feet high, with a mutilated inscription on it. This, however, is the principal part of it, viz., "Aśôka-râja with a firm principle of faith has thrice bestowed Jambudvîpa as a religious offering on Buddha, the Dharma and the assembly, and thrice he has redeemed it with his jewels and treasure; and this is the record thereof." Such is the purport of the record.

To the north of the old palace is a large stone house. It looks outside like a great mountain, and within it is many tens of feet wide. This is the house which Aśôka-râja commanded the genii to build for his brother who had become a recluse. Early in his life Aśôka had a half-brother (*mother's brother*) called **Mahêndra**[27] (Mo-hi-in-to-lo), who was born of a noble tribe. In dress he arrogated the style of the king; he was extravagant, wasteful, and cruel. The people were indignant, and the ministers and aged officers of the king came to him (*the king*), and remonstrated thus, "Your proud brother assumes a dignity as though he were some great one in comparison with others. If the government is impartial,

[27] Mahêndra (translated *Ta-ti*, great ruler) is generally spoken of as the son of Aśôka. The Simhalese historical works speak of him as the first Buddhist missionary sent to Ceylon. See *Mahawanso*, Turnour's transl., p. 76. Dr. Oldenberg doubts the truth of this tradition. *Vinayapitaka*, i., *Introduction*, lii.

then the country is contented; if men are agreed, then the ruler is in peace: these are the principles which have been handed down to us from our fathers. We desire that you will preserve the rules of our country, and deliver to justice those who would change them." Then Aśôka-râja addressed his brother as he wept, and said, 'I have inherited (*as my rule of*) government the duty of protecting and cherishing the people; how then have you, my brother, forgotten my affection and my kindness? It is impossible at the very beginning of my reign to neglect the laws. If I punish you, I fear the anger of my ancestors; on the other hand, if I excuse you, I fear the opinion of the people."

Mahêndra, bowing his head, replied, "I have not guarded my conduct, and have transgressed the laws of the country; I ask only an extension of my life for seven days."

On this the king placed him in a dark dungeon, and placed over him a strict guard. He provided him with every kind of exquisite meat and every necessary article. At the end of the first day the guard cried out to him, "One day has gone; there are six days left." The sixth day having expired, as he had greatly sorrowed for his faults and had afflicted (*disciplined*) his body and his heart, he obtained the fruit of sanctity (*became an Arhat*); he mounted into the air and exhibited his miraculous powers (*spiritual traces*). Then separating himself from the pollution of the world, he went afar, and occupied the mountains and valleys (*as a recluse*).

Aśôka-râja, going in his own person, addressed him as follows, "At first, in order to put in force the laws of the country, I desired to have you punished, but little did I think you would have attained to this highest rank of holiness.[28] Having, however, reached this condition of detachment from the world, you can now return to your country."

[28] That you would have mounted up in pure conduct to attain to and possess this holy fruit.

The brother replied, "Formerly I was ensnared in the net of (*worldly*) affections, and my mind was occupied with love of sounds (*music*) and beauty; but now I have escaped all this (*the dangerous city*), and my mind delights in (*the seclusion of*) mountains and valleys. I would fain give up the world for ever (*men's society*) and dwell here in solitude."

The king said, "If you wish to subdue your heart in quiet, you have no need to live in the mountain fastnesses. To meet your wishes I shall construct you a dwelling."

Accordingly he summoned the genii to his presence and said to them, "On the morrow I am about to give a magnificent feast. I invite you to come together to the assembly, but you must each bring for your own seat a great stone."[29] The genii having received the summons, came at the appointed time to the assembly. The king then addressed them and said, "The stones which are now arranged in order on the ground you may pile up, and, without any labour to yourselves, construct of them for me an empty house." The genii having received the order, before the day was over finished the task. Aśôka-râja then himself went to invite his brother to fix his abode in this mountain cell.

To the north of the old palace, and to the south of "the hell," is a great stone with a hollow trough in it. Aśôka-râja commissioned the genii as workmen to make this hollow (*vase*) to use for the food which he gave to the priests when he invited them to eat.

To the south-west of the old palace there is a little mountain. In the crags and surrounding valleys there are several tens of stone dwellings which Aśôka-râja made for Upagupta and other Arhats, by the intervention of the genii.

By the side of it is an old tower, the ruins of which are a mass of heaped-up stones. There is also a pond, the gentle ripples of which play over its surface as pure as a

[29] Compare *Fa-hian*, chap. xxvii.

mirror. The people far and near call it the sacred water. If any one drinks thereof or washes in it, the defilement of their sins is washed away and destroyed.

To the south-west of the mountain is a collection of five *stûpas.* The foundations are lofty but ruinous; what remains, however, is a good height. At a distance they look like little hills. Each of them is several tens of paces in front. Men in after-days tried to build on the top of these little *stûpas.* The records of India state, "In old time, when Aśôka-râja built the 84,000 *stûpas,* there was still remaining five measures of relics. Therefore he erected with exceptional grandeur five other *stûpas,* remarkable for their spiritual portents (*miraculous exhibitions*), with a view to indicate the fivefold spiritual body of Tathâgata.[30] Some disciples of little faith talking together argued thus, 'In old time Nanda-râja[31] built these five (*stûpas*) as treasure-places for his wealth (*seven precious substances*).' In consequence of this gossip, in after-time a king of insincere faith, and excited by his covetousness, put his troops in movement, and came with his followers to dig (*the stûpas*). The earth shook, the mountains bent (*fell*), and the clouds darkened the sun, whilst from the *stûpas* there came a great sound like thunder. The soldiers with their leaders fell backward, and the elephants and horses took to flight. The king thus defeated, dared no longer to covet (*the treasures*). It is said, moreover (*i.e., in the Indian records*), 'With respect to the gossip of the priests there has been some doubt expressed, but we believe it to be true according to the old tradition.'"

[30] Literally, the body of the law of Tathâgâta (*Ju-lai*) divided into five parts. It may refer to the five skandhas; these are *rûpa* (*sih*), *vêdanâ* (*sheu*), *saṁjñâna* (*siang*), *sâñskâra* (*hing*), *vijñâna* (*chi*).

[31] This refers to Nanda, the son of Mahânanda, called Mahâpadma, who was exceedingly avaricious. He was the son of a woman of the Sûdra class. He brought the whole earth under one umbrella (*Vishnu-Purâna*, p. 466, Wilson's translation). In the *Mahâvanso* he is called Dhana-nando, because he personally devoted himself to the hoarding of treasure (Max Müller, *Hist. Anc. Sansc. Lit.*, p. 281). The statement in the text, derived from "the old records of India," appears to identify Nanda with Aśôka, *i.e.*, Kâlâśôka.

To the south-east of the old city there is the *saṅghârâma* called K'iu-cha-'o-lan-mo[32] (Kukkuṭârâma), which was built by Aśôka-râja when he first became a believer in the religion of Buddha. It was a sort of first-fruit (*preparation in planting the root of virtue*), and a pattern of majestic construction (*lofty building*). He gathered there a thousand priests; a double congregation of lay people and saints made their offerings of the four necessary things, and provided gratuitously all the articles for use. This building has long been in ruins, but the foundation walls are still preserved.

By the side of the *saṅghârâma* is a great *stûpa* called 'O-mo-lo-kia (Âmalaka), which is the name of a fruit used as a medicine in India. King Aśôka having fallen sick and lingering for a long time, felt that he would not recover, and so desired to offer all his possessions (*gems and valuables*) so as to crown his religious merit (*to plant high the field of merit*). The minister[33] who was carrying on the government was unwilling to comply with his wish. Some time after this, as he was eating part of an Âmalaka fruit, he playfully[34] put the half of it (*in the hand of the king*) for an offering. Holding the fruit in his hand he said with a sigh to his minister, "Who now is lord of Jambudvîpa?"

The minister replied, "Only your majesty."

The king answered, "Not so! I am no longer lord; for I have only this half fruit to call my own! Alas! the wealth and honour of the world are as difficult to keep as

[32] This convent or *saṅghârâma* must not be confounded with the Kukkuṭapâdagiri, near Gayâ. See *Fa-hian*, cap. xxxiii. p. 132 n., also *Arch. Survey of India*, vol. xv. p. 4; *Ind. Ant.*, vol. xii. p. 327; compare also Julien's remark (p. 428, n. 1).

[33] It may be "ministers;" the story of the text is found among Aśvaghôsha's sermons. It is No. 26 as given in the *Abstract of Four Lectures*, p. 103.

[34] In a trifling way. This translation is difficult. Julien translates it as though the king were amused as he played with the fruit, until he had reduced it to a half. This translation is more agreeable to the text. But, on the other hand, in Aśvaghôsha's rendering of the story, he says that the minister offered the king a half Âmala fruit, to bestow in charity. The translation I have given requires the substitution of *tan* (to give in charity) for *lan* (cooked or thoroughly dressed).

it is to preserve the light of a lamp in the wind! My wide-spread possessions, my name and high renown, at close of life are snatched from me, and I am in the hands of a minister violent and powerful. The empire is no longer mine; this half fruit alone is left!"

Then he commanded an attendant officer to come, and he addressed him thus: "Take this half fruit and offer it in the garden (*ârâma*) of the cock (*monastery*) to the priests, and speak thus to the venerable ones, 'He who was formerly lord of Jambudvîpa, but now is master of only this half Âmala fruit, bows down before the priests (*chief priest*). I pray you (*on behalf of the king*) receive this very last offering. All that I have is gone and lost, only this half fruit remains as my little possession. Pity the poverty of the offering, and grant that it may increase the seeds of his religious merit.'"

The Sthavira, in the midst of the priests, spake thus in reply: "Aśôka-râja by his former deeds may hope to recover. Whilst the fever has held his person, his avaricious ministers have usurped his power and amassed wealth not their own. But this offering of half a fruit will secure the king an extension of life." The king having recovered from his sickness, gave large offerings to the priests. Moreover he ordered the manager of the affairs of the convent (Tin-see—Karmmadâna) to preserve the seeds[35] of the fruit in a vessel of liquid fit for the purpose, and he erected this *stûpa* as a mark of gratitude for his prolonged life.[36]

To the north-west of Âmalaka *stûpa*, in the middle of an old *saṅghârâma*, is a *stûpa*; it is called "establishing the sound of the *ghaṇṭâ* (*Kin-t'i*)." At first there were about 100 *saṅghârâmas* in this city; the priests were grave

[35] Or, the stone or kernel. The Karmmadâna is the steward of the convent.

[36] This passage is obscure, and the translation I give is not in agreement with M. Julien's. He makes the words of the Sthavira to be addressed to the other priests, and not to the messenger from the king. It appears to me that they were made in reply to the king's message, and include in them a promised anticipation of the king's recovery.

and learned, and of high moral character. The scholars among the heretics were silent and dumb. But afterwards, when that generation of priests had died out, their successors were not equal to those gone before. Then the teachers of the heretics, during the interval, gave themselves to earnest study with a view to the mastery. Whereupon they summoned their partisans, numbering 1000 to 10,000, to assemble together within the priest's precincts, and then they addressed them saying, with a loud voice, "Strike loudly the *ghaṇṭâ* and summon all the learned men; let the foolish ones also stop and dispute; if we are wrong, let them overthrow us" (*or*, to overthrow their errors).

They then addressed the king and asked him to decide between the weak and the strong. And now the heretical masters were men of high talent and marked learning; the priests, although numerous, were weak in their points of verbal discussion.

The heretics said, "We have got the victory; from this time forth let no *saṅghârâma* dare to sound the *ghaṇṭâ* to call together a congregation." The king confirmed this result of the discussion, and, in agreement with it, bound the priests to the penalty. They on their part retired with shame and chagrin. For twelve years the *ghaṇṭâ* was not sounded.

At this time lived (Na-kia-'o-la-chu-na) Nâgârjuna Bôdhisattva in Southern India, as a youth of high renown for scholarship. When grown up he assumed a lofty title. Giving up his home and its pleasures, he practised himself in the acquisition of the deepest and most excellent principle of learning, and arrived at the first earth (*the first degree*). He had a great disciple called (Ti-po) Dêva, a man illustrious for wisdom and spiritual energy. This man, arousing himself to action, said, "At Vaiśâlî the followers of learning (*Buddhist learners*) have been defeated in argument by the heretics, and now for twelve years, days, and months together, they have not sounded the *ghaṇṭâ*. I am bold enough to wish to overturn the mountain of heresy and to light the torch of true religion."

Nâgârjuna replied, "The heretics of Vaiśâlî are singularly learned; you are no match for them. I will go myself."

Dêva said, "In order to trample down some rotten stems why should we overthrow a mountain? I am bold enough to think that by the instructions I have received I can silence all the heretics. But let my master assume the side of the heretics, and I will refute you according to the points of the thesis; and according as the question is decided, let my purpose to go or not be settled."

Then Nâgârjuna took the side of the heretics, and Dêva set himself to overthrow his arguments. After seven days Nâgârjuna lost his superiority (*was defeated*), and said with a sigh, "False positions are easily lost; erroneous doctrines are defended with difficulty. You yourself can go; you will overthrow those men."

Dêva Bôdhisattva's early reputation being known to the heretics of Vaiśâlî, they forthwith called an assembly, and went at once to the king, saying, "Mahârâja! you formerly condescended to attend to us and bind the Śramaṇas, not to sound the *ghaṇṭâ*. We pray you issue an order that no foreign Śramaṇa be allowed to enter the city, lest they should combine together to bring about an alteration in the former law." The king consented to their request, and gave strict orders to his officers to carry it out (*to spy narrowly*).

Dêva having come to the city, was not able to enter it; having understood the order, he made arrangements to change his garments, and wrapped up his *kashâya* robe in a bundle of grass (*shrubs*); then tucking up his garments, he went straight on with his bundle on his back, and entered the city. Having come to the middle of the city, he threw away his grass bundle, put on his robes, and came to this *saṅghârâma*, intending to stop there.

Knowing few people there, he had no place to lodge, and so he took up his night's rest in the Ghaṇṭâ Tower, and at early dawn he struck it (*the ghaṇṭâ*) with all his might.

The people hearing it, on investigating the matter, found that the stranger of yesternight was a travelling Bhikshu. Forthwith all the *saṅghârâmas* repeated the sounds (*of the ghaṇṭâ*).

The king hearing the noise, and inquiring about it closely, could not ascertain the origin of it all; coming to this *saṅghârâma*, they at length charged Dêva with the deed. Dêva answering said, "The *ghaṇṭâ* is struck to assemble the congregation; if it is not used for that purpose, what use is it?"

The king's people answered, "In former days the congregation of priests having been defeated in argument, it was decided the *ghaṇṭâ* should not be sounded any more, and this is twelve years since."

Dêva said, "Is it so? Nevertheless, I venture to sound afresh the drum of the law."

The messenger told the king saying, "There is a strange Śramaṇa who wishes to wipe out the former disgrace (*of the priests*)."

Then the king assembled the men of learning (*the Buddhists*), and said, by way of decree, "Whoever is defeated shall die, as a proof of his inferiority."

Then the heretics came together with their flags and drums, and began to discuss together with respect to their opinions; each displayed the point of his argument to his best ability. Then Dêva Bôdhisattva, having mounted the preaching-throne, attending to their former arguments, and following each point, refuted them one by one. In less than one hour he refuted the sectaries, and the king and his ministers being satisfied, raised this venerable monument in honour of his extreme virtue (*reverence*).

To the north of the *stûpa* built where the *ghaṇṭâ* was

sounded is an old foundation. This was the dwelling-place of a Brâhmaṇ that was inspired by demons. At the beginning there was in this city a Brâhmaṇ who had constructed for himself a hut in a wild and desert spot far from the haunts of men; he sacrificed to demons, seeking religious merit. By the assistance of such spiritual connection he discoursed in a high tone and disputed with eagerness. The report (*echo*) of his eloquent discourses resounded through the world. If any one came to propose a difficult question, he answered him after letting down a curtain. Old men of learning and of high talent could not wrest from him his precedence. Officers and people were silenced in his presence, and looked on him as a saint. At this time lived Aśvaghôsha Bôdhisattva (*'O-shi-po-kiu-sha-pu-sa*).[87] His wisdom embraced all subjects, and in his career he had traversed the arguments of the three Vehicles (*Little, Great, and Middle Vehicle?*). He constantly spoke (*about the Brâhmaṇ*) thus: "This Brâhmaṇ is learned without a master; he is skilful without examining the ancients; he lives apart in the gloomy desert, and arrogates a great name. It is all done by the connivance of the evil spirits and the assistance of occult powers; this is the way he does it! Men, therefore, on account of his eloquence derived from the devil, are unable to reply, and exalt his renown and say he is invincible. I will go to his place, and see what all this means, and expose it."

Forthwith he went to his cabin and addressed him thus: "I have long felt respect for your illustrious qualities; pray keep up your curtain whilst I venture to

[87] Translated into Chinese by *Ma-ming*, "the voice of the horse." For some remarks respecting him, see *Abstract of Four Lectures*, p. 95 ss. He is spoken of as the twelfth Buddhist patriarch. According to Tibetan accounts, he is the same as Mâtṛijeta (mother-child), who composed hymns for Buddhist worship (*op. cit.*, p. 141). Nâgârjuna also was a poet, and composed a work called *Suhṛid lêkha* (or *likh*), which he dedicated to his patron, Sadvaha, king of Southern Kôsala (*I-tsing*, k. iv. fol. 5 b.)

express my mind to you." But the Brâhmaṇ, maintaining an air of proud indifference, let down his curtain in order to reply, and to the end would not face his adversary.

Aśvaghôsha feeling in his heart the presence of the evil spirits, his feelings revolted, and he finished the discussion; but as he retired he said, "I have found him out, and he shall be overthrown." Going straightway to the king, he said, "Pray condescend to permit me to propose a subject and discuss it with that lay-doctor!"

The king, hearing the request, said with feeling, "Do you know your man? Unless well learned in the three *vidyâs* and in the six supernatural faculties, who can discuss with him?" Giving permission, he himself ordered his chariot in order to be present during the discussion, and to decide as to the victory.

Then Aśvaghôsha discoursed on the minute words of the three *Piṭakas*, and alluded to the great principles of the five *Vidyâs*, and nicely divided the length and breadth of his argument with a high and various discourse. Then the Brâhmaṇ following in the argument, Aśvaghôsha said, "You have lost the thread of the subject. You must follow my points consecutively."

The Brâhmaṇ then was silent and closed his mouth.

Aśvaghôsha finding fault, said, "Why do you not solve the difficulty? Call the spirits to your help to give you words as quickly as you can;" and then he lifted up his curtain to see how he looked.

The Brâhmaṇ, terrified, cried out, "Stop! stop!"

Aśvaghôsha, retiring, said, "This doctor has forfeited his high renown. 'A hollow fame lasts not long,' as the saying is."

The king answered and said, "Without the eminent ability of a master, who can detect the errors of the ignorant! The acumen of the person who knows men casts honour on his ancestors, and shuts out possibility of superiority among his successors. The country has a standing rule that such a person should ever be honoured and remembered."

Leaving the south-west angle of the city and going about 200 li,[38] there is an old ruined *saṅghârâma*, by the side of which is a *stûpa* which from time to time reflects a divine light and displays many miracles. This place is frequented by crowds from a distance and near by, who offer up their prayers[39] in worship. There are traces where the four past Buddhas sat and walked to and fro.

To the south-west of the old *saṅghârâma* about 100 li is the *saṅghârâma* of Tilaḍaka (Ti-lo-shi-kia).[40] This building has four halls, belvideres of three stages, high towers, connected at intervals with double gates that open inwards (*deeply*). It was built by the last descendant of Bimbisâra-râja (Pin-pi-sha-lo).[41] He made much of high talent and exalted the virtuous. Learned men from different cities and scholars from distant countries flock

[38] In the French translation the distance given is 200 *paces*. The text does not require the distance of 200 li to be reckoned in a south-westerly direction from the city; the construction, indeed, is unusual, and it is possible that the symbol *yu* (corner) is an error for *hing* (going); but as it stands, the text reads, "about two hundred li (from) the south-west angle of the city there is," &c. If the text be correct, some of the difficulties noticed by Cunningham (*Anc. Geog. of Ind.*, p. 456) will be explained.

[39] Make their requests in worship. Whatever the theory is as to the possibility of prayer in the Buddhist religion, the fact remains that prayer was offered up.

[40] So Cunningham restores it. And the symbol *shi* may represent *ḍa* as in Chanḍaka. It might also be made to represent Darśika, and as the last descendant of Bimbisâra-râja was Nâga-dâsaka, I thought at one time that this might be the right restoration. But I-tsing gives *Ti-lo-ch'a* as an alternative reading (*Nan hae*, k. iv. fol. 12 b.), which can only represent Tilaḍa (as in *Man ch'a* for *Manḍaka*, &c.) This monastery of Tilaḍaka was three yôjanas west of Nâlanda, or about twenty-one miles (*Vie de H. T.*, p. 211). In this last passage Hiuen Tsiang notices that there was an eminent priest called Prajñabhadra residing in this monastery when he visited it. When I-tsing was there a few years later, there was a priest called Prajñachandra there. Prof. Max Müller by some mistake has placed this temple of Tilaḍaka in Surat (*India*, p. 312), and he speaks of it as *Si-ra-chu*, but it is not so in I-tsing.

[41] Or Vimbasâra, juice of the *Bimba'* (*Bryonia grandis*), (see *ante*, p. 85) his descendant Nâgadâśaka, who appears to have preceded the nine Nandas; he seems to be the same as Mahâ-Nandin. Conf. R. David's *Numis. Orient.*, pp. 50 and 45. Is he the same as Kâlâśôka? Lassen, *Ind. Alt.*, vol. i. p. 859, and *Anh.*, p. xxxviii.

together in crowds, and reaching so far, abide in this *saṅghârâma*. There are 1000 priests in it who study the Great Vehicle. In the road facing the middle gate there are three *vihâras*, above which are placed the connected succession of metal rings (*circles*) with bells suspended in the air; below they are constructed storey above storey, from the bottom to the top. They are surrounded by railings, and the doors, windows, the pillars, beams, and staircases are all carved with gilt copper in relief, and in the intervals highly decorated. The middle *vihâra* contains an erect image of Buddha about thirty feet high. On the left is an image of Târa (*To-lo*) Bôdhisattva;[42] on the right, one of Avalôkitêsvara (Kwan-tsz'-tsai) Bôdhisattva. Each of these images is made of metallic stone; their spiritually composed appearance inspires a mysterious awe, and their influence is felt from far (*or*, spreads far). In each *vihâra* there is a measure of relics which emit a supernatural brilliancy, and from time to time shed forth miraculous indications.

To the south-west of the Tilaḍaka *saṅghârâma* about 90 li we come to a great mountain of blue-clouded (*variegated*) marble,[43] dark and tangled with wood. Here the divine Ṛishis dwell; poisonous snakes and savage dragons inhabit their dens, whilst numerous beasts and birds of prey dwell in the forests. On the top is a large and remarkable rock, on which is built a *stûpa* about ten feet or so high. This is the place where Buddha entered on ecstatic meditation. Of old, when Tathâgata descended as a spirit (*to be born*),[44] he rested on this rock, and entered here the *samâdhi* called "perfectly destroyed," and passed the night so. Then the Dêvas and spiritual saints offered

[42] Târa, said to be a female deity of Tibetan origin, worshipped by the followers of the Yôgachara school (Eitel). Târâvatî is also a form of Durgâ. *Ind. Ant.*, vol. x. p. 273.

[43] *Yun shih* is "variegated marble" (cloud-stone). Whether this be the meaning in the text it is difficult to say. Julien gives "enveloped with dark clouds." This may be so; the original is literally, "cloud-rock-dark-tangled."

[44] The phrase *Kiang shin*, descend spiritually, is generally applied to the incarnation of Buddha; in this passage, however, it may simply mean "descended as a spirit"

their offerings to Tathâgata, and sounded the drums and heavenly music, and rained down great flowers. Tathâgata leaving his ecstasy, the Dêvas all reverenced him, and raised a *stûpa* composed of gold, silver, and precious stones. Now so long time has elapsed since then, that the precious substances are changed into stone. No one has visited the spot for ages; but looking at the mountain from a distance, one can see different kinds of beasts and snakes turning round it to the right. The Dêvas and Rĭshis and spiritual saints accompany them in a body, praising and worshipping.

On the eastern summit of the mountain there is a *stûpa*. Here Tathâgata formerly stood for a time beholding the country of Magadha.

To the north-west of the mountain 30 li or so, on a declivity of the mountain, is a *saṅghârâma;* it is flanked by a high precipice, and the lofty walls and towers stand up in intervals of the rocks. The priests are about fifty in number, who all study the great Vehicle. This is the place where Guṇamati (Kiu-na-mo-ti) Bôdhisattva overcame the heretic. In the early time there was in this mountain a heretic called Mâdhava (Mo-ta-po), who at first followed the law of the Saṅkhyâ (Seng-kie) system, and practised the acquirement of wisdom. He had studied to the bottom the doctrine of "the extreme void," as found in the orthodox and erroneous (*books*). His fame was great, and surpassed that of former teachers, and outweighed all then living. The king honoured him exceedingly, and named him "the treasure of the country." The ministers and people regarded him with admiration, and spoke of him as "the teacher of the household." The learned men of the neighbouring countries acknowledged his merits and honoured his virtue, and compared him to the most eminent of his predecessors; a man, verily! highly accomplished. He had as his means of subsistence two towns of the district, and the surrounding houses paid him for the privilege of building (*tenant dues?*).

At this time in Southern India there lived Guṇamati[45] Bôdhisattva, who in his youth had displayed great talents and acquired in early life a brilliant reputation. By close study he had penetrated the meaning of the three *Piṭakas*, and investigated the four truths.[46] Hearing that Mâdhava discussed on the most mysterious and subtle questions, he desired to humble him by overcoming him (*in argument*). He ordered one of his followers to carry a letter thus written (*to his adversary*): "I have heard with all respect of Mâdhava's virtuous ease. You must now, without thought of fatigue, take up again your ancient studies, for in three years' time I intend to overthrow your brilliant reputation."

And so in the second and third years he sent a messenger with the same tidings; and now when he was about to go to meet him, he again wrote a letter, saying: "The appointed period has expired; your studies, such as they are, I am now coming (*to investigate*); you ought to know the fact."

Mâdhava now was alarmed, and gave orders to his disciples and to the inhabitants of the towns:[47] "From this time forth give no hospitality to the Śramaṇa heretics; let this order be generally known and obeyed."

At this time Guṇamati Bôdhisattva, with his staff in hand, arrived at the town of Mâdhava. The people who guarded the town, in agreement to the order, would give him no hospitality.[48] The Brâhmaṇs, moreover, deriding him, said, "What mean you by your shaven head and your singular dress? Begone from this! there is no place here for you to stop."

[45] Translated by the Chinese "virtue and wisdom" (*Tih hwui*).

[46] The four truths, the foundation of the Buddhist dogma, are—(1) the truth of "suffering" (*duḥkha*); (2) the increase or accumulation of misery from the passions (*samudaya*); (3) the extinction or destruction of suffering is possible (*nirôdha*); (4) the way or means (*mârga*). See Childers, *Pali Dict.*, sub voc. *Ariyasaccam*; Burnouf, *Lotus*, p. 517; *Manual of Budhism*, p. 496; also Julien *in loco*, n. 1.

[47] That is, the two towns he held in feoffment.

[48] Would have no intercourse with him.

Guṇamati Bôdhisattva desiring to overthrow the heretic, sought to remain the night in the town, and so he said with gentle words, "You, in pursuing your worldly studies, observe a pure conduct. I also, in studying higher truth, observe a pure line of conduct.[49] Our life being alike,[50] why do you exclude me?"

But the Brâhmaṇs would have no words with him, and only drove him from the place. Leaving the town, he went into a great forest in which savage beasts prowled about to destroy all passers-by. At this time there was a faithful brother[51] who, fearing (*the risk he ran from*) the beasts and the prickly thorns, hastened to him, staff in hand. Having met him, he said to the Bôdhisattva, "In Southern India there is a Bôdhisattva called Guṇamati, of far-spread renown; because this man wants to come here to discuss principles of belief, the master of the town, being afraid of him and his fame, has strictly enjoined to give no shelter to the Śramaṇas, and because I am afraid lest some accident should happen to him, I have come to accompany him in his journey, and to assure him of safety (*that he may rest free from fear of the other*)."

Guṇamati replied, "Most kind believer, I am Guṇamati." The disciple having heard this, with the greatest reverence replied to Guṇamati thus: "If what you say be true, you must go quickly (*onwards*)." Leaving the deep forest, they stopped awhile on the open plain; the faithful believer, following with his torch (?) and holding his bow, kept guard on the right and left. The (*first*) division of the night being past, he addressed Guṇamati and said, "It is better for us to go, lest men, knowing that you have come, should plot together to kill you."

Guṇamati, expressing his gratitude, said, "I dare not disobey you!" On this, following him, they came to the king's palace and said to the door-keeper, there is a

[49] They were both men of "pure conduct." The expression "pure brother" is applied to the Buddhist convert. The word Brâhmaṇ also is explained by "a pure-lived man."

[50] As we both aim at pure conduct.

[51] A pure believer.

Śramaṇa here who has come from a distance; he prays the king to agree in condescension to permit him to discuss with Mâdhava.

The king hearing the news, moved by his feelings, said, "This man is bereft of reason," and then he ordered an officer to go to the place where Mâdhava was, with this royal order: "There is a foreign Śramaṇa come here who seeks to discuss with you. I have now ordered the hall for the discussion to be prepared and watered; I have told those in the neighbourhood and far off to await the usual arrangements after your coming. Pray condescend to come forthwith."

Mâdhava asked the messenger of the king, "This surely is the doctor Guṇamati of South India." "Yes," he said, "it is he."

Mâdhava hearing this, his heart was very sad, but as he could not well avoid the difficulty, he set out for the hall of discussion, where the king, the ministers, and the people were all assembled desiring to hear this great controversy. Guṇamati first laid down the principles of his school, and continued his speech till the setting of the sun. Then Mâdhava excusing himself on account of his age and infirmities, to defer his answer, asked permission to retire and meditate. He would then return and answer every objection (*difficulty*) in order.[52] At the early morn he returned and ascended the throne, and so they went on to the sixth day, but on that day he vomited blood and died. When on the point of death he gave this command to his wife, "You have high talent; do not forget the affront paid to me." When Mâdhava was dead, she concealed the fact and had no funeral ceremonies; and clothing herself in shining apparel, she entered forthwith the assembly where the discussion was held, and a general clamour was raised as the people said one to another, "Mâdhava, who boasted of his talents, is unable to reply

[52] This sentence appears to be parenthetical, and is introduced to explain the language used by Guṇamati.

to Guṇamati, and so he sends his wife to make up for his deficiency."

Guṇamati, addressing the wife, said, "He who could bind you, has been bound by me."

Mâdhava's wife, seeing the difficulty, retired. The king then said, "What secret words are these at which she remains silent?"

Guṇamati said, "Alas! Mâdhava is dead! and his wife desires to come and discuss with me!"

The king said, "How know you this? Pray explain it to me."

Then Guṇamati said, "When the wife came her face was pale as death, and her words were toned in bitter enmity. I knew therefore that Mâdhava is dead! 'Able to bind you,' is a phrase applicable to her husband."

The king having sent a messenger to verify the statement, he found it even so; then the king in gratitude said, "The law of Buddha is a mysterious one! Eminent sages succeed one another without interruption; with no personal object they guard themselves in wisdom and use their secret knowledge for the purpose of converting (*transforming the world*). According to the old rules of the country the praises of such a sage (*or*, of your virtue) should be ever celebrated."

Guṇamati replied, "Whatever poor talents I have, I reserve them for the benefit of all that lives; and when I would draw them to the truth first of all I subdue their pride, then use the influences of converting power. Now then, in this case, O king, let the descendants of Mâdhava's territory for a thousand generations employ themselves in the service of a *saṅghârâma*. Your instructions will extend, then, from age to age, and your reputation will be immortal. Persons of a pure faith, conscious of protection, their religious merit will benefit the country for ages. They will be nourished as the priests are, and so the faithful will be encouraged to honour their virtue."

On this he founded the *saṅghârâma* to celebrate the victory.

At first, after the defeat of Mâdhava, six Brâhmaṇs (*pure-lived men*), fleeing to the frontiers, told the heretics of the reverse they had suffered, and they selected men of eminent talent with a view hereafter to wipe out their disgrace.

The king having a sincere respect for Guṇamati, went in person, and addressed the following invitation to him: "Now the heretics, not measuring their strength aright, have plotted together, and dare to sound the drum of discussion. Pray, sir, condescend to crush these heretics."

Guṇamati replied, "Let those who wish to discuss come together!"

Then the learned men among the heretics were rejoiced, and said, "We shall be sure of the victory to-day!" The heretics then laid down their principles with energy for the purpose of opening the discussion.

Guṇamati Bôdhisattva replied, "Now those heretics who fled from the difficulty they were in of obeying the king's command, these are mean men. What have I to do to discuss with and answer such persons?" Then he added, "There is a young servant here by the pulpit who has been accustomed to listen to these discussions. He is well acquainted with abstract questions from attending by my side and listening to the high language of the disputants."

Then Guṇamati, leaving the pulpit, said to the servant, "Take my place, and carry on the discussion." Then all the assembly was moved with astonishment at this extraordinary proceeding. But the servant, sitting by the pulpit, immediately proceeded to examine the difficulties proposed. His arguments were clear like the water that wells from the fountain, and his points were true as the sound of the echo. After three replies the heretics were defeated, and once more they were obliged to hide their disgrace and clip their wings. From this time forth the *saṅghârâma* enjoyed the endowment of the town and dwellings.

South-west of the convent of Guṇamati about 20 li we come to a solitary hill on which is a convent called (the *saṅghârâma* of) Śîlabhadra (Shi-lo-po-t'o-lo).[53] This is the convent which the master of *śâstras* after his victory caused to be built out of the funds of a village which were given up. It stands by the side of a single sharp crag like a *stûpa*. It contains some sacred relics of Buddha. This master of *śâstras* belonged to the family of the king of Samataṭa (San-mo-ta-ch'a), and was of the Brâhmaṇ caste. He loved learning and had gained a wide reputation. Travelling through the Indies to examine into and seek after religious truth, he came to this kingdom, and in the *saṅghârâma* of Nâlanda (Na-lan-t'o) he encountered Dharmapâla Bôdhisattva (Hu-fa-pu-sa). Hearing him explain the law, his understanding was opened, and he requested to become a disciple.[54] He inquired into the most subtle questions,[55] and investigated the way of deliverance to its conclusion; and thus having reached the highest point of intelligence, he estab-

[53] In Chinese, Kiai hien, "the sage of moral conduct."

[54] To assume the soiled or coloured robes of a mendicant.

[55] He inquired as to "the extreme point of the end of all." This idea of "a terminal fixed point of all things" (*yih-tsai-sse kau-keng kin-ku*) corresponds to the Sanskṛit *dhruva*, and may be rendered "final truth." It is the name of a Samâdhi; it is also used as a definition of *Nirvâṇa*; it is the formal definition of the title of a well-known Buddhist *sûtra*, the *Śuraṅgama*. In this connection it denotes the investigation of the highest (mystical) truth. This *sûtra* was written at Nâlanda; it was probably the work of Dharmapâla (it must not be confused with another work of the same name translated by Kumârajîva, and recited by Fa-hian at the Vulture Peak near Râjagṛiha); it was brought to China and translated A.D. 705. In the commentary (k. viii. fol. 30 b) it is said, "This *sûtra* was brought from India and belongs to the Mûrdhâbhishikta school (*Kun teng pu*). According to Colebrooke (Essays, p. 272), the Mûrdhâbhishiktas were a mixed class sprung from a Brâhmaṇa and a Kshatriya girl. The school named, therefore, was probably founded on a mixture of Brâhmaṇ and Buddhist doctrine. Now Nâlanda was especially a place of study both for the Brahmanical and Buddhist books (Edkins, *Chinese Buddhism*, p. 289). This school, therefore, probably originated there.

lished his fame over men of his time, even to distant countries.

There was a heretic of South India who delighted in examining profound questions and searching out hidden matters, in penetrating obscure and abstruse points of doctrine. Hearing of Dharmapâla's fame, the pride of self rose up within him, and, moved by profound envy, he passed over mountains and rivers in order to sound the drum [56] and seek discussion. He said, "I am a man of Southern India. It is reported that in the king's country there is a great master of *śâstras;* [57] I am but ignorant, yet I would wish to discuss with him."

"It is true, as you affirm," the king said; and forthwith he sent a messenger to ask Dharmapâla thus: "There is a heretic of Southern India who has come from a long distance here, and desires to discuss with you. Will you condescend to come to the hall of assembly and discuss with him?"

Dharmapâla having heard the tidings, gathered up his garments and went, whilst Śîlabhadra and the inferior disciples surrounded him as he advanced. Then Śîlabhadra (the chief disciple) addressed him thus: "Whither goest thou so quickly?" Dharmapâla answered, "Since the sun of wisdom went down,[58] and only the lamp of the inherited doctrine burns quietly, the heretics like clouds of ants and bees have risen; therefore I am now going to crush that one in discussion."

Śîlabhadra said, "As I have myself attended at various discussions, let me destroy this heretic." Dharmapâla, knowing his history, allowed him to have his way.

At this time Śîlabhadra was just thirty years old. The assembly, despising his youth, feared that it would be difficult for him alone to undertake the discussion. Dharmapâla knowing that the mind of his followers was

[56] To sound the drum is an expression for a challenge to discuss the law.

[57] *Ta lun sse*, explained by Julien (note 1, p. 453) to be equivalent to *Mahâvâdî*.

[58] That is, since the death of Buddha.

disturbed, hastened to relieve them and said, "In honouring the conspicuous talent of a person we do not say, 'He has cut his teeth' (*count his years according to his teeth*). As I see the case before us now, I feel sure that he will defeat the heretic; he is strong enough."

On the day of discussion (*assembly for discussion*) the people came together from far and near; both old and young in numbers assembled. Then the heretical teacher on his part laid open his case with great emphasis, and penetrated to the utmost the abstruse points (*of his argument*). Śîlabhadra followed his arguments (*principles*), and refuted them by profound and subtle allegations. The heretic, his words being exhausted, was covered with shame and retired.

The king, in order to reward the virtue (*of Śîlabhadra*), gave him the revenues of this town as a bequest. The master of *śâstras*, declining the offer, said, "A master who wears the garments of religion (*dyed garments*) knows how to be contented with little and to keep himself pure. What would he do with a town?"

The king in reply said, "The King of the Law has passed into the obscure (*abode*), and the vessel of wisdom has been engulfed in the stream. If there are no distinctions now made (*between the learned and ignorant*), then no encouragement is given to the scholar to press forward in the attainment of religion. Pray, of your pity, accept my offering."

The doctor, not persisting in his refusal, accepted the town and built this *saṅghârâma*, vast and magnificent, and endowed it with the revenues of the town,[59] as a means of providing it with the offerings necessary for religious service.

Going to the south-west of the *saṅghârâma* of Śîlabhadra about 40 or 50 li, and crossing the Nairañjanâ[60]

[59] Of the houses of the town. I understand it to mean the revenues of the *saṅghârâma* were derived from the rentals of the place; not that the people or the inhabitants were bound to the service of the priests.

[60] This river is now called Phalgu; the name Lilâjan or Nilâñjana is confined to the western branch, which joins the Mohâni five miles above Gayâ (Cunningham, *Anc. Geog.*, p. 457).

river we come to the town of Gayâ.[61] This town is naturally strong (*situated amid crags or precipices*). It has but few inhabitants; there are about 1000 families of Brâhmaṇs only; they are the offspring (*successors*) of a Ṛishi. The king does not regard them as vassals and the people everywhere highly respect them.

To the north of the town 30 li or so there is a pure fountain of water. The tradition handed down in India is that it is called "holy water;" all who bathe or drink thereof are cleansed from whatever defilement of sin they have.

To the south-west of the town 5 or 6 li we come to Mount Gayâ (Kia-ye), with its sombre valley, streams, and steep and dangerous crags. In India the name commonly given to this is the divine (*spiritual*) mountain. From old days it has been the custom for the ruling sovereign when he comes to the throne, with a view to conciliate his subjects at a distance and to cause his renown to exceed previous generations, to ascend (*this mountain*) and declare his succession with accompanying ceremonies (*religious ceremonies*). On the top of the mountain is a *stûpa* about 100 feet high, which was built by Aśôka-râja. Divine prodigies are exhibited by it, and a sacred effulgency often shines from it. In old days Tathâgata here delivered the *P'ao-yun*[62] and other *sûtras*.

To the south-east of Mount Gayâ is a *stûpa*. This is the spot where Kâśyapa (Kia-she-po) was born. To the south of this *stûpa* are two others. These are the spots where Gayâkâśyapa (Kia-ye-kia-she-po) and Nadîkâśyapa (Nai-ti-kia-she-po) sacrificed as fire-worshippers.[63]

[61] Now called Brahma-Gayâ to distinguish it from Bauddha-Gayâ, the place where Buddha reached enlightenment. The distance from Pâtna to Gayâ is 60 miles by the highroad, about 70 by the route of Hiuen Tsiang. We do not know the direction of the "old convent," 200 li from Pâtna, and therefore cannot test the correctness of Hiuen Tsiang's figures.

[62] Restored to *Ratnamêgha Sûtra* by Julien.

[63] For an account of the three Kâśyapas and their conversion see *Fo-sho-hing-tsan-king*, varga 16, vv. 1304 ss. For the scene of the "fire grot" see *Tree and Serpent Worship*, pl. xxiv. fig. 1.

To the east of the place where Gayâkâśyapa sacrificed to fire, crossing a great river, we come to a mountain called Prâgbôdhi (Po-lo-ki-po-ti).[64] Tathâgata, after diligently seeking for six years and not yet obtaining supreme wisdom, after this gave up his penance and accepted the rice-milk (*of Sujatâ*). As he went to the north-east he saw this mountain that it was secluded and dark, whereupon he desired to seek enlightenment thereon. Ascending the north-east slope and coming to the top, the earth shook and the mountain quaked, whilst the mountain Dêva in terror spake thus to Bôdhisattva: "This mountain is not the fortunate spot for attaining supreme wisdom. If here you stop and engage in the '*Samadhi* of diamond,'[65] the earth will quake and gape and the mountain be overthrown upon you."

Then Bôdhisattva descended, and half-way down the south-west slope he halted. There, backed by the crag and facing a torrent, is a great stone chamber. Here he sat down cross-legged. Again the earth quaked and the mountain shook. Then a Dêva of the pure abode (*Śuddhavâsas*) cried out in space, "This is not the place for a Tathâgata to perfect supreme wisdom. From this south-west 14 or 15 li, not far from the place of penance, there is a *Pippala* (*Pi-po-lo*) tree under which is 'a diamond throne.'[66] All the past Buddhas seated on this throne have obtained true enlightenment, and so will those yet to come. Pray, then, proceed to that spot."[67]

Then Bôdhisattva, rising up, the dragon dwelling in the cave said, "This cave is pure and excellent. Here you

[64] In Chinese *Tsin-ching-kio-shan*, *i.e.*, "the mountain leading to (before) perfect intelligence." When Tathâgata was about to attain to enlightenment he first ascended this mountain; hence the name.

[65] *Vajra samâdhi*, because it penetrates all conditions of being (*fa*).

[66] Vajrâsana, an imperishable throne. It was supposed to be the centre of the earth, and the spot where all the Buddhas arrived at complete wisdom.

[67] The whole of this passage is spoken by the Dêva. Julien translates it differently.

may accomplish the holy (*aim*). Would that of your exceeding love you would not leave me."

Then Bôdhisattva having discovered that this was not the place for accomplishing his aim, to appease the dragon, he left him his shadow and departed. The Dêvas going before, led the way, and accompanied him to the *Bôdhi* tree. When Aśôka-râja came into power, he signalised each spot up and down this mountain which Bôdhisattva had passed, by erecting distinguishing posts and *stûpas*. These, though of different sizes, yet are alike in spiritual manifestations. Sometimes flowers fall on them from heaven; sometimes a bright light illumines the dark valleys. Every year, on the day of breaking up the season of *Wass* (*Varshâs*), religious laymen from different countries ascend this mountain for the purpose of making religious offerings to the faithful. They stop one night and return.

Going south-west from Mount Prâgbôdhi about 14 or 15 li, we come to the Bôdhi tree. It is surrounded by a brick wall (*a wall of piled bricks*) of considerable height, steep and strong. It is long from east to west, and short from north to south. It is about 500 paces round. Rare trees with their renowned flowers connect their shade and cast their shadows; the delicate *sha*[68] herb and different shrubs carpet the soil. The principal gate opens to the east, opposite the Nairañjanâ river. The southern gate adjoins a great flowery bank. The western side is blocked up and difficult of access (*steep and strong*). The northern gate opens into the great *saṅghârâma*. Within the surrounding wall the sacred traces touch one another in all directions. Here there are *stûpas*, in another place *vihâras*. The kings, princes, and great personages throughout all Jambudvîpa, who have accepted the bequeathed teaching as handed down to them, have erected these monuments as memorials.

In the middle of the enclosure surrounding the *Bôdhi*

[68] The *Sha t'so* is the *Cyperus iria* of Linnæus (Doolittle's *Handbook*, ii. 432).

tree is the diamond throne (*Vajrâsana*). In former days, when the Bhadra-kalpa was arriving at the period of perfection (*vivartta*), when the great earth arose, this (*throne*) also appeared. It is in the middle of the great *chiliocosm;* it goes down to the limits of the golden wheel (*the gold circle*), and upwards it is flush with the ground. It is composed of diamond. In circuit it is 100 paces or so. On this the thousand Buddhas of the Bhadra-kalpa have sat and entered the diamond *Samâdhi;* hence the name of the diamond throne. It is the place where the Budddas attain the holy path (*the sacred way of Buddhahood*). It is also called the *Bôdhimaṇḍa.* When the great earth is shaken, this place alone is unmoved. Therefore when Tathâgata was about to reach the condition of enlightenment, and he went successively to the four angles of this enclosure, the earth shook and quaked; but afterwards coming to this spot, all was still and at rest. From the time of entering on the concluding portion of the kalpa, when the true law dies out and disappears, the earth and dust begin to cover over this spot, and it will be no longer visible.

After the *Nirvâṇa* of Buddha, the rulers of the different countries having learned by tradition the measurement of the diamond throne, decided the limits from north to south by two figures of Kwan-tsz'-tsai (Avalôkitêśvara) Bôdhisattva, there seated and looking eastward.

The old people say that "as soon as the figures of this Bôdhisattva sink in the ground and disappear, the law of Buddha will come to an end." The figure at the south angle is now buried up to its breast. The *Bôdhi* tree above the diamond throne is the same as the *Pippala* tree. In old days, when Buddha was alive, it was several hundred feet high. Although it has often been injured by cutting, it still is 40 or 50 feet in height. Buddha sitting under this tree reached perfect wisdom, and therefore it is called the (*Samyak sambôdhi*) tree of knowledge (*Pu-ti-Bôdhi*). The bark is of a yellowish-white colour, the leaves and twigs of a dark green. The leaves wither not either in winter or summer, but they remain shining and glistening all the year round without change. But at every successive *Nirvâṇa*-day (*of the Buddhas*) the leaves wither and fall, and then in a moment revive as before. On this day (of the *Nirvâṇa* ?) the princes of different countries and the religious multitude from different quarters assemble by thousands and ten thousands unbidden, and bathe (*the roots*) with scented water and perfumed milk; whilst they raise the sounds of music and scatter flowers and perfumes, and whilst the light of day is continued by the burning torches, they offer their religious gifts.

After the *Nirvâṇa* of Tathâgata, when Aśôka-râja began to reign, he was an unbeliever (*a believer in heresy*), and he desired to destroy the bequeathed traces of Buddha; so he raised an army, and himself taking the lead, he came here for the purpose of destroying (*the tree*). He cut through the roots; the trunk, branches, and leaves were all divided into small bits and heaped up in a pile a few tens of paces to the west of the place. Then he ordered a Brâhmaṇ who sacrificed to fire to burn them in the discharge of his religious worship. Scarcely had the smoke cleared away, when lo! a double tree burst forth from the flaming fire, and because the leaves and branches were shining like feathers, it was called the "ashes bôdhi tree." Aśôka-râja, seeing the miracle, repented of his crime. He bathed the roots (*of the old tree*) with perfumed milk to fertilise them, when lo! on the morning of the next day, the tree sprang up as before. The king, seeing the miraculous portent, was overpowered with deep emotion, and himself offered religious gifts, and was so overjoyed that he forgot to return (*to the palace*). The queen, who was an adherent of the heretics, sent secretly a messenger, who, after the first division of night, once more cut it down. Aśôka-râja in the morning coming again to worship at the tree, seeing only the mutilated trunk, was filled with exceeding grief. With the utmost sincerity he prayed as he worshipped; he bathed the roots with perfumed milk, and in less than a day again the tree was restored. The king, moved by deep reverence at the prodigy, surrounded the tree with a stone (*brick*) wall above 10 feet, which still remains visible. In late times Śaśâṅka-râja (She-shang-kia), being a believer in heresy, slandered the religion of Buddha, and through envy destroyed the convents and cut down the *Bôdhi* tree, digging it up to the very springs of the earth; but yet he did not get to the bottom of the roots. Then he burnt it with fire and sprinkled it with the juice of the sugar-cane, desiring to destroy it entirely, and not leave a trace of it behind.

Some months afterwards, the king of Magadha, called Pûrṇavarmâ (Pu-la-na-fa-mo), the last of the race of Aśôka-râja, hearing of it, sighed and said, "The sun of wisdom having set, nothing is left but the tree of Buddha, and this they now have destroyed, what source of spiritual life is there now?" He then cast his body on the ground overcome with pity; then with the milk of a thousand cows he again bathed the roots of the tree, and in a night it once more revived and grew to the height of some 10 feet. Fearing lest it should be again cut down, he surrounded it with a wall of stone 24 feet high. So the tree is now encircled with a wall about 20 feet high.

To the east of the *Bôdhi* tree there is a *vihâra* about 160 or 170 feet high. Its lower foundation-wall is 20 or more paces in its face. The building (*pile*) is of blue tiles (*bricks*) covered with chunam (*burnt stone, lime*); all the niches in the different storeys hold golden figures.[69] The four sides of the building are covered with wonderful ornamental work; in one place figures of stringed pearls (*garlands*), in another figures of heavenly Ṛishis. The whole is surrounded by a gilded copper *Âmalaka* fruit.[70] The eastern face adjoins a storeyed pavilion, the projecting eaves of which rise one over the other to the height

[69] There is no mention made of "figures of Buddha."

[70] *Myrobolan-embilc*; it is also called "a precious pitcher" or "a precious gourd." But see note at end of this Book.

of three distinct chambers; its projecting eaves, its pillars, beams, doors, and windows are decorated with gold and silver ornamental work, with pearls and gems let in to fill up interstices. Its sombre chambers and mysterious halls have doors in each of the three storeys. To the right and left of the outside gate are niches like chambers; in the left is a figure of Avalôkitêśvara Bôdhisattva, and in the right a figure of Maitrêya (T'se-shi) Bôdhisattva. They are made of white silver, and are about 10 feet high. On the site of the present *vihâra* Aśôka-râja at first built a small *vihâra*. Afterwards there was a Brâhmaṇ who reconstructed it on a larger scale. At first this Brâhmaṇ was not a believer in the law of Buddha, and sacrificed to Mahêśvara. Having heard that this heavenly spirit (*god*) dwelt in the Snowy Mountains, he forthwith went there with his younger brother to seek by prayer (*his wishes*). The Dêva said, "Those who pray should aim to acquire some extensive religious merit. If you who pray have not this ground (*of merit*), then neither can I grant what you pray for."

The Brâhmaṇ said, "What meritorious work can I set about, to enable me to obtain my desire?"

The god said, "If you wish to plant a superior root (*growth*) of merit, then seek a superior field (*in which to acquire it*). The *Bôdhi* tree is the place for attaining the fruit of a Buddha. You should straightway return there, and by the *Bôdhi* tree erect a large *vihâra*, and excavate a large tank, and devote all kinds of religious offerings (*to the service*). You will then surely obtain your wishes."

The Brâhmaṇs having received the divine communication, conceived a believing heart, and they both returned to the place. The elder brother built the *vihâra*, the younger excavated the tank, and then they prepared large religious offerings, and sought with diligence their heart's desire (*vow*). The result followed at once. The Brâhmaṇ became the great minister of the king. He devoted all his emoluments to the work of charity. Having finished the *vihâra*, he invited the most skilful artists to make a figure (*likeness*) of Tathâgata when he first reached the condition of Buddha. Years and months passed without result; no one answered the appeal. At length there was a Brâhmaṇ who came and addressed the congregation thus: "I will thoroughly execute (*paint and mark*) the excellent figure (*or* distinguishing points) of Tathâgata."

They replied, "For the purpose of doing this, what do you require?"

"Place in the *vihâra* a pile of scented earth and a lighted lamp; then when I have gone in, fasten the doors. After six months you may open them again."

Then the priests did as he directed. After four months, the six not being passed, the priests being astonished at the strange circumstance, opened the door to see what had happened. In the *vihâra* they found a beautiful figure of Buddha in a sitting position, the right foot uppermost, the left hand resting, the right hand hanging down. He was sitting facing the east, and as dignified in appearance as when alive. The throne was 4 feet 2 inches high, and 12 feet 5 inches broad. The figure was 11 feet 5 inches high; the two knees were 8 feet 8 inches apart, and the two shoulders 6 feet 2 inches. The signs and marks (*of a Buddha*) were perfectly drawn. The loving expression of his face was like life, only above his right breast the material was not yet completely rounded off. Having seen no man, they were satisfied that this was a miracle, and all of them were filled with strong emotion (*piteously sighed*) as they diligently sought to find out the secret (*earnestly inquired in order to know*). Now there was a Śramana who was passing the night there. He was of an honest and truthful heart, and being affected by the circumstance (*just related*), he had a dream, in which he saw the forementioned Brâhmaṇ, who addressed him thus: "I am Maitrêya Bôdhisattva. Fearing that the mind of no artist could conceive the beauty of the sacred features, therefore I myself have come to paint and

delineate the figure of Buddha. His right hand hangs down[71] in token that when he was about to reach the fruit of a Buddha, and the enticing Mâra came to fascinate him, then the earth-spirits came to tell him thereof. The first who came forth advanced to help Buddha to resist Mâra, to whom Tathâgata said, 'Fear not! By the power of patience he must be subdued!' Mâra-râja said, 'Who will bear witness for you?' Tathâgata dropped his hand and pointed to the ground, saying, 'Here is my witness.' On this a second earth-spirit leapt forth to bear witness (*to testify*). Therefore the present figure is so drawn, in imitation of the old posture of Buddha."

The brethren having understood this sacred miracle (*spiritual reflection*), were all moved with a tender emotion, and they placed above the breast, where the work was as yet unfinished, a necklace of precious stones and jewels, whilst on the head they placed a diadem of encircling gems, exceedingly rich.

Śaśâṅka-râja having cut down the *Bôdhi* tree, wished to destroy this image; but having seen its loving features, his mind had no rest or determination, and he returned with his retinue homewards. On his way he said to one of his officers, "We must remove that statue of Buddha and place there a figure of Mahêśvara."

The officer having received the order, was moved with fear, and, sighing, said, "If I destroy the figure of Buddha, then during successive kalpas I shall reap misfortnne; if I disobey the king, he will put me to a cruel death and destroy my family; in either case, whether I obey or disobey, such will be the consequences; what, then, shall I do?"

On this he called to his presence a man with a believing heart (*i.e., a believer in Buddha*) to help him, and sent him to build up across the chamber and before the figure of Buddha a wall of brick. The man, from a feeling of shame at the darkness, placed a burning lamp (*with the*

[71] This is the *Bhûmisparśa mudrâ*.

concealed figure); then on the interposing wall he drew a figure of (*or*, he made a figure of)[72] Mahêśvara-dêva.

The work being finished, he reported the matter. The king hearing it, was seized with terror; his body produced sores and his flesh rotted off, and after a short while he died. Then the officer quickly ordered the intervening wall to be pulled down again, when, although several days had elapsed, the lamp was still found to be burning (*unextinguished*).

The figure still exists in its perfect state as it was made by the sacred art of the god. It stands in a dark chamber; lamps and torches are kept burning therein; but those who wish to see the sacred features cannot do so by coming into the chamber; they should in the morning reflect the sunlight by means of a great mirror on the interior of the room; the sacred marks may then be seen. Those who behold them find their religious emotions much increased. Tathâgata obtained complete enlightenment (*Samyak sambodhi*) on the eighth day of the latter half of the Indian month Vaiśâkha (Fei-she-ḳie), which is with us the eighth day of the third month. But the Sthavira school (Shang-tso-pu) say on the fifteenth day of the second half of Vaiśâkha, which corresponds with us to the fifteenth day of the third month. Tathâgata was then thirty years old, or, according to others, thirty-five years.

To the north of the *Bôdhi* tree is a spot where Buddha walked up and down. When Tathâgata had obtained enlightenment, he did not rise from the throne, but remained perfectly quiet for seven days, lost in contemplation. Then rising, he walked up and down during seven days to the north of the tree; he walked there east and west for a distance of ten paces or so. Miraculous flowers sprang up under his foot-traces to the number of eighteen. Afterwards this space was covered in by a brick wall about three feet high. According to the old belief, these

[72] Julien thinks a translation should be adopted that would apply equally to a statue or a picture.

holy traces thus covered in, indicate the length or shortness of a man's life. First of all, having offered up a sincere prayer, then count the measurement (*or*, pace the distance and measure); according as the person's life is to be long or short, so will the measurement be greater or less.

On the left side of the road, to the north of the place where Buddha walked, is a large stone, on the top of which, as it stands in a great *vihâra*, is a figure of Buddha with his eyes raised and looking up Here in former times Buddha sat for seven days contemplating the *Bôdhi* tree; he did not remove his gaze from it during this period, desiring thereby to indicate his grateful feelings towards the tree by so looking at it with fixed eyes.

Not far to the west of the *Bôdhi* tree is a large *vihâra* in which is a figure of Buddha made of *teou-shih* (*brass*), ornamented with rare jewels; he stands with his face to the east. Before it is a blue stone with wonderful marks upon it and strangely figured. This is (*the place where*) Buddha sat on a seven-gemmed throne made by Śakra Dêva-râja when Brahma-râja built a hall for him of seven precious substances, after he had arrived at complete enlightenment. Whilst he thus sat for seven days in reflection, the mysterious glory which shone from his person lit up the *Bôdhi* tree. From the time of the holy one till the present is so long that the gems have changed into stone.

Not far to the south of the *Bôdhi* tree is a *stûpa* about 100 feet high, which was built by Aśôka-râja. Bôdhisattva having bathed in the Nairañjanâ river, proceeded towards the *Bôdhi* tree. Then he thought, "What shall I do for a seat? I will seek for some pure rushes when the day breaks." Then Śakra-râja (Shi) transformed himself into a grass-cutter, who, with his burden on his back, went along the road. Bôdhisattva addressing him said, "Can you give me the bundle of grass you are carrying on your back?"

The assumed grass-cutter, hearing the request, offered the grass with respect. Bôdhisattva having received it, went onwards to the tree.

Not far to the north of this spot is a *stûpa*. Bôdhisattva, when about to obtain enlightenment (*the fruit of Buddha*), saw a flock of blue birds rising up (*rohin?*)[73] according to the lucky way. Of all the good omens recognised in India this is the most so. Therefore the Dêvas of the pure abodes (*Śuddhavâsas* accommodated their proceedings to the customary modes of the world, and caused the birds thus to encircle him as spiritually (*miraculously*) indicating his holiness.

To the east of the *Bôdhi* tree, on the left and right of the great road, there are two *stûpas* (*one on each side*). This is the place where Mâra-râja tempted Bôdhisattva. Bôdhisattva, when on the point of enlightenment, was tempted by Mâra to become a Chakravarttin (Lun-wang) monarch.[74] On his refusing, he went away heavy and sorrowful. On this his daughters, asking him, went to try to entice the Bôdhisattva, but by his spiritual power he changed their youthful appearance into that of decrepit old women. Then leaning together on their sticks they went away.[75]

To the north-west of the *Bôdhi* tree in a *vihâra* is the image of Kâśyapa Buddha. It is noted for its miraculous and sacred qualities. From time to time it emits a glorious light. The old records say, that if a man actuated by sincere faith walks round it seven times, he obtains the power of knowing the place and condition of his (*former?*) births.

[73] The expression in the text seems to be phonetic. Julien translates "*luh*" literally by "deer." But the reference is to the blue birds rising up and circling round Bôdhisattva in a fortunate way, vid. *Tree and Serpent Worship*, pl. lviii. fig. 2, *first section*. The account of these signs is to be found in *Wong Pûh*, and in other legendary lives of Buddha.

[74] To accept the letter inviting him to be a Chakravarttin, or the *lot* cast by the soothsayers with respect to his being a Chakravarttin (Ch'uen-lun-wang).

[75] The temptation scene is represented in all the sculptures. See, *e.g.*, *Cave Temples*, by Dr. Burgess, pl. xx. For an account of the different events named in the text and a description of the great temple of Gayâ built by a king of Ceylon, see *Buddha Gayâ*, by Dr. Raj. Mitra.

To the north-west of the *vihâra* of Kâśyapa Buddha there are two brick chambers, each containing a figure of an earth-spirit. Formerly, when Buddha was on the point of obtaining enlightenment, Mâra came to him, and each one (*or* one) became witness for Buddha. Men afterwards, on account of his merit, painted or carved this figure of him with all its points of excellence.

To the north-west of the wall of the *Bôdhi* tree is a *stûpa* called Yuh-kin-hiang (the saffron scent, Kuṅkuma); it is about 40 feet high; it was built by a merchant chief (*srêshṭhî*) of the country of Tsao-kiu-ch'u (Tsaukuṭa). In old days there was a merchant-prince of this country who worshipped the heavenly spirits and sacrificed to them with a view to seek religious merit. He despised the religion of Buddha, and did not believe in the doctrine of "deeds and fruits." After a while, he took with him some merchants to engage in commercial transactions (*to take goods for having or not having, i.e., for exchange*). Embarking in a ship on the southern sea, a tempest arising, they lost their way, whilst the tumultuous waves encircled them. Then after three years, their provisions being gone and their mouths parched with thirst, when there was not enough to last the voyagers from morning till evening, they employed all their energies with one mind in calling on the gods to whom they sacrificed. After all their efforts no result followed (*their secret desire not accomplished*), when unexpectedly they saw a great mountain with steep crags and precipices, and a double sun gleaming from far. Then the merchants, congratulating themselves, said, "We are fortunate indeed in encountering this great mountain; we shall here get some rest and refreshment." The merchant-master said, "It is no mountain; it is the *Makara* fish; the high crags and scarped precipices are but its fins and mane; the double suns are its eyes as they shine." Scarce had he finished when the sails of the ship began to draw; on which the merchant-master said to his companions, "I have heard say that Kwan-tsz'-tsai Bôdhisattva is able to come to the help of those in difficulties and give them rest; we ought then with all faith to call upon that name." So with one accord and voice they paid their adorations[76] and called on the name. The high mountains disappeared, the two suns were swallowed up, and suddenly they saw a Śramaṇa with dignified mien and calm demeanour holding his staff, walking through the sky, and coming towards them to rescue them from shipwreck, and in consequence they were at their own country immediately.[77] Then because their faith was confirmed, and with a view not to lose the merit of their condition, they built a *stûpa* and prepared their religious offerings, and they covered the *stûpa* from top to bottom with saffron paste. After thus, conceiving a heart of faith, those who were like-minded resolved to pay their adoration to the sacred traces; beholding the *Bôdhi* tree, they had no leisure for words about returning; but now, a month having elapsed, as they were walking together, they said in conversation, "Mountains and rivers separate us from our native country, and now as to the *stûpa* which we built formerly, whilst we have been here, who has watered and swept it?" On finishing these words and coming to the spot (*where this stûpa stands*), they turned round in token of respect; when suddenly they saw a *stûpa* rise before them, and on advancing to look at it, they saw it was exactly like the one they had built in their own country. Therefore now in India they call it the Kuṅkuma stûpa.

At the south-east angle of the wall of the *Bôdhi* tree is a *stûpa* by the side of a Nyagrôdha (*ni-ken-liu*) tree. Beside it there is a *vihâra* in which is a sitting figure of Buddha. This is the spot where the great Brahmadêva exhorted Buddha, when he had first acquired enlightenment, to turn the wheel of the excellent law.[78]

[76] *Kwai-ming*, pay their adorations; the same as *kwai-i*. Julien translates it "placed their lot in his hands."

[77] Can this be the scene represented in the Ajaṇṭa frescoes? See Burgess, *Cave Temples*, pl. xvi.

[78] Buddha was in doubt whether

Within the walls of the *Bôdhi* tree at each of the four angles is a great *stûpa*. Formerly, when Tathâgata received the grass of good omen (*Santi*), he walked on the four sides of the *Bôdhi* tree from point to point; then the great earth trembled. When he came to the diamond throne, then all was quiet and peaceable again. Within the walls of the tree the sacred traces are so thick together that it would be difficult to recite each one particularly.

At the south-west of the *Bôdhi* tree, outside the walls, there is a *stûpa;* this is where the old house of the two shepherd-girls stood who offered the rice-milk to Buddha. By the side of it is another *stûpa* where the girls boiled the rice; by the side of this *stûpa* Tathâgata received the rice. Outside the south gate of the *Bôdhi* tree is a great tank about 700 paces round, the water of which is clear and pure as a mirror. Nâgas and fishes dwell there. This was the pond which was dug by the Brâhmaṇs, who were uterine brothers, at the command of Mahêśvara (Ta-thseu-thsaï).

Still to the south there is a tank; formerly, when Tathâgata had just acquired perfect enlightenment, he wished to bathe; then Śakra (Shi), king of Dêvas, for Buddha's sake, caused a pond to appear as a phantom.

On the west is a great stone where Buddha washed his robes, and then wished to dry them; on this, Śakra, king of Dêvas, brought this rock from the great Snowy Mountains. By the side of this is a *stûpa;* this is where Tathâgata put on (?) the old garments offered him. Still to the south in a wood is a *stûpa;* this is where the poor old woman gave the old garments which Tathâgata accepted.

any were fit to hear him preach. On this, Brahmâ (Fan), the lord of the "Saha world" (Mahâbrahmâ Sahâmpati), came and exhorted him to "turn the wheel," for, he said, "as on the surface of a pond there are white and blue lotus flowers, some only in bud, some opening, others fully opened; thus it is with men; some are not yet fit to be taught, others are being made fit, whilst some are ready to receive the saving doctrine." See the account in the *Chung-hu-mo-ho-ti Sûtra*. See also *Fo-sho*, varga 14, v. 1183.

To the east of the pond which Śakra caused to appear, in the midst of a wood, is the lake of the Nâga king Muchilinda (Mu-chi-lin-t'o). The water of this lake is of a dark blue colour, its taste is sweet and pleasant; on the west bank is a small *vihâra* in which is a figure of Buddha. Formerly, when Tathâgata first acquired complete enlightenment, he sat on this spot in perfect composure, and for seven days dwelt in ecstatic contemplation. Then this Muchilinda Nâga-râja kept guard over Tathâgata; with his folds seven times round the body of Buddha, he caused many heads to appear, which overshadowed him as a parasol; therefore to the east of this lake is the dwelling of the Nâga.

To the east of the tank of Muchilinda in a *vihâra* standing in a wood is a figure of Buddha, which represents him as thin and withered away.

At the side of this is the place where Buddha walked up and down, about 70 paces or so long, and on each side of it is a *Pippala* tree.

Both in old times and now, among the better classes and the poor, those who suffer from disease are accustomed to anoint the figure with scented earth, on which they get cured in many cases. This is the place where Bôdhisattva endured his penance. Here it was Tathâgata subdued the heretics and received the request of Mâra, and then entered on his six years' fast, eating a grain of millet and of wheat each day; his body then became thin and withered and his face marred. The place where he walked up and down is where he took the branch of the tree (*as he left the river*) after his fast.

By the side of the *Pippala* tree which denoted the place of Buddha's fast is a *stûpa;* this is where Ajñâta-Kauṇḍinya and the rest, to the number of five, resided. When first the prince left his home, he wandered through the mountains and plains; he rested in forests and by wells of water. Then Suddhôdana-râja ordered five men to follow him and wait on his person. The prince having entered on his penance, then Ajñâta Kauṇḍinya and the rest gave themselves also to a diligent practice of the same.

To the south-west of this spot there is a *stûpa*. This is where Bôdhisattva entered the Nairañjanâ river to bathe. By the side of the river, not far off, is the place where Bôdhisattva received the rice-milk.

By the side of this is a *stûpa* where the merchant-prince (*householder*) offered him the wheat and honey. Buddha was seated with his legs crossed beneath a tree, lost in contemplation, experiencing in silence the joys of emancipation. After seven days he aroused himself from his ecstasy. Then two merchant-princes travelling by the side of the wood were addressed by the Dêva of the place thus: "The prince-royal of the Śâkya family dwells in this wood, having just reached the fruit of a Buddha. His mind fixed in contemplation, he has for forty-nine days eaten nothing. By offering him whatsoever you have (*as food*) you will reap great and excellent profit."

Then the two merchants offered some wheat-flour and honey from their travelling store. The World-honoured accepted and received it.

By the side of the merchant-offering place is a *stûpa*. This is the spot where the four Dêva-râjas presented (*Buddha*) with a *pâtra*. The merchant-princes having made their offering of wheat-flour and honey, the Lord thought with himself in what vessel he should receive it. Then the four Dêva-râjas coming from the four quarters, each brought a golden dish and offered it. The Lord sat silently and accepted not the offerings, on the ground that such a costly dish became not the character of a hermit. The four kings casting away the golden dishes, offered silver ones; afterwards they offered vessels of crystal (*po-ch'i*), lapis-lazuli (*liu-li*), cornelian (*ma-nao*), amber (*ku-ch'i*), ruby (*chin chu*), and so on. The Lord of the World would accept neither of them. The four kings then returned to their palaces and brought as an offering stone *pâtras*, of a deep blue colour and translucent. Again presenting these, the Lord, to avoid accepting one and rejecting the others, forthwith joined them all in one and accepted them thus. Putting them one within the other, he made one vessel of the four. Therefore may be seen the four borders on the outside of the rim (*of the dish*).

Not far from this spot is a *stûpa*. This is the place where Tathâgata preached the law for the sake of his mother. When Tathâgata had acquired complete enlightenment, he was termed "the teacher of gods and of men." His mother, Mâyâ, then came down from heaven to this place. The Lord of the World preached to her according to the occasion, for her profit and pleasure.

Beside this spot is a dry pool, on the border of which is a *stûpa*. This is where in former days Tathâgata displayed various spiritual changes to convert those who were capable of it.

By the side of this spot is a *stûpa*. Here Tathâgata converted Uravilvâ-Kâśyapa (Yeu-leu-pin-lo-kia-she-po) with his two brothers and a thousand of their followers. Tathâgata, for the purpose of following out his office as "illustrious guide," according to his opportunity (*or* in a suitable way), caused him (*i.e.*, Kâśyapa) to submit to his teaching. On this occasion, when 500 followers of Uravilvâ-Kâśyapa had requested to receive the instruction of Buddha, then Kâśyapa said, "I too with you will give up the way of error." On this, going together, they came to the place where Buddha was. Tathâgata, addressing them, said, "Lay aside your leather garments and give up your fire-sacrificing vessels." Then the disciples, in obedience to the command, cast into the Nairañjanâ river their articles of worship (*service* or *use*). When Nadî-Kâśyapa (Nai-ti-kia-she-po) saw these vessels following the current of the river, he came with his followers to visit his brother. Having seen his conduct and changed behaviour, he also took the yellow robes. Gayâ-Kâśyapa also, with two hundred followers, hearing of his brother's change of religion, came to the place where Buddha was, and prayed to be allowed to practise a life of purity.

To the north-west of the spot where the Kâśyapa brothers were converted is a *stûpa*. This is the place where Tathâgata overcame the fiery Nâga to which Kâśyapa sacrificed. Tathâgata, when about to convert these men, first subdued the object of their worship, and rested in the house of the fiery Nâga of the Brahmachârins. After the middle of the night the Nâga vomited forth fire and smoke. Buddha having entered *Samâdhi*, likewise raised the brilliancy of fire, and the house-cell seemed to be filled with fiery flames. The Brahmachârins, fearing that the fire was destroying Buddha, all ran together to the spot with piteous cries, commiserating his fate. On this Uravilvâ-Kâśyapa addressed his followers and said, "As I now gather (*see*), this is not a fire, but the Śramaṇa subduing the fiery Nâga." Tathâgata having got the fiery dragon firmly fixed in his alms-bowl, on the morrow came forth holding it in his hand, and showed it to the disciples of the unbelievers. By the side of this monument is a *stûpa*, where 500 Pratyêka Buddhas at the same time entered *Nirvâṇa*.

To the south of the tank of Muchilinda Nâga is a *stûpa*. This indicates the spot where Kâśyapa went to save Buddha during an inundation. The Kâśyapa brothers still opposing the divine method,[79] all who lived far off or near reverenced their virtue, and submitted themselves to their teaching. The Lord of the World, in his character as guide of those in error, being very intent on their conversion, raised and spread abroad the thick clouds and caused the torrents to fall. The fierce waves surrounded the place where Buddha dwelt; but he alone was free from the flood. At this time Kâśyapa, seeing the clouds and

[79] *I.e.*, the methods Buddha had used for their conversion.

rain, calling his disciples, said, "The place where the Shaman dwells must be engulfed in the tide!"

Embarking in a boat to go to his deliverance, he saw the Lord of the World walking on the water as on land; and as he advanced down the stream, the waters divided and left the ground visible. Kâśyapa having seen (*the miracle*), his heart was subdued, and he returned.[80]

Outside the eastern gate of the wall of the *Bôdhi* tree, 2 or 3 li distant, there is the house of the blind Nâga. This Nâga, by the accumulated effect of his deeds during former existences, was born blind, as a punishment, in his present birth. Tathâgata going on from Mount Prâgbôdhi, desired to reach the *Bôdhi* tree. As he passed this abode, the eyes of the Nâga were suddenly opened, and he saw Bôdhisattva going on to the tree of intelligence (*Bôdhi*). Then addressing Bôdhisattva, he said, "O virtuous master! erelong you will become perfectly enlightened! My eyes indeed have long remained in darkness; but when a Buddha appears in the world, then I have my sight restored. During the Bhadra-kalpa, when the three past Buddhas appeared in the world, then I obtained light and saw (*for a while*); and now when thou, O virtuous one! didst approach this spot, my eyes suddenly opened; therefore I know that you shall become a Buddha."

By the side of the eastern gate of the wall of the *Bôdhi* tree is a *stûpa*. This is where Mâra-râja tried to frighten Bôdhisattva. When first Mâra-râja knew that Bôdhisattva was about to obtain perfect enlightenment, having failed to confuse him by his enticements or to terrify him by his arts, he summoned his host of spirits and arranged his demon army, and arrayed his soldiers, armed with their weapons, as if to destroy the Bôdhisattva. On this the winds arose and the rains descended, the thunders rolled in space and the lightning gleamed, as it lit up the darkness; flames of fire and clouds of smoke burst forth;

80 See *Tree and Serpent Worship*, pl. xxxi. fig. 2.

sand and hailstones fell like lances, and were as arrows flying from the bow. Whereupon the Bôdhisattva entered the *samâdhi* of "great love," and changed the weapons of the host to lotus flowers. Mâra's army, smitten by fear, retreated fast and disappeared.

Not far from this are two *stûpas* built by Śakra, king of Dêvas, and by Brahma-râja.

Outside the northern gate of the wall of the *Bôdhi* tree is the Mahâbodhi *saṅghârâma*. It was built by a former king of Siṁhala (*Ceylon.*) This edifice has six halls, with towers of observation (temple towers) of three storeys; it is surrounded by a wall of defence thirty or forty feet high. The utmost skill of the artist has been employed; the ornamentation is in the richest colours (*red and blue*). The statue of Buddha is cast of gold and silver, decorated with gems and precious stones. The *stûpas* are high and large in proportion, and beautifully ornamented; they contain relics of Buddha. The bone relics are as great as the fingers of the hand, shining and smooth, of a pure white colour and translucent. The flesh relics are like the great true pearl, of a bluish-red tint. Every year on the day of the full moon of (*the month when*) Tathâgata displayed great spiritual changes, they take these relics out for public exhibition.[81] On these occasions sometimes a bright light is diffused, sometimes it rains flowers. The priests of this convent are more than 1000 men; they study the Great Vehicle and belong to the Sthavira (Shang-tso-pu) school. They carefully observe the *Dharma Vinaya*, and their conduct is pure and correct.

In old days there was a king of Ceylon, which is a country of the southern sea, who was truthful and a believer in the law of Buddha. It happened that his brother, who had become a disciple of Buddha (*a houseless one*), thinking on the holy traces of Buddha, went forth to wander through India. At all the convents he visited,

[81] In India, the thirtieth day of the twelfth month; in China, the fifteenth day of the first month.

he was treated with disdain as a foreigner (*a frontier countryman*). On this he returned to his own country. The king in person went out to a distance to meet him, but the Śramaṇa was so affected that he could not speak. The king said, "What has so afflicted you as to cause this excessive grief?" The Śramaṇa replied, "I, relying on the dignity of your Majesty's kingdom, went forth to visit the world, and to find my way through distant regions and strange cities. For many years all my travels, during heat and cold, have been attended with outrage, and my words have been met with insults and sarcasm. Having endured these afflictions, how can I be light-hearted?"

The king said, "If these things are so, what is to be done?"

He replied, "In truth, I wish your Majesty in the field of merit would undertake to build convents throughout all India. You would thus signalise the holy traces, and gain for yourself a great name; you would show your gratitude for the advantage derived from your predecessors, and hand down the merit thereof to your successors."

He replied, "This is an excellent plan; how have I but just heard of it?"

Then he gave in tribute to the king of India all the jewels of his country. The king having received them as tribute, from a principle of duty and affection to his distant ally, he sent messengers to say, "What can I now do in return for the decree?"

The minister said, "The king of Siṁhala salutes the king of India (Mahâ Śrî râja). The reputation of the Mahârâja has spread far and wide, and your benefits have reached to distant regions. The Śramaṇas of this inferior country desire to obey your instructions and to accept your transforming influences. Having wandered through your superior country in visiting the sacred traces, I called at various convents and found great difficulty in getting entertainment, and so, fatigued and very much worn by affronts, I returned home. I have therefore formed a plan for the benefit of future travellers; I desire to build in all the Indies a convent for the entertainment of such strangers, who may have a place of rest between their journey there and back. Thus the two countries will be bound together and travellers be refreshed."

The king said, "I permit your royal master to take (*for this purpose*) one of the places in which Tathâgata has left the traces of his holy teaching."

On this the messenger returned home, having taken leave of the king, and gave an account of his interview. The ministers received him with distinction and assembled the Śramâṇas and deliberated as to the foundation of a convent. The Śramaṇas said, "The (*Bôdhi*) tree is the place where all the past Buddhas have obtained the holy fruit and where the future ones will obtain it. There is no better place than this for carrying out the project."

Then, sending all the jewels of the country, they built this convent to entertain priests of this country (*Ceylon*), and he caused to be engraved this proclamation on copper, "To help all without distinction is the highest teaching of all the Buddhas; to exercise mercy as occasion offers is the illustrious doctrine of former saints. And now I, unworthy descendant in the royal line, have undertaken to found this *saṅghârâma*, to enclose the sacred traces, and to hand down their renown to future ages, and to spread their benefits among the people. The priests of my country will thus obtain independence, and be treated as members of the fraternity of this country. Let this privilege be handed down from generation to generation without interruption."

For this cause this convent entertains many priests of Ceylon. To the south of the *Bôdhi* tree 10 li or so, the sacred traces are so numerous that they cannot be each named. Every year when the Bhikshus break up their yearly rest of the rains, religious persons come here from every quarter in thousands and myriads, and during seven days and nights they scatter flowers, burn incense, and sound music as they wander through the district[82] and pay their worship and present their offerings. The priests of India, according to the holy instruction of Buddha, on the first day of the first half of the month Śrâvaṇa enters on *Wass*. With us this is the sixteenth day of the fifth month; they give up their retreat on the fifteenth day of the second half of the month *Âśvayuja*, which is with us the fifteenth day of the eighth month.

In India the names of the months depend on the stars, and from ancient days till now there has been no change in this. But as the different schools have translated the accounts according to the dialects of the countries without distinguishing one from the other, mistakes have arisen, and as a consequence contradictions are apparent in the division of the seasons. Hence it is in some places they enter on *Wass* on the sixteenth day of the fourth month, and break up on the fifteenth day of the seventh month.

NOTE 1, p. 102.

The pilgrim's route from Pâtna to Gayâ is difficult to settle. I think we must omit the passage on p. 102, l. 5, "going about 200 li," and consider the "old *saṅghârâma*" as being perhaps 10 li beyond the south-west angle of the city. This 10 li, together with the two distances of 100 li + 90 li to the "cloud-stone mountain," will thus make up 200 li (put down by mistake), and correspond with the 6 or 7 *yojanas* in Hwui-lih from Patna to the *Ti lo-chi-kia* convent. This last place I should identify with the Barabar Hills; but we must place the Tilaḍaka convent at Tilâra. Hiuen Tsiang did not actually visit the spots named between the Barabar Hills and Gayâ (see Ferguson's remarks, *J. R. A. S.*, vol. vi. part 2).

NOTE 2, p. 118.

With reference to the translation on p. 118, where the Chinese symbols *'O-mo-lo-kia-ko* have been rendered the "Âmalaka fruit," as though this were the surmounting ornament of the great *vihâra* at

[82] The district of the penance of Buddha.

Buddha Gayâ, it is to be noticed that in the Chinese text these symbols are explained as being equivalent to "precious pitcher or vase" (*pao p'ing*). This phrase is frequently explained as "the sweet-dew dish or vase," or, "the immortal dish." M. Julien, in his note on the passage in question, restores the phonetic symbols, in deference to the Chinese explanation, to *Amalakarka*, that is, "*pure dish or vase.*" But the right restoration is doubtless *Amara Karka*, "the immortal dish or vase," for, as before stated, "sweet-dew" is always rendered by "immortal" or "immortality." This "sweet-dew dish or vessel" is represented in Chinese drawings as an oval bottle with a long narrow neck (see the illustration in the Liturgy of Avalôkitêśvara, "possessed of a thousand hands and a thousand eyes"). This explains the statement of Dr. Burgess (*Ajantâ Caves*, xvii. § iv.): "Avalôkitêśvara holds the palm of his right hand forward and has a bottle with oval body and narrow neck in his left." This is the *Amara Karka*. In the illustration of the pavement slab of the great temple of Gayâ (*i.e.*, the *vihâra* under present notice) given in the first volume of the *Archæological Survey of India*, pl. vi. (following p. 8), there is the figure of a devotee praying in front of a *stûpa*, which is crowned with flags and a bottle or vase, doubtless the same as the *Amara Karka*. This illustrates the inscription found at Buddha Gayâ and translated by Sir Charles Wilkins, in which the building of the temple is attributed to Amara Kosha; one of the nine gems of the court of King Vikramâditya. General Cunningham, then, is probably correct in saying that this great temple of Buddha Gayâ was built between the time of Fa-hian and Hiuen Tsiang. The crowning member or stone of a temple spire is called *Amalaśilâ*, or "pure stone."

END OF BOOK VIII.

BOOK IX.

The Second Part of the Country Magadha.

To the east of the Bôdhi tree, crossing the Nairañjanâ (Ni-len-shan-na) river, in the middle of a wood, is a *stûpa*. To the north of this is a pool. This is the spot where a perfume elephant (Gandhahastî)[1] waited on his mother. Formerly when Tathâgata was practising discipline as a Bôdhisattva, he was born as the offspring of a *perfume-elephant*, and lived in the mountains of the north. Wandering forth, he came to the border of this pool. His mother being blind, he gathered for her the sweet lotus roots, and drew pure water for her use, and cherished her with devotion and filial care. At this time there was a man who had changed his home,[2] who wandered here and there in the wood without knowing his way, and in his distress raised piteous cries. The elephant-cub heard him and pitied him; leading him on, he showed him his way to the road. The man having got back, forthwith went to the king and said, "I know of a wood[3] in which a *perfume-elephant* lives and roams. It is a very valuable animal. You had better go and take it."

The king, assenting to his words, went with his soldiers to capture it, the man leading the way. Then pointing

[1] See *ante*, vol. i. p. 5, note 25. Consult also Monier Williams, *Sansc. Dict.*, sub voc. *Gandhadvipa*.

[2] *Tui i shuh* seems to imply that he had changed his place of abode, and so was at a loss to find his way about; or it may simply mean, "In the lapse of time it happened that," &c. So Julien translates it.

[3] The ruins of the *stûpa* and the lower portion of the shaft of the pillar raised on the spot where the young elephant was taken still exist at Bakror, on the eastern bank of the Lilâjan river, about one mile to the south-east of Buddha Gayâ (Cunningham, *Anc. Geog.*, p. 459).

to the elephant to show it to the king, immediately both his arms fell off as if cut by a sword. The king, though he saw this miracle, yet captured the elephant-cub, and bound it with cords, and returned to his palace. The young elephant having been bound (in order to tame it), for a long time would neither eat nor drink. The stable-keeper stated the matter to the king, who, on his part, came to see for himself, and asking the elephant the reason.[4] "Lo!" he answered and said, "my mother is blind, and now for days together is without food or drink, and here I am bound in a dreary dungeon. How can I take my food with relish!" The king, pitying his feelings and resolution, therefore ordered him to be set free.

By the side of this (*pool*) is a *stûpa,* before which is built a stone pillar. In this place the Buddha Kaśyapa (Kia-she-po) long ago sat in meditation. By its side are traces where the four past Buddhas sat down and walked.

To the east of this spot, crossing the Mo-ho[5] (Mahî) river, we come to a great forest in which is a stone pillar. This is the place where a heretic entered a condition of ecstasy and made a wicked vow. In old days there was a heretic called Udra-Râmaputtra (U-teou-lan-tseu). In mind he soared above the vapoury clouds, whilst he left his body among the wilds and marshes. Here in this sacred forest, restraining his spirit, he left his traces.[6] Having acquired the five supernatural faculties,[7] he reached the highest condition of *Dhyâna,* and the king of Magadha greatly respected him. Each day at noon he invited him to his palace to eat. Udra-Râmaputtra, mounting through space, walking in the air, came and went without hindrance.

[4] In a fond way, as we speak to dumb creatures.

[5] The Mohana Nadî river.

[6] Udra-Râmaputtra was one of the teachers to whom Bôdhisattva went before his penance (*Fo-sho-hing-tsan-king*, varga 12); but it is uncertain whether he is the one referred to in the text. The expression, "restraining his spirit" means that when he confined his spirit within his body he left here bodily traces.

[7] *Pañchâbhijñâs*; see Childers, *Pali Dict.*, sub voc. *Abhiññâ*; Burnouf, *Introd.*, p., 263; *Lotus*, pp. 820 ff.

The king of Magadha, expecting the moment of his arrival, kept watch for him, and, on his coming, respectfully placed for him his seat. The king being about to go forth on a tour, wished to put this affair in charge of some one during his absence, but he found no one in his inner palace whom he could select, capable of undertaking his commands.[8] But (amongst his attendants) there was a little pet girl of modest appearance and well-mannered, so that in the whole palace none of his followers (*wise folk*) was able to excel her.[9] The king of Magadha summoned this one, and said to her, "I am going some distance on a tour of observation, and I desire to put you in charge of an important business; you must, on your part, give all your mind to do thoroughly as I direct in the matter. It relates to that celebrated Ṛĭshi Udra-Râmaputtra, whom I have for a long time treated with reverence and respect. Now when he comes here at the appointed time to dine, do you pay him the same attention that I do." Having left these instructions, the king forthwith gave notice of his absence (*non-attendance*).

The little girl, according to her instructions, waited in expectation as usual. The great Ṛĭshi having come, she received him, and placed a seat for him. Udra-Râmaputtra having touched the young female, felt within him the impure risings of earthly passion (*of the world of desire*), and so he lost his spiritual capabilities. Having finished his meal, he spoke of going, but he was unable to rise in the air. Then feeling ashamed, he prevaricated, and addressing the maiden said, "I am able, as the result of the discipline I practise, to enter *Samâdhi*, and then, my mind at rest, I can ascend into the air, and come and go without a moment's delay. I have heard long ago, however, that the people of the country desire to see me. In agreement with the rule of the olden time, our

[8] That is, none of the females of the palace.

[9] Could take her place of precedence.

utmost aim should be to benefit all that lives. How shall I regard only my own benefit and forget to benefit others? I desire, therefore, on this occasion, to go through the gate and walk on the ground, to bring happiness and profit to all those who see me going."

The royal maiden hearing this, straightway spread the news far and wide. Then the people began with all their hearts to water and sweep the roads, and thousands upon thousands awaited to see him come. Udra-Râma-puttra, stepping from the royal palace, proceeded on foot to that religious forest. Then sitting down in silence, he entered *Samâdhi.* Then his mind, quickly escaping outside, was yet limited within the boundaries of the forest.[10] And now (as it wandered through the woods) the birds began to scream and flutter about, and as it approached the pond, the fishes began to jump and splash, till at last his feelings being wrought up, and his mind becoming confused, he lost his spiritual capabilities. Giving up his attempt at ecstasy,[11] he was filled with anger and resentment, and he made this wicked vow, "May I hereafter be born as a fierce and wicked beast, with the body of a fox and the wings of a bird, that I may seize and devour living creatures. May my body be 3000 li long, and the outspread of my wings each way 1500 li; then rushing into the forest, I will devour the birds, and entering the rivers, I will eat the fish."

When he had made this vow his heart grew gradually at rest, and by earnest endeavours he resumed his former state of ecstasy. Not long after this he died, and was born in the first of the Bhuvâni heavens,[12] where his years

[10] That is, although his spirit was able to leave his body, yet, owing to his evil thoughts, it was unable to rise as before "above the vapoury clouds."

[11] This seems to show that although his spirit quickly passed "outside," it was unable to obtain complete independence of his body.

[12] That is, in the highest of the Arupa heavens. This heaven is called in Chinese *fi-seang-fi-fi-siang-tin*, *i.e.*, the heaven where there is neither thought (consciousness) nor an absence of thought; in Pâli,

would be 80,000 kalpas. Tathâgata left this record of him: "The years of his life in that heaven being ended, then he will reap the fruit of his old vow and possess this ignoble body. From the streams of the evil ways of birth he may not yet expect to emerge."[13]

To the east of Mahî river we enter a great wild forest, and going 100 li or so, we come to the Ki'u-ki'u-cha-po-to-shan (Kukkuṭapâdagiri, the Cock's-foot Mountain). It is also called Kiu-liu-po-to-shan (Gurupâdâḥ giri[14]). The sides of this mountain are high and rugged, the valleys and gorges are impenetrable. Tumultuous torrents rush down its sides, thick forests envelope the valleys, whilst tangled shrubs grow along its cavernous heights. Soaring upwards into the air are three sharp peaks; their tops are surrounded by the vapours of heaven, and their shapes lost in the clouds. Behind these hills the venerable Mahâ-Kâśyapa dwells wrapped in a condition of *Nirvâṇa*. People do not dare to utter his name, and therefore they speak of the "Guru-pâdâḥ" (*the venerable teacher*.)[15] Mahâ-Kâśyapa was a Śrâvaka and a disciple (*or*

"Nevasaññânâsaññâ" (see Childers, *Pâli Dict.* sub voc. From the history given in the *Fo-sho-king*, it would seem that this refinement of language as to the character of the highest heaven is due to Udra-Râmaputtra.

[13] That is, although he is now in the highest heaven of substance (*bhuva*), where his life will last 80,000 great kalpas (an incalculable period), yet he is not saved from future misery. This exhibits the character of Buddha's conception of *Nirvâṇa*, that it is a condition free from any possibility of a return to mundane or other bodily form of existence.

[14] That is, the Mountain of the Venerable Master, *i.e.*, Kâśyapa. Pâda is here added as a token of respect, as in Dêva-pâdâḥ, Kumârila-pâdâḥ, &c. It seems to have been called the Cock's-foot from its shape, the three peaks or spurs resembling the foot of the cock. Fa-hian places it 3 *li* to the south of Gayâ, probably a mistake for 3 *yôjanas* to the east (see *Fa-hian*, Beal's ed., cap. xxxiii. n. 1). It has been identified by Cunningham with the village of Kurkihâr (vid. *Arch. Survey*, vol. i. pp. 14–16; vol. xv. p. 4; and *Anc. Geog. Ind.*, p. 460). This *hill* of the cock's foot must not be confused with the *saṅghârâma* of the cock-*garden* near Patna. There is no evidence that there was a hill near this last establishment, and it is nowhere called the Kukkuṭa-*pâda* vihâra. The quotation made by Julien (vol. ii. 428 n.) refers to the hill near Gayâ; so also does the note of Burnouf, *Introd.*, p. 366. See also Schiefner's *Lebensbeschreibung Çâkyamuni's*, p. 278; *Ind. Ant.*, vol. xii. p. 327.

[15] This is a difficult passage, but the sense is evident. Kâśyapa dwells in the mountain awaiting the arrival of Maitrêya; he cannot therefore have passed into complete *Nirvâṇa*.

a Śrâvaka disciple) perfectly possessed of the six supernatural faculties and the eight enfranchisements[16] (*ashṭau vimôkshas*).[17] Tathâgata, his work of conversion being done, and just on the point of attaining *Nirvâṇa*, addressed Kâśyapa and said, "Through many[18] kalpas I have undergone (*diligently borne*) painful penances for the sake of all that lives, seeking the highest form of religion. What I have all along prayed for (*desired*) I have now obtained to the full. Now, as I am desirous to die (*enter Mahânirvâṇa*), I lay on you the charge of the *Dharma Piṭaka*. Keep and disseminate (*this doctrine*) without loss or diminution. The golden-tissued *Kashâya* robe given me by my foster-mother (*mother's sister*)[19] I bid you keep and deliver to Maitrêya (T'se-chi) when he has completed the condition of Buddha.[20] All those who engage in the profession of my bequeathed law, whether they be Bhikshus, Bhikshunîs, Upâsakas, or Upâsikas, must first (*i.e., before this be accomplished*) cross over and escape the stream of transmigration."

Kâśyapa having received this commission to undertake to preserve the true law, summoned an assembly[21] (*council or convocation*). This done, he continued twenty years (*in charge of the order*), and then, in disgust at the imperma-

In fact, the subsequent narrative shows that he will only reach that condition when Maitrêya comes. I take the expression *chung tsie mih* to denote the indefinite character of his present condition, which cannot be called *Nirvâṇa*, but is a middle state of existence. *Pâda*, as stated above, is an honorary affix; the expression *ki-heou* refers to the inner recesses of the mountain. Julien translates the passage thus: "In the sequence of time the great Kâśyapa dwelt in this mountain, and there entered *Nirvâṇa*. Men dare not call him by his name, and so they say "the foot of the venerable."

16 *Shaḍabhijñâs*. See Childers, *Pâli Dict.*, s. v. *Abhiññâ*, and *ante*, vol. i. p. 104, n. 73.

17 See Childers, *u. s.*, s. v. *Vimokho*; Burnouf, *Lotus*, pp. 347, 824 f. and *ante*, vol. i. p. 149, n. 90.

18 Mahâprajâpatî.

19 The word means "waste" or "distant;" as we might say, through "a waste of ages," or "dreary ages."

20 This passage is translated by Julien thus: "Which Maitrêya after he became Buddha left, that it might be transmitted to you." But this cannot be correct. Maitrêya has not become Buddha. I translate it, "I deliver to you to keep, awaiting the time when Maitrêya shall become perfect Buddha."

21 This is the usual phrase used for "calling a convocation.'

nence of the world, and desiring to die, he went towards Cock's-foot Mountain. Ascending the north side of the mountain, he proceeded along the winding path, and came to the south-west ridge. Here the crags and precipices prevented him going on. Forcing his way through the tangled brushwood, he struck the rock with his staff, and thus opened a way. He then passed on, having divided the rock, and ascended till he was again stopped by the rocks interlacing one another. He again opened a passage through, and came out on the mountain peak on the north-east side. Then having emerged from the defiles, he proceeded to the middle point of the three peaks. There he took the *Kashâya* garment (*chîvara*) of Buddha, and as he stood he expressed an ardent vow. On this the three peaks covered him over; this is the reason why now these three rise up into the air. In future ages, when Maitrêya shall have come and declared the threefold law,[22] finding the countless persons opposed to him by pride, he will lead them to this mountain, and coming to the place where Kâśyapa is, in a moment (*the snapping of the finger*) Maitrêya will cause it to open of itself, and all those people, having seen Kâśyapa, will only be more proud and obstinate. Then Kâśyapa, delivering the robe, and having paid profound reverence, will ascend into the air and exhibit all sorts of spiritual changes, emitting fire and vapour from his body. Then he will enter *Nirvâṇa*. At this time the people, witnessing these miracles, will dismiss their pride, and opening their minds, will obtain the fruit (*of holiness*). Now, therefore, on the top of the mountain is a *stûpa* built. On quiet evenings those looking from a distance see sometimes a bright light as it were of a torch; but if they ascend the mountain there is nothing to be observed.[23]

[22] The thrice-repeated law; see *ante*, p. 47, n. 10.

[23] The three-peaked mountain here referred to has been identified by General Cunningham with the three peaks of the Murali mountain, which stands three miles north-north-east of the town of Kurkihâr. There is still a square basement surrounded by quantities of bricks on the highest or middle peak of the three. *Arch. Survey*, vol. xv. p. 5.

Going to the north-east of the Cock's-foot Mountain about 100 li, we come to the mountain called Buddhavana (Fo-to-fa-na), with its peaks and cliffs lofty and precipitous. Among its steep mountain cliffs is a stone chamber where Buddha once descending stayed; by its side is a large stone where Śakra (Shih), king of Dêvas, and Brahma-râja (Fan-wang) pounded some ox-head (*gôśîrsha*)[24] sandal-wood, and anointed Tathâgata with the same. The scent (*of this*) is still to be perceived on the stone. Here also five hundred Arhats secretly dwell[25] in a spiritual manner, and here those who are influenced by religious desire to meet with them sometimes see them, on one occasion under the form of Samaṇêras just entering the village to beg food, at other times as withdrawing (*to their cells*), on some occasions manifesting traces of their spiritual power in ways difficult to describe in detail.

Going about 30 li to the east, amongst wild valleys of the Buddhavana (Fo-to-fa-na) mountain, we come to the wood called Yashṭivana (Ye-sse-chi).[26] The bamboos that grow here are large; they cover the hill and extend through the valley. In former days there was a Brâhmaṇ, who hearing that the body of Śâkya Buddha (Shih-kia-fo) was sixteen feet in height, was perplexed with doubt and would not credit it. Then taking a bamboo sixteen feet long, he desired to measure the height of Buddha; the body constantly overtopped the bamboo and exceeded the sixteen feet. So going on increasing, he could not find the right measurement. He then threw the bamboo on

[24] "In Pâli called *gosisam*, among the Tibetans *gorshi-sha*, and among the Mongols *gurshosha*. It is apparently applied to sandal-wood having the odour of the cow's head" (Burnouf, *Introd.*, p. 557). But perhaps its name is derived from its appearance, viz., a centre of silvery white wood within a darker outside circle. Compare the description of the bull that carried off Europa—κύκλος δ' αργυφέος μέσσῳ μάρμαιρε μετώπῳ. *Abstract of Four Lectures*, p. 158. For the circle on the forehead, see the figures "from the oldest painting in Cave X. at Ajaṇṭâ" (*Burgess*, plates viii. ix. x., *Report on the Paintings at Ajaṇṭâ*).

[25] I do not find in the text that they entered *Nirvâṇa* here.

[26] "The forest of the staff."

the ground and departed; but because of this it stood upright and took root.

In the midst of this wood is a *stûpa* which was built by Aśôka-râja. Here Tathâgata displayed for seven days great spiritual wonders (*miracles*) for the sake of the Dêvas, and preached the mysterious and excellent law.

In the forest of the staff (Yashṭivana) not long since there was an Upâsaka named Jayasêna (She-ye-si-na), a Kshattriya of Western India. He was exceedingly simple-minded and moderate. He amused himself amid the forests and hills, dwelling in a sort of fairyland, whilst his mind wandered amid the limits of truth (*true limits*). He had deeply studied the mysteries both of orthodox and other treatises (*inside and outside books*). His language and observations were pure, and his arguments elevated; his presence was quiet and dignified. The Śramaṇas, Brâhmaṇas, heretics of different schools, the king of the country, the great ministers and householders, and persons of rank came together to visit him and personally to ask him questions. His pupils occupied sixteen apartments;[27] and although nearly seventy years of age, he read with them diligently and without cessation, and applied their minds only to the study of Buddhist *sûtras*, rejecting all other engagements. Thus night and day he gave up body and mind to this pursuit alone.

It is a custom in India to make little *stûpas* of powdered scent made into a paste; their height is about six or seven inches, and they place inside them some written extract from a *sûtra;* this they call a *dharma-śarîra*[28] (*fa-shi-li*). When the number of these has become large, they then build a great *stûpa*, and collect all the others within it, and continually offer to it religious

[27] The text here seems to be faulty.

[28] See the seals found at Birdâban; *Arch. Surv.*, vol. iii. p. 157, pl. xlvi.; see also *J. Bom. B. R. A. S.*, vol. vi. p. 157 f.

offerings. This then was the occupation of Jaya-sêna (Ching-kian); with his mouth he declared the excellent law, and led and encouraged his students, whilst with his hand he constructed these *stûpas*. Thus he acquired the highest and most excellent religious merit. In the evening, again, he would walk up and down worshipping and repeating his prayers, or silently sit down in meditation. For eating or sleeping he had little time, and relaxed none of his discipline night or day. Even after he was an hundred years old his mind and body were in full activity. During thirty years he had made seven *kôṭis* of these *dharma-śarîra stûpas*, and for every *kôṭi* that he made he built a great *stûpa* and placed them in it. When full, he presented his religious offerings and invited the priests; whilst they, on their part, offered him their congratulations.[29] On these occasions a divine light shone around and spiritual wonders (*miracles*) exhibited themselves; and from that time forth the miraculous light has continued to be seen.

South-west of the Yashṭivana[30] about 10 li or so, on the south side of a great mountain, are two warm springs;[31] the water is very hot. In old days, Tathâgata caused this water to appear, and washed himself therein. The pure flow of these waters still lasts without diminution. Men far and near flock here to bathe, after which those who have suffered from disease or chronic affections are often healed. By the side of the springs is a *stûpa*, to mark the place where Tathâgata walked for exercise.

To the south-east of the Yashṭivana about six or seven

[29] *Or*, invited the congregation of priests to a religious assembly to consecrate the service.

[30] The Bamboo forest (Chang-lin) is still known as the Jakhti-ban; it lies to the east of the Buddhain hill (Buddhavana), and is frequented by the people for the purpose of cutting bamboos (Cunningham, *Anc. Geog.*, p. 461).

[31] These springs are about two miles to the south of Jakhti-ban, at a place called Tapoban, which name is a common contraction of Tapta-pâṇi, or the "hot water" (*Ibid.*)

li we come to a great mountain. Before a cross-ridge[32] of this mountain is a *stûpa*. Here in old days Tathâgata explained the law during the three months of rain for the benefit of men and Dêvas. Then Bimbisâra-râja (Pin-pi-so-lo) wished to come to hear the law. He cut away the mountain, and piled up the stones to make steps in order to ascend. The width is about twenty paces and the length 3 or 4 li.[33]

To the north of the great mountain 3 or 4 li is a solitary hill. Formerly the Ṛishi Vyâsa[34] (Kwang-po) lived here in solitude. By excavating the side of the mountain he formed a house. Some portions of the foundations are still visible. His disciples still hand down his teaching, and the celebrity of his bequeathed doctrine still remains.

To the north-east of the solitary hill 4 or 5 li there is a small hill, also standing alone. In the side of this hill (*has been excavated*) a stone chamber. In length and breadth[35] it is enough to seat 1000 persons or so. In this place Tathâgata, when living in the world, repeated the law for three months. Above the stone chamber is a great and remarkable rock, on which Śakra, king of Dêvas, and Brahma-râja pounded some *ox-head* sandal-wood, and with the dust sprinkled the body of Tathâgata. The surface of the stone still emits the scent of the perfume.

At the south-west angle of the stone house there is a lofty cavern which the Indians call the palace of the Asuras ('O-su-lo). Formerly there was a good-natured fellow who was deeply versed in the use of magic formulæ. He engaged with some companions, fourteen altogether, to covenant with one another to enter this lofty cavern. After going about 30 or 40 li, suddenly the whole place was

[32] *Or* it may be "a transverse pass."

[33] The great mountain referred to in the text corresponds with the lofty hill of Handia, 1463 feet in height (Cunningham).

[34] This restoration rests on M. Julien's authority, as explained in his note (iii. 13).

[35] *Kwang mow*, see Medhurst, *Chin. Dict.*, sub *Mow*, p. 994.

lighted up with great brilliancy, and they saw a walled city before them, with towers and look-outs all of silver and gold and lapis-lazuli (*lieu-li*). The men having advanced to it, there were some young maidens who stationed themselves at the gates, and with joyful laughing faces greeted them and paid them reverence. Going on a little farther they came to the inner city-gates, where there were two slave-girls holding each of them a golden vessel full of flowers and scents. Advancing with these, they waited the approach of the visitors, and then said, "You must first bathe yourselves in yonder tank, and then anoint yourselves with the perfumes and crown yourselves with the flowers, and then you may enter the city. Do not hasten to enter yet; only that master of magic can come in at once." Then the other thirteen men went down at once to bathe. Having entered the tank, they all at once became confused, and forgot all that had taken place, and were (*found*) sitting in the middle of a rice field distant from this due north, over a level country, about 30 or 40 li.

By the side of the stone-house there is a wooden way (*a road made with timber*)[36] about 10 paces wide and about 4 or 5 li. Formerly Bimbisâra-râja, when about to go to the place where Buddha was, cut out a passage through the rock, opened up the valleys, levelled the precipices, and led a way across the river-courses, built up walls of stone, and bored through the opposing crags, and made ladders up the heights to reach the place where Buddha was located.

From this spot proceeding eastward through the mountains about 60 li, we arrive at the city Kuśâgâra-pura (Kiu-she-kie-lo-pu-lo), or "the royal city of best grass (*lucky grass*)." This is the central point of the kingdom of Magadha.[37] Here the former kings of the country

[36] *Chan-tau*, wooden bridges over mountain chasms (Khang-hi, quoted by Julien, note *in loco*).

[37] Kuśâgârapura was the original capital of Magadha, and was called Râjagṛiha, or the "royal residence." It was also named Girivraja, or the "hill surrounded." (See Cunningham, *Anc. Geog.*, p. 462).

fixed their capital. It produces much of the most excellent, scented, fortunate grass, and therefore it is called "the city of the superior grass." High mountains surround it on each side, and form as it were its external walls.[38] On the west it is approached through a narrow pass, on the north there is a passage through the mountains. The town is extended from east to west and narrow from north to south. It is about 150 li in circuit. The remaining foundations of the wall of the inner city are about 30 li in circuit. The trees called *Kie-ni-kia* (Kanakas) border all the roads, their flowers exhale a delicious perfume, and their colour is of a bright golden hue. In the spring months the forests are all of a golden colour.

Outside the north gate of the palace city is a *stûpa.* Here Dêvadatta (Ti-p'o-to-to) and Ajâtaśatru-râja Wi-sing-yun), having agreed together as friends, liberated the drunken elephant for the purpose of killing Tathâgata. But Tathâgata miraculously caused five lions to proceed from his finger-ends; on this the drunken elephant was subdued and stood still before him.[39]

To the north-east of this spot is a *stûpa.* This is where Śâriputra (She-li-tseu) heard Aśvajita ('O-shi-p'o-shi) the Bhikshu declare the law, and by that means reached the fruit (*of an Arhat*). At first Śâriputra was a layman; he was a man of distinguished ability and refinement, and was highly esteemed by those of his own time. At this time, with other students, he accepted the traditional teaching as delivered to him. On one occasion, being about to enter the great city of Râjagṛĭha, the Bhikshu Aśvajita (Ma-shing) was also just going his round of begging. Then Śâriputra, seeing him at a distance, addressed his disciples, saying, "Yonder man who comes, so full of dignity and nobleness, if he has not reached the fruit of sanctity

[38] So also Fa-hian states that the five hills which surround the town are like the walls of a city (cap. xxviii.)

[39] This is a perversion of the simple story found in the *Fo-sho-king*, vv. 1713 ss., and compare p. 246, n. 4.

(*Arhatship*), how is he thus composed and quiet? Let us stop awhile and observe him as he approaches." Now as Aśvajita Bhikshu had reached the condition of an Arhàt, his mind was self-possessed, his face composed and of an agreeable refinement; thus, holding his religious staff, he came along with a dignified air. Then Śâriputra said, "Venerable sir! are you at ease and happy? Pray, who is your master, and what the system you profess, that you are so gladsome and contented?"

Aśvajita answering him said, "Know you not the royal prince, the son of Śuddhôdana-râja, who gave up the condition of a Chakravarttin monarch, and from pity to the six kinds of creatures for six years endured penance and reached the condition of *Sambôdhi*, the state of perfect omniscience? This is my master! As to his law, it has respect to a condition including the absence of existence, without nonentity;[40] it is difficult to define; only Buddhas with Buddhas can fathom it; how much less can foolish and blind mortals, such as I, explain its principles. But for your sake I will recite a stanza in praise of the law of Buddha."[41] Śâriputra having heard it, obtained forthwith the fruit of Arhatship.

To the north of this place, not far off, there is a very deep ditch, by the side of which is built a *stûpa;* this is the spot where Śrîgupta (She-li-kio-to) wished to destroy Buddha by means of fire concealed in the ditch and poisoned rice. Now Śrîgupta (Shing-mi) greatly honoured (*believed in*) the heretics, and his mind was deeply possessed by false views. All the Brahmachârins said, "The men of the country greatly honour Gautama (Kiao-ta-mo), and in consequence he causes our disciples to be without support. Invite him then to your house to eat, and before the door make a great ditch and fill it with fire, and cover it over slightly with wooden planks to conceal the fire; moreover,

[40] The opposite of existence (*yau*, material or conditioned existence), and also of not-being.

[41] The stanza he recited is given in the *Fo-sho-king*, v. 1392. See also p. 194, n. 2.

poison the food, so that if he escape the fire (*fiery ditch*), he will take the poison."

Śrîgupta, according to his directions, caused the poison to be prepared, and then all the people in the town, knowing the evil and destructive design of Śrîgupta against the Lord of the World, entreated Buddha not to go to the house. The Lord said, "Be not distressed; the body of Tathâgata cannot be hurt by such means as these." He therefore accepted the invitation and went. When his foot trod on the threshold of the door the fire in the pit became a tank of pure water with lotus flowers on its surface.

Śrîgupta having witnessed this, being filled with shame and fear lest his project should fail, said to his followers, "He has by his magical power escaped the fire; but there is yet the poisoned food!" The Lord having eaten the rice, began to declare the excellent law, on which Śrîgupta, having attended to it, himself became a disciple.

To the north-east of this fiery ditch of Śrîgupta (Shing-mi), at a bend of the city, is a *stûpa*; this is where Jîvaka (Shi-fo-kia),[42] the great physician, built a preaching-hall for Buddha. All round the walls he planted flowers and fruit trees. The traces of the foundation-walls and the decayed roots of the trees are still visible. Tathâgata, when he was in the world, often stopped here. By the side of this place are the remains of the house of Jîvaka, and the hollow of an old well also exists there still.

To the north-east of the palace city going 14 or 15 li, we come to the mountain Gṛîdhrakûṭa (Ki-li-tho-kiu-ch'a). Touching the southern slope of the northern mountain, it rises as a solitary peak to a great height, on which vultures make their abode. It appears like a high tower on which the azure tints of the sky are reflected, the colours of the mountain and the heaven being commingled.

[42] For the history of Jivaka see S. Hardy's *Manual of Buddhism*, p. 238.

When Tathâgata had guided the world for some fifty years, he dwelt much in this mountain, and delivered the excellent law in its developed form (*kwang*).[43] Bimbisâra-râja, for the purpose of hearing the law, raised a number of men to accompany him from the foot of the mountain to its summit. They levelled the valleys and spanned the precipices, and with the stones made a staircase about ten paces wide and 5 or 6 li long. In the middle of the road there are two small *stûpas*, one called "Dismounting from the chariot" (*Hia-shing*), because the king, when he got here, went forward on foot. The other is called "Sending back the crowd" (*T'ui-fan*), because the king, separating the common folk, would not allow them to proceed with him. The summit of this mountain is long from the east to the west and narrow from north to south. There is a brick *vihâra* on the borders of a steep precipice at the western end of the mountain. It is high and wide and beautifully constructed. The door opens to the east. Here Tathâgata often stopped in old days and preached the law. There is now a figure of him preaching the law of the same size as life.

To the east of the *vihâra* is a long stone, on which Tathâgata trod as he walked up and down for exercise. By the side of it is a great stone about fourteen or fifteen feet high and thirty paces round. This is the place where Dêvadatta[44] flung a stone from a distance to strike Buddha.

South of this, below the precipice, is a *stûpa*. Here

[43] A great number of the later developed *sûtras* are said to have been delivered here. There is also a late form of belief which connects the spiritual form of Buddha with this mountain. It is barely possible that Buddha did in his later years declare a developed (mystical) form of his doctrine, and perhaps this mountain was the scene of his teaching; but the greater portion of the *sûtras* claiming the authority of his utterance here are fabulous. Compare *Fa-hian*, cap. xxix. The Vulture Peak is a part of the lofty hill now called Śaila-giri, but no caves have been discovered there (Cunningham, *Anc. Geog.*, p. 466).

[44] The story of Dêvadatta rolling down the stone will be found in Fa-hian, chap. xxix., also in the *Fo-sho-king*, p. 246, and in the *Manual of Buddhism*, p. 383. The accounts, however, slightly differ.

Tathâgata, when alive in old time, delivered the *Saddharma Puṇḍarîka Sûtra.*[45]

To the south of the *vihâra*, by the side of a mountain cliff, is a great stone house. In this Tathâgata, when dwelling in the world long ago, entered *Samâdhi*.

To the north-west of the stone house and in front of it is a great and extraordinary stone. This is the place where Ânanda (O-nan) was frightened by Mâra. When the venerable Ânanda had entered *Samâdhi* in this place, Mâra-râja, assuming the form of a vulture, in the middle of the night, during the dark portion of the month, took his place on this rock, and flapping his wings and uttering loud screams, tried to frighten the venerable one.[46] Ânanda, filled with fear, was at a loss to know what to do; then Tathâgata, by his spiritual power, seeing his state, stretched out his hand to compose him. He pierced the stone wall and patted the head of Ânanda, and with his words of great love he spoke to him thus: "You need not fear the assumed form which Mâra has taken." Ânanda in consequence recovered his composure, and remained with his heart and body at rest and in peace.

Although years and months have elapsed since then, yet the bird traces on the stone and the hole in the rock[47] still remain visible.

By the side of the *vihâra* there are several stone houses,[48] where Śâriputra and other great Arhats entered *Samâdhi*. In front of the stone house of Śâriputra is a

[45] Fa-hian relates how he visited the cave on this peak, and wept in recollection of Buddha's residence therein. Here also, he adds, "he delivered the *Sheu-ling-yan Sûtra.*" This is the *S'uraṅgama Sûtra.* Hiuen Tsiang says he also delivered here the *Saddharma Puṇḍarîka Sûtra.* These *sûtras*, belonging to the last stage of Buddhist development, are referred to this mountain, as it was the scene of Buddha's latest teaching. See Cunningham, *Anc. Geog.*, p. 467; see also Fergusson, *Cave Temples of India*, p. 50.

[46] Fa-hian, chap. xxix.

[47] Julien translates "The long cavern which traverses the flanks of the mountain." But the "long cavern" is the hole referred to, piercing the side of the rock.

[48] Probably caves or cells. Cunningham understands them to be small rooms built against the cliff (*Anc. Geog.*, p. 467). The Chinese quite bears out this idea.

great well, dry and waterless. The hollow (*shaft*) still remains.

To the north-east of the *vihâra*, in the middle of a rocky stream, is a large and flat stone. Here Tathâgata dried his *Kashâya* garment. The traces of the tissue of the robe still remain, as though they were cut out on the rock.

By the side of this, and upon a rock, is a foot-trace of Buddha. Although the "wheel" outline is somewhat obscure, yet it can be distinctly traced.

On the top of the northern mountain is a *stûpa*. From this point Tathâgata beheld the town of Magadha,[49] and for seven days explained the law.

To the west of the north gate of the mountain city is the mountain called Pi-pu-lo (Vipula-giri).[50] According to the common report of the country it is said, "On the northern side of the south-western crags of this mountain there were formerly five hundred warm springs; now there are only some ten or so; but some of these are warm and others cold, but none of them hot." These springs have their origin to the south of the Snowy Mountains from the Anavatapta (Wu-jeh-no-c'hi) lake,[51] and flowing underground, burst forth here. The water is very sweet and pure, and the taste is like that of the water of the lake. The streams (*from the lake*) are five hundred in number (*branches*), and as they pass by the lesser underground fire-abodes (*hells*), the power of the flames ascending causes the water to be

[49] That is, as it seems, the capital of Magadha, viz., Râjagṛiha.

[50] I have restored *Pi-pu-lo* to Vipula in deference to Julien. But it might be equally well restored to Vaibhâra or Baibhâr, and as Cunningham in his map of Râjgîr (*Arch. Survey*, vol. i. pl. xiv.) places Baibhâr to the west of the north gate of the town, it would be more agreeable to the account in the text to restore it so. On the other hand, as Hiuen Tsiang places the hot springs on the south-western slopes of *Pi-po-lo*, and as we are told that "the hot springs of Râjagṛiha are found at the eastern foot of Mount Baibhâr and the western foot of Mount Vipula" (Cunningham, *Anc. Geog.*, p. 466), it would seem that he must be speaking of Vipula.

[51] Râvaṇahrad; in Pali, Anavatatta, in Tibetan, Ma-dros, in Chinese, Wu-je-nao. See *Asiat. Res.*, vol. xx. p. 65, or *Ann. Musée Guimet*, tom. ii. p. 168; Burnouf, *Introd.*, pp. 152, 154; and *ante*, vol. i. pp. 11–13.

hot. At the mouths of the various hot springs there are placed carved stones, sometimes shaped like lions, and at other times as the heads of white elephants; sometimes stone conduits are constructed, through which the water flows on high (*aqueducts*), whilst below there are stone basins, in which the water collects like a pond. Here people of every region come, and from every city, to bathe; those who suffer from any disease are often cured. On the right and left of the warm springs[52] are many *stûpas* and the remains of *vihâras* close together. In all these places the four past Buddhas have sat and walked, and the traces of their so doing are still left. These spots being surrounded by mountains and supplied with water, men of conspicuous virtue and wisdom take up their abode here, and there are many hermits who live here also in peace and solitude.

To the west of the hot springs is the Pippala (Pi-po-lo) stone house.[53] When the Lord of the World was alive in olden times, he constantly dwelt here. The deep cavern which is behind the walls of this house is the palace abode of an Asura (*or*, the Asuras). Many Bhikshus who practise *Samâdhi* dwell here. Often we may see strange forms, as of Nâgas, serpents, and lions, come forth from it. Those who see these things lose their reason and become dazed. Nevertheless, this wonderful place (*excellent land*) is one in which holy saints dwell, and occupying the spot consecrated by such sacred

[52] The names of these warm springs are given by Cunningham (*Anc. Geog.*, p. 466).

[53] This stone house is mentioned also by Fa-hian, chap. xxx. He places it to the south of the new city, west about three hundred paces. It would therefore be in Mount Baibhâr, and Cunningham suggests that Pi-pu-lo may be an equivalent for Vaibhâra (*Arch. Survey*, i. p. 21 n.). It may be so, but it is usually restored to Pippala. This stone house is supposed to be the same as the present Sonbhândâr, or "treasury of gold" (*ibid.*) General Cunningham also identifies the Sonbhândâr cave with the Sattapanni cave. But this seems impossible. Mr. Fergusson's remarks on this perplexing subject are intelligible and satisfactory. See *Cave Temples of India*, pp. 49, 50, and *note*.

traces, they forget the calamities and evils that threaten them.

Not long ago there was a Bhikshu of a pure and upright life, whose mind was enamoured of solitude and quiet; he desired to practise *Samâdhi* concealed in this house. Some one protested and said, "Go not there! Many calamities happen there, and strange things causing death are frequent. It is difficult to practise *Samâdhi* in such a spot, and there is constant fear of death. You ought to remember what has happened before time, if you would not reap the fruits of after-repentance." The Bhikshu said, "Not so! My determination is to seek the fruit of Buddha and to conquer the Dêva Mâra. If these are the dangers of which you speak, what need to name them?" Then his took his pilgrim's staff and proceeded to the house. There he reared an altar and began to recite his magic protective sentences. After the tenth day, a maiden came forth from the cave and addressed the Bhikshu, saying, "Sir of the coloured robes! you observe the precepts, and, with full purpose, you adopt the refuge (*found in Buddha*); you aspire after (*prepare*) wisdom, and practise *Samâdhi*, and to promote in yourself spiritual power, so that you may be an illustrious guide of men, you dwell here and alarm me and my fellows! But how is this in agreement with the doctrine of Tathâgata?" The Bhikshu said, "I practise a pure life, following the holy teaching (*of Buddha*). I conceal myself among the mountains and dells to avoid the tumult of life. In suddenly bringing a charge against me, I ask where is my fault?" She replied, "Your reverence! when you recite your prayers, the sound causes fire to burst into (*my house*) from without, and burns my abode; it afflicts me and my family! I pray you, pity us, and do not say your charmed prayers any more!"

The Bhikshu said, "I repeat my prayers to defend myself, and not to hurt any living thing. In former days, a religious person (*a disciple*) occupied this place and practised *Samâdhi* with a view to obtain the holy fruit and to help the miserable;[54] then with unearthly sights he was frightened to death and gave up his life. This was your doing. What have you to say?"

She replied, "Oppresed with a weight of guilt, my wisdom is small indeed; but from this time forth I will bar my house and keep the partition (*between it and this chamber*). Do you, venerable one, on your part, I pray, repeat no more spiritual formulæ."

On this the Bhikshu prepared himself in *Samâdhi*, and from that time rested in quiet, none hurting him.

On the top of Mount Vipula (Pi-pu-lo) is a *stûpa*. This is where in old times Tathâgata repeated the law. At the present time naked heretics (Nirgranthas) frequent this place in great numbers; they practise penance night and day without intermission, and from morn till night walk round (*the stûpa*) and contemplate it with respect.

To the left of the northern gate of the mountain city (Girivjaja, *Shan-shing*), going east, on the north side of the southern crag (*precipice or cliff*), going 2 or 3 li, we come to a great stone house in which Dêvadatta formerly entered *Samâdhi*.

Not far to the east of this stone house, on the top of a flat stone, there are coloured spots like blood. By the side of this rock a *stûpa* has been built. This is the place where a Bhikshu practising *Samâdhi* wounded himself and obtained the fruit of holiness.

There was formerly a Bhikshu who diligently exerted himself in mind and body, and secluded himself in the practice of *Samâdhi*. Years and months elapsed, and he had not obtained the holy fruit. Retiring from the spot, he upbraided himself, and then he added with a sigh, "I despair of obtaining the fruit of Arhatship (*freedom from learning*). What use to keep this body, the source of im-

[54] *I.e.*, to succour the people in the dark ways of birth, *i.e.*, demons and pretas and "the lost."

pediment from its very character." Having spoken thus, he mounted on this stone and gashed his throat. Forthwith he reached the fruit of an Arhat, and ascended into the air and exhibited spiritual changes; finally, his body was consumed by fire, and he reached *Nirvâṇa.*[55] Because of his noble resolution they have built (*this stûpa*) as a memorial. To the east of this place, above a rocky crag, there is a stone *stûpa.* This is the place where a Bhikshu practising *Samâdhi* threw himself down and obtained the fruit. Formerly, when Buddha was alive, there was a Bhikshu who sat quietly in a mountain wild, practising the mode of *Samâdhi* leading to Arhatship. For a long time he had exercised the utmost zeal without result. Night and day he restrained his thoughts, nor ever gave up his quiet composure. Tathâgata, knowing that his senses were fit for the acquirement (*of emancipation*), went to the place for the purpose of converting him (*perfecting him*). In a moment[56] he transported himself from the garden of bamboos (Vêṇuvana) to this mountain-side, and there calling him,[57] stood standing awaiting him.

At this time the Bhikshu, seeing from a distance the holy congregation, his heart and body ravished with joy, he cast himself down from the mountain. But by his purity of heart and respectful faith for Buddha's teaching before he reached the ground he gained the fruit of Arhatship. The Lord of the World then spoke and said, "You ought to know the opportunity." Immediately he ascended into the air and exhibited spiritual transformation. To show his pure faith they have raised this memorial.

Going about one li from the north gate of the mountain city we come to the Karaṇḍavêṇuvana (Kia-lan-t'o-chuh-yuen),[58] where now the stone foundation and the

[55] This incident is also related by Fa-hian, cap. xxx.

[56] So I understand *tan c'hi,* "in the snapping of a finger." Julien translates it as though Buddha called the Bhikshu by cracking his fingers.

[57] It may be either "calling him" or "calling an assembly."

[58] The bamboo garden of Karaṇḍa, or Kalaṇḍa. For an account of this garden see Fa-hian, (Beal's edit., p. 117, n. 2), and also Julien *in loco,* n. 1; see also Burnouf, *Introd.*, 1st ed. p. 456; *Lalita Vistara,* p. 415.

brick walls of a *vihâra* exist. The door faces the east. Tathâgata, when in the world, frequently dwelt here, and preached the law for the guidance and conversion of men and to rescue the people. They have now made a figure of Tathâgata the size of life. In early days there was in this town a great householder (*gṛihapati*) called Karaṇḍa; at this time he had gained much renown by giving to the heretics a large bamboo garden. Then coming to see Tathâgata and hearing his law, he was animated by a true faith. He then regretted that the multitude of unbelievers should dwell in that place. "And now," he said, "the leader of gods and men has no place in which to lodge." Then the spirits and demons, affected by his faithfulness, drove away the heretics, and addressing them said, "Karaṇḍa, the householder, is going to erect a *vihâra* here for the Buddha; you must get away quickly, lest calamity befall you!"

The heretics, with hatred in their heart and mortified in spirit, went away; thereupon the householder built this *vihâra*. When it was finished he went himself to invite Buddha. Thereon Tathâgata received the gift.

To the east of the Karaṇḍaveṇuvana is a *stûpa* which was built by Ajâtaśatru-râja. After the *Nirvâṇa* of Tathâgata the kings divided the relics (*she-li*); the king Ajâtaśatru returned then with his share, and from a feeling of extreme reverence built (*a stûpa*) and offered his religious offerings to it. When Aśôka-râja (Wu-yau) became a believer, he opened it and took the relics, and in his turn built another *stûpa*. This building constantly emits miraculous light.

By the side of the *stûpa* of Ajâtaśatru-râja is another *stûpa* which encloses the relics of half of the body of Ânanda. Formerly, when the saint was about to reach *Nirvâṇa*, he left the country of Magadha and proceeded to the town of Vaiśâlî (Fei-she-li). As these two countries disputed (*about him*) and began to raise troops, the venerable one, from pity, divided his body into two parts. The king of Magadha, receiving his share, returned and offered to it his religious homage, and immediately prepared in this renowned land, with great honour, to raise a *stûpa*. By the side of this building is a place where Buddha walked up and down.

Not far from this is a *stûpa*. This is the place where Śâriputra and Mudgalaputra dwelt during the rainy season.

To the south-west of the bamboo garden (Vêṇuvana) about 5 or 6 li, on the north side of the southern mountain, is a great bamboo forest. In the middle of it is a large stone house. Here the venerable Kâśyapa with 999 great Arhats, after Tathâgata's *Nirvâṇa*, called a convocation (*for the purpose of settling*) the three *Piṭakas*.[59] Before it is the old foundation-wall. King Ajâtaśatru made this hall[60] for the sake of accommodating the great Arhats who assembled to settle the *Dharma-piṭaka*.

At first, when Mahâ Kâśyapa was seated in silent (*study*) in the desert (*mountain forests*), suddenly a bright light burst forth, and he perceived the earth shaking. Then he said, "What fortunate change of events is there, that this miracle should occur?" Then exerting his divine sight, he saw the Lord Buddha between the two trees entering *Nirvâṇa*. Forthwith he ordered his followers to accompany him to the city of Kuśinagara (Ku-shi). On the way they met a Brâhmaṇ holding in his hands a divine flower. Kâśyapa, addressing him, said, "Whence come you? Know you where our great teacher is at present?" The Brâhmaṇ replied and said, "I have but just come from yonder city of Kuśinagara, where I saw your great master just entered into *Nirvâṇa*. A vast

[59] This is the famous Sattapanni cave, in which the "first Buddhist council" was held "At the entrance of the Sattapaṇṇa cave in the Magadha town (compare *ante*, n. 45) Giribbaja (*i.e.*, Girivraja or Râjagṛiha) the first council was finished after seven months" (*Dîpavaṁśa* (Oldenberg) v. 5). In connection with this extract I would refer to the sentence preceding it (4), where we have named "the *second* beginning of the Vassa season." This seems to explain the constant use of the expression, the "double resting season," by Hiuen Tsiang. See below, n. 61.

[60] The hall appears to have been structural; the cave at the back was natural. See Fergusson, *Cave Temples of India*, p. 49.

multitude of heavenly beings were around him offering their gifts in worship, and this flower, which I hold, I brought thence."

Kâśyapa having heard these words said to his followers, "The sun of wisdom has quenched his rays. The world is now in darkness. The illustrious guide has left us and gone, and all flesh must fall into calamity."

Then the careless Bhikshus said one to another with satisfaction, "Tathâgata has gone to rest. This is good for us, for now, if we transgress, who is there to reprove or restrain us?"

Then Kâśyapa, having heard this, was deeply moved and afflicted, and he resolved to assemble (*collect*) the treasure of the law (*Dharma-piṭaka*) and bring to punishment the transgressors. Accordingly he proceeded to the two trees, and regarding Buddha, he offered worship.

And now the King of the Law having gone from the world, both men and Dêvas were left without a guide, and the great Arhats, moreover, were cleaving to (*the idea of their*) *Nirvâṇa*. Then the great Kâśyapa reflected thus: "To secure obedience to the teaching of Buddha, we ought to collect the *Dharma-piṭaka*." On this he ascended Mount Sumeru and sounded the great gong (*ghaṇṭâ*), and spake thus: "Now then, in the town of Râjagṛiha there is going to be a religious assembly.[61] Let all those who have obtained the fruit (*of arhatship*) hasten to the spot."

In connection with the sounding of the gong the direction of Kâśyapa spread far and wide through the great chiliocosm, and all those possessed of spiritual capabilities, hearing the instructions, assembled in convocation. At this time Kâśyapa addressed the assembly and said, "Tathâgatâ having died (*attained to extinction* or *Nirvâṇa*), the world is empty. We ought to collect the *Dharma-piṭaka*, in token of our gratitude to Buddha. Now then, being about to accomplish this, there should be profound composure (*quiet*). How can this be done in the midst of

[61] A business relating to religion; a religious proceeding.

such a vast multitude? Those who have acquired the three species of knowledge (*trividyâ*), who have obtained the six supernatural faculties (*shaḍabhijñâs*), who have kept the law without failure, whose powers of discrimination (*dialectic*) are clear, such superior persons as these may stop and form the assembly. Those who are learners with only limited fruit, let such depart to their homes."

On this 999 men were left; but he excluded Ânanda, as being yet a learner. Then the great Kâśyapa, calling him, addressed him thus: "You are not yet free from defects; you must leave the holy assembly." He replied, "During many years I have followed Tathâgata as his attendant; every assembly that has been held for considering the law, I have joined; but now, as you are going to hold an assembly after his death (*wai*), I find myself excluded; the King of the Law having died, I have lost my dependence and helper."

Kâśyapa said, "Do not cherish your sorrow! You were a personal attendant on Buddha indeed, and you therefore heard much, and so you loved (*much*), and therefore you are not free from all the ties that bind (*the soul* or *affections*)."

Ânanda, with words of submission, retired and came to a desert place, desiring to reach a condition "beyond learning;" he strove for this without intermission, but with no result. At length, wearied out, he desired one day to lie down. Scarcely had his head reached the pillow[62] when lo! he obtained he condition of an Arhat.

He then went to the assembly, and knocking at the door, announced his arrival. Kâśyapa then asked him, saying, "Have you got rid of all ties? In that case exercise your spiritual power and enter without the door being opened!" Ânanda, in compliance with the order, entered through the keyhole,[63] and having paid reverence to the priesthood, retired and sat down.

[62] For a similar account of Ânanda's illumination, see *Abstract of Four Lectures*, p. 72, and compare the whole account.

[63] In other accounts it is stated he entered through the wall.

At this time fifteen days of the summer rest (*Varshâvasâna*) had elapsed. On this Kâśyapa rising, said, "Consider well and listen! Let Ânanda, who ever heard the words of Tathâgata, collect by singing through[64] the *Sûtra-piṭaka*. Let Upâli (Yeu-po-li), who clearly understands the rules of discipline (*Vinaya*), and is well known to all who know, collect the *Vinaya-piṭaka*; and I, Kâśyapa, will collect the *Abhidharma-piṭaka*." The three months of rain[65] being past, the collection of the *Tripiṭaka* was finished. As the great Kâśyapa was the president (*Sthavira*) among the priests, it is called the Sthavira (Chang-tso-pu) convocation.[66]

North-west of the place where the great Kâśyapa held the convocation is a *stûpa*. This is where Ânanda, being forbidden by the priests to take part in the assembly, came and sat down in silence and reached the fruit (*position*) of an Arhat. After this he joined the assembly.

Going west from this point 20 li or so, is a *stûpa* built by Aśôka-râja. This is the spot where the "great assembly" (*Mahâsaṅgha*) formed their collection of books (*or*, held their assembly). Those who had not been permitted to join Kâśyapa's assembly, whether learners or those above learning (*Arhats*), to the number of 100,000 men, came together to this spot and said, "Whilst Tathâgata was alive we all had a common master, but now the King of the Law is dead it is different. We too wish to show our gratitude to Buddha, and we also will hold an assembly for collecting the scriptures." On this the common folk with the holy disciples came to the assembly (*all assembled*), the foolish and wise alike flocked together and collected the *Sûtra-piṭaka*, the *Vinaya-piṭaka*, the *Abhidharma-piṭaka*, the miscellaneous *Piṭaka* (*Khuddakanikâya*),[67] and

[64] Chanting or rehearsing, *saṅgîti*.

[65] Or, the second "three months." It is to be noted that the season of *Wass* was twofold, either the first "three months," or, the second "three months."

[66] This is contrary to the usual explanation, which makes the Sthavira school date from the second convocation at Vaiśâli.

[67] Or perhaps the *Sannipâtanikâya*.

the *Dhâraṇî-piṭaka.* Thus they distinguished five *Piṭakas.* And because in this assembly both common folk and holy personages were mixed together, it was called "the assembly of the great congregation" (*Mahâsaṅgha*).[68]

To the north of the Vêṇuvana Vihâra about 200 paces we come to the Karaṇḍa lake (Karaṇḍahrada). When Tathâgata was in the world he preached often here. The water was pure and clear, and possessed of the eight qualities.[69] After the *Nirvâṇa* of Buddha it dried up and disappeared

To the north-west of the Karaṇḍahrada, at a distance of 2 or 3 li, is a *stûpa* which was built by Aśôka-râja It is about 60 feet high; by the side of it is a stone pillar on which is a record engraved relating to the foundation of the *stûpa.* It is about 50 feet high, and on the top has the figure of an elephant.

To the north-east of the stone pillar, not far, we come to the town of Râjagṛiha[70] (Ho-lo-shi-ki-li-hi). The outer walls of this city have been destroyed, and there are no remnants of them left; the inner city (*walls*),[71] although in a ruined state, still have some elevation from the ground, and are about 20 li in circuit. In the first case, Bimbisâra-râja established his residence in Kuśâgâra; in this place the houses of the people, being close together, were frequently burned with fire and destroyed. When one house was in flames, it was impossible to prevent the whole neighbourhood sharing in the calamity, and consequently the whole was burned up. Then the people made loud complaints, and were unable to rest quietly in their dwellings. The king said, "By my demerit the lower people are afflicted;

[68] This account, too, differs from the common tradition, which makes this school of the great assembly date from the schism at Vaiśâlî. The statement, however, of Hiuen Tsiang, that the additional *piṭakas* were collated at this assembly is a useful and suggestive one.

[69] For the eight qualities of water see *J. R. A. S.*, vol. ii. pp. 1, 141.

[70] "The royal abode" (*Wang she*). This is what Fa-hian calls "the new city." It was to the north of the mountains.

[71] That is, the walls of the royal precincts or the citadel.

what deed of goodness (*meritorious virtue*) can I do in order to be exempt from such calamities?" His ministers said, "Mahârâja, your virtuous government spreads peace and harmony, your righteous rule causes light and progress. It is by want of due attention on the part of the people that these calamities of fire occur. It is necessary to make a severe law to prevent such occurrences hereafter. If a fire breaks out, the origin must be diligently sought for, and to punish the principal guilty person, let him be driven into the cold forest. Now this cold forest (*Śîtavana*) is the place of corpses abandoned (*cast out*) there. Every one esteems it an unlucky place, and the people of the land avoid going there and passing through it. Let him be banished there as a cast-out corpse. From dread of this fate, the people will become careful and guard (*against the outbreak of fire*)." The king said, "It is well; let this announcement be made, and let the people attend to it."

And now it happened that the king's palace was the first to be burned with fire. Then he said to his ministers, "I myself must be banished;" and he gave up the government to his eldest son in his own place. "I wish to maintain the laws of the country (*he said*); I therefore myself am going into exile."

At this time the king of Vaiśâlî hearing that Bimbisâra-râja was dwelling alone in the "cold forest," raised an army and put it in movement to invade (*make a foray*) when nothing was ready (*to resist him*). The lords of the marches (*frontiers*), hearing of it, built a town,[72] and as the king was the first to inhabit it, it was called "the royal city" (Râjagṛiha). Then the ministers and the people all flocked there with their families.

It is also said that Ajâtaśatru-râja first founded this

[72] That is, as it seems, in the place where the king was living. From this it would appear that the site of the new town of Râjagṛiha had been before used as a burial-place for the people of the "old town."

city, and the heir-apparent of Ajâtaśatru having come to the throne, he also appointed it to be the capital, and so it continued till the time of Aśôka-râja, who changed the capital to Pâṭaliputra, and gave the city of Râjagṛĭha to the Brâhmaṇs, so that now in the city there are no common folk to be seen, but only Brâhmaṇs to the number of a thousand families.

At the south-west angle of the royal precincts[73] are two small *saṅghârâmas;* the priests who come and go, and are strangers in the place, lodge here. Here also Buddha, when alive, delivered the law (*preached*). North-west from this is a *stûpa;* this is the site of an old village where the householder Jyôtishka[74] (Ch'u-ti-se-kia) was born.

Outside the south gate of the city, on the left of the road, is a *stûpa.* Here Tathâgata preached and converted Râhula (Lo-hu-lo).[75]

Going north from this 30 li or so, we come to Nâlanda *saṅghârâma.*[76] The old accounts of the country say that to the south of this *saṅghârâma,* in the middle of an Âmra ('An-mo-lo) grove, there is a tank. The Nâga of this tank is called Nâlanda.[77] By the side of it is built the *saṅghârâma,* which therefore takes the name (*of the Nâga*). But the truth is that Tathâgata in old days practised the life of a Bôdhisattva here, and became the king of a great country, and established his capital in this land. Moved by pity for living things, he delighted in continually relieving them. In remembrance of this virtue he was called[78] "charity without intermission;" and the *saṅg-*

[73] *I.e.*, of the inner city of Râjagṛĭha.

[74] In Chinese Sing lih, "constellation" or "star collection."

[75] If this Lo-hu-lo be the son of Buddha, his conversion is generally stated to have occurred at Kapilavastu (*Manual of Budhism*, p. 206).

[76] Nâlanda has been identified with the village of Baragaon, which lies seven miles north of Râjgîr (Cunningham, *Anc. Geog.*, p. 468).

[77] According to I-tsing the name Nâlanda is derived from Nâga Nanda (see *J. R. A. S.*, N.S., vol. xiii. p. 571). For a description of this temple of Nâlanda see "Two Chinese Buddhist Inscriptions found at Buddha Gayâ," *J. R. A. S.*, N.S., vol. xiii. *l. c.* See also *Abstract of Four Lectures*, p. 140.

[78] So I understand the passage.

hârâma was called in perpetuation of this name. The site was originally an Âmra garden. Five hundred merchants bought it for ten *kôṭis* of gold pieces and gave it to Buddha. Buddha preached the law here during three months, and the merchants and others obtained the fruit of holiness. Not long after the *Nirvâṇa* of Buddha, a former king of this country named Śakrâditya (Shi-kia-lo-'o-t'ie-to) respected and esteemed the (*system of the*) one Vehicle,[79] and honoured very highly the three treasures.[80] Having selected by augury a lucky spot, he built this *saṅghârâma*. When he began the work he wounded, in digging, the body of the Nâga. At this time there was a distinguished soothsayer belonging to the heretical sect of the Nirgranthas. He having seen the occurrence, left this record: "This is a very superior site. If you build here a *saṅghârâma*, it must of necessity become highly renowned. Throughout the five Indies it will be a model. For a period of a thousand years it will flourish still. Students of all degrees will here easily accomplish their studies. But many will spit blood because of this wound given to the Nâga."

His son, Buddhagupta-râja (Fo-t'o-kio-to), who succeeded him, continued to labour at the excellent undertaking of his father. To the south of this he built another *saṅghârâma*.

Tathâgatagupta-râja (Ta-tha-kie-to-kio-lo) vigorously practised the former rules (*of his ancestors*), and he built east from this another *saṅghârâma*.

Balâditya-râja (P'o-lo-'o-tie-lo) succeeded to the empire. On the north-east side he built a *saṅghârâma*.

It has no reference to the Nâga. The word Nâlanda would thus appear to be derived from *na* + *alam* + *da*, "not giving enough," or "not having enough to give."

[79] The "one Vehicle," according to the authority quoted by Julien (n. 2 *in loco*) is "the vehicle of Buddha, which is compared to a car formed of seven precious substances, and drawn by a white ox." But the expression, "one Vehicle," is a common one in later Buddhist books to denote the *nature* of Buddha, to which we all belong, and to which we all shall return.

[80] *Triratnâni* Buddha, dharma, saṅgha.

The work being done, he called together an assembly for congratulation. He respected equally the obscure and the renowned, and invited common folk and men of religion (*holiness*) without distinction. The priests of all India came together for the distance of 10,000 li. After all were seated and at rest, two priests arrived. They led them up the three-storeyed pavilion. Then they asked them, saying, "The king, when about to call the assembly, first asked men of all degrees (*common and holy*). From what quarter do your reverences come so late?" They said, "We are from the country of China. Our teacher[81] was sick. Having nourished him, we set out to accept the king's far-off invitation.[82] This is the reason why we have arrived so late."

The assembly hearing this, were filled with astonishment, and proceeded at once to inform the king. The king knowing that they were holy persons, went himself to interrogate them. He mounted the pavilion, but he knew not where they had gone.[83] The king then was affected by a profound faith; he gave up his country and became a recluse. Having done so, he placed himself as the lowest of the priests, but his heart was always uneasy and ill at rest. "Formerly (*he said*) I was a king, and the highest among the honourable; but now I have become a recluse, I am degraded to the bottom of the priesthood." Forthwith he went to the priests, and said words to the above effect. On this the *saṅgha* resolved that they who had not received the full orders should be classed according to their natural years of life.[84] This *saṅghârâma* is the only one in which this law exists.

[81] It is true the symbol *shang* in this phrase is not the same as that forming the second member of the word *hoshang* (upâdhyâya), but they are the same in sound, and therefore I think *ho-shang* in the text should be translated "teacher."

[82] That is, the invitation coming from a long distance.

[83] That is, he ascended the pavilion with three stages where the strangers from China had been received; but when he arrived he found they had departed.

[84] The usual order was that they should be classed according to the number of years they had been "professed disciples;" but in the convent of Balâditya the order was that they should be classed accord-

This king's son, called Vajra (Fa-she-lo), came to the throne in succession, and was possessed of a heart firm in the faith. He again built on the west side of the convent a *saṅghârâma.*

After this a king of Central India built to the north of this a great *saṅghârâma.* Moreover, he built round these edifices a high wall with one gate.[85] A long succession of kings continued the work of building, using all the skill of the sculptor, till the whole is truly marvellous to behold. The king[86] said, "In the hall of the monarch who first began the *saṅghârâma* I will place a figure of Buddha, and I will feed forty priests of the congregation every day to show my gratitude to the founder."

The priests, to the number of several thousands, are men of the highest ability and talent. Their distinction is very great at the present time, and there are many hundreds whose fame has rapidly spread through distant regions. Their conduct is pure and unblamable. They follow in sincerity the precepts of the moral law. The rules of this convent are severe, and all the priests are bound to observe them. The countries of India respect them and follow them. The day is not sufficient for asking and answering profound questions. From morning till night they engage in discussion; the old and the young mutually help one another. Those who cannot discuss questions out of the *Tripiṭaka* are little esteemed, and are obliged to hide themselves for shame. Learned men from different cities, on this account, who desire to acquire quickly a renown in discussion, come here in multitudes to settle their doubts, and then the streams (*of their wisdom*) spread far and wide. For this reason some persons usurp the name (*of Nâlanda students*), and in going to and fro receive honour in consequence. If men

ing to their natural age, up to the time of their full ordination. The king, although he had become a disciple, was not fully ordained.

[85] That is, to enter the whole area.

[86] But it is not said what king. The symbol, too, is *ti*, not *wang*. Is Śîlâditya referred to? He was not to take the name of *wang* or *ta wang* (see vol. i. p. 213 n 21).

of other quarters desire to enter and take part in the discussions, the keeper of the gate proposes some hard questions; many are unable to answer, and retire. One must have studied deeply both old and new (*books*) before getting admission. Those students, therefore, who come here as strangers, have to show their ability by hard discussion; those who fail compared with those who succeed are as seven or eight to ten. The other two or three of moderate talent, when they come to discuss in turn in the assembly, are sure to be humbled, and to forfeit their renown. But with respect to those of conspicuous talent of solid learning, great ability, illustrious virtue, distinguished men, these connect (*their high names*) with the succession (*of celebrities belonging to the college*), such as Dharmapâla (Hu-fa)[87] and Chandrapâla (Hu-yueh),[88] who excited by their bequeathed teaching the thoughtless and worldly; Guṇamati (Tih-hwui)[89] and Sthiramati (Kin-hwui),[90] the streams of whose superior teaching spread abroad even now; Prabhamitra (Kwang-yeu),[91] with his clear discourses; Jinamitra (Shing-yeu),[92] with his exalted eloquence; the pattern and fame (*sayings and doings*) of Jñânachandra (Chi-yueh)[93] reflect his brilliant activity; Śigrabuddha (?) (Ming-min), and Śilabhadra (Kiaï-hien),[94] and other eminent men whose names are lost. These illustrious personages, known to all, excelled in their attainments (*virtue*) all their distinguished predecessors, and passed the bounds of the ancients in their learning. Each of these composed some tens of treatises and commentaries

[87] A native of Kâñchipura, author of the *S'abdavidya-samyukta S'âstra* (Max Müller, pp. 308 n., 309–310 and n., 346, 348–349, 361).

[88] See Vassilief; Max Müller, *India*, p. 311.

[89] Max Müller, *India*, p. 305 and n., pp. 309–310 n., p. 362.

[90] Pupil of Ârya Asaṅga (Max Müller, pp. 305, 310 n., 318 n.; Vassilief, pp. 59 78, 226–227, 305).

[91] Po-lo-pho-mi-to-lo of Central India, by caste a Kshattriya. He reached China in A.D. 627, and died in 633 at the age of sixty-nine (Beal, *Abs. Four. Leet.*, p. 28; Max Müller, *Ind.*, p. 312).

[92] Eitel, p. 37.

[93] Max Müller, *Ind.*, pp. 312–361; Eitel, *Djñânatchandra.*

[94] The favourite teacher of Hiuen Tsiang. *Vie*, pp. 144, 212, 215, 225; Max Müller, *India*, pp. 310, 343; Eitel, *s. v.*

which were widely diffused, and which for their perspicuity are passed down to the present time.

The sacred relics on the four sides of the convent are hundreds in number. For brevity's sake we will recount two or three. On the western side of the *saṅghârâma*, at no great distance, is a *vihâra*. Here Tathâgata in old days stopped for three months and largely expounded the excellent law for the good of the Dêvas.

To the south 100 paces or so is a small *stûpa*. This is the place where a Bhikshu from a distant region saw Buddha. Formerly there was a Bhikshu who came from a distant region. Arriving at this spot, he met the multitude of disciples accompanying Buddha, and was affected inwardly with a feeling of reverence, and so prostrated himself on the ground, at the same time uttering a strong desire that he might obtain the position of a Chakravarttî monarch. Tathâgata having seen him, spoke to his followers thus: "That Bhikshu ought much to be pitied. The power (*character*) of his religious merit is deep and distant;[95] his faith is strong. If he were to seek the fruit of Buddha, not long hence he would obtain it; but now that he has earnestly prayed to become a Chakravarttî king, he will in future ages receive this reward: as many grains of dust as there are from the spot where he has thrown himself on the earth down to the very middle of the gold wheel,[96] so many Chakravarttî kings will there be for reward;[97] but having fixed his mind on earthly joys, the fruit of holiness is far off."[98]

On this southern side is a standing figure of Kwan-tsz'-tsai (Avalôkitêśvara) Bôdhisattva. Sometimes he is seen holding a vessel of perfume going to the *vihâra* of Buddha and turning round to the right.

[95] This is the literal meaning of the symbols. Julien translates, "he has a profound virtue." It may mean that his religious merit, though deep, will have but a distant reward.

[96] *I.e.*, to the middle of the earth where the gold wheel is.

[97] *I.e.*, so many times will he be a Chakravarttî king.

[98] This seems to explain the words "deep and distant." See above n. 95.

To the south of this statue is a *stûpa*, in which are remains of Buddha's hair and nails cut during three months. Those persons afflicted with children's complaints,[99] coming here and turning round religiously, are mostly healed.

To the west of this, outside the wall, and by the side of a tank, is a *stûpa*. This is where a heretic, holding a sparrow in his hand, asked Buddha questions relating to death and birth.

To the south-east about 50 paces, within the walls, is an extraordinary tree, about eight or nine feet in height, of which the trunk is twofold. When Tathâgata of old time was in the world, he flung his tooth-cleaner (*dantakâshṭha*) on the ground here, where it took root. Although many months and years have elapsed since then, the tree neither decreases nor increases.[100]

Next to the east there is a great *vihâra* about 200 feet in height. Here Tathâgata, residing for four months, explained various excellent laws.

After this, to the north 100 paces or so, is a *vihâra* in which is a figure of Kwan-tsz'-tsai Bôdhisattva. The disciples of pure faith, who offer their religious gifts, do not all see the place he occupies alike; it is not fixed.[101] Sometimes he (*i.e., the figure*) seems to be standing by the side of the door; sometimes he goes out in front of the eaves. Religious people, both clerics and laics, from all parts come together in numbers to offer their gifts.

To the north of this *vihâra* is a great *vihâra*, in height about 300 feet, which was built by Balâditya-râja (Po-lo-'o-tie-to-wang). With respect to its magnificence,

[99] Or it may be translated, "those afflicted with complicated diseases." The symbol *ying* means either "a babe" or "to add or increase."

[100] After having used the dantakâshṭha for cleaning the teeth, it was usual to divide it into two parts, hence the double trunk of the tree (compare Julien *in loc.*, n. 1). The *dantakâshṭha* in the original is "chewing-willow-twig." The wood used in India is the *Acacia catechu*; see *ante*, vol. i. p. 68 n.; and Julien's note, tome I., p. 55.

[101] Or, "do not all see what they see alike. The place he occupies is not fixed."

its dimensions, and the statue of Buddha placed in it, it resembles (*is the same as*) the great *vihâra* built under the *Bôdhi* tree.[102]

To the north-east of this is a *stûpa*. Here Tathâgata in days gone by explained the excellent law for seven days.

To the north-west is a place where the four past Buddhas sat down.

To the south of this is a *vihâra* of brass[102] built by Śîlâditya-râja. Although it is not yet finished, yet its intended measurement, when finished (*to plan*), will be 100 feet.[104]

Next to the eastward 200 paces or so, outside the walls, is a figure of Buddha standing upright and made of copper. Its height is about 80 feet. A pavilion of six stages is required to cover it. It was formerly made by Pûrṇavarma-râja (Mwan-cheu).

To the north of this statue 2 or 3 li, in a *vihâra* constructed of brick, is a figure of Târa Bôdhisattva (To-lo-p'u-sa). This figure is of great height, and its spiritual appearance very striking. Every fast-day of the year large offerings are made to it. The kings and ministers and great people of the neighbouring countries offer exquisite perfumes and flowers, holding gem-covered flags

[102] This is the great *vihâra* supposed to have been built by Amaradêva. With respect to this and the whole subject, the controversies and theories respecting its date, see Dr. Rajêndralâl Mitra's work on the *stûpa* at Buddha Gayâ.

[103] *Yu-shih*, "calamine stone, used in the formation of brass" (Medhurst). There is much confusion in the use of the symbols *teou shi* and *yu shi*. The former is explained by Medhurst (sub voc. *t'how*) "as a kind of stone resembling metal, which the Chinese call the finest kind of native copper. It is found in the Posse country and resembles gold. On the application of fire it assumes a red colour, and does not turn black." But *yu shi* (which seems to be intended in the passage in the text, although Julien renders it *theou chi*) is explained by Medhurst (sub voc. *shih*) to be "calamine stone, used in the formation of brass." The calamine stone is the *cadmia* of Pliny—"fit et e lapide æroso, quem vocant cadmiam" (vol. ii. cap. xxxiv. § 2). Cadmus is fabled to have discovered its use in the composition of brass, and hence the name. It may be called calamine from its place of exportation, Calamina, at the mouth of the Indus; hence the Chinese say it comes from Po-ssc. Brass being capable of being rolled into thin sheets (*latten* or *Dutch metal*), might easily be used in covering the walls of a building. It was so used probably by Śîlâditya in the case under notice.

[104] Not in height, but in length.

and canopies, whilst instruments of metal and stone resound in turns, mingled with the harmony of flutes and harps. These religious assemblies last for seven days.

Within the southern gate of the wall is a large well. Formerly, when Buddha was alive, a great company of merchants parched with thirst came here to the spot where Buddha was. The Lord of the World, pointing to this place, said, "You will find water there." The chief of the merchants, piercing the earth with the end of the axle of his cart, immediately water rushed out from the ground. Having drunk and heard the law, they all obtained the fruit of holiness.

Going south-west 8 or 9 li from the *saṅghârâma*, we come to the village of Kulika (Kiu-li-kia). In it is a *stûpa* built by Aśôka-râja. This is where the venerable Mudgalaputra (Mo-te-kia-lo-tseu) was born. By the side of the village is a *stûpa*. This is where the Venerable One reached complete *Nirvâṇa*,[105] and in it are placed the remains of his bequeathed body. The venerable (Mahâmudgalaputra) was of a great Brâhmaṇ family, and was an intimate friend of Śâriputra when they were young. This Śâriputra was renowned for the clearness of his dialectic skill; the other for his persevering and deep penetration. Their gifts and wisdom were alike, and moving or standing they were always together.[106] Their aims and desires from beginning to end were just the same. They had together left the world from distaste to its pleasures, and as hermits had followed Sañjaya (Shen-she-ye) as their master.[107] Śâriputra having met Aśvajita (Ma-shing) the Arhat, hearing the law, understood its holy (*meaning*).[108] On returning he repeated what he had

[105] Literally, *Nirvâṇa* "without remains" (anupâdiseśa). For the meaning of this phrase consult Childers, *Pali Dict.*, sub voc. *Nibbânaṁ*. Julien renders it *Parinirvâna*.

[106] For an account of these two disciples, see *Fo-sho-king*, varga 17. They are called Seriyut and Mugalan in Pâli,—Hardy, *Manual of Budhism*, p. 181.

[107] "There was at this time in Rajagaha a famous paribrajika called Saṅga. To him they (Seriyut and Mugalan) went, and they remained with him some time."—*Manual of Budhism*, p. 195.

[108] Or, understood the holy one, *i.e.*, Aśvajita.

heard for the sake of the venerable (Mudgalaputra). On this he understood the meaning of the law and reached the first fruit.[109] Then with 250 followers he went to the place where Buddha was. The Lord of the World, seeing him at a distance, pointing him out, said to his disciples, "That one coming here will be the first among my followers in the exercise of spiritual faculties (*miraculous powers*)." Having reached the place where Buddha was, he requested to enter the law (*the society*). The Lord replying, said, "Welcome, O Bhikshu; carefully practise a pure life, and you shall escape the limits of sorrow." Hearing this his hair fell off, and his common robes were changed into others. Observing in their purity the sections of the rules of moral discipline, and being in his exterior behaviour faultless, after seven days, getting rid of all the bonds of sin, he reached the condition of an Arhat and the supernatural powers.

East of the old village of Mudgalaputra, going 3 or 4 li, we come to a *stûpa*. This is the place where Bimbisâra-râja went to have an interview with Buddha. When Tathâgata first obtained the fruit of a Buddha, knowing that the hearts of the people of the Magadha were waiting for him athirst, he accepted the invitation of Bimbisâra-râja, and early in the morning, putting on his robes, he took his begging-dish, and with a thousand Bhikshus around him, on the right hand and the left (*he advanced*). In front and behind these there were a number of aged Brâhmaṇs who went with twisted hair (*jâlina*), and being desirous of the law, wore their dyed garments (*chîvara*). Followed by such a throng, he entered the city of Râjagṛiha.

Then Lord Śakra (Ti-shih), king of Dêvas, changing his appearance into that of a Mânava (Ma-na-p'o) youth,[110] with a crown upon his head and his hair bound up, in his left hand holding a golden pitcher and in his right a precious staff, he walked above the earth four fingers

[109] *I.e.*, became a Śrotâpanna.

[110] That is, a young Brâhmaṇ.

high, leading Buddha along the road in front, in the midst of the vast assembly. Then the king of the Magadha country, Bimbisâra (Pin-pi-so-lo) by name, accompanied by all the Brâhmaṇ householders within the land, and the merchants (*ku-sse*), 100,000 myriads in all, going before and behind, leading and following, proceeded from the city of Râjagṛiha to meet and escort the holy congregation.

South-east from the spot where Bimbasâra-râja met Buddha, at a distance of about 20 li, we come to the town of Kâlapinâka (*Kia-lo-pi-na-kia*). In this town is a *stûpa* which was built by Aśôka-râja. This is the place where Śâriputra, the venerable one, was born. The well[111] of the place still exists. By the side of the place[112] is a *stûpa*. This is where the venerable one obtained *Nirvâṇa;* the relics of his body, therefore, are enshrined therein. He also was of a high Brâhmaṇ family. His father was a man of great learning and erudition; he penetrated thoroughly the most intricate questions. There were no books he had not thoroughly investigated. His wife had a dream and told it to her husband. "Last night," said she, "during my sleep my dreams were troubled by a strange man[113] whose body was covered with armour; in his hand he held a diamond mace with which he broke the mountains; departing, he stood at the foot of one particular mountain." "This dream," the husband said, "is extremely good. You will bear a son of deep learning; he will be honoured in the world, and will attack the treatises of all the masters and break down their teaching (*schools*). Being led to consider, he will become the disciple of one who is more than human."[114]

[111] This may also mean "the stone foundation."

[112] Julien says, "by the side of the well." But refer to the account of Mudgalaputra's birthplace. The original is "the well of the village," *not* "of the house."

[113] By intercourse with a strange man.

[114] This is an obscure sentence, but it seems to correspond with the dream of the man standing at the foot of a mountain. Buddha is constantly spoken of as "a mountain of gold;" and the expression *puh ju yih jin*, "not as one man," seems to allude to the superhuman character of Śâriputra's future teacher.

And so in due course she conceived a child. All at once she was greatly enlightened. She discoursed in high and powerful language, and her words were not to be overthrown. When the venerable one began to be eight years old, his reputation was spread in every direction. His natural disposition was pure and simple, his heart loving and compassionate. He broke through all impediments in his way, and perfected his wisdom. He formed a friendship when young with Mudgalaputra, and being deeply disgusted with the world, and having no system to adopt as a refuge, he went with Mudgalaputra to the heretic Sañjaya's abode, and practised (*his mode of salvation*). Then they said together, "This is not the system of final deliverance,[115] nor is it able to rescue us from the trammels of sorrow. Let us each seek for an illustrious guide. He who first obtains *sweet dew*,[116] let him make the taste common to the other."[117]

At this time the great Arhat Aśvajita, holding in his hand his proper measure bowl (*pâtra*), was entering the city begging for food.

Śâriputra seeing his dignified exterior and his quiet and becoming manner, forthwith asked him, "Who is your master?" He answered, "The prince of the Śâkya tribe, disgusted with the world, becoming a hermit, has reached perfect wisdom. This one is my master." Śâriputra added, "And what doctrine does he teach? May I find a way to hear it?" He said, "I have but just received instruction, and have not yet penetrated the deep doctrine." Sâriputra said, "Pray tell me (*repeat*) what you have heard." Then Aśvajita, so far as he could, explained it and spoke. Śâriputra having heard it, immediately

On the other hand, Julien translates it, "there will not be a greater honour for a man than to become his disciple;" or, "nothing will be considered so great an honour to a man as to become his disciple," and this perhaps is the meaning of the passage.

[115] "The highest" or "absolute truth."

[116] That is, "the water of immortality;" the doctrine of Buddha.

[117] *I.e.*, let him communicate the knowledge of that system of salvation (sweet dew).

reached the first fruit, and went forthwith with 250 of his followers, to the place where Buddha was dwelling.

The Lord of the World, seeing him afar off, pointing to him and addressing his followers, said, "Yonder comes one who will be most distinguished for wisdom among my disciples." Having reached the place, he bent his head in worship and asked to be permitted to follow the teaching of Buddha. The Lord said to him, "Welcome, O Bhikshu."

Having heard these words, he was forthwith ordained.[118] Half a month after, hearing Buddha preach the law on account of a Brâhmaṇ [119] called "Long-nails" (Dîrghanakha), together with other discourses,[120] and understanding them with a lively emotion, he obtained the fruit of an Arhat. After this, Ânanda hearing Buddha speak about his *Nirvâṇa*, it was noised abroad and talked about (*by the disciples*). Each one was affected with grief. Śâriputra was doubly touched with sorrow, and could not endure the thought of seeing Buddha die. Accordingly, he asked the Lord that he might die first. The lord said, "Take advantage of your opportunity."

He then bade adieu to the disciples and came to his native village. His followers, the Śrâmaṇêras, spread the news everywhere through the towns and villages. Ajâtaśatru-râja and his people hastened together as the wind, and assembled in clouds to the assembly, whilst Śâriputra repeated at large the teaching of the law. Having heard it, they went away. In the middle of the following night, with fixed (*correct*) thought, and mind restrained, he entered the *Samâdhi* called "final extinction." After awhile, having risen out of it, he died.

[118] Admitted to undertake the duties of the moral code of discipline.

[119] This Brâhman or Brahmachârin (ch'ang-chao-fan-chi) is well known, as there is a work called *Dîrghanakha parivrâjaka paripṛichchha* (Jul. note *in loc.*)

[120] *Or*, the end of the discourse; but the symbol *chu* generally means "the rest."

Four or five li to the south-east of the town Kâlapinâka[121] is a *stûpa*. This is the spot where a disciple of Śâriputra reached *Nirvâṇa*. It is otherwise said, "When Kâśyapa Buddha was in the world, then three *kôṭis* of great Arhats entered the condition of complete *Nirvâṇa* in this place."

Going 30 li or so to the east of this last-named *stûpa*, we come to Indraśailaguhâ mountain (In-t'o-lo-shi-lo-kia-ho-shan).[122] The precipices and valleys of this mountain are dark and gloomy. Flowering trees grow thickly together like forests. The summit has two peaks, which rise up sharply and by themselves. On the south side of the western peak[123] between the crags is a great stone house,[124] wide but not high. Here Tathâgata in old time was stopping when Śakra, king of Dêvas, wrote on the stone matters relating to forty-two doubts which he had, and asked Buddha respecting them.[125]

Then Buddha explained the matters. The traces of these figures still exist. Persons now try to imitate by comparison these ancient holy figures (*figure forms*).[126]

[121] For some remarks on Kâlapinâka, see *Fa-hian* Beal's edition), p. 111, n. 2.

[122] "The-cavern-of-Indra mountain." The "rocky hill standing by itself," named by Fa-hian, chap. xxviii., has been identified by General Cunningham (*Arch. Survey*, vol. i. p. 18) with the western peak of this hill. The northern range of hills, that stretch from the neighbourhood of Gayâ to the bank of the Pañchâna river, a distance of about thirty-six miles, end abruptly in two lofty peaks; the higher of the two on the west is called Giryek. This is the one referred to by Fa-hian. (See Cunningham, *Arch. Survey*, vol. i. pp. 16, 17, and vol. iii. p. 150.)

[123] Julien has omitted the symbol for west.

[124] Now called Gidha-dwar; in Sanskrit, Gṛídhradwâra, "the vulture's opening."

[125] That is, at it seems, he drew certain figures or letters on the stone, and asked Buddha to explain some difficulties he had as to the subject of these figures. These forty-two difficulties have no reference to the *Book of Forty-two Sections*.

[126] This translation appears to me the only justifiable one. Julien has, "Now there is a statue there which resembles the ancient image of the saint (*i.e.*, of the Buddha)." But if the symbol *ts'z* (this) be taken for the adverb "here," the natural translation would be: "Now there are here figures in imitation of these ancient sacred symbols or marks." The only doubt is whether *ts'z siang*, "these marks or figures," or "the figures here," be not an error for "*Fo-siang*," "the figure of Buddha," which occurs a little farther on.

Those who enter the cave to worship are seized with a sort of religious trepidation.

On the top of the mountain ridge are traces where the four former Buddhas sat and walked, still remaining. On the top of the eastern peak is a *saṅghârâma;* the common account is this: when the priests who dwell here look across in the middle of the night at the western peak, where the stone chamber is, they see before the image of Buddha lamps and torches constantly burning.

Before the *saṅghârâma* on the eastern peak of the Indraśailaguhâ mountain is a *stûpa* which is called Haṅsa (Keng-sha).[127] Formerly the priests of this *saṅghârâma* studied the doctrine of the Little Vehicle, that is, the Little Vehicle of the "gradual doctrine."[128] They allowed therefore the use of the three pure articles of food, and they followed this rule without fail. Now afterwards, when it was not time to seek for the three pure articles of food, there was a Bhikshu who was walking up and down; suddenly he saw a flock of wild geese flying over him in the air. Then he said in a jocose way, "To-day the congregation of priests has not food sufficient, Mahâsattvas! now is your opportunity." No sooner had he finished, than a goose, stopping its flight, fell down before the priest and died. The Bhikshu having seen this, told it to the priests, who, hearing it, were affected with pity, and said one to the other, "Tathâgata framed his law as a guide and en-

[127] Keng-so-kia-lan, in Chinese Keng-sha. The lower peak on the east is crowned with a solid tower of brickwork, well known as Jârasandha-ka-baithak, or "Jârasandha's throne." This tower, the ruins of which still exist, is probably the *stûpa* alluded to in the text (comp. Cunningham, *Arch. Survey,* i. 19). But I am at a loss how to explain General Cunningham's remark (*Arch. Survey,* iii. 141), that "close to the hot springs on the north-east slope of the Baibhâr hill there is a massive foundation of a stone house 83 feet square, called Jarâsandha-ka-baithak, or "Jarâsandha's throne." This is explained, however, in Fergusson and Burgess' *Cave Temples of India,* by the statement that there are two sites so named.

[128] The advanced doctrine of the Little Vehicle (Hînayâna); compare Julien's note, tome i. p. 3.

courageement (*suitable to*) the powers (*springs*) of each person ;[129] now we, following 'the gradual doctrine,' are using a foolish guide. The Great Vehicle is the true doctrine. We ought to change our former practice, and follow more closely the sacred directions. This goose falling down is, in truth, a true lesson for us, and we ought to make known its virtue by handing down the story to other ages, the most distant." On this they built a *stûpa* to hand down to future ages the action they had witnessed, and they buried the dead goose beneath it.

Going 150 or 160 li to the north-east of the Indraśila-guhâ mountain, we come to the Kapôtika (*pigeon*) convent.[130] There are about 200 priests, who study the principles of the Sarvâstavâda school of Buddhism.

To the east is a *stûpa* which was built by Aśôka-râja. Formerly Buddha residing in this place, declared the law for one night to the great congregation. At this time there was a bird-catcher who was laying his snares for the feathered tribe in this wood. Having caught nothing for a whole day, he spoke thus, "My bad luck to-day is owing to a trick somewhere." Therefore he came to the place where Buddha was, and said in a high voice, "Your speaking the law to-day, O Tathâgata, has caused me to catch nothing in all my nets. My wife and my children at home are hungry; what expedient shall I try to help them?" Then Tathâgata replied, "If you will light a fire, I will give you something to eat."

Then Tathâgata made to appear a large dove, which fell in the fire and died. Then the bird-catcher taking it, carried it to his wife and children, and they ate it

[129] *I.e.*, Buddha's law was intended to be adapted to circumstances.

[130] This Kapôtika (pigeon) convent is identified by General Cunningham with the village of Pârbati, just 10 miles to the north-east of Giriyek. This would require us to change the 150 or 160 li of Hiuen Tsiang into 50 or 60.

together. Then he went back to the place where Buddha was, on which, by the use of expedients, he framed his discourse so as to convert the bird-catcher. Having heard the discourse, he repented of his fault and was renewed in heart. Then he left his home, and practising wisdom, reached the holy fruit, and because of this the *saṅghârâma* was called Kapôtika.

To the south of this 2 or 3 li we come to a solitary hill,[131] which is of great height, and covered with forests and jungle. Celebrated flowers and pure fountains of water cover its sides and flow through its hollows. On this hill are many *vihâras* and religious shrines, sculptured with the highest art. In the exact middle of the *vihâra* is a figure of Kwan-tsz'-tsai Bôdhisattva. Although it is of small size, yet its spiritual appearance is of an affecting character. In its hand it holds a lotus flower; on its head is a figure of Buddha.

There are always a number of persons here who abstain from food desiring to obtain a view of the Bôdhisattva. For seven days, and fourteen days, and even for a whole month (*do they fast*). Those who are properly affected see this Kwan-tsz'-tsai Bôdhisattva with its beautiful[132] marks, and thoroughly adorned with all its majesty and glory. It comes forth from the middle of the statue, and addresses kind words to these men.

In old days the king of the Siṁhala country, in the

[131] This solitary hill is supposed to be "the hill standing by itself," named by Fa-hian (Cunningham, *Reports*, vol. xv. p. 7). Dr. Fergusson, on the other hand, identifies the hill of Behar with that site (*J. R. A. S.* N.S., vol. vi. p. 229), and this hill with the Shêkhpura range (*ibid.*, p. 232).

[132] One form of the worship of Kwan-yin will probably be found to have been derived from the Persian Anaitis or Anâhita; the descriptions given of each are too similar to be attributed to accident. Especially on this point of "beauty" compare *Sacred Books of the East*, vol. xxiii. p. 82; also Bunyiu Nanjio, *Catalogue of Jap. and Chin. Books lately added to the Bodleian*, col. 7, to show that Kwan-yin is identified with "pure water." Note also Edkin's *Chinese Buddhism*, p. 262, "Kwan-yin from beyond the sea." The description of Anâhita's dress in the *Abân Yasht* (*S. B. E.*, vol. xxiii.), §§ 126–131, corresponds with the representations in the *Liturgy of Kwan-yin*. The subject is too copious for a note.

early morning reflecting his face in a mirror, was not able to see himself, but he saw in the middle of a Tâla wood, on the top of a little mountain in the Magadha country of Jambudvîpa, a figure of this Bôdhisattva. The king, deeply affected at the benevolent appearance of the figure, diligently searched after it. Having come to this mountain,[133] he found in fact a figure resembling the one he had seen. On this he built a *vihâra* and offered to it religious gifts. After this the king still recollecting the fame of the circumstance, according to his example, built *vihâras* and spiritual shrines. Flowers and incense with the sound of music are constantly offered here.

Going south-east from this shrine on the solitary mountain about 40 li, we come to a convent with about fifty priests,[134] who study the teaching of the Little Vehicle. Before the *saṅghârâma* is a great *stûpa*, where many miracles are displayed. Here Buddha in former days preached for Brahma-dêva's sake and others during seven days. By the side of it are traces where the three Buddhas of the past age sat and walked. To the north-east of the *sanghârâma* about 70 li, on the south side of the Ganges river, we come to a large village, thickly populated.[135] There are many Dêva temples here, all of them admirably adorned.

Not far to the south-east is a great *stûpa*. Here Buddha for a night preached the law. Going east from this we enter the desert mountains; and going 100 li or so, we come to the convent of the village of Lo-in-ni-lo.[136]

Before this is a great *stûpa* which was built by Aśôka-

[133] The worship of Kwan-yin as a mountain deity has been alluded to in the *J. R. A. S.*, N.S., vol. xv. pp. 333 f. I would remark here that it seems the worship of this deity was partly connected with Ceylon. The argument of the paper in the *J. R. A. S.* is to the same purport.

[134] General Cunningham suggests the substitution of *four* li for *forty*. In that case the place indicated would be Aphsar (see *Arch. Survey*, vol. xv. p. 10).

[135] Both distance and direction point to the vicinity of Shekhpura (*op. cit.* p. 13).

[136] Identified by Cunningham with Rajjâna. In Gladwin's *Ayin-Akbari* it is found under the form "Rowbenny," which closely resembles the Chinese. Julien proposes Rôhinîla doubtfully. See also Fergusson (*op. cit.*), p. 233.

râja. Here Buddha formerly preached the law for three months. To the north of this 2 or 3 li is a large tank about 30 li round. During the four seasons of the year a lotus of each of the four colours opens its petals.

Going east we enter a great forest wild, and after 200 li or so we come to the country of I-lan-na-po-fa-to (Hiranyaparvata).

BOOK X.

Contains an account of seventeen countries, viz., (1) *I-lan-na-po-fa-to;* (2) *Chen-po;* (3) *Kie-chu-hoh-khi-lo;* (4) *Pun-na-fa-tan-na;* (5) *Kia-mo-lu-po;* (6) *San-mo-ta-cha;* (7) *Tan-mo-li-ti;* (8) *Kie-lo-na-su-fa-la-na;* (9) *U-cha;* (10) *Kong-u-t'o;* (11) *Kie-ling-kia;* (12) *Kiao-sa-lo;* (13) *'An-ta-lo;* (14) *To-na-kie-tse-kia;* (15) *Chu-li-ye;* (16) *Ta-lo-pi-ch'a;* (17) *Mo-lo-kiu-cha.*

I-LAN-NA-PO-FA-TO (HIRANYA-PARVATA).[1]

THIS country is about 3000 li in circuit. The capital of the country is 20 li or so round, and is bounded on the north by the river Ganges.[2] It is regularly cultivated, and is rich in its produce. Flowers and fruits also are abundant. The climate is agreeable in its temperature. The manners of the people are simple and honest. There are ten *saṅghârâmas,* with about 4000 priests. Most of them study the Little Vehicle of the Sammatîya (Ching-liang-pu) school. There are some twelve Dêva temples, occupied by various sectaries.

[1] Hiraṇya-parvata, or the Golden Mountain, is identified by General Cunningham with the hill of Mongir. This hill (and the kingdom to which it gave its name) was from early date of considerable importance, as it commanded the land route between the hills and the river, as well as the water route by the Ganges. It is said to have been originally called Kashṭaharaṇa Parvata, as it overlooked the famous bathing-place on the Ganges called Kashṭaharaṇa Ghât, or "the pain-expelling bathing-place," because all people afflicted with either grief or bodily pain were at once cured by bathing there. Cunningham remarks that "this name of Haraṇa Parvata is clearly the original of Hwen Thsang's *I-lan-na-Pa-fo-to*" (see the whole section, *Arch. Survey of India,* vol. xv. pp. 16, 17). The hill was also called Mudgalagiri. This may have originated the story of Mudgalaputra and the householder, *Srutaviṁśatikôṭi.*

[2] There seems to be a confusion in the text. Literally it is, "The capital (*has*) as a northern road or way the river Ganges." There is a note in the original saying that the order is misprinted.

Lately the king of a border country deposed the ruler of this country, and holds in his power the capital. He is benevolent to the priests, and has built in the city two *saṅghârâmas*, each holding something less than 1000 priests. Both of them are attached to the Sarvâstivâdin school of the Little Vehicle.

By the side of the capital and bordering on the Ganges river is the Hiraṇya (I-lan-na) mountain, from which is belched forth masses of smoke and vapour which obscure the light of the sun and moon. From old time till now Ṛĭshis and saints have come here in succession to repose their spirits. Now there is a Dêva temple here, in which they still follow their rules handed down to them. In old days Tathâgata also dwelt here, and for the sake of the Dêvas preached at large the excellent law.

To the south of the capital is a *stûpa*. Here Tathâgata preached for three months. By the side of it are traces of the three Buddhas of the past age, who sat and walked here.

To the west of this last-named spot, at no great distance, is a *stûpa*. This denotes the spot where the Bhikshu Śrutaviṁśatikôṭi[3] (Shi-lu-to-p'in-she-ti-ku-chi) was born. Formerly there was in this town a rich householder (*gṛĭhapati*), honoured and powerful. Late in life he had an heir born to his estate. Then he gave as a reward to the person who told him the news 200 lakhs of gold pieces. Hence the name given to his son was Śûtraviṁ-

[3] This translated into Chinese is *Wen urh pih yih*, that is, "hearing-two-hundred lakhs." The note adds that formerly it was translated by *yih-urh*, that is, *laksha-karṇa*. The reference in the story is to Soṇa Kolivisi, who, according to the Southern account, lived at Champâ (see *Sacred Books of the East*, vol. xvii. p. 1). He is said to have been worth eighty cart-loads of gold, *asîti-sakaṭa-vâhe hiraññaṃ* (*op. cit.*, p. 13). But in the following section of the *Mahâvaggâ* (*op. cit.* 32) there is reference to another Soṇa called Kuṭikaṇṇa, which Buddhaghôsha explains by saying that his ear-ornaments were worth a kôṭi; but Rhys Davids thinks this may be explained by his having *pointed ears* (p. 13, n. 3). It seems evident that the old form in Chinese, viz., *yih urh*, *i.e.*, *lakshakarṇa*, refers to this Soṇa. The symbol *yih* is frequently used for kôṭi, in which case the translation would be *kôṭi karṇa*. Compare Cunningham's remarks about Râja Karṇa (*Arch. Surv.*, vol. xv. p. 16). Compare also Julien, tome ii. *errata*, p. 573, col. 1, line 16.

śatikôṭi (Wen-urh-pih-yih). From the time of his birth till he grew up his feet never touched the ground. For this reason there grew on the bottom of his feet hairs a foot long, shining and soft, and of a yellow gold colour. He loved this child tenderly, and procured for him objects of the rarest beauty. From his house to the Snowy Mountains he had established a succession of rest-houses from which his servants continually went from one to the other. Whatever valuable medicines were wanted, they communicated the same to each other in order, and so procured them without loss of time, so rich was this family. The world-honoured one, knowing the root of piety in this man was about to develop, ordered Mudgalaputra to go there and to instruct him. Having arrived outside the gate, he had no way to introduce himself (*to pass through*). Now the householder's family (*or* simply the householder) worshipped Sûrya-dêva. Every morning when the sun rose he turned towards it in adoration. At this time Mudgalaputra, by his spiritual power, caused himself to appear in the disc of the sun and to come down thence and stand in the interior. The householder's son took him to be Sûrya-dêva, and so offered him perfumed food (*rice*) and worshipped him.[4] The scent of the rice, so exquisite was it, reached even to Râjagṛiha. At this time Bimbisâra-râja, astonished at the wonderful perfume, sent messengers to ask from door to door whence it came. At length he found that it came from the Vêṇuvana-vihâra, where Mudgalaputra had just arrived from the abode of the (*rich*) householder. The king finding out that the son of the householder had such miraculous (*food*), sent for him to come to court. The householder, receiving the order, considered with himself what was the easiest mode of transport; a galley (*boat with banks of oars*) is liable to accidents from wind and waves; a chariot is liable to accident from the frightened elephants

[4] The symbol *kwei*, "to return," is probably a mistake for *kwei*, "to worship." The translation I have given differs from the French.

running away. On this he constructed from his own house to Rajâgṛiha a canal basin, and filled it full of mustard seed.[5] Then placing gently on it a lordly boat furnished with ropes with which to draw it along, he went thus to Râjagṛiha.

First going to pay his respects to the Lord of the World, he (*i.e.*, *Buddha*) addressed him and said, "Bimbasâra-râja has sent for you, no doubt desiring to see the hair beneath your feet. When the king desires to see it, you must sit cross legged with your feet turned up. If you stretch out your feet towards the king, the laws of the country exact death."[6]

The householder's sôn, having received the instruction of Buddha, went. He was then led into the palace and presented (*to the king*). The king desiring to see the hair, he sat cross-legged with his feet turned up. The king, approving of his politeness, formed a great liking for him. Having paid his final respects, he then returned to the place where Buddha was.

Tathâgata at that time was preaching the law and teaching by parables. Hearing the discourse and being moved by it, his mind was opened, and he forthwith became a disciple. Then he applied himself with all his power to severe thought, with a view to obtain the fruit (*of Arhatship*). He walked incessantly up and down,[7] until his feet were blood-stained.

The Lord of the World addressed him, saying, "You, dear youth, when living as a layman, did you know how to play the lute?"[8] He said, "I knew." "Well, then,"

[5] In the *Mahâvagga* it is simply said, "and they carried Soṇa Kolivisa in a palanquin to Râjagṛiha" (*S. B. E.*, xvii. 2).

[6] This advice is given him by his parents in the Southern account. On the other hand, the visit of the eighty thousand overseers to Buddha and the miracles of Sâgata resulting in their conversion, are quite omitted here.

[7] Walking up and down, thinking, is represented as a constant habit of the early Buddhist Śramaṇas" (*S. B. E.*, xvii. 17, n. 3). It is constantly referred to in Hiuen Tsiang, and the spots where the Buddhas had walked up and down appear to have been accounted sacred.

[8] The *viṇâ*, as in the Pâli.

said Buddha, "I will draw a comparison derived from this. The cords being too tight, then the sounds were not in cadence; when they were too loose, then the sounds had neither harmony nor charm; but when not tight and not slack, then the sounds were harmonious. So in the preparation for a religious life, the case is the same; too severe, then the body is wearied and the mind listless; too remiss, then the feelings are pampered and the will weakened."[9]

Having received this instruction from Buddha, he moved round him in a respectful way,[10] and by these means he shortly obtained the fruit of Arhatship.

On the western frontier of the country, to the south of the river Ganges, we come to a small solitary mountain, with a double peak rising high.[11] Formerly Buddha in this place rested during the three months of rain, and subdued the Yaksha Vakula (Yo-c'ha Po-khu-lo).[12]

Below a corner of the south-east side of the mountain is a great stone. On this are marks caused by Buddha sitting thereon. The marks are about an inch deep, five feet two inches long, and two feet one inch wide. Above them is built a *stûpa*.

Again to the south is the impression on a stone where Buddha set down his *kiun-chi-kia* (*kuṇḍikâ* or water-vessel). In depth the lines are about an inch, and are like a flower with eight buds (*or* petals).[13]

Not far to the south-east of this spot are the foot-traces of the Yaksha Vakula. They are about one foot five or

[9] This comparison is found in the *Sûtra of Forty-two Sections*, No. xxxiii.

[10] That is, keeping his right shoulder towards him (*pradakshina*).

[11] This mountain is identified by Cunningham with the hill of Mahâdêva, which is situated east from the great irregular central mass of the Mongir hills (*Arch. Surv.*, vol. xv. p. 19). Hiuen Tsiang does not appear himself to have visited this spot, as the symbol used is *chi*, not *hing*. The passage might be translated, "there is a small solitary hill with successive crags heaped up." For an account of the neighbouring hot springs see Cunningham (*op. cit.* Appendix).

[12] Vakula or Vâkkula was also the name of a Sthavira, one of Buddha's disciples. Burnouf, *Introd.*, p. 349; *Lotus*, pp. 2, 126.

[13] Many of these marks or figures might probably be explained by a knowledge of the character of the rock formation. Buchanan describes the rock of Mahâdêva as quartz or silicious hornstone.

six inches long, seven or eight inches wide, and in depth less than two inches. Behind these traces of the Yaksha is a stone figure of Buddha in sitting posture, about six or seven feet high.

Next, to the west, not far off, is a place where Buddha walked for exercise.

Above this mountain top is the old residence of the Yaksha.

Next, to the north is a foot-trace of Buddha, a foot and eight inches long, and perhaps six inches wide, and half an inch deep. Above it is a *stûpa* erected. Formerly when Buddha subdued the Yaksha, he commanded him not to kill men nor eat their flesh. Having respectfully received the law of Buddha, he was born in heaven.

To the west of this are six or seven hot springs. The water is exceedingly hot.[14]

To the south the country is bounded by great mountain forests in which are many wild elephants of great size.

Leaving this kingdom, going down the river Ganges, on its south bank eastwards, after 300 li or so, we come to the country of Chen-po (Champâ).

CHEN-PO (CHAMPÂ).[15]

This country (Champâ) is about 4000 li in circuit. The capital is backed to the north by the river Ganges, it is about 40 li round. The soil is level and fertile (*fat*

[14] These springs as described by a recent visitor in the *Pioneer*, 17th August 1882 (see Cunningham, *op. cit.* Appendix); they are still so hot as to fill the valley with clouds of steam "like a cauldron."

[15] Champâ and Champâpuri in the *Purâṇas* is the name of the capital of Aṅga or the country about Bhâgalpur (Wilson, *Vishṇu-pur.*, vol. ii. p. 166; vol. iv. p. 125; *J. R. A. S.*, vol. v. p. 134; *Hari-vaṁ.*, 1699; *Mahâbh.*, iii. 8141, &c.) See Lassen, *I. A.*, vol. i. pp. 175, 176. Champânagar and Karnâgarh are close to Bhâgalpur. M. Martin, *East India*, vol. ii. pp. 39 f. (Hunter's *Statistical Ac. of Bengal*, vol. xiv. p. 82, only copies the preceding). Fa-hian, chap. xxxvii.; Burnouf, *Introd.* (2d ed.), p. 132.

or *loamy*); it is regularly cultivated and productive; the temperature is mild and warm (*moderately hot*); the manners of the people simple and honest. There are several tens of *saṅghârâmas*, mostly in ruins, with about 200 priests. They follow the teaching of the Little Vehicle. There are some twenty Dêva temples, which sectaries of every kind frequent. The walls of the capital are built of brick, and are several "tens of feet" high. The foundations of the wall are raised on a lofty embankment, so that by their high escarpment, they can defy (*stop*) the attack of enemies. In old times at the beginning of the kalpa, when things (*men and things*) first began, they (*i.e., people*) inhabited dens and caves of the desert. There was no knowledge of dwelling-houses. After this, a Dêvî (*divine woman*) descending in consequence of her previous conduct, was located amongst them. As she sported in the streams of the Ganges, she was affected by a spiritual power, and conceiving, she brought forth four sons, who divided between them the government of Jambudvîpa. Each took possession of a district, founded a capital, built towns, and marked out the limits of the frontiers. This was the capital of the country of one of them, and the first of all the cities of Jambudvîpa.

To the east of the city 140 or 150 li, on the south of the river Ganges, is a solitary detached rock,[16] craggy and steep, and surrounded by water. On the top of the peak is a Dêva temple; the divine spirits exhibit many miracles (*spiritual indications*) here. By piercing the rock, houses have been made; by leading the streams (*through each*), there is a continual flow of water. There are wonderful trees (*forming*) flowering woods; the large rocks and dangerous precipices are the resort of men of

[16] Either an islet or a detached rock. Cunningham identifies it with the picturesque rocky island opposite Patharghâṭa with its temple-crowned summit (*Anc. Geog. of India*, p. 477). The same writer (*Arch. Surv.*, vol. xv. p. 34) states, "Both bearing and distance point to the rocky hill of Kahalgaon (Kolgong of the maps), which is just 23 miles to the east of Bhâgalpur (Champâ)."

wisdom and virtue; those who go there to see the place are reluctant to return.

In the midst of the desert wilds, that form the southern boundary of the country, are wild elephants and savage beasts that roam in herds.

From this country going eastwards 400 li or so, we come to the kingdom of Kie-chu-hoh-khi-lo (Kajûghira).

KIE-CHU-HOH-KHI-LO (KAJÛGHIRA OR KAJIṄGHARA).

This kingdom[17] is about 2000 li or so in circuit. The soil is level and loamy; it is regularly cultivated, and produces abundant crops; the temperature is warm; the people are simple in their habits. They greatly esteem men of high talent, and honour learning and the arts. There are six or seven *saṅghârâmas* with about 300 priests; and there are some ten Dêva temples frequented by sectaries of all sorts. During the last few centuries the royal line has died out, and the country has been ruled by a neighbouring state, so that the towns are desolate, and most of the people are found scattered in villages and hamlets. On this account, Śîlâditya-râja, when roaming through Eastern India, built a palace in this place, in which he arranged the affairs of his different states. It was built of branches and boughs for a temporary residence, and burnt on his departure. On the southern frontiers of the country are many wild elephants.

On the northern frontiers, not far from the Ganges river, is a high and large tower made of bricks and stone. Its foundation, wide and lofty, is ornamented with rare

[17] In a note we are told that the common pronunciation of this country is "*Kie-ching-kie-lo.*" M. V. de St. Martin (*Mémoire*, p. 387) notices that in the *Mahâbhârata* there is a country Kajiṅgha named among the people of Eastern India; also in the Sinhalese Chronicles a town called Kajaṅghêlê-Niyaṅgamê, in the eastern region of Jambudvipa. There is also a village called Kajéri marked in Rennell's map, just 92 miles (460 li) from Champâ.

sculptures. On the four faces of the tower are sculptured figures of the saints, Dêvas, and Buddhas in separate compartments.

Going from this country eastward, and crossing the Ganges, after about 600 li we come to the kingdom of Pun-na-fa-tan-na (Puṇḍravarddhana).

PUN-NA-FA-TAN-NA (PUṆḌRAVARDDHANA).[18]

This country is about 4000 li in circuit. Its capital is about 30 li round. It is thickly populated. The tanks and public offices and flowering woods are regularly connected at intervals.[19] The soil is flat and loamy, and rich in all kinds of grain-produce. The *Panasa* [20] (*Pan-na-so*) fruit, though plentiful, is highly esteemed. The fruit is as large as a pumpkin.[21] When it is ripe it is of a yellowish-red colour. When divided, it has in the middle many tens of little fruits of the size of a pigeon's egg; breaking these, there comes forth a juice of a yellowish-red colour and of delicious flavour. The fruit sometimes collects on the tree-branches as other clustering fruits, but sometimes at the tree-roots, as in the case of the earth-growing *fu ling*.[22] The climate (*of this country*) is temperate; the people

[18] Prof. H. H. Wilson includes in the ancient Puṇḍra the districts of Râjashâhi, Dinâjpur, Raṅgpur, Nadiyâ, Bîrbhum, Bardwân, Midnâpur, Jangal Mahâls, Râmgaḍh, Pachît, Palaman, and part of Chunâr. It is the country of "sugar-cane," *puṇḍra*, Bangâli *puṇri-akh*. The Pauṇḍra people are frequently mentioned in Sanskrit literature, and Puṇḍravarddhana was evidently a portion of their country. *Quart. Orient. Mag.*, vol. ii. p. 188; *Vishṇu-pur.*, vol. ii. pp. 134, 170. Mr. Westmacott proposed to identify Puṇḍra-varddhana with the adjacent parganâs or districts of Pâñjara and Borddhonkûti (or Khêttâl) in Dinâjpur, about 35 miles N.N.W. from Raṅgpur; but also suggested, as an alternative, Poṇḍua or Poṅrowâ, afterwards Firzupur or Firuzâbâd, 6 miles north-east of Mâldâ, and 18 N.N.E. from Gauḍa. Mr. Fergusson assigned it a place near Raṅgpur. See *Ind. Ant.*, vol. iii. p. 62; Hunter, *Stat. Acc. Bengal*, vol. viii. pp. 59 f., 449; *J. R. A. S.*, N.S., vol. vi. pp. 238 f.; conf. *Râja-Taraṅgiṇi*, tom. iv. p. 421; *Mahabh.*, ii. 1872. General Cunningham has more recently fixed on Mahâsthânagadha on the Karatoyâ, 12 miles south of Bardhaukûṭi and 7 miles north of Bagraha, as the site of the capital (*Report*, vol. xv. pp. v., 104, 110 f.)

[19] This passage may also be translated thus: "Maritime offices (offices connected with the river navigation?) with their (surrounding) flowers and groves occur at regular intervals."

[20] Jack or bread fruit.

[21] "A large and coarse squash." Williams' *Tonic Dict.*, sub *Kwd.*[21]

[22] The *radix China*, according to

esteem learning. There are about twenty *saṅghârâmas*, with some 3000 priests; they study both the Little and Great Vehicle. There are some hundred Dêva temples, where sectaries of different schools congregate. The naked Nirgranthas are the most numerous.

To the west of the capital 20 li or so is the Po-chi-p'o *saṅghârâma*.[23] Its courts are light and roomy; its towers and pavilions are very lofty. The priests are about 700 in number; they study the law according to the Great Vehicle. Many renowned priests from Eastern India dwell here.

Not far from this is a *stûpa* built by Aśôka-râja. Here Tathâgata, in old days, preached the law for three months for the sake of the Dêvas. Occasionally, on fast-days, there is a bright light visible around it.

By the side of this, again, is a place where the four past Buddhas walked for exercise and sat down. The bequeathed traces are still visible.

Not far from this there is a *vihâra* in which is a statue of Kwan-tsz'-tsai Bôdhisattva. Nothing is hid from its divine discernment; its spiritual perception is most accurate; men far and near consult (*this being*) with fasting and prayers.

From this going east 900 li or so, crossing the great river, we come to the country of Kia-mo-lu-po (Kâmarûpa).

KIA-MO-LU-PO (KÂMARÛPA).

The country of Kâmarûpa[24] is about 10,000 li in circuit. The capital town is about 30 li. The land lies

Julien; the *pachyma cocos*, according to Doolittle's *Vocabulary*, vol. ii. 423. Medhurst (sub voc. *ling*) names "the China root" which grows under old fir trees.

[23] Julien restores this (with a query) to Vâśibhâsaṅghârâma, "the convent which has the brightness of fire."

[24] Kâmarûpa (its capital is called in the *Purâṇas*, Prâgjyôtisha) extended from the Karatôyâ river in Raṅgpur to the eastward (*Stat. Acc. Bengal*, vol. vii. pp. 168, 310; or M. Martin, *East Ind.*, vol. iii. p. 403). The kingdom included Manipur, Jayntîya, Kachhâr, West Asâm, and parts of Maymansiṅgh, and Silhet (Śrîhaṭṭa). The modern district extends from Goalpâra to Gauhaṭṭi. Lassen, *I. A.*, vol. i. p. 87, vol. ii. p. 973; Wilson, *V. P.*, vol. v. p. 88;

low, but is rich, and is regularly cultivated. They cultivate the *Panasa* fruit and the *Na-lo-ki-lo* (Nârîkêla)[25] fruit. These trees, though numerous, are nevertheless much valued and esteemed. Water led from the river or from banked-up lakes (*reservoirs*) flows round the towns. The climate is soft and temperate. The manners of the people simple and honest. The men are of small stature, and their complexion a dark yellow. Their language differs a little from that of Mid-India. Their nature is very impetuous and wild; their memories are retentive, and they are earnest in study. They adore and sacrifice to the Dêvas, and have no faith in Buddha; hence from the time when Buddha appeared in the world even down to the present time there never as yet has been built one *saṅghârâma* as a place for the priests to assemble. Such disciples as there are are of a pure faith, say their prayers (*repeat the name of Buddha*) secretly, and that is all. There are as many as 100 Dêva temples, and different sectaries to the number of several myriads. The present king belongs to the old line (*tso yan*) of Nârâyaṇa-dêva. He is of the Brâhman caste. His name is Bhâśkaravarman,[26] his title Kumâra (Keu-mo-lo). From the time that this family seized the land and assumed the government till the present king, there have elapsed a thousand successions (*generations*). The king is fond of learning, and the people are so likewise in imitation of him. Men of high talent from distant regions aspiring after office (?) visit his dominions as strangers. Though he has no faith in Buddha, yet he much respects Śramaṇas of learning. When he first heard that a Śramaṇa from China[27] had come to Magadha to the Nâlanda *saṅghârâma* from such a distance, to study with diligence the

As. Res., vol. xiv. p. 422; *Lalita Vis.*, p. 416.

[25] The bread-fruit and the cocoa-nut.

[26] P'o-se-kie-lo-fa-mo, in Chinese, Yih-cheu, "helmet of the sun." See Hall's *Vâsavadattâ*, p. 52.

[27] The French translation is very confused. Julien appears to have overlooked the symbols *Chi-na-kwŏ* (the country of China).

profound law of Buddha, he sent a message of invitation by those who reported it as often as three times, but yet the Śramaṇa (*i.e.*, Hiuen Tsiang) had not obeyed it. Then Śîlabhadra (Shi-lo-po-t'o-lo), master of *śâstras*, said, "You desire to show your gratitude to Buddha; then you should propagate the true law; this is your duty. You need not fear the long journey. Kumâra-râja's family respect the teaching of the heretics, and now he invites a Śramaṇa to visit him. This is good indeed! We judge from this that he is changing his principles, and desires to acquire merit (*or*, from merit acquired) to benefit others. You formerly conceived a great heart, and made a vow with yourself to travel alone through different lands regardless of life, to seek for the law for the good of the world.[28] Forgetful of your own country, you should be ready to meet death; indifferent to renown or failure, you should labour to open the door for the spread of the holy doctrine, to lead onwards the crowds who are deceived by false teaching, to consider others first, yourself afterwards; forgetful of renown, to think only of religion (*enlarge the law*)."

On this, with no further excuses, he hastened in company with the messengers to present himself to the king. Kumâra-râja said, "Although I am without talents myself, I have always been fond of men of conspicuous learning. Hearing, then, of your fame and distinction, I ventured to ask you here to visit me."

He replied, "I have only moderate wisdom, and I am confused to think that you should have heard of my poor reputation."

Kumâra-râja said, "Well, indeed! from regard for the law and love of learning to regard oneself as of no account, and to travel abroad regardless of so great dangers, to wander through strange countries! This is the result of the transforming power of the king's government, and the exceeding learning, as is reported, of the country. Now,

[28] To save all creatures (Jul.)

through the kingdoms of India there are many persons who sing about the victories of the Tsin king of the Mahâchîna country. I have long heard of this. And is it true that this is your honourable birthplace?"

He said, "It is so. These songs celebrate the virtues of my sovereign."

He replied, "I could not think that your worthy self was of this country. I have ever had an esteem for its manners and laws. Long have I looked towards the east, but the intervening mountains and rivers have prevented me from personally visiting it."

In answer I said, "My great sovereign's holy qualities are far renowned, and the transforming power of his virtue reaches to remote districts. People from strange countries pay respect at the door of his palace, and call themselves his servants."

Kumâra-râja said, "If his dominion is so great (*covering thus his subjects*), my heart strongly desires to bear my tribute to his court. But now Śîlâditya-râja is in the country of Kajûghira (Kie-chu-hoh-khi-lo), about to distribute large alms and to plant deeply the root of merit and wisdom. The Śramaṇs and Brâhmaṇs of the five Indies, renowned for their learning, must needs come together. He has now sent for me. I pray you go with me!"

On this they went together.

On the east this country is bounded by a line of hills. so that there is no great city (*capital*) to the kingdom. Their frontiers, therefore, are contiguous to the barbarians of the south-west (*of China*). These tribes are, in fact, akin to those of the Man[29] people in their customs. On inquiry I ascertained that after a two months' journey we reach the south-western frontiers of the province of Sz'chuen (*Shuh*). But the mountains and rivers present obstacles, and the pestilential air, the poisonous vapours,

[29] The 'Man people' (*man lo*) are the south-west barbarians (so named by the Chinese).

the fatal snakes, the destructive vegetation, all these causes of death prevail.

On the south-east of this country herds of wild elephants roam about in numbers; therefore, in this district they use them principally in war.

Going from this 1200 or 1300 li to the south, we come to the country of San-mo-ta-cha (Samataṭa).

SAN-MO-TA-CHA (SAMATAṬA).

This country[30] is about 3000 li in circuit and borders on the great sea. The land lies low and is rich. The capital is about 20 li round. It is regularly cultivated, and is rich in crops, and the flowers and fruits grow everywhere. The climate is soft and the habits of the people agreeable. The men are hardy by nature, small of stature, and of black complexion; they are fond of learning, and exercise themselves diligently in the acquirement of it. There are professors (*believers*) both of false and true doctrines. There are thirty or so *saṅghârâmas* with about 2000 priests. They are all of the Sthavira (Shang-tso-pu) school. There are some hundred Dêva temples, in which sectaries of all kinds live. The naked ascetics called Nirgranthas (Ni-kien) are most numerous.

Not far out of the city is a *stûpa* which was built by Aśôka-râja. In this place Tathâgata in former days preached the deep and mysterious law for seven days for the good of the Dêvas. By the side of it are traces where the four Buddhas sat and walked for exercise.

Not far from this, in a *saṅghârâma*, is a figure of Buddha of green jade. It is eight feet high, with the marks on its person perfectly shown, and with a spiritual power which is exercised from time to time.

Going north-east from this to the borders of the

[30] Eastern Bengal: Samôtaṭa or Samataṭa means "the shore country" or "level country" (Lassen *Ind. Alt.*, iii. 681). It is named by Varâha Mihira (*Br. Saṁh.*, xiv. 6) along with Mithilâ and Orissa.

ocean, we come to the kingdom of Śrîkshêtra (Shi-li-ch'a-ta-lo).[31]

Farther on to the south-east, on the borders of the ocean, we come to the country of Kâmalaṅkâ (Kia-mo-lang-kia);[32] still to the east is the kingdom of Dvârapati (To-lo-po-ti);[33] still to the east is the country of Îśânapura (I-shang-na-pu-lo); still to the east is the country of Mahâchampâ (Mo-ho-chen-po), which is the same as Lin-i. Next to the south-west is the country called Yamanadvîpa[34] (Yavanadvîpa—Yen-nio-na-cheu). These six countries are so hemmed in by mountains and rivers that they are inaccessible;[35] but their limits and the character of the people and country could be learned by inquiry.

From Samataṭa going west 900 li or so, we reach the country of Tan-mo-li-ti (Tâmralipti).

TAN-MO-LI-TI (TÂMRALIPTI).[36]

This country is 1400 or 1500 li in circuit, the capital about 10 li. It borders on the sea. The ground is low and rich; it is regularly cultivated, and produces flowers and fruits in abundance. The temperature is hot. The manners of the people are quick and hasty. The men are hardy and brave. There are both heretics and believers. There are about ten *saṅghârâmas*, with about 1000 priests. The Dêva temples are fifty in number, in

[31] Śrîkshêtra or Tharekhettarâ is the name of an ancient Burmese kingdom, whose capital city of the same name near Prome, on the Irâwâdi; but this is *south-east*, whilst *north-east*, towards Śrîbatta or Silhet, does not lead to "the borders of the ocean."

[32] Kâmalaṅkâ: Pegu (Haṅsâwâdi) and the delta of the Irâwâdi, called Ramanya, and earlier Aramana

[33] Dwâravatî is the classic name for the town and district of Sandowê, but in Burmese history it is also applied to Siam (Phayre, *Hist. of Burma*, p. 32).

[34] Yamadvîpa is an island mentioned in the *Vâyu-purâṇa*, but probably fabulous.

[35] *I.e.*, the pilgrim did not enter them.

[36] Ταμαλίτης in Ptol., lib. vii. c. 1, 73. Tâmalitti or Tâmraliptî, the modern Tamluk, on the Selai, just above its junction with the Hughli. *Jour R. A. S.* vol. v. p. 135; Wilson, *Vishṇu-pur.*, vol. ii. p. 177; Lassen, *I. A.*, vol. i. p. 177; Varâha Mih., *Br. S.*, x. 14; Turnour, *Mahavanso*, pp. 70, 115.

which various sectaries dwell mixed together. The coast of this country is formed by (or in) a recess of the sea; the water and the land embracing each other.[37] Wonderful articles of value and gems are collected here in abundance, and therefore the people of the country are in general very rich.

By the side of the city is a *stûpa* which was built by Aśôka-râja; by the side of it are traces where the four past Buddhas sat and walked.

Going from this north-west 700 li or so, we come to the country Kie-lo-na-su-fa-la-na (Karṇasuvarṇa).

KIE-LO-NA-SU-FA-LA-NA (KARṆASUVARṆA).[38]

This kingdom is about 1400 or 1500 li in circuit; the capital is about 20 li. It is thickly populated. The householders are very (*rich and in ease*). The land lies low and is loamy. It is regularly cultivated, and produces an abundance of flowers, with valuables numerous and various. The climate is agreeable; the manners of the people honest and amiable. They love learning exceedingly, and apply themselves to it with earnestness. There are believers and heretics alike amongst them. There are ten *saṅghârâmas* or so, with about 2000 priests. They study the Little Vehicle of the Sammatîya (*Ching-tiang-pu*) school. There are fifty Dêva temples. The heretics are very numerous. Besides these there are three *saṅghârâmas* in which they do not use thickened milk (*ü lok*), following the directions of Dêvadatta (Ti-p'o-ta-to).[39]

By the side of the capital is the *saṅghârâma* called

[37] *I.e.*, the coast of the country is that of a large bay.

[38] Karṇa was the king of Aṅga, whose capital is placed at Karṇagaṛh near Bhâgalpur (M. Martin, *E. Ind.*, vol. ii. pp. 31, 38 f., 46, 50.

[39] Dêvadatta appears to have had a body of disciples; in consequence of his inferiority in point of influence to Buddha, he became his enemy. One of the rules of his sect was not to use butter. A sect revering him as a Buddha existed up to A.D. 400 (Eitel, *s. v.*) For an account of his more rigorous ascetic praxis, see Oldenberg, *Buddha*, pp. 160, 161.

Lo-to-wei-chi (Raktaviṭi),[40] the halls of which are light and spacious, the storeyed towers very lofty. In this establishment congregate all the most distinguished, learned, and celebrated men of the kingdom. They strive to promote each other's advancement by exhortations, and to perfect their character.[41] At first the people of this country did not believe in Buddha; at this time[42] there was a heretic of Southern India who wore over his belly copper-plates and on his head a lighted torch. With lofty steps, staff in hand, he came to this country. Sounding aloud the drum of discussion, he sought an adversary in controversy. Then a man said to him, "Why are your head and your body so strangely (*arrayed*)?" He said, "My wisdom is so great, I fear my belly will burst, and because I am moved with pity for the ignorant multitude who live in darkness, therefore I carry this light on my head."

After ten days, no one was found to question him. Among all the learned and professed scholars there was not a single person to discuss with him. The king said, "Alas! what ignorance[43] prevails in my territories, that no one should be able to challenge the difficult propositions[44] of this stranger. What a disgrace to the country! We must scheme and seek through the most obscure retreats."

Then one said to him, "In the forest there is a strange man who names himself a Śramaṇa, he is most diligent in study. He is now living apart in silence and obscurity, and so he has lived for a long time; who so well able

[40] Meaning "*red mud*." I adopt the Sanskrit restoration from Julien.

[41] Literally, "to promote their mutual perfection by shaping and smoothing (*in the sense of polishing*) their reason and virtue."

[42] Julien refers this expression to the time when Hiuen Tsiang was there (p. 85, n. 3); in this case, it is possible that the allusion in vol. i. p. 4, n. 22, is to this encounter. But as the *saṅghârâma* was already built when Hiuen Tsiang visited the capital, it is difficult to understand how the event occurred at that time.

[43] *Wou ming*—darkness.

[44] It may also mean "the difficulty" resulting from the stranger's challenge.

by his united virtue to controvert this irreligious man as he ?"[45]

The king hearing this, went himself to invite him to come. The Śramaṇa replying, said, "I am a man of South India; I stop here on my travels merely as a stranger. My abilities are small and commonplace; I fear lest you should not know it, but yet I will come according to your wish, though I am by no means certain as to the character of the discussion. If, however, I am not defeated, I will ask you to erect a *saṅghârâma,* and summon the fraternity to glorify and extol the law of Buddha." The king said, "I accept your terms, nor could I dare to forget your virtue."[46]

Then the Śramaṇa, having accepted the king's invitation, proceeded to the arena of controversy. Then the heretic went through (*chanted*) some 30,000 words of his school. His arguments were profound, his illustrations (*figures* or *writing*) ample; his whole discourse, both as to names and qualities, was captivating to sight and hearing.

The Śramaṇa, after listening, at once fathomed his meaning; no word or argument deceived him. With a few hundred words he discriminated and explained every difficulty, and then he asked (*the heretic*) as to the teaching (*the principles*) of his school. The words of the heretic were confused and his arguments devoid of force, and so his lips were closed and he could not reply. Thus he lost his reputation, and, covered with confusion, retired.

The king, deeply reverencing the priest, founded this

[45] Julien translates this passage thus: "Could he conduct himself thus if he was not attached to the law and devoted to virtue?" The passage is difficult; literally it runs thus: "With this no-master, who is able so well as this (Śramaṇa) to embody the law, to unite virtue?" "To embody the law" means "to represent, or, vindicate, religion;" and "to unite virtue" means "so virtuously or fully."

[46] The symbol *tih* (virtue) sometimes stands for *bhadanta, i.e.,* "your reverence" or "your excellency." It may also refer to the priesthood generally. It is applied in inscriptions to Sthaviras or priests.

convent; and from that time and afterwards the teaching of the law widely extended (*through the kingdom*).[47]

By the side of the *saṅghârâma*, and not far off, is a *stûpa* which was built by Aśôka-râja. When Tathâgata was alive in the world he preached here for seven days, explaining (*the law*) and guiding (*men*). By the side of it is a *vihâra*; here there are traces where the four past Buddhas sat down and walked. There are several other *stûpas* in places where Buddha explained the excellent law.[48] These were built by Aśôka-râja.

Going from this 700 li or so in a south-westerly direction, we come to the country of U-cha.

U-CHA (UḌRA).

This country[49] is 7000 li or so in circuit; the capital city[50] is about 20 li round. The soil is rich and fertile, and it produces abundance of grain, and every kind of fruit is grown more than in other countries. It would be difficult to name the strange shrubs and the famed flowers that grow here. The climate is hot; the people are uncivilised, tall of stature, and of a yellowish black complexion. Their words and language (*pronunciation*) differ from Central India. They love learning and apply themselves to it without intermission. Most of them believe in the law of Buddha. There are some hundred *saṅghârâmas*, with 10,000 priests. They all study the Great Vehicle. There are fifty Dêva temples in which sectaries of all sorts make their abodes. The *stûpas*,

[47] *Or*, he widely extended the teaching of the law.

[48] The original has *king fǎ*, the law of the *sûtras*; perhaps *king* is a mistake for *miu*, "excellent."

[49] Uḍra or Oḍra is Orissa (*Mahâbh.*, ii. 1174, iii. 1988); also called Uṭkala (*Mahâbh.*, vii. 122; *Vishṇu-pur.*, vol. ii. p. 160).

[50] This capital is generally identified with Jajipura on the Baitani: Mr. Fergusson suggests Midnâpur (*J. R. A. S.*, N.S., vol. vi. p. 249); his remarks (in this paper) on the whole of this part of the pilgrim's route are of great interest. He first noticed that the journey of Hiuen Tsiang to Kâmarûpa was made from Nâlanda on his return to that monastery from South India; he also points out the errors made by his predecessors in the same inquiry and corrects them.

to the number of ten or so, point out spots where Buddha preached. They were all founded by Aśôka-râja.

In a great mountain on the south-west frontiers[51] of the country is a *saṅghârâma* called Pushpagiri (Pu-se-po-k'i-li); the stone *stûpa* belonging to it exhibits very many spiritual wonders (*miracles*). On fast-days it emits a bright light. For this cause believers from far and near flock together here and present as offerings beautifully embroidered (*flower*) canopies (*umbrellas*); they place these underneath the vase[52] at the top of the cupola,[53] and let them stand there fixed as needles in the stone. To the north-west of this, in a convent on the mountain, is a *stûpa* where the same wonders occur as in the former case. These two *stûpas* were built by the demons,[54] and hence are derived the extraordinary miracles.

On the south-east frontiers of the country, on the borders of the ocean, is the town Charitra (Che-li-ta-lo),[55] about 20 li round. Here it is merchants depart for distant countries, and strangers come and go and stop here on their way. The walls of the city are strong and lofty. Here are fonnd all sorts of rare and precious articles.

[51] Remains, probably of a *stûpa*, have been found near Âska (*J. R. A. S.*, vol. xx. p. 105).

[52] Literally, "underneath the dew-vessel or vase." Here we have another instance of the custom of crowning the *stûpa* with a dew-vase, or "vessel of immortality" (*amara karka*). The custom would appear to have originated in the idea that "sweet dew" thus collected in a vessel had miraculous qualities as "the water of life." Dr. Burgess remarks that these flags were probably fixed "on the capital of the *stûpa*, on which was placed the relic-casket (when not enshrined inside the capital over the *garbha* of the *stûpa*)."

[53] It is satisfactory to find that Julien in this passage translates the "inverted vase or alms-dish" by *cupola*. It should have been so rendered throughout.

[54] The expression *shin kwei* does not mean demons in a bad sense, but spiritual or divine beings. It might also be rendered "spirits and demons." Cunningham supposes the two hills named in the text to be Udayagiri and Khandagiri, in which many Buddhist caves and inscriptions have been discovered. These hills are 20 miles to the south of Kaṭak and 5 miles to the west of the grand group of temples at Bhuvanêśwara (*Anc. Geog. of India*, p. 512).

[55] In Chinese, *Fa-hing*, "city of departure." This is exactly Ptolemy's *τὸ ἀφετήριον των εἰς τὴν Χρυσῆν ἐμπλεόντων* (lib. vii. c. 1,15). Comp. Lassen, *I. A.*, vol. i. p. 205, and vol. iii. p. 202. It is plain

Outside the city there are five convents[56] one after the other; their storeyed towers are very high, and carved with figures of saints exquisitely done.

Going south 20,000 li or so is the country of Siṁhala (Seng-kia-lo). In the still night, looking far off, we see the surmounting precious stone of the tooth-stûpa of Buddha brilliantly shining and scintillating as a bright torch burning in the air.

From this going south-west about 1200 li through great forests, we come to the kingdom of Kong-u-t'o (Kônyôdha).

KONG-U-T'O (KÔNYÔDHA ?).

This kingdom[57] is about 1000 li in circuit; the capital is 20 li round. It borders on a bay (*angle of the sea*). The ranges of mountains are high and precipitous. The ground is low and moist. It is regularly cultivated and productive. The temperature is hot, the disposition of the people brave and impulsive. The men are tall of stature and black complexioned and dirty. They have some degree of politeness and are tolerably honest. With respect to their written characters, they are the same as those of Mid-India, but their language and mode of pronunciation are quite different. They greatly respect the teaching of heretics and do not believe in the law of Buddha. There are some hundred Dêva temples, and there are perhaps 10,000 unbelievers of different sects.

(from Hiuen Tsiang's remark, that the precious stone could be seen at a distance of 20,000 li) that he is confusing *this* Charitrapura with the one farther south, two days' sail from Ceylon.

[56] M. Julien renders it "five *stûpas*" by mistake.

[57] See *J. R. A. S.*, N.S., vol. vi. p. 250. Cunningham supposes this place to be Ganjam. The origin of the name Ganjam is not known. When Hiuen Tsiang returned to Magadha he found that Harshavardhana had just returned from a successful expedition against the king of Ganjam. Cunningham thinks that Ganjam was then annexed to the province of Orissa (Robert Sewell, *Lists*, vol. i. p. 2). Mr. Fergusson remarks that "Khordhagar in the neighbourhood of Bhuvanêśwar is just 170 miles south-west from Midnâpur, and it is impossible to mistake the Chilka Lake as the great bay and the two seas of the text. Perhaps Hiuen Tsiang stopped here to visit the caves in the Khandagiri and Udayagiri hills" (*J. R. A. S.*, loc. cit.)

Within the limits of this country there are several tens of small towns which border on the mountains and are built contiguous to the sea.[58] The cities themselves are strong and high; the soldiers are brave and daring; they rule by force the neighbouring provinces, so that no one can resist them. This country, bordering on the sea, abounds in many rare and valuable articles. They use cowrie shells and pearls in commercial transactions. The great greenish-blue[59] elephant comes from this country. They harness it to their conveyances and make very long journeys.

From this going south-west, we enter a vast desert, jungle, and forests, the trees of which mount to heaven and hide the sun. Going 1400 or 1500 li, we come to the country of Kie-ling-kia (Kaliṅga).

KIE-LING-KIA (KALINGA).

This country[60] is 5000 li or so in circuit; its capital is 20 li or so round. It is regularly cultivated and is productive. Flowers and fruits are very abundant. The forests and jungle are continuous for many hundred li. It produces the great tawny[61] wild elephant, which are much prized by neighbouring provinces. The climate is

[58] The phrase *hai kiau* does not necessarily imply "the confluence of two seas." It seems to mean that the towns were built near the mountains (the Mahêndra Malê?), but in communication with the sea-coast. So along the west coast of South America the towns built at the foot of the hills are in communication with the sea by ports of embarcation (*embarcadores*).

[59] It may mean simply "dark coloured;" but *ts'ing* generally means "the colour of nature, as the azure of the sky or the green of growing plants" (Wells Williams). The phrase for *black* is *un ts'ing*.

[60] The frontier line of Kaliṅga cannot have extended beyond the Gôdâvarî river on the south-west, and the Gaoliyâ branch of the Indrâvati river on the north-west (Cunningham). For an account of the Kaliṅga dêśa, see Sewell, *op. cit.*, p. 19. The chief town was probably Râjamahêndri, where the Chalukyas perhaps established their capital. Either this place or Koriṅga, on the sea-coast, agrees with the bearing and distance given in the text. If, however, we accept Mr. Fergusson's hypothesis that the capital of Kônyôdha was near Kaṭak, and calculating the *li* to be one-seventh of a mile, we shall have to seek for the capital of Kaliṅga near Vijayanagram. For a notice respecting Râjamahêndri see Sewell, *Lists*, &c., vol. i. p. 22.

[61] The same word is used in the previous section; see n. 60.

burning; the disposition of the people vehement and impetuous. Though the men are mostly rough and uncivilised, they still keep their word and are trustworthy. The language is light and tripping,[62] and their pronunciation distinct and correct. But in both particulars, that is, as to words and sounds, they are very different from Mid-India. There are a few who believe in the true law, but most of them are attached to heresy. There are ten *saṅghârâmas*, with about 500 priests, who study the Great Vehicle according to the teaching of the Sthavira school. There are some 100 Dêva temples with very many unbelievers of different sorts, the most numerous being the Nirgranthas[63] [Ni-kin followers].

In old days the kingdom of Kaliṅga had a very dense population. Their shoulders rubbed one with the other, and the axles of their chariot wheels grided together, and when they raised their arm-sleeves a perfect tent was formed.[64] There was a Ṛishi possessed of the five supernatural powers,[65] who lived (*perched*) on a high precipice,[66] cherishing his pure (*thoughts*). Being put to shame (insulted) because he had gradually lost his magic powers, he cursed the people with a wicked imprecation, and caused all dwelling in the country, both young and old, to perish; wise and ignorant alike died, and the population disappeared. After many ages the country was gradually repeopled by emigrants, but yet it is not properly inhabited. This is why at the present time there are so few who dwell here.

Not far from the south of the capital there is a *stûpa* about a hundred feet high; this was built by Aśôka-râja. By the side of it there are traces where the four past Buddhas sat down and walked.

[62] This description of their language will appear natural to those who have had Kling boys about them.

[63] Digambara Jainas, *ante*, vol. i. p. 145, n. 74.

[64] *I.e.*, by stretching out their arms one to another, so close were they, there would be a continuous tent formed.

[65] Explained by Julien as referring to the *pañchâbhijñâs*.

[66] Julien translates *gan* by "cavern;" but it means "a rocky or precipitous mountain."

Near the northern frontier of this country is a great mountain precipice,[67] on the top of which is a stone *stûpa* about a hundred feet high. Here, at the beginning of the kalpa, when the years of men's lives were boundless, a Pratyêka [68] Buddha reached *Nirvâṇa*.

From this going north-west through forests and mountains about 1800 li, we come to the country of Kiao-sa-lo (Kôsala).

KIAO-SA-LO (KÔSALA).

This country[69] is about 5000 li in circuit; the frontiers consist of encircling mountain crags; forests and jungle are found together in succession. The capital [70] is about 40 li round; the soil is rich and fertile, and yields abundant crops. The towns and villages are close together. The population is very dense. The men are tall and black complexioned. The disposition of the people is hard and violent; they are brave and impetuous. There are both heretics and believers here. They are earnest in study and of a high intelligence. The king is of the Kshattriya race; he greatly honours the law of Buddha, and his virtue and love are far renowned. There are about one hundred *saṅghârâmas*, and somewhat less than 10,000

[67] Perhaps Mahêndragiri

[68] A Pratyêka Buddha is one who has reached enlightenment "for himself alone;" that is, he is not able to enlighten others by preaching or guiding. In Chinese it is rendered *tuh hioh*, "a solitary Buddha," for the same reason.

[69] To be distinguished from Śrâvastî or Ayôdhyâ, which district was also called Kôśala or Kôsala. See Wilson, *Vishṇu-pur.*, vol. ii. p. 172; Lassen, *I. A.*, vol. i. p. 160, vol. iv. p. 702. It lay to the south-west of Orissa and in the district watered by the upper feeders of the Mahânadî and Gôdâvarî.

[70] There is some uncertainty as to the capital of this country. General Cunningham, who identifies the ancient Kôsala with the modern province of Berâr or Gondwâna, places it at Chândâ, a walled town 290 miles to the north-west of Râjamahêndri, with Nâgpur, Amarâvatî, or Ilichpur as alternatives; the three last-named towns appear to be too far from the capital of Kalinga. But if we allow five li to the mile, the distance either of Nâgpur or Amarâvatî from Râjamahêndri would agree with the 1800 or 1900 li of Hiuen Tsiang. There is much mention in I-tsing's memoirs of priests visiting and remaining at a place called Amarâvatî; it may refer to Kôsala. Mr. Fergusson, calculating the *li* at one-sixth of a mile, suggests either Wairagaṛh or Bhândak, both of them sites of old cities, as the capital. He prefers the former for reasons stated (*J. R. A. S.*, N.S., vol. vi. p. 260).

priests: they all alike study the teaching of the Great Vehicle. There are about seventy Dêva temples, frequented by heretics of different persuasions.

Not far to the south of the city is an old *saṅghârâma*, by the side of which is a *stûpa* that was built by Aśôka-râja. In this place Tathâgata, of old, calling an assembly, exhibited his supernatural power and subdued the unbelievers. Afterwards Nâgârjuna Bôdhisattva (*Long-meng-p'u-sa*) dwelt in the *saṅghârâma*. The king of the country was then called Sadvaha.[71] He greatly prized and esteemed Nâgârjuna, and provided him with a city-gate hut.[72]

At this time Ti-p'o (Dêva) Bôdhisattva coming from the country of Chi-sse-tseu (Ceylon), sought to hold a discussion with him. Addressing the gate-keeper he said, "Be good enough to announce me." Accordingly the gate-keeper entered and told Nâgârjuna. He, recognising his reputation, filled up a *pâtra* with water and commanded his disciple to hold the water before this Dêva. Dêva, seeing the water, was silent, and dropped a needle into it. The disciple held the *pâtra*, and with some anxiety and doubt returned to Nâgârjuna. "What did he say," he asked. The disciple replied, "He was silent and said nothing; he only dropped a needle into the water."

Nâgârjuna said, "What wisdom! Who like this man! To know the springs of action (*motives*), this is the privilege of a god! to penetrate subtle principles is the privilege of an inferior saint.[73] Such full wisdom as this entitles him to be allowed to enter forthwith." He (the disciple) replied, "What a saying is this! is this then the sublime eloquence (*skill*) of silence?"

"This water," he (Nâgârjuna) went on to say, "is shaped according to the form of the vessel that holds it;

71 Expressed phonetically by So-to-p'o-ho, with the meaning, "he who draws the good."

72 Placed guards round his hut (Julien).

73 An inferior saint (ya shing) is an expression applied to Mencius compared with Confucius (Julien). In this passage the title is referred to Dêva in comparison with Buddha.

it is pure or dirty according to the character of things (*in it*); it fills up every interstice; in point of clearness and comprehensiveness[74] he, on beholding the water, compared it to the wisdom which I have acquired by study. Dropping into it a needle, he pierced it, as it were, to the bottom. Show this extraordinary man in here at once, and let him be presented."

Now the manner and appearance of Nâgârjuna were imposing, and inspired all with respect. In discussion all were awed by it, and submitted (*bowed the head*). Dêva being aware of his excellent characteristics, had long desired to consult him, and he wished to become his disciple. But now as he approached he felt troubled in mind, and he was abashed and timid. Mounting the hall, he sat down awkwardly and talked darkly; but at the end of the day his words were clear and lofty. Nâgârjuna said, "Your learning exceeds that of the world and your fine distinctions shine brighter than the former (*teachers*). I am but an old and infirm man; but having met with one so learned and distinguished, surely it is for the purpose of spreading the truth and for transmitting without interruption the torch of the law, and propagating the teaching of religion. Truly this is one who may sit on the upper seat to expound dark sayings and discourse with precision."

Dêva hearing these words, his heart conceived a degree of self-confidence, and being about to open the storehouse of wisdom, he first began to roam through the garden of dialectic and handle fine sentences; then having looked up for some indication of approval (*confirmation of his argument*), he encountered the imposing look of the master; his words escaped him; his mouth was closed; and leaving his seat, he made some excuse, and asked to be instructed.

Nâgârjuna said, "Sit down again; I will communicate

[74] I have translated it thus; literally it runs "clear and limpid and of unfathomable fulness, as you showed it to him."

to you the truest and most profound principles which the king of the law himself verily handed down (*taught for transmission*)." Dêva then prostrated himself on the ground, and adored with all his heart, and said, "Both now and for ever I will dare to listen to your instructions."

Nâgârjuna Bôdhisattva was well practised in the art of compounding medicines; by taking a preparation (*pill* or *cake*), he nourished the years of life for many hundreds of years,[75] so that neither the mind nor appearance decayed. Sadvaha-râja had partaken of this mysterious medicine, and his years were already several hundred in number. The king had a young son who one day addressed his mother thus, "When shall I succeed to the royal estate?" His mother said, "There seems to me to be no chance of that yet; your father the king is now several hundred years old, his sons and grandsons are many of them dead and gone through old age. This is the result of the religious power of Nâgârjuna, and the intimate knowledge he has of compounding medicines. The day the Bôdhisattva dies the king will also succumb. Now the wisdom of this Nâgârjuna is great and extensive, and his love and compassion very deep; he would give up for the benefit of living creatures his body and life. You ought, therefore, to go, and when you meet him, ask him to give you his head. If you do this, then you will get your desire."

The king's son, obedient to his mother's instructions, went to the gate of the convent. The doorkeeper, alarmed, ran away,[76] and so he entered at once. Then Nâgârjuna Bôdhisattva was chanting as he walked up and down. Seeing the king's son he stopped, and said, "It is evening time now; why do you at such a time come so hastily to the priests' quarters? has some accident happened, or are

[75] Some attribute 600 years to Nâgârjuna as his term of life (*Vassilief*, *Bouddisme*, p. 76). This writer says, "In my opinion the 400 or 600 years of life given to Nâgârjuna refer to the development of the system of the Great Vehicle" (*op. cit.*, p. 77, n. 1).

[76] To announce the arrival of the king's son (Julien). But it would seem to mean he ran away through fear.

you afraid of some calamity that you have hastened here at such a time?"

He answered, "I was considering with my dear mother the words of different *śâstras*, and the examples (*therein given*) of sages who had forsaken (*given up*) the world, and I was led to remark on the great value set on life by all creatures, and that the scriptures, in their examples given of sacrifice, had not enforced this duty of giving up life readily for the sake of those who desired it. Then my dear mother said, 'Not so; the Sugatas (*shen shi*) of the ten regions, the Tathâgatas of the three ages, whilst living in the world and giving their hearts to the object, have obtained the fruit. They diligently sought the way of Buddha; practising the precepts, exercising patience, they gave up their bodies to feed wild beasts, cut their flesh to deliver the dove. Thus Râja Chandraprabha [77] (Yueh-kwang) gave up his head to the Brâhmaṇ; Maitribâla (Ts'e li) râja fed the hungry Yaksha with his blood. To recite every similar example would be difficult, but in searching through the history of previous sages, what age is there that affords not examples? And so Nâgârjuna Bôdhisattva is now actuated by similar high principles; as for myself, I have sought a man who for my advantage would give me his head, but have never yet found such a person for years. If I had wished to act with violence and take the life of a man (*commit murder*), the crime would have been great and entailed dreadful consequences. To have taken the life of an innocent child would have been infamous and disgraced my character. But the Bôdhisattva diligently practises the holy way and aspires after a while to the fruit of Buddha. His love extends to all beings and his goodness knows no bounds. He esteems life as a bubble, his body as decaying wood. He would not contradict his purpose in refusing such a gift, if requested."

[77] For the story of Chandraprabha see R. Mitra's *Nepalese Buddhist Lit.*, p. 310; for Maitribâla, *ibid.*, p. 50.

Nâgârjuna said, "Your comparisons and your words are true. I seek the holy fruit of a Buddha. I have learnt that a Buddha is able to give up all things, regarding the body as an echo, a bubble, passing through the four forms of life,[78] continually coming and going in the six ways.[79] My constant vow has been not to oppose the desires of living things. But there is one difficulty in the way of the king's son, and what is that? If I were to give up my life your father also would die. Think well of this, for who could then deliver him?"

Nâgârjuna, irresolute, walked to and fro, seeking for something to end his life with; then taking a dry reed leaf, he cut his neck as if with a sword, and his head fell from his body.

Having seen this, he (*the royal prince*) fled precipitately and returned. The guardian of the gate informed the king of the event from first to last, who whilst listening was so affected that he died.

To the south-west about 300 li we came to the Po-lo-mo-lo-ki-li (Brahmaragiri) mountain.[80] The solitary peak of this mountain towers above the rest, and stands out with its mighty precipices as a solid mass of rock without approaches or intervening valleys. The king, Sadvaha, for the sake of Nâgârjuna Bôdhisattva, tunnelled out this rock through the middle, and built and fixed therein (*in*

[78] The four modes of life are described as creatures oviparous, viviparous, born from spawn or by transformation. See *Vajrachhêdikâ*, cap. 2.

[79] The six ways of birth are (1.) as Dêvas, (2.) as men, (3.) as Asuras, (4.) as Prêtas, (5.) as beasts, (6.) in hell.

[80] It would seem that this is the right restoration. The Chinese explanation is "the black peak," but here *fung*, "a peak," is probably a mistake for *fung*, "a bee." Brahmarâ is an epithet of Durgâ or Chaṇḍâ. Assuming Bhândak to have been the capital of Kôsala, the Winjhâsanî and Dewâlâ Hills, with the footprint of Bhîma, *i.e.*, Śiva (or, if Bhîmâ, then Durgâ), would answer to the hill of Sadvahâ. It is tolerably certain that the Po-lo-yu of Fa-hian is intended for Pârvatî (his interpretation of "pigeon" (Pârâvata) being derived from *hearsay* at Bânâras), and this corresponds with "Brahmara." Altogether it seems probable that the worship of Durgâ, or Chaṇḍâ, or Bhîmâ, or Pârvatî, was affected in this part of India, and probably gave rise to, or at any rate fostered, the worship of Avalokiteśvara or Kwan-yin. (See the question discussed, *J. R. A. S* N.S., vol. xv. p. 344.)

the middle) a *saṅghârâma;* at a distance of some 10 li, by tunnelling, he opened a covered way (*an approach*). Thus by standing under the rock (*not knowing the way in*) we see the cliff excavated throughout, and in the midst of long galleries (*corridors*) with eaves for walking under and high towers (*turrets*), the storeyed building reaching to the height of five stages, each stage with four halls with *vihâras* enclosed (*united*).[81] In each *vihâra* was a statue of Buddha cast in gold, of the size of life, wrought (*cast*) with consummate art and singularly adorned and specially ornamented with gold and precious stones. From the high peak of the mountain descending streamlets, like small cascades, flow through the different storeys, winding round the side galleries, and then discharging themselves without. Scattered light-holes illumine the interior (*inner chambers*).[82]

When first Sadvaha-râja excavated this *saṅghârâma*, the men (*engaged in it*) were exhausted and the king's treasures emptied. His undertaking being only half accomplished, his heart was heavily oppressed. Nâgârjuna addressing him said, "For what reason is the king so sad of countenance?" The king replied, "I had formed in the course of reflection a great purpose.[83] I ventured to undertake a meritorious work of exceeding excellence which might endure firm till the coming of Maitrêya, but now before it is completed my means are exhausted. So I sit disconsolate day by day awaiting the dawn, cast down at heart."

Nâgârjuna said, "Afflict not yourself thus; the returns consequent on the high aims of a lofty religious purpose

[81] It seems to mean that in each platform there were four halls, and each of these halls had a *vihâra* which were connected.

[82] The description of this rock-monastery in the text shows that it is the same as that described by Fa-hian (pp. 139, 140, Beal's edition). Neither Fa-hian nor Hiuen Tsiang personally visited the spot. It would seem to have been utterly deserted and waste even in Fa-hian's time. This favours the record of its early construction in the time of Nâgârjuna (about the first century B.C.)

[83] Or, "as my great heart was revolving in chance thoughts."

are not to be foiled: your great resolve shall without fail be accomplished. Return then to your palace; you shall have abundance of joy. To-morrow, after you have gone forth to roam through and observe the wild country round (*the mountain wilds*), then return to me and quietly discuss about the buildings." The king having received these instructions left him after proper salutation (*turning to the right*).

Then Nâgârjuna Bôdhisattva, by moistening all the great stones with a divine and superior decoction (*medicine* or *mixture*), changed them into gold. The king going forth and seeing the gold, his heart and his mouth mutually congratulated each other.[84] Returning, he went to Nâgârjuna and said, "To-day as I roamed abroad, by the influence of the divine spirits (*genii*) in the desert, I beheld piles of gold." Nâgârjuna said, "It was not by the influence of the genii, but by the power of your great sincerity; as you have this gold, use it therefore for your present necessities, and fulfil your excellent work." So the king acted and finished his undertaking, and still he had a surplus. On this he placed in each of the five stages four great golden figures. The surplus still remaining he devoted to replenish the necessitous (*deficient*) branches of the exchequer.

Then he summoned 1000 priests to dwell (*in the building he had constructed*), and there to worship and pray. Nâgârjuna Bôdhisattva placed in it all the authoritative works of instruction spoken by Śâkya Buddha, and all the explanatory compilations (*commentaries*) of the Bôdhisattvas, and the exceptional collection of the miscellaneous school.[85] Therefore in the first (*uppermost*) storey they

[84] That is, his words were in agreement with the happy thoughts entertained in his heart.

[85] If this be the right rendering of the passage, then the "miscellaneous school" will refer to the *sannipâta* class of books. If, however, we adopt M. Julien's rendering, the passage will simply mean, "he collected these books (viz., the *sûtras* and *śâstras*) and divided them into sections." But if we examine the entire passage, it seems to imply that Nâgârjuna collected (1.) The books claiming the authority of Buddha's utterance; (2.) the writ-

placed only the figure of Buddha, and the *sûtras* and *śâstras;* in the fifth stage from the top (*i.e., in the lowest*), they placed the Brâhmaṇs (*pure men*) to dwell, with all necessary things provided for them; in the three middle storeys they placed the priests and their disciples. The old records state that when Sadvaha-râja had finished, he calculated that the salt consumed by the workmen cost nine *koṭis* of gold pieces. Afterwards the priests having got angry and quarrelled, they went to the king to get the question settled. Then the Brâhmaṇs said amongst themselves, "The Buddhist priests have raised a quarrel on some question of words." Then these wicked men consulting together, waiting for the occasion, destroyed the *saṅghârâma*, and afterwards strongly barricaded the place in order to keep the priests out.

From that time no priests of Buddha have lived there. Looking at the mountain caves (*or heights*) from a distance, it is impossible to find the way into them (*the caves*). In these times, when they (*the Brâhmaṇs*) introduce a physician into their abodes to treat any sickness, they put a veil over his face on going in and coming out, so that he may not know the way.

From this, going through a great forest south, after 900 li or so, we come to the country of 'An-ta-lo (Andhra).

'AN-TA-LO (ANDHRA).

This country is about 3000 li in circuit; the capital is about 20 li round. It is called P'ing-k'i-lo (Vingila?)[86] The soil is rich and fertile; it is regularly cultivated, and produces abundance of cereals. The temperature is hot, and the manners of the people fierce and impulsive. The language and arrangement of sentences differ from Mid-India, but with reference to the shapes of the letters, they

ings of the Bôdhisattvas; (3.) the other miscellaneous books.

[86] This is probably the old city of Veṅgi, north-west of Elur lake, between the Gôdâvarî and Kṛishnâ rivers, which was certainly in the early Andhra dominions. In the neighbourhood are said to be rock temples and other remains.

are nearly the same. There are twenty *saṅghârâmas* with about 3000 priests. There are also thirty Dêva temples with many heretics.

Not far from Viṅgila (?) is a great *saṅghârâma* with storeyed towers and balconies beautifully carved and ornamented. There is here a figure of Buddha, the sacred features of which have been portrayed with the utmost power of the artist. Before this convent is a stone *stûpa* which is several hundred feet high; both the one and the other were built by the Arhat 'O-che-lo (Achala).[87]

To the south-west of the *saṅghârâma* of the Arhat 'O-che-lo not a great way is a *stûpa* which was built by Aśôka-râja. Here Tathâgata in old days preached the law, and exhibited his great spiritual powers, and converted numberless persons.

Going 20 li or so to the south-west of the *saṅghârâma* built by Achala (*So-hing*), we reach a solitary mountain on the top of which is a stone *stûpa*. Here Jina[88] Bôdhisattva composed the *In-ming-lun* (*Nyâyadvâra-târaka Śâstra* or *Hêtuvidyâ Śâstra?*).[89] This Bôdhisattva, after Buddha had left the world, received the doctrine and assumed the vestments (*of a disciple*). His wisdom and his desires (*prayers* or *vows*) were vast. The power of his great wisdom was deep and solid. Pitying the world, which was without any support (*reliance*), he designed to spread the sacred doctrine. Having weighed[90] the character of

[87] The Chinese translation of the Arhat's name is "he who acts," it should therefore be restored to Âchâra. The restoration otherwise might be Achala, who is mentioned in an inscription at Ajaṇṭa. See *infra*.

[88] The phonetic symbols for Jina are *Ch'in-na*; it is translated by *t'ong sheu*, "youth-received," which Julien restores to Kumâralabdha. But thus *Jina* cannot be translated by either of these phrases. (For an account of the works of this Bôdhisattva, see Bunyiu Nanjio, *Catalogue*, Appendix i. No. 10). In Hwui-li (iv. fol. 5, b.) the translation of Ch'in-na is simply *sheu*.

[89] There is much confusion here. The text gives only *In-ming-lun*, which must be restored to *Hêtuvidyâ Śâstra*; but Julien, in his list of *errata*, p. 568, corrects the text, and supplies the title of the work, *In-ming-ching-li-men-lun*, *i.e.*, *Nyâyadvâra-târaka Śâstra*. This may be so, but this work is not named in Bunyiu Nanjio's *Catalogue* among those written by Jina.

[90] I do not see in the text that he composed this *śâstra*, but considering its character (*i wei*), he, &c.

the *Hêtuvidyâ Śâstra,* its words so deep, its reasonings so wide, and (*having considered*) that students vainly endeavoured to overcome its difficulties in their course of study, he retired into the lonely mountains and gave himself to meditation to investigate it so as to compose a useful compendium, that might overcome the difficulties (*obscurities*) of the work, its abstruse doctrines and complicated sentences. At this time the mountains and valleys shook and reverberated; the vapour and clouds changed their appearance, and the spirit of the mountain, carrying the Bôdhisattva to a height of several hundred feet, then repeated (*chanted*) these words, "In former days the Lord of the World virtuously controlled and led the people; prompted by his compassionate heart, he delivered the *Hêtuvidya Śâstra,*[91] and arranged in due order its exact reasonings and its extremely deep and refined words. But after the *Nirvâṇa* of Tathâgata its great principles became obscured; but now Jina Bôdhisattva, whose merit and wisdom are so extensive, understanding to the bottom the sacred well, will cause the *Hêtuvidyâ Śâstra* to spread abroad its power (*to add its weight*) during the present day."

Then the Bôdhisattva caused a bright light to shine and illumine the dark places (*of the world*), on which the king of the country conceived a deep reverence as he saw the sign of this brilliancy, and being in doubt whether he (*i.e., Bôdhisattva*) had not entered the *Vajrasamâdhi* (or, diamond *Samâdhi*); then he asked the Bôdhisattva to obtain the fruit of "no further birth."[92]

Jina said, "I have entered *Samâdhi* from a desire to explain a profound *sûtra;* my heart awaits perfect enlightenment (*samyak sambôdhi*), but has no desire for this fruit that admits of no rebirth."

The king said, "The fruit of 'no-birth' is the aim of

[91] It does not necessarily mean that Buddha composed this work, but delivered (*shwo*) or spake it.

[92] That is, to acquire the privilege of an Arhat.

all the saints. To cut yourself off from the three worlds, and to plunge into the knowledge of the 'three vidyâs,' how grand such an aim![93] May you soon attain it!"

Then Jina Bôdhisattva, pleased at the request of the king, conceived the desire to reach the holy fruit which "exempts from learning."[94]

At this time Mañjuśrî Bôdhisattva (Miu-ki-ts'iang-p'u-sa), knowing his purpose, was moved with pity. Wishing to arouse him to the truth and to awaken him in a moment, he came and said, "Alas! how have you given up your great purpose, and only fixed your mind on your own personal profit, with narrow aims, giving up the purpose of saving all! If you would really do good, you ought to transmit and explain the rules of the *Yu-kia-sse-ti-lun* (*Yôgachârya-bhûmi Śâstra*) of Maitrêya Bôdhisattva. By that you may lead and direct students, and cause them to receive great advantage."

Jina Bôdhisattva receiving these directions, respectfully assented and saluted the saint. Then having given himself to profound study, he developed the teaching of the *Hêtuvidyâ Śâstra;* but still fearing that the students thereof would dread its subtle reasonings and its precise style, he composed the *Hêtuvidyâ Śâstra*,[95] exemplifying the great principles and explaining the subtle language, in order to guide the learners. After that he explained fully the Yôga discipline.

From this going through the desert forest south[96] 1000 li or so, we come to To-na-kie-tse-kia (Dhanakaṭaka).[97]

[93] "This is the chief, or complete, thing."

[94] This also is a phrase to denote the condition of Arhatship.

[95] The title is defective. It probably refers to the *Nyâyadvâra-târaka S'âstra;* but, on the other hand, this work was composed by Nâgârjuna (see B. Nanjio's *Catalogue*, 1223). The whole of the passage in the text referring to Jina is obscure, and probably corrupt.

[96] In the translation of Hwui-lih, Julien gives "vers le sud," which expression is quoted by Fergusson (*J. R. A. S.*, N.S., vol. vi. p. 262); but it is simply "going south" in the original.

[97] Called also the Great Andhra country. Julien has Dhanakachêka; the Pâli inscriptions at Amarâvatî and Nâsik give Dhaṁñakaṭaka, for which the Sanskrit would be Dhanyakaṭaka or Dhânyakaṭaka; and in

T'O-NA-KIE-TSE-KIA (DHANAKAṬAKA).

This country is about 6000 li in circuit, and the capital [98] some 40 li round. The soil is rich and fertile, and is regularly cultivated, affording abundant harvests. There is much desert country, and the towns are thinly populated. The climate is hot. The complexion of the people is a yellowish black, and they are by nature fierce and impulsive. They greatly esteem learning. The convents (*saṅghârâmas*) are numerous, but are mostly deserted and ruined; of those preserved there are about twenty, with 1000 or so priests. They all study the law of the Great Vehicle. There are 100 Dêva temples, and the people who frequent them are numerous and of different beliefs.

To the east of the capital (*the city*) bordering on (*leaning against*) [99] a mountain is a convent called the Pûrvaśilâ (*Fo-p'o-shi-lo-seng*).[100] To the west of the city leaning against (*maintained by*) a mountain is a convent called Avaraśilâ.[101] These were (*or*, this was) built by a former king to do honour to (*for the sake of*) Buddha.

an inscription of 1361 A.D. we have Dhânyavâtîpura, and these would identify the city of Dhaṁñakaṭaka with Dhara-ikṭ.ṭa close to Amarâvatî (*Ind. Ant.*, vol. xi. pp. 95 f.) The symbol *tse* is equivalent to the Sanskrit *ṭa*.

[98] Mr. Fergusson concludes from a report addressed to Government by the late J. A. C. Boswell, and also from some photographs by Captain Ross Thompson, that almost beyond the shadow of a doubt Bejwâḍâ is the city described by Hiuen Tsiang (*op. cit.*, p. 263). But see *Ind. Ant.*, ut cit.

[99] The word is *keu*, to hold, to rely on. In the *Analects* (vii. 6, 2) there is the expression *keu yu tih*, which Dr. Legge translates, "let every attainment in what is good be *firmly grasped.*" I should suppose, therefore, the text means that the Pûrvaśilâ convent was supported by or enclosed by a mountain on the east of the city.

[100] The symbol *lo* appears to be omitted. *Fo-lo-po* would be equal to Purva.

[101] *'O-fa-lo-shi-lo*, Aparaśilâ or West Mount. Fergusson identifies this with the Amarâvatî tope. The tope is 17 miles west of Bejwâḍâ. It stands to the south of the town of Amarâvatî, which again is 20 miles north-north-west of Guṇṭûr. The old fort called Dharṇikôṭa (which appears at one time to have been the name of the district) is just one mile west of Amarâvatî. "This celebrated Buddhist tope was first discovered by Râja Veṅkaṭâdri Nâyuḍu's servants in A.D. 1796: it was visited by Colonel Mackenzie and his survey staff in 1797; it was greatly demolished by the Râja, who utilised the sculptured

He hollowed the valley, made a road, opened the mountain crags, constructed pavilions and long (*or*, lateral) galleries; wide chambers supported the heights and connected the caverns.[102] The divine spirits respectfully defended (*this place*); both saints and sages wandered here and reposed. During the thousand years following the *Nirvâṇa* of Buddha, every year there were a thousand laymen[103] and priests who dwelt here together during the rainy season. When the time was expired, all who had[104] reached the condition of Arhats mounted into the air and fled away. After the thousand years the lay-

marbles for building materials up to the year 1816. It was again visited by Colonel Mackenzie, who made large excavations, in 1816. Further excavations in 1835 (?); examined by Sir Walter Elliot, who unearthed the ruins of the western gateway in 1840. Excavations recommenced (by Mr. R. Sewell) in May 1877. Further excavations (by Dr. James Burgess) in 1882–83. Sewell's *List of Antiquarian Remains in Madras*, vol. i. p. 63. For a full and valuable account of the sculptures of this tope see Fergusson, *Tree and Serpent Worship*, also Burgess, *Report on the Amarâvatî Stûpa*. An inscription discovered by Dr. Burgess among the stones of the *stûpa* proves "beyond doubt that the Amarâvatî *stûpa* was either already built or was being built in the second century A.D., if not earlier" (Burgess, *op. cit.*, p. 27).

[102] This would appear to refer to his work in constructing a sort of "sacred way" leading to the tope. But the text does not supply any information beyond the fact of the excavations in connection with this western *saṅghârâma*. But were these excavations confined to "the high mountain on the west of the town, full of caves, abutting on the river?" Perhaps an explanatoin may be found by supposing that the excavation of the mountain, &c., was independent of the building of the *saṅghârâma*. In Hwui-lih there is nothing said about the caverns, galleries, and tunnels; he simply states that "the eastern and western *saṅghârâmas* were built by a former king of the country, and he thoroughly searched through all the examples (*kw'ai shih*, rules and patterns) [of similar buildings] to be found in Ta-hia." Hiuen Tsiang says that "the eastern and western convents were built [the symbol *ch'a* in the text is *lih* in Hwui-lih; I regard it as a misprint] by a former king," and then he goes on to say that "he moreover bored through the river valley, hollowed out a road, divided the crags, raised pavilions (turreted chambers) with lateral galleries, whilst wide chambers supported (pillowed) the heights and connected the caves." This is all independent of building the *saṅghârâmas*. I must confess, however, that the position of the *stûpa*, seventeen miles west of the town, and on the other side of the river, seems to be a difficulty. With reference to Ta-hia, it is generally translated Baktria (Bretschneider, *Notices of Mediæval Geography*, &c., p. 197). The rules and patterns of buildings in Baktria would, I should suppose, be those of the Greeks.

[103] *Fan fu*, common disciples.

[104] Or, it may mean all of them attained the condition of Arhats.

men and saints dwelt together; but for the last hundred years there have been no priests (*dwelling here*) in consequence of the spirit of the mountain changing his shape, and appearing sometimes as a wolf, sometimes as a monkey, and frightening the disciples; for this reason the place has become deserted and wild, with no priests to dwell there.

To the south[105] of the city a little way is a great mountain cavern. It is here the master of *śâstras* P'o-pi-feï-kia (Bhâvavivêka)[106] remains in the palace of the Asuras ('O-ssu-lo), awaiting the arrival of Maitrêya Bôdhisattva as perfect Buddha.[107] This master of *śâstras* was widely renowned for his elegant scholarship and for the depth of his vast attainments (*virtue*). Externally he was a disciple of Kapila[108] (Sâṅkhya), but inwardly he was fully possessed of the learning of Nâgârjuna. Having heard that Dharmapâla (Hu-fa-p'u-sa) of Magadha was spreading abroad the teaching of the law, and was making many thousand disciples, he desired to discuss with him. He took his religious staff in hand and went. Coming to Pâṭaliputra (Po-ch'a-li) he ascertained that Dharmâpala Bôdhisattva was dwelling at the *Bôdhi* tree. Then the master of *śâstras* ordered his disciples thus: "Go you to the place where Dharmapâla resides near the *Bodhi* tree, and say to him in my name, 'Bôdhisattva (*i.e.*, Dharmapâla) publishes abroad the doctrine (*of Buddha*) bequeathed to the world: he leads and directs the

[105] According to the report quoted by Mr. Fergusson (*op. cit.*, p. 263), "immediately south of the town (*i.e.*, of Bejwâḍâ) is a singular isolated rock or hill, along whose base and sides there are the remains of a considerable number of rock-caves, &c."

[106] In Chinese Tsing-pin, "he who discusses with clearness" (Jul.); but in Wong-Pûh (§ 193) he is called *Ming-pin*, which seems more accurate. For the story of this doctor see Wong-Pûh (*loc. cit.*)

[107] In this passage, as in the one relating to Kâśyapa in the Kukkutapâda-giri, Julien has quite missed the sense; he translates as though Bhâvavivêka had become a Buddha.

[108] In the text it is "externally he wore the clothes or costume of the Sâṅkhya (*Săng-k'ie*), that is, he was a follower of Kapila by outward profession. Julien has translated it as though *Săng-k'ie* were equivalent to *Săng-kia-chi*, but the symbols are quite different, and he himself gives *Sâṅkhya* as the equivalent of *Săng-k'ie* (pp. 470, 527).

ignorant. His followers look up to him with respect and humility, and so it has been for many days; nevertheless his vow and past determination have borne no fruit! Vain is it to worship and visit the *Bôdhi* tree. Swear to accomplish your object, and then you will be in the end guide of gods and men.'"[109]

Dharmapâla Bôdhisattva answered the messenger thus: "The lives of men (*or*, generations of men) are like a phantom; the body is as a bubble. The whole day I exert myself; I have no time for controversy; you may therefore depart—there can be no meeting."

The master of *śâstras* having returned to his own country, led a pure (*quiet*) life and reflected thus: "In the absence of[110] Maitrêya as a Buddha, who is there that can satisfy my doubts?" Then in front of the figure of the Bôdhisattva Kwan-tsz'-tsai,[111] he recited in order the *Sin-to'-lo-ni* (*Hṛidaya-dhâraṇi*),[112] abstaining from food and drink. After three years Kwan-tsz'-tsai Bôdhisattva appeared to him with a very beautiful[113] body, and

[109] This passage is obscure, and I offer my translation only as tentative. It appears to me that the message to the Bôdhisattva was couched ironically. Bhâvavivêka challenges Dharmapâla on the ground that his aim has not yet been accomplished, and to go to the Bôdhi tree to worship is foolish and inoperative. "Vow to accomplish your purpose, and it shall be accomplished irrespective of worship or humility." This would seem to have been the tendency of Nâgârjuna's teaching, and Bhâvavivêka, though outwardly a follower of Kapila, was yet full of Nâgârjuna's spirit.

[110] That is, until Maitrêya becomes Buddha, who is there that can answer my doubts? It is not that Maitréya *has* become Buddha, but until he does so become.

[111] This is indirectly a most important passage. It shows that Bhâvavivêka, who was imbued "with the spirit of Nâgârjuna," although professedly a follower of Kapila, exhibited his faith by going to Avalôkitêśvara. This, joined with the story of Sadvaha excavating the Brahmara (Durgâ) convent for Nâgârjuna, shows that the worship of Durgâ (the *many-armed and the high*) was the chief feature in the spirit of Nâgârjuna's teaching; in other words, that the fusion between Buddhism and the native worship of hill gods dates from Nâgârjuna's time, and was brought about by his influence.

[112] This is a well-known *sûtra* or mantra, has been translated in the *Journal of the R. A. S.*, 1875, p. 27; see also Bendall, *Catalogue of MSS.*, &c., p. 117, add. 1485. The composition of this *sûtra* may, I think be attributed to Nâgârjuna, as the founder of the Mahâyâna doctrine.

[113] This "beautiful body" of Avalôkitêśvara seems to be derived from foreign sources. The character of

addressed the master of *śâstras* thus: "What is your purpose (*will*)?" He said, "May I keep my body till Maitrêya comes." Kwan-tsz'-tsai Bôdhisattva said, "Man's life is subject to many accidents. The world is as a bubble or a phantom. You should aim at the highest resolve to be born in the Tushita heaven, and there, even now,[114] to see him face to face and worship."

The master of *śâstras* said, "My purpose is fixed; my mind cannot be changed."[115] Bôdhisattva said, "If it is so, you must go to the country of Dhanakaṭaka, to the south of the city, where in a mountain cavern a diamond-holding (*Vajrapâṇi*) spirit dwells, and there with the utmost sincerity reciting the *Chi-king-kang-t'o-lo-ni* (*Vajrapâṇidhâraṇî*), you ought to obtain your wish."

On this the master of *śâstras* went and recited (the *dhâraṇi*). After three years the spirit said to him, "What is your desire, exhibiting such earnest diligence?" The master of *śâstras* said, "I desire that my body may endure till Maitrêya comes, and Avalôkitêśvara Bôdhisattva directed me to come here to request the fulfilment (*of my desire*). Does this rest with you, divine being?"

The spirit then revealed to him a formula and said, "There is an Asura's palace in this mountain; if you ask according to the rule given you, the walls will open, and then you may enter and wait there till you see (*Maitrêya*)." "But," said the master of *śâstras*, "dwelling in the dark, how shall I be able to see or know when the Buddha

the beauty may be seen from the plates supplied by Mr. B. Hodgson in the *J. R. A. S.*, vol. vi. p. 276. There can be little doubt that we have here a link connecting this worship with that of Ardhvisura-anâhita, the Persian representative of the beautiful goddess of "pure water." Compare Anaitis as Venus, and the Venus-mountains in Europe (Fensberg), the survival of the worship of hill-gods. (See Karl Blind on "water-gods," &c., in the *Contemporary Review*.)

[114] This is the aim of the true Buddhist convert, to be born in the heaven of Maitrêya after death, and there to hear his doctrine, so as to be able at his advent to receive his instruction and reach *Nirvâṇa*. Opposed to this is the foreign theory of a Western paradise.

[115] This exhibits the character of Bhâvavivêka, who had charged Dharmapâla with want of a strong determination (*oath*). See *ante*, n. 109.

appears?" Vajrapâṇi said, "When Maitrêya comes into the world, I will then advertise you of it." The master of *śâstras* having received his instructions, applied himself with earnestness to repeat the sentences, and for three years, without any change of mind, he repeated the words to a nicety (*mustard-seed*).[116] Then knocking at the rock-cavern, it opened out its deep and vast recesses. Then an innumerable multitude appeared before him looking about them, but forgetful of the way to return. The master of *śâstras* passed through the door, and addressing the multitude said, "Long have I prayed and worshipped with a view to obtain an opportunity to see Maitrêya. Now, thanks to the aid of a spiritual being, my vow is accomplished. Let us therefore enter here, and together await the revelation of this Buddha."

Those who heard this were stupified, and dared not pass the threshold. They said, "This is a den of serpents; we shall all be killed." Thrice he addressed them, and then only six persons were content to enter with him. The master of *śâstras* turning himself and advancing, then all the multitude followed him with their gaze as he entered. After doing so the stone walls closed

[116] Julien translates this "*sur* un graine de sénevé." Referring to my translation in Wong-Pûh, § 193, I had the honour to correspond with M. Julien on the subject, he only allowed that the point was worthy of consideration. His words are these: "Il me semble au contraire que cela signifie que la puissance des *dhâraṇi* recités sur une graine de sénevé fut telle que cette graine, malgré sa légérité extrême, put, etant projetée sur la pierre, la faire s'entrouvrir comme si elle avait été frappée avec un instrument d'une force, d'un poids extraordinaire." But there is something to be said on the other side. To repeat a formula "to a mustard-seed," is to repeat it perfectly (*ad unguem*); hence the name of Siddhârtha, "the perfect" (*yih-tsai-i-shing*), the son of Śuddhôdana, the promised Buddha, was just this, "the white mustard-seed" (Siddhârtha), because he was "perfectly endowed." Whether the phrase, "faith as a grain of mustard-seed" (*ὥς κόκκον σινάπεως*) does not mean "perfect *faith*" (an Orientalism introduced into Palestine, *ὥς* used for *ἕως, or πρός*) is a point I shall not urge; but probably the familiar story of "Open Sesame" is derived from the legend of Bhâvavivêka and the "mustard-seed." Both Ali Baba and the master of *śâstras* succeeded in opening the cavern gate by a "mustard-seed" formula. Cunningham connects the name of the place, Dhâraṇi-kôṭa, with this legend (*Anc. Geog.*, p. 538).

behind them, and then those left without chided themselves for neglecting his words addressed to them.

From this going south-west 1000 li or so, we come to the kingdom of Chu-li-ye (Chulya).

Chu-li-ye (Chulya or Chôla).

The country of Chulya (Chôḷa) is about 2400 or 2500 li in circuit; the capital is about 10 li round. It is deserted and wild, a succession of marshes and jungle. The population is very small, and troops of brigands go through the country openly. The climate is hot; the manners of the people dissolute and cruel. The disposition of the men is naturally fierce; they are attached to heretical teaching. The *sâṅghârâmas* are ruined and dirty as well as the priests. There are some tens of Dêva temples, and many Nirgrantha heretics.

At a little distance south-east of the city is a *stûpa* built by Aśôka-râja. Here Tathâgata in old time dwelt, and exhibited his spiritual power, and preached the sublime law, and defeated the heretics, delivering both men and Dêvas.

Not far to the west of the city there is an old *saṅghârâma*. This was the place where Ti-p'o (Dêva) Bôdhisattva discussed with an Arhat. In the first instance, Dêva Bôdhisattva heard that in this convent there was an Arhat called Uttara (Wu-ta-lo) who possessed the six supernatural powers (*shaḍabhijñâs*), and the eight *vimôkshas* (*means of deliverance*); forthwith he came from a distance to observe his manner as a model. Having arrived at the convent, he asked the Arhat for a night's lodging. Now in the place where the Arhat lived (*in his cell*) there was only one bed. Having entered, in the absence of a mat, he spread some rushes on the ground, and showing it to him, begged him to be seated. Having taken the seat, the Arhat entered into *samâdhi*, and came out of it after midnight. Then Dêva proposed to him his doubts, and prayed him to answer them. The Arhat took up each difficulty and explained it. Dêva, closely examining each word, pressed his difficulties in the way of cross-examination, till after the seventh round of discussion the Arhat closed his mouth and declined (*was unable*) to reply. Then using secretly his divine faculties, he passed into the Tushita heaven, and there questioned Maitrêya. Maitrêya gave the required explanations, but because of their character he added, "This is the celebrated Dêva who for a succession of kalpas has practised religion, and in the middle of the Bhadra-kalpa ought to attain the condition of Buddha. You do not know this.[117] You should greatly honour him and pay him reverence."

In a moment he returned to his seat, and once more entered on a clear explanation (*of the difficulties*), which he expressed in great precision and language. Dêva addressing him said, "This is the explanation of the holy wisdom of Maitrêya Bôdhisattva. It is not possible for you, reverend sir, to have discovered such profound answers." Then the Arhat said, "It is so, in truth; the will of Tathâgata." On this, rising from his mat, he offered him worship and profound reverence and praise.

Going from this south, we enter a wild forest district, and passing 1500 or 1600 li, we come to the country of Ta-lo-pi-ch'a (Drâviḍa).

TA-LO-PI-CH'A (DRÂVIḌA).

This country is about 6000 li in circuit; the capital of the country is called Kâñchîpura (Kin-chi-pu-lo),[118] and is about 30 li round. The soil is fertile and regularly cultivated, and produces abundance of grain. There are

[117] Or, do you not know this?

[118] This must be Conjiveram. I do not think the text in Hwui-lih can be construed as Julien takes it "the town of *Kin-chi* is situated or a port of the sea." The original runs thus: "The town of *Kin-chi* is the opening (mouth) of the southern sea of India, and in the direction of Siṅhala the water journey is three days." It seems to imply that Conjiveram was the central town from which the traffic to Ceylon was conducted.

also many flowers and fruits. It produces precious gems and other articles. The climate is hot, the character of the people courageous. They are deeply attached to the principles of honesty and truth, and highly esteem learning; in respect of their language and written characters, they differ but little from those of Mid-India. There are some hundred of *saṅghârâmas* and 10,000 priests. They all study the teaching of the Sthavira (*Chang-tso-pu*) school belonging to the Great Vehicle. There are some eighty Dêva temples, and many heretics called Nirgranthas. Tathâgata in olden days, when living in the world, frequented this country much; he preached the law here and converted men, and therefore Aśôka-râja built *stûpas* over all the sacred spots where these traces exist. The city of Kâñchîpura is the native place of Dharmapâla Bôdhisattva.[119] He was the eldest son of a great minister of the country. From his childhood he exhibited much cleverness, and as he grew up it increased and extended. When he became a young man,[120] the king and queen condescended to entertain him at a (*marriage*) feast. On the evening of the day his heart was oppressed with sorrow, and being exceedingly afflicted, he placed himself before a statue of Buddha and engaged in earnest prayer (*supplication*). Moved by his extreme sincerity, the spirits removed him to a distance, and there he hid himself. After going many hundred li from this spot he came to a mountain convent, and sat down in the hall of Buddha. A priest happening to open the door, and seeing this youth, was in doubt whether he was a robber or not. After interrogating him on the point, the Bôdhisattva completely unbosomed himself and told him the cause; moreover he asked permission to become a disciple. The priests were much astonished at the wonderful event, and forthwith granted his request. The king ordered search to be made for him in every direction, and at length finding out that Bôdhi-

[119] Ta-mo-po-lo-p'u-sa, in Chinese Hu-fa, "defender of the law."
[120] Assumed the cap, *toga virilis.*

sattva had removed to a distance from the world, driven[121] by the spirit (*or*, spirits), then he redoubled his deep reverence and admiration for him. From the time that Dharmapâla assumed the robes of a recluse, he applied himself with unflagging earnestness to learning. Concerning his brilliant reputation we have spoken in the previous records.[122]

To the south of the city not a great way is a large *saṅghârâma*, in which men of the same sort, renowned for talent and learning, assemble and stop. There is a *stûpa* about 100 feet high which was built by Aśôka-râja. Here Tathâgata, dwelling in old days, repeated the law and subdued the heretics, and converted both men and Dêvas in great number.

Going 3000 li or so south from this, we come to the country of Mo-lo-kiu-ch'a (Malakûṭa).

Mo-lo-kiu-ch'a (Malakûṭa).

This country[123] is about 5000 li in circuit; the capital is about 40 li. The land and fields are impregnated with

[121] Both here and in the preceding portion of the narrative the phrase used is *shin fu*, which may either mean "carried by spirits" (in the sense of divine spirits) or "driven by his own spirit." Julien adopts the former rendering. We should in this case have expected to find the phrase *kwei shin*, instead of *shin*. Hwui-lih, however, tells us that it was "a great king of the spirits" (one of the Mahâdêva-râjas) that carried him away.

[122] See *ante*, vol. i. p. 238. For some account of his writings, compare *Hwui-lih*, book iv. p. 191 (Jul.); see also note 87, book ix.

[123] The distance given (3000 li or so) south from Conjiveram seems to be excessive. But none of the distances given by Hiuen Tsiang from *hearsay* are to be depended on. Compare, for example, the distance given from Charitra, in Orissa, to Ceylon, viz., about 20,000 li. This part of the pilgrim's itinerary is beset with difficulties. In the text before us, the use of the symbol *hing* would denote that he went personally to the Malakûṭa kingdom, but in Hwui-lih we are told that he heard only of this country, and his intention was evidently to embark, probably at the mouth of the Conjiveram river, for Ceylon, when he heard from the priests who came from that country to Kin-chi of the death of the king Râja Buna Mugalân and the famine. Mr. Fergusson, assuming Nellore to have been the capital of Chôḷa (I may here notice, by the way, that the symbols used for this country are the same both in *Hwui-lih* and the *Si-yu-ki*, so that the "Djourya" adopted by Julien in the *Life* of Hiuen-Tsiang is the same as "Tchoulya" in the *Si-yu-ki*), is

salt, and the produce of the earth is not abundant. All the valuables that are collected in the neighbouring islets are brought to this country and analysed. The temperature is very hot. The men are dark complexioned. They are firm and impetuous in disposition. Some follow the true doctrine, others are given to heresy. They do not esteem learning much, but are wholly given to commercial gain. There are the ruins of many old convents, but only the walls are preserved, and there are few religious followers. There are many hundred Dêva temples, and a multitude of heretics, mostly belonging to the Nirgranthas.

Not far to the east of this city is an old *saṅghârâma* of which the vestibule and court are covered with wild shrubs; the foundation walls only survive. This was built by Mahêndra, the younger brother of Aśôka-râja.

To the east of this is a *stûpa*, the lofty walls of which are buried in the earth, and only the crowning part of the cupola remains. This was built by Aśôka-râja. Here

disposed to refer Kin-chi-pu-lo to Nâgapaṭṭaṇam, and so get over the difficulty which arises from Hwui-lih's remark that "the town of Kin-chi is at the sea-mouth on the water-road to Ceylon," and also the distance from Nellore of 1500 or 1600 li. But this would involve us in subsequent difficulties; the name of Kâñchîpura, moreover, is the well-known equivalent for Conjiveram, and it is impossible to disregard this. M. V. de St. Martin, relying on Hwui-lih, says (*Mémoire*, p. 399) that Hiuen-Tsiang did not go farther south than Kâñchîpura, but, on the other hand, Dr. Burnell is of opinion that Hiuen-Tsiang returned from Malakûṭa to Kâñchîpura (*Ind. Ant.*, vii. p. 39). It is certain that on his way to the Koṅkaṇ he started from Drâviḍa; I am disposed, therefore, to think that he did not go farther south than Kin-chi. In this case the subsequent account he gives us of Malakûṭa, Mount Malaya, and Potaraka, is derived from hearsay. With regard to Malakûṭa, Dr. Burnell has shown (*loc. cit.*) that "this kingdom was comprised roughly in the delta of the Kâvêrî." This would lead us to suppose that the capital was somewhere near Kumbhaghôṇam or Âvûr; but how then shall we account for the 3000 li of Hiuen-Tsiang? the actual distance south from Conjiveram to this neighbourhood being only 150 miles, or, at most, 1000 li. For an account of Kumbhaghôṇam, see Sewell, *Lists of Antiq. Remains in Madras*, vol. i. p. 274. Dr. Burnell gives the name Malaikûṟṟam as possibly that by which Kumbhaghôṇam was known in the seventh century (*ibid.*) In a note the Chinese editor remarks that Malakûṭa is also called Chi-mo-lo; Julien restores this to Tchimor (p. 121, n.), and also to Tchimala "the Simour of M. Reinaud" (Jul., iii. 530). I have given reasons for thinking that Chi-mo-lo is the equivalent for Kûmâr (*J. R. A. S.*, vol. xv. p. 337).

Tathâgata in old days preached the law and exhibited his miraculous powers, and converted endless people. To preserve the traces of this event, this memorial tower was built. For years past it has exhibited spiritual signs, and what is wished for in its presence is sometimes obtained.

On the south of this country, bordering the sea, are the Mo-la-ye (Malaya) mountains,[124] remarkable for their high peaks and precipices, their deep valleys and mountain torrents. Here is found the white sandal-wood tree and the *Chan-t'an-ni-p'o* (*Chandanêva*)[125] tree. These two are much alike, and the latter can only be distinguished by going in the height of summer to the top of some hill, and then looking at a distance great serpents may be seen entwining it: thus it is known. Its wood is naturally cold, and therefore serpents twine round it. After having noted the tree, they shoot an arrow into it to mark it.[126] In the winter, after the snakes have gone, the tree is cut down. The tree from which *Kie-pu-lo* (*Karpûra*) scent is procured,[127] is in trunk like the pine, but different leaves and flowers and fruit. When the tree is first cut down and sappy, it has no smell; but when the wood gets dry, it forms into veins and splits; then in the middle is the scent, in appearance like mica, of the colour of frozen snow. This is what is called (in Chinese) *long-nao-hiang*, the dragon-brain scent.

124 These mountains, or this mountain, bordering on the sea, may either represent the Malabâr Ghâṭs generally, or, more probably, the detached mass of the Ghâṭs south of the Koimbatur gap, apparently the true Malaya of the Pauranik lists. See *Ind. Ant.*, vol. xiii. p. 38; Sewell, *op. cit.*, p. 252. The term *Ma-la-yo* is also applied to a mountainous district in Ceylon, of which Adam's Peak is the centre (Childers, *Pâli Dict.*, sub voc.); compare *J. R. A. S.*, N.S., vol. xv. p. 336. It would seem, at any rate, if this district of Malaya, "bordering on the sea," was a part of the kingdom of Malakûṭa, that the latter cannot be confined to the delta of the Kâvêrî, but must be extended to the southern sea-coast. This would explain the alternative name of Chi-mo-lo (Kumâr). *Malaya* means any "mountainous region."

125 That is, a tree "*like* the sandal-wood" (Jul., n. 1).

126 Compare Julien, note 2 (*in loco*), and Burnouf, *Introd. to Buddhism*, p. 620. The Malaya mountain is called Chandanagiri, part of the southern range of the Ghâts, because of the sandal-wood found there (Monier Williams, *Sansc. Dict.* s. v. *Chandana*).

127 That is, *camphor*.

To the east of the Malaya mountains is Mount Po-ta-lo-kia (Pôtalaka).[128] The passes of this mountain are very dangerous; its sides are precipitous, and its valleys rugged. On the top of the mountain is a lake; its waters are clear as a mirror. From a hollow proceeds a great river which encircles the mountain as it flows down twenty times and then enters the southern sea. By the side of the lake is a rock-palace of the Dêvas. Here Avalôkitêśvara[129] in coming and going takes his abode. Those who strongly desire to see this Bôdhisattva do not regard their lives, but, crossing the water (*fording the streams*), climb the mountain forgetful of its difficulties and dangers; of those who make the attempt there are very few who reach the summit. But even of those who dwell below the mountain, if they earnestly pray and beg to behold the god, sometimes he appears as Tsz'-tsaï-t'ien (Îśvâra-dêva), sometimes under the form of a yôgi (*a Pâmśupata*); he addresses them with benevolent words and then they obtain their wishes according to their desires.

Going north-east from this mountain, on the border[130] of the sea, is a town;[131] this is the place from which they

[128] The situation of this mountain has been discussed (*J. R. A. S.*, N.S., vol. xv. p. 339 ff.

[129] See vol. i. p. 60, n. 210.

[130] The symbol used implies "a division of the sea," as though it were at a point where the sea divided into an eastern and western ocean.

[131] There is no name given; it is simply stated there is a town from which they go to Ceylon. If it were intended to give the name Charitrapura to it, there would be no symbol between the word for "city or town" and the word "go." M. Julien's parenthesis has misled Dr. Burnell and others. Dr. Burnell has also argued on a mistaken translation as to the position of this town, which he identifies with Kâvêripaṭṭanam (*Ind. Ant.*, vol. vii. p. 40). Julien says, "Going from Malakûṭa in a north-eastern direction, on the borders of the sea is a town (called Che-li-ta-to, Charitrapura)." Conf. *ante*, p. 05, n. 55. But, in fact, the original states, "Going from this mountain, *i.e.*, Mount Malaya, in a north-eastern direction, there is a town at the sea-dividing." So that Dr. Burnell's conclusions, so for as this part of his argument goes, are not supported by the text. On the other hand, it is stated by I-tsing that "going west thirty days from Quedâh, merchants used to arrive at Nâgavadana, whence after two days' voyage they reach Ceylon" (*J. R. A. S.*, N.S., vol. xiii. p. 562). This looks as though Nâgapaṭṭanam were the town referred to by Hiuen Tsiang.

start for the southern sea and the country of Săng-kia-lo (Ceylon). It is said commonly by the people that embarking from this port and going south-east about 3000 li we come to the country of Siṁhala.

END OF BOOK X.

BOOK XI.

Contains an account of twenty-three kingdoms, viz., (1) *Săng-kia-lo;* (2) *Kong-kien-na-pu-lo;* (3) *Mo-ho-la-c'ha;* (4) *Po-lu-kie-che-p'o;* (5) *Mo-la-p'o;* (6) *O-c'ha-li;* (7) *Kie-ch'a;* (8) *Fa-la-pi;* (9) *'O-nan-to-pu-lo;* (10) *Su-la-ch'a;* (11) *Kiu-che-lo;* (12) *U-she-yen-na;* (13) *Shi-kie-tu;* (14) *Mo-hi-chi-fa-lo-po-lo;* (15) *Sin-to;* (16) *Mo-lo-san-pu-lo;* (17) *Po-fa-to;* (18) *O-tien-p'o-chi-lo;* (19) *Long-kie-lo;* (20) *Po-la-sse;* (21) *Pi-to-shi-lo;* (22) *O-fan-c'ha;* (23) *Fa-la-na.*

SĂNG-KIA-LO (SIṀHALA).[1]

THE kingdom of Siṁhala is about 7000 li in circuit;[2] the capital is about 40 li round. The soil is rich and fertile; the climate is hot; the ground is regularly cultivated; flowers and fruits are produced in abundance. The population is numerous; their family possessions are rich in revenues. The stature of the men is small. They are black complexioned[3] and fierce by nature. They love learning and esteem virtue. They greatly honour religious excellence, and labour in the acquisition of religious merit.

[1] Siṁhala or Ceylon was not visited by Hiuen Tsiang, for reasons given in the last book. Fa-hian, however, resided in the island for two years (cap. 40). For the various names by which this island has been known, we may refer to Vincent (*Navigation of the Ancients*, &c.) Colonel Yule doubts whether we owe the name Ceylon or Seilan to Siṁhala (*Marco Polo*, ii. p. 254, note 1). Childers traces the derivation of the word Elu to this name Sīhala (*Notes on the Sinhalese Language*). See *Ind. Ant.*, vol. xiii. pp. 33 ff.

[2] For the exaggerated reports concerning the size of this island, we may refer to Tennent's *Ceylon*, cap. i., and Yule, *Marco Polo* (vol. ii. p. 254, n. 1). The circuit of the island is really under 700 miles. We must therefore allow 10 li to the mile if Hiuen Tsiang's statement is to be received. Fa-hian is much more nearly correct in his figures, but in his account we must substitute *length* for *breadth* (cap. 37).

[3] This must refer to the Tamil population. The Siṅhalese are tall and comparatively fair.

This country was originally (*called*) Pâo-chu[4] (Ratnadvîpa), because of the precious gems found there. It was occupied by evil spirits.[5]

After this there was a king of a country of Southern India, whose daughter was affianced in a neighbouring country. On a fortunate day, having paid a complimentary visit, she was returning when a lion met her on the way. The servants of the guard left her and fled from the danger. Resting alone in her car, her heart was resigned to death. At this time the lion king, taking the woman on his back, went away and entered a lone valley in the deep mountains.[6] He caught the deer and gathered the fruits according to their season, with which to nourish her. In the course of time she brought into the world a boy and a girl. In form and features they resembled human beings, but in disposition they were like the beast tribes.

The youth gradually grew up, and was possessed of great bodily strength, so that he could subdue the wildest

[4] That is, the "isle or islet of gems." So it was called by the Arabs of the ninth century (Yule, *op. cit.*, p. 255). The Javanese word for precious stone is *sela*, and from this, some think, comes the word Sailán or Ceylon (*ibid.*) In any case the name itself, "gem-island," was an old one; the regular formation would give us Ratnadvîpa.

[5] The construction of the text and context is a little unusual. It seems to imply that because the island abundantly possessed gems and precious stones, it was a resting-place for demons and spirits, or demons. Of course it refers to the Rakshasîs or Yakkhiṇîs. Comp. Weber, *Râmâyaṇa*, p. 25 (Boyd's translation).

[6] For notices of this legend see Prof. Vasconcellos Abreu, *Fragmentos d'uma tentativa de Estudo scoliastico da Epopeia Portugueza* (Lisboa, 1880), pp. 40–75; or *Ind. Ant.*, vol. xiii. pp. 33 ff.; *Dîpavaṁśa*, ch. ix.; Lassen, *Ind. Alt.*, vol. i. p. 241 n.; Burnouf, *Introd.*, pp. 198 f. It owes its origin probably to the rape of a woman during a seaboard raid. Some of the northern tribes (invaders of India) affected the name of *lion* (siṁha or li). Compare *Fo-sho*, v. 1788. There are three events (obscure in themselves, yet perhaps connected) which happened in India about the time of Buddha: (1.) The invasion of north-west of India by the Vṛījjis; (2.) the incursion of Yavanas into Orissa; (3.) the invasion and conquest of Ceylon by Vijaya. These events may have had a mutual relationship; the pressure of the Vṛījjis from the north-west would drive the intermediate tribes on Orissa, and from Orissa some of the adventurers would start for fresh conquests by sea. Precisely similar events occurred in the west a few centuries afterwards. Compare Fergusson, *Cave Temples of India*, p. 58; Beal, *Abstract of Four Lectures*, Introduction, ix., x., xi., and also the sculptures in the Gaṇêśa Gumpha and

beasts. When he came to man's estate,[7] the wisdom of his manhood also came, and he asked his mother, saying, "What am I to be called? My father is a savage beast, and my mother is a human creature. But as you differ in kind, how can you have lived together?" Then the mother related the old story, and told it to her son. Her son, replying, said, "Men and beasts are of different kinds. We ought to hasten away from this." The mother replied, "I should have fled long ago, but I cannot help myself." Then the son from that time forth stopped at home whenever his father, the lion, roamed forth through the mountain passes, with a view to escape the difficult (*position in which they were placed*). And now on a certain occasion, his father having gone forth, he proceeded to carry away his mother and sister to a village inhabited by men. The mother then said, "You ought, both of you, to keep this matter secret, and say nothing about the first transaction, for if people were to come to hear of it, they would lightly esteem us."

On this she returned to her father's country, but it no longer belonged to her family, and the sacrifices of her ancestors had all died out. Having taken refuge in the town, all the men addressed her, saying, "From what kingdom do you come?" She said, "I belong to this country. Having wandered through strange places, we have come back, mother and son together (*to our home*)."

Then the village people were moved with pity, and provided them with necessary food. And now the lion king returning to his place, saw no one there. Thinking with affection of his son and daughter, he was moved with rage, and went away through the mountains and valleys, and roamed through the towns and villages, roaring frightfully and destroying the people, slaughtering and mangling every living thing. The town-folk went forth,

Rani ka Nur caves, Fergusson, *op. cit.*, pl. 1.

[7] Reached the age of twenty years.—Julien.

therefore, to pursue and capture him, in order to kill him. They beat the drums, sounded the conch, and with their bows and spears formed a large company; but yet they lagged behind (*delayed*) in order to escape danger. Then the king, fearing that their courage was little,[8] organised a band of hunters to capture the lion. He himself went with an army consisting of the four kinds of troops, amounting to tens of thousands, and beat through the woods and jungle, and traversed the mountains and valleys (*in search of their prey*). The lion raising his terrible roar, men and beasts flee in consternation.

Not being captured in the hunt, the king again made a proclamation, and promised that whoever captured the lion and freed the country from the affliction should be largely rewarded and his reputation widely published.

The son, hearing the royal decree, spake to his mother and said, "We have suffered much from hunger and cold. I certainly will answer to the appeal. Perhaps we may thus get enough to support us."

The mother said, "You ought not to think of it; for though he is a beast, yet he is still your father. What though we be wretched through want? this is no reason why you should encourage a wicked and murderous thought."[9]

The son said, "Men and beasts are of a different kind. What room is there for the question of propriety in such a matter as this? Why should such a thought interfere with my plan?" So seizing a knife and concealing it in his sleeve, he went forth to answer to the appeal. On this a thousand people and ten thousand horsemen assembled in crowds (*like the clouds and vapour*). The lion lay hid in the forest, and no one dared to approach him. On this the son forthwith advanced to him, and the father, tame and crouching, forgot in his sense of loving affection all

[8] The virtue (viz., of manliness) which influenced them did not prevail (far).

[9] Wicked, *i.e.*, unnatural, against nature.

his previous hate. Then he (*the son*) plunged the knife into the middle of his bowels, but he still exhibited the same love and tenderness, and was free from all anger or revengeful feeling even when his belly was ripped up, and he died in agony.[10]

The king then said, "Who is this man who has done such a wonderful deed?" Allured by promises of reward on the one hand, and alarmed by fear of punishment on the other, if he kept back anything, he at last revealed the whole from beginning to end, and told the touching story without reserve. The king said, "Thou wretch! if thou wouldest kill thy father, how much more those not related to thee! Your deserts indeed are great for delivering my people from the savage cruelty of a beast whose (*passions*) it is difficult to assuage, and whose hateful tempers are easily aroused; but to kill your own father, this is a rebellious (*unnatural*) disposition. I will reward your good deed largely, but you shall be banished from the country as the punishment of your crime. Thus the laws will not be infringed and the king's words not violated." On this he prepared two large ships (*boats*) in which he stored much provision (*cured rice or other grain*). The mother he detained in the kingdom, and provided her with all necessary things as the reward of the service done. The son and daughter each were placed in a separate boat, and abandoned to the chance of the waves and the wind. The boat in which the son was embarked, driven over the sea, came to this Ratnadvîpa. Seeing it abounded in precious gems, he took up his abode here.

Afterwards merchants seeking for gems frequently came to the island. He then killed the merchant chief and detained his children. Thus he extended his race. His sons and grandsons becoming numerous, they pro-

[10] The cave pictures from Ajaṇṭâ given in Mrs. Speir's *Life in Ancient India*, pp. 300 ff. seem to refer to the history of Vijaya and the "lion" legend; see also Burgess, *Cave Temples*, &c., pp. 312 f.

ceeded to elect a king and ministers and to divide the people into classes. They then built a city and erected towns, and seized on the territory by force; and because their original founder got his name by catching a lion,[11] they called the country (*after his name*) Siṁhala.

The boat in which the girl was embarked was driven over the sea till it reached Persia (Po-la-sse), the abode of the western demons, who by intercourse with her engendered a clan of women-children, and therefore the country is now called the Country of the Western Women;—this is the reason.

The men of the Siṁha kingdom are small in stature and black-complexioned; they have square chins and high foreheads; they are naturally fierce and impetuous, and cruelly savage without hesitation. This is from their inherited disposition as descended from a beast; but another version of the story is that they are very brave and courageous.

The records of the Buddhist religion say: In the middle of a great iron city of this Ratnadvîpa (P'ao-chu) was the dwelling of the Râkshasî women (Lo-t'sa). On the towers of this city they erected two high flagstaffs with lucky or unlucky signals, which they exhibited according to circumstances[12] (*to allure mariners*), when merchants came to the island (*Ratnadvîpa*). Then they changed themselves into beautiful women, holding flowers and scents, and with the sound of music[13] they went forth to meet them, and caressingly invited them

[11] *Chih-sse-tseu*, lion-catching; this seems also to be the meaning of *siṁhala*, where *la* means *to catch* or *take*. The *Dipavaṁsa* brings Vijaya, the son of 'Siṁha, from Siṁhapura in Lâḷa (Gujarât).

[12] "If circumstances were propitious, they agitated the lucky flag or drapery; if they were unfortunate or unlucky, they moved the unpropitious signal." It would seem to mean that if a ship drew near the shore as if to anchor, then the favourable flag or signal was shown; but if she kept away on her voyage, then the unfavourable signal was displayed. Or it may mean that the signal was to allure mariners.

[13] The curious parallel between the ways of these Râkshasîs and the Sirens has attracted frequent notice. Compare Pausanias, book x. cap. vi. Σειρήνων νῆσος ἀνάπλεως ὀστεῶν, viz., of those who had listened to their songs. Homer, Odys.,

to enter the iron city; then having shared with them all sorts of pleasure, they shut them up in an iron prison, and devoured them at their leisure.

At this time there was a great merchant of Jambudvîpa called Săng-kia (Siṁha) whose son was called Săng-kia-la (Siṁhala). His father having grown old, he was deputed to take charge of the house (*family*); he embarked, therefore, with 500 merchants to seek for precious stones; driven by the winds and waves, they came to Ratnadvîpa.

Then the Râkshasîs, displaying the lucky signal, began to wave it, and went forth with scents and flowers and the sound of music to meet them, and invite them to enter the iron city. The prince of the merchants accordingly, matched with the queen of the Râkshasîs, gave himself up to pleasure and indulgence. The other merchants also selected each one a companion, and so, in the course of time, a son was born to each. After this, the Râkshasîs, feeling tired of their old partners' love, (*were preparing to*) shut them up in the iron prison, and to seek new companions among other merchants.

At this time, Săng-kia-la, moved in the night by an evil dream, and impressed with a sense of its bad augury, sought some mode of escape, and coming to the iron stronghold, he heard the sounds of piteous cries within. Forthwith he climbed a great tree, and questioned them, saying, "Who are you thus bound, and why these miserable cries?" They replied, "Do you not know then that the women who occupy this place are all Râkshasîs? In former days, they allured us to enter the city with festive sounds of music, but when you arrived, they shut us up in this prison, and are gradually devouring our flesh. Now we are half eaten up; your turn too will soon come."

xii. 178, &c., with the account in the text and in the *Romantic Legend of Buddha*, p. 339. See also *Ind. Antiq.*, vol. x. p. 291, and the *Academy*, Aug. 13, 1881, pp. 120, 121.

Then Săng-kia-la (Siṁhala) said, "By what device then may we escape this danger?" They replied, and said, "We hear that on the sea-board there is a divine horse,[14] and whoever prays with supreme faith he will safely carry him across."

Siṁhala having heard this, secretly told the merchants his companions to assemble altogether on the sea-shore and there to offer up fervent prayers for deliverance. Then the divine horse came and addressed the men and said, "Each one of you grasp my hairy coat and look not behind; then will I deliver you and transport you across the sea out of danger's way. I will conduct you back to Jambudvîpa, to your happy homes (*country*)."

Then the merchants, obeying his directions, did each one implicitly as commanded. They seized the hairy coat (*of the divine horse*). Then he mounted aloft, traversed through the clouds, and passed the sea to the other side.

Then the Râkshasîs, perceiving all at once their husbands had escaped, spake one to another in surprise, and asked where they had gone. Then, taking each her child, they traversed to and fro the air. Perceiving, then, that the merchants had just left the shore, they issued a general order to unite in their flight to follow them. Not an hour had passed but they encountered them, and then, with mingled joy and tears, they came, and for a time restraining their grief they said, "We thought ourselves happy when first we met you, and made it our care to provide you homes, and for long have loved and cherished you, but now you are departing and deserting your wives and children, leaving them desolate. Who can bear the terrible grief that afflicts us! We pray you stay your departure and turn again with us to the city."

[14] The horse is called Kêśî in the *Abhinishkramana Sûtra* (*Romantic Legend*, loc. cit.) The reference appears to be to the change of monsoon, which would favour the departure of merchants (see note in the *Romantic Legend*). Avalôkitêśvara is often spoken of as a white horse, *i.e.*, as one who came across the sea.

But the minds of the merchants were as yet unwilling to consent. The Râkshasîs, seeing their words had no effect, had recourse to seductive blandishments, and by their conduct excited the feelings of the merchants; in consequence of which, being unable to suppress their tender emotions, their steadfastness forsook them, and, hesitating to go on, they paused, and at length returned in company with the Râkshasîs. The women, saluting and congratulating each other, closely holding to the men, went back.

Now the wisdom of Siṁhala was deep, and his firm purpose remained unchanged, and so he succeeded in traversing the ocean, and thus escaped the danger.

Then the queen of the Râkshasîs returned alone to the iron city; on which the other women addressing her said, "You are without wisdom or astuteness, and so you are abandoned by your husband; since you have so little cleverness or capacity you cannot dwell here." On this the Râkshasî queen, taking her child, hastened her flight after Siṁhala. She indulged before him in excessive blandishments and entreated him tenderly to return. But Siṁhala repeated with his mouth some spiritual charms, and with his hand brandishing a sword, he said, "You are a Râkshasî and I am a man, men and demons belong to different classes, there can be no union between such; if you trouble me further with your entreaties I will take your life."

The Râkshasî woman, knowing the uselessness of further parley, darted through the air and disappeared. Coming to Siṁhala's house, she addressed his father Siṁha, and said, "I am a king's daughter belonging to such and such a country. Siṁhala took me as his wife, and I have borne him a son. Having collected gems and goods, we were returning to my lord's country when the ship, driven by the winds and the sea, was lost, and only I, my child, and Siṁhala were saved. After crossing rivers and mountains with great difficulty, hungry and worn out, I said a word displeasing to my husband, and I found myself deserted, and as he left me he let fall bitter words and raged on me as if he were a Râkshasa.[15] If I attempt to return, my native country is a very long distance off; if I stop, then I am left alone in a strange place: staying or returning I am without support. I have, therefore, dared to tell you the true state of things."

Siṁha said, "If your words be true, you have done right." Then she entered the king's house to dwell there. Not long after Siṁhala came, and his father addressing him said, "How is it you esteemed riches and gems so much and made so little of your wife and child?" Siṁhala said, "This is a Râkshasî." Then he related the whole previous history to his father and mother; then his relatives, angry on account of the whole affair, turned on her to drive her away; on which the Râkshasî went to the king and entreated him. The king wished to punish Siṁhala, but Siṁhala said, "The delusive influence of Râkshasîs is very great."

Moreover, the king, regarding his son's words as untrue, and being moved in his mind (*feelings*) by her fascination, addressed Siṁhala and said, "Since you have decided to reject this woman, I will now protect her in my after-palace." Siṁhala said, "I fear she will cause you some misfortune, for the Râkshasas eat only flesh and blood."

But the king would not listen to Siṁhala's words, and accordingly took her as his wife. In the middle of the night following this, flying away, she returned to Ratnadvîpa, and calling together 500 Râkshasa demon women, they all came to the king's palace, and there, by means of destructive charms and sorceries, they killed all living things within the building and devoured their flesh and

[15] Or, it may be, "as if I were a Râkshasî," and so Julien translates it. In this case we should supply the symbol *niu* (woman); but I observe that in the previous sentence where Siṁhala draws his sword he calls her a Râkshasa, not a Râkshasî, so that either translation is correct.

drank their blood, whilst they carried off the rest of the corpses and with them returned to the "island of gems."

The next day, early, all the ministers were assembled at the king's gates, which they found fast closed, and not able to be opened. After waiting a long time, and not hearing any sounds of voices within, they burst open the doors and gates, and pressed forward together (*into the house*). Coming to the palace hall, they found no living thing therein but only gnawed bones. The officers looking at one another in astonishment, then bent down their heads in their confusion, and uttered lamentable cries. Being unable to fathom the cause of the calamity that had happened, Siṁhala related to them from beginning to end the whole story. The ministers and people then saw from whence the evil came.

On this, the ministers of the country, the aged men and different officers, inquired in order as to the best person to appoint to the high dignity (*of the throne*). All looked in the direction of Siṁhala, (*so conspicuous for*) religious merit and wisdom. Then speaking together, they said, "With respect to a ruler, the selection is no trivial matter; he needs to be devout and wise, and at the same time of quick natural parts. If he be not good and wise, he would not be able to give lustre to the succession; if he have no natural parts (*skill or tact*), how could he direct the affairs of state? Now this Siṁhala appears to be such a man: he discovered in a dream the origin of the calamity;[16] by the effect of his virtue he encountered the divine horse, and he has loyally warned the king of his danger. By his prudence he has preserved himself; the succession should be his."

The result of the deliberation being known, the people joyfully raised him to the honourable position of king. Siṁhala was desirous of declining the honour, but was

[16] Viz., of the Râkshasîs.

not able to do so. Then keeping to the middle course, he respectfully saluted the different officers of state, and forthwith accepted the kingly estate. On this, he corrected the former abuses, and promoted to honour the good and virtuous; then he made the following decree, "My old merchant friends are in the country of the Râkshasîs, but whether alive or dead I cannot tell. But in either case I will set out to rescue them from their danger; we must equip an army. To avert calamities and to help the unfortunate, this is the merit of a kingdom; to preserve treasures of precious stones and jewels, is the advantage of a state."

On this he arrayed his troops and embarked. Then on the top of the iron city the evil flag was agitated.[17]

Then the Râkshasîs seeing it, were filled with fear, and putting in practice their seducing arts, went forth to lead and cajole them. But the king, thoroughly understanding their false artifices, commanded the soldiers to recite some charmed words and to exhibit their martial bearing Then the Râkshasîs were driven back, and fled precipitately to rocky islets of the sea; others were swallowed up and drowned in the waves. On this they destroyed the iron city and broke down the iron prison; they delivered the captive merchants, obtained large stores of jewels and precious stones, and then summoning the people to change their abodes, he (*Siṁhala*) founded his capital in the "island of gems," built towns, and so found himself at the head of a kingdom. Because of the king's name the country was called Siṁhala. This name is also connected with the *Jâtakas*, relating to Śâkya Tathâgata.

The kingdom of Siṁhala formerly was addicted to immoral religious worship, but after the first hundred years following Buddha's death the younger brother of Aśôkarâja, Mahêndra by name, giving up worldly desires,

[17] It would seem that "the evil flag" was a signal to warn the Râkshasîs of danger.

sought with ardour the fruit of Arhatship. He gained possession of the six supernatural powers and the eight means of liberation; and having the power of instant locomotion, he came to this country. He spread the knowledge of the true law and widely diffused the bequeathed doctrine. From his time there has fallen on the people a believing heart, and they have constructed 100 convents, containing some 20,000 priests. They principally follow the teaching of Buddha, according to the *dharma* of the Sthavira (Shang-ts'o-pu) school of the Mahâyâna sect.[18] When 200 years had elapsed,[19] through discussion, the one school was divided into two. The former, called the Mahâvihâravâsinas[20] (Mo-ho-pi-ho-lo-chu-pu), was opposed to the Great Vehicle and adhered to the teaching of the Little Vehicle; the other was called Abhayagirivâsinas ('O-p'o-ye-k'i-li-chu-pu);[21] they studied both vehicles, and widely diffused the *Tripiṭakas*. The priests attended to the moral rules, and were distinguished for their power of abstraction and their wisdom.[22] Their correct conduct was an example for subsequent ages; their manners grave and imposing.

[18] The Mahâyâna, or Great Vehicle, is generally supposed to have been unknown in the Southern school; but it is an elastic term, and in the present instance would refer probably to the developed doctrine (in what direction we hardly know) of the old school of the Sthaviras or elders.

[19] That is, as it seems, two hundred years after the introduction of Buddhism into Ceylon. If so, the period referred to would be about the time of the reduction of the three *piṭakas* to writing in Ceylon, viz., B.C. 75. Does the phrase just following this, "they widely diffused the *Tripiṭakas*," refer to this event?

[20] This school evidently followed the teaching of the Mahâvihâra priests. The Mahâvihâra was about 7 li to the south of the capital Anurâdhapura. It was built by Dêvanampiyatissa, about 250 B.C. (*Fa-hian*, c. 39.) Compare *Dîpavaṁsa* (Oldenberg), xix. 10. Oldenberg makes some remarks respecting the *Aṭṭhakathâ* preserved in this monastery, *op. cit. Introd.*, pp. 6, 7. See for some notice of the vihâra, Beal, *Fa-hian*, p. 159, n. 1.

[21] For some account of the Abhayagiri vihâra see *Dîpavaṁsa*, xix. 14, 17; Beal's *Fa-hian*, p. 151, n. 1. It seems to have been the vihâra in which the tooth-relic was exhibited, *Fa-hian*, 157.

[22] "Meditative powers" and "wisdom." This would indicate a developed form of belief. It corresponds to the *chi kwan* school of Tien-tai in China. The same steps which led to the formation of the school there may have marked the development in Ceylon. It represents a compromise between quietism and practice of rules.

By the side of the king's palace is the *vihâra* of Buddha's tooth, several hundred feet high, brilliant with jewels and ornamented with rare gems. Above the *vihâra* is placed an upright pole on which is fixed a great Padma râja (*ruby*) jewel.[23] This gem constantly sheds a brilliant light, which is visible night and day for a long distance, and afar off appears like a bright star. The king three times a day washes the tooth of Buddha with perfumed water,[24] sometimes with powdered perfumes. Whether washing or burning, the whole ceremony is attended with a service of the most precious jewels.

[The country of Siṁhala,[25] formerly called the Kingdom of Lions, is also called the Sorrowless Kingdom;[26] it is the same as South India. This country is celebrated for its precious gems; it is also called Ratnadvîpa. Formerly, when Śâkyamuni Buddha took an apparitional body called Siṁhala, all the people, and priests, in honour of his character, made him king,[27] and therefore the country was called Siṁhala. By his mighty spiritual power he destroyed the great iron city and subdued the Râkshasî women, and rescued the miserable and distressed, and then founded a city, and built towns, and converted this district. In order to disseminate the true doctrine, he left a tooth to be kept in this land, firm as a diamond, indestructible through ages. It ever scatters its light like the stars or the moon in the sky, or, as brilliant as the sun, it lights up the night. All those who fast and pray in its presence obtain answers, like the echo (*answers the voice*). If the country is visited by calamity, or famine, or other plague, by use of earnest religious prayer, some

[23] For some notice of the rubies of Ceylon, see *Marco Polo*, book iii. cap. xiv.

[24] Or, every day thrice washes, &c.

[25] This and the following paragraphs are interpolated in the text; they belong to the time of the Ming dynasty (third year of Yung-lo, A.D. 1405). I have translated a portion of the passage, the rest will be found in a note at the end of this Book xi.

[26] Or the Aśôka kingdom. Compare the Aśôka garden of Râvaṇa, in the *Râmâyaṇa*.

[27] To do him honour.

spiritual manifestation ever removes the evil. It is now called Si-lan-mount,[28] but formerly Simhala country.

By the side of the king's palace is the *vihâra* of Buddha's tooth,[29] which is decorated with every kind of gem, the splendour of which dazzles the sight like that of the sun. For successive generations worship has been respectfully offered to this relic, but the present king of the country, called A-li-fun-nai-'rh (Alibunar' ?), a man of So-li (Chôḷa),[30] is strongly attached to the religion of the heretics and does not honour the law of Buddha ; he is cruel and tyrannical, and opposed to all that is good. The people of the country, however, still cherish the tooth of Buddha.[31]]

By the side of the *vihâra* of Buddha's tooth is a little *vihâra* which is also ornamented with every kind of precious stone. In it is a golden statue of Buddha ; it was cast by a former king of the country, and is of the size of life. He afterwards ornamented the head-dress (the *ushṇisha*) with a precious gem.

In course of time there was a robber who formed the design to carry off the precious stone, but as it was guarded by a double door and a surrounding balustrade, the thief resolved to tunnel out an entrance underneath the obstacles, and so to enter the *vihâra* and take the jewel. Accordingly he did so, but on attempting to seize the gem, the figure gradually raised itself higher, and outreached the grasp of the thief. He, then, finding his efforts of no avail, in departing sighed out thus, "Formerly when Tathâgata was practising the life of a Bôdhisattva, he cherished in himself a great heart and vowed that for

[28] Si-lan-shan. *Shan* corresponds to *giri*, the name therefore would be Silangiri, reminding us of the *Sirenum scopuli* of Virgil, *Æn.* v. 864. It is evident that this name was given to Ceylon before the Portuguese arrived in India

[29] This has been already stated in the previous section. For an account of Buddha's tooth and the *vihâra*, see Beal's *Fahian*, p. 153, n. 1.; *Eastern Monachism*, by Spence Hardy, pp. 224, 226.

[30] For Soli see *Marco Polo* (Yule), vol. ii. p. 272. The Chôḷas had just before this conquered the Pallavas.

[31] The rest of this passage will be found at the end of this book (xi.)

the sake of the four kinds of living things he would of his compassion give up everything, from his own life down to his country and its towns. But now the statue which stands in his place (*bequeathed*) grudges to give up the precious stone. His words, weighed against this, do not seem to illustrate his ancient conduct." On this the statue lowered its head and let him take the gem. The thief having got it, went to the merchants to sell it; on which they all exclaimed and said, "This is the gem which our former king placed on the head-dress of the golden statue of Buddha. Where have you got it from, that you want to sell it surreptitiously to us?" Then they took him to the king and stated the case. The king then asked him from whom he had procured the gem, on which the thief said, "Buddha himself gave it to me. I am no robber." The king not believing him, ordered a messenger to be sent immediately to ascertain the truth. On arriving he found the head of the statue still bent down. The king seeing the miracle, his heart was affected by a sincere and firm faith. He would not punish the man, but bought the gem again from him, and ornamented with it the head-dress of the statue. Because the head of the figure was thus bent on that occasion, it remains so until now.

By the side of the king's palace there is built a large kitchen, in which daily is measured out food for eight thousand priests. The meal-time having come, the priests arrive with their *pâtras* to receive their allowance.[82] Having received and eaten it, they return, all of them, to their several abodes. Ever since the teaching of Buddha reached this country, the king has established this charity, and his successors have continued it down to our times. But during the last ten years or so the country has been in confusion, and there has been no established ruler to attend to this business.

[82] Fa-hian also alludes to this charitable mode of feeding the priests, p. 155, *op. cit.*

In a bay on the coast of the country the land is rich in gems and precious stones.[33] The king himself goes (*there*) to perform religious services, on which the spirits present him with rare and valuable objects. The inhabitants of the capital come, seeking to share in the gain, and invoke the spirits for that purpose. What they obtain is different according to their religious merit. They pay a tax on the pearls they find, according to their quantity.

On the south-east corner of the country is Mount Laṅkâ.[34] Its high crags and deep valleys are occupied by spirits that come and go; it was here that Tathâgata formerly delivered the *Ling-kia-king* (*Laṅka Sûtra* or *Laṅkâvatâra*).[35]

Passing seawards to the south of this country some

[33] Marco Polo (cap. xvi.) alludes to the pearl-fisheries off the west coast of Ceylon. He mentions Bettelar as the place of rendezvous. Colonel Yule thinks that this is Putlam, the Pattâla of Ibu Batuta. With reference to the account given by Marco Polo of the fishery, it is curious how, in all its particulars (except that of the charmers) it agrees with the arrangements of the pearl-fishery at La Paz, on the coast of Lower California. I have visited that fishery, and inquired into its management. The merchants fit out the boats and pay the gangs of drivers (*buzos*); the shells are brought up in the same way as described by Marco Polo. The heap each day is divided into three parts—one for the State (estado), one for the Church (The Virgin), one for the chief merchant (armador), or sometimes, when the divers do not receive pay, they have a proportion of the last heap for themselves. The sharks which abound at La Paz can be seen swimming in the neighbourhood (so clear is the water under a cloudless and rainless sky), but the divers fear only one kind, which they call the *Tintero* (*the tiger shark*). They dive just as Marco Polo describes, and I may add that I never found one of them (experts though they were) remain down more than 58 seconds.

[34] Laṅkâ is sometimes spoken of as a city, sometimes as a mountain, and at other times applied to the whole island. Moreover, it is sometimes distinguished from Ceylon, and described as on the same meridian as Ujjayinî. The mountain is spoken of as three-peaked (*trikûṭa*) in the *Râmâyaṇa*. It was the abode of Râvaṇa.

[35] The *Laṅkâvatâra Sûtra* or the *Saddharma Laṅkâvatâra Sûtra* belongs to the later development and is of a mystical character. It refers everything to "the heart," which is simply the all-pervading *âtman*. There are three translations of the *sûtra* in China; see B. Nanjio, *Catalogue*, 175, 176, 177. The title of 176, the "entering-Laṅkâ-sûtra," would almost justify us in considering this *sûtra* as belongiug to Vaishṇavism. Bodhidharma, who arrived in China, A.D. 526, from South India, attached his faith to the teaching of this *sûtra*; it was therefore composed before his time. The earliest translation in China (No. 175) dates from A.D. 443, but this is

thousands of li, we arrive at the island of Narakira (Na-lo-ki-lo). The people of this island[36] are small of stature, about three feet high; their bodies are those of men, but they have the beaks of birds; they grow no grain, but live only on cocoa-nuts.

Crossing the sea westward from this island several thousands of li, on the eastern cliff of a solitary island is a stone figure of Buddha more than 100 feet high. It is sitting facing the east. In the head-ornament (*ushṇîsha*) is a stone called *Yueh-ngai-chu* (Chandrakânta). When the moon begins to wane, water immediately runs down from this in a stream along the sides of the mountain, and along the ravines of the precipices.[37]

At one time there was a band of merchants who were driven by the winds and waves during a storm, till they reached this solitary island. The sea-water being salt, they were unable to drink it, and were parched with thirst for a long time. But now on the fifteenth day, when the moon was full, from the head of the image water began to trickle forth, and they obtained deliverance. They all thought that a miracle had been wrought, and were affected with a profound faith; they

incomplete; the next (No. 176) dates from A.D. 513; the third from A.D. 700. The following quotation from Csoma Korösi is found in Spence Hardy's *Manual of Buddhism*, p. 356. "The second treatise or *sûtra* in the fifth volume of the *Mdo* is entitled in Sanskrit *Ârya Laṅkâvatâra mahâyâna Sûtra*, a venerable *sûtra* of high principles (or speculation) on the visiting of Lankâ. This was delivered at the request of the lord of Lankâ by Shâkya, when he was in the city of Lanâkâ on the top of the Malaya mountain, on the sea-shore, together with many priests and Bôdhisattvas." It is stated by Hodgson that the *Laṅkâvatâra* is regarded in Nepal as the fourth *dharma*; "it consists of 3000 slocas, and states that Râvaṇa, lord of Lankâ, having gone to the Malayagiri mountain, there heard the history of the Buddhas from Śakya Sinha, and obtained Beddhynàna" (*ibid.*) Laṅkâgiri, then, is probably the same as Mount Potaraka spoken of at the end of the tenth book.

[36] Perhaps the Maldive Islands; but see Yule, *Marco Polo*, ii. 249. Nârikera means *cocoa-nut*.

[37] Julien translates, "when the moon is about to reflect its light from this jewel (*d'y reflichir sa lumière*); " but the literal rendering is, "when the moon is about to turn back its light," that is, "to wane."

determined then to delay on the island. Some days having elapsed, as soon as the moon began to be hidden behind the high steeps, the water did not flow out. Then the merchant-chief said, "It cannot have been specially on our account that the water ran down. I have heard that there is a pearl 'loved by the moon,' when the moon's rays shine full on it, then the water begins to flow from it. The gem on the top of the statue of Buddha must be one of this sort." Then having climbed the mountain to examine the case, they saw that it was a Chandrakânta pearl in the head-ornament of the figure. This is the origin of the story as it was told by those men.

Crossing the sea many thousand li to the west of this country, we come to a large island renowned for its precious stones (*or* Mahâratnadvîpa); it is not inhabited, except by spirits. Seen from a distance on a calm night, a light seems to shine from mountains and valleys. Merchants going there are much surprised to find nothing can be procured.

Leaving the country of Ta-lo-pi-ch'a (Drâviḍa) and travelling northwards,[38] we enter a forest wild, in which are a succession of deserted towns, or rather little villages.[39] Brigands, in concert together, wound and capture (or delay) travellers. After going 2000 li or so we come to Kong-kin-na-pu-lo (Koṅkanâpura).[40]

KONG-KIN-NA-PU-LO (KOṄKANÂPURA).

This country is about 5000 li in circuit. The capital is

[38] Both General Cunningham and Mr. Fergusson give the direction north-west. This is a mistake (*Anc. Geog.*, p. 552; *J. R. A. S.*, vi. 266); but Hwui-lih has north-west. He moreover says that the pilgrim *returned* to the north-west. If we adopt the reading *north*, then the route would be a return one. The origin, as it seems, of the error in direction must be traced to M. V. de St. Martin (*Mémoire*, p. 400), who seems to adopt Hwui-lih's text as his guide.

[39] The passage may also be translated "passing through (or by) a deserted town and many little villages."

[40] Hwui-lih gives Kin-na-pu-lo, although in Julien we find Kong-kin-na-pu-lo. It may be an error in the text. In the passage before us

3000 li or so round. The land is rich and fertile; it is regularly cultivated, and produces large crops. The climate is hot; the disposition of the people ardent and quick. Their complexion is black, and their manners fierce and uncultivated. They love learning, and esteem virtue and talent. There are about 100 *saṅghârâmas*, with some 10,000 priests (*followers*). They study both the Great and the Little Vehicle. They also highly reverence the Dêvas, and there are several hundred temples in which many sectaries dwell together.

By the side of the royal palace is a great *saṅghârâma* with some 300 priests, who are all men of distinction. This convent has a great *vihâra*, a hundred feet and more in height. In it is a precious tiara belonging to Sarvârthasiddha (Yih-tsai-i-sh'ing) the prince. It is somewhat less than two feet in height, and is ornamented with gems and precious stones. It is kept in a jewelled casket. On fast-days it is brought out and placed on a high throne. They offer to it flowers and incense, on which occasions it is lit up with radiance.

By the side of the city is a great *saṅghârâma* in which is a *vihâra* about 50 feet high. In this is a figure of Maitrêya Bôdhisattva carved out of sandal-wood. It is about ten feet high. This also on fast-days reflects a bright light. It is the work of the Arhat Wen-'rh-pih-i (Śrutaviṁśatikôṭi).[41]

the country is Kong-kin-na-pu-lo, which is restored by Julien to Koṅkaṇâpura. It is stated that this country is in Southern India. There is no agreement as to the site of the capital. V. de St. Martin takes the pilgrim north-west to Vânavâsi (*Mémoire*, p. 401). General Cunningham thinks that Anagundi on the northern bank of the Tûṅgabhadrâ river is the place indicated (*Anc. Geog.*, p. 552), whilst Mr. Fergusson would take the pilgrim from Nâgapaṭṭaṇ to the centre of the Maisûr plateau somewhere east of Bednore (*J. R. A. S.*, N.S., vol. vi. p. 267). Assuming, however, that his route was north, and that he was returning towards the neighbourhood of Chânda, we should have to look for the capital of Kong-kin-na near Golkonda.

[41] For some reference to this person see *ante*, p. 187, n. 3. It seems likely that the allusion in the text is to Soṇa Kutikaṇṇa, as he was a disciple of Kâtyâyana, who dwelt in Southern India (*S. B. E.*, xvii. p. 32).

To the north of the city not far is a forest of *Tâla* trees about 30 li round. The leaves (*of this tree*) are long and broad, their colour shining and glistening. In all the countries of India these leaves are everywhere used for writing on. In the forest is a *stûpa*. Here the four former Buddhas sat down and walked for exercise, and traces of them still remain. Beside this is a *stûpa* containing the bequeathed relics of the Arhat Śrutaviṁśatikôṭi.

Not far to the east of the city is a *stûpa* which has sunk down into the ground from its foundations, but is still about thirty feet high. The old tradition says, In this *stûpa* is a relic of Tathâgata, and on religious days (*holy days*) it exhibits a miraculous light. In old days, when Tathâgata was in the world, he preached in this place, and exhibited his miraculous powers and converted a multitude of men.

Not far to the south-west of the city is a *stûpa* about a hundred feet high, which was built by Aśôka-râja. Here the Arhat Śrutaviṁśatikôṭi exhibited great miraculous powers and converted a great many people. By the side of it is a *saṅghârâma*, of which only the foundations remain. This was built by the fore-named Arhat.

From this going north-west, we enter a great forest wild, where savage beasts and bands of robbers inflict injury on travellers. Going thus 2400 or 2500 li, we come to the country of Mo-ho-la-ch'a (Mahârâshṭra).[42]

MO-HO-LA-CH'A (MAHÂRÂSHṬRA).

This country is about 5000 li in circuit. The capital[43] borders on the west on a great river. It is about 30 li

[42] "The great kingdom;" the country of the Marâṭhas.

[43] There have been various surmises as to the name of this capital. M. V. de St. Martin names Devagiri or Daulatâbâd, but this is not on a river. General Cunningham thinks Kalyâṇ or Kalyâṇî is the place intended, to the west of which flows the Kailâsâ river; but this is due south of Bharoch (the next station) instead of east. Mr. Fergusson names Toka, Phulthamba, or Paitan. However, the distance and direction from the capital of Koṅkaṇâpura is about 400 miles N.W. This seems to bring us near the river Tapti, or perhaps the Ghirnâ river.

round. The soil is rich and fertile; it is regularly cultivated and very productive. The climate is hot; the disposition of the people is honest and simple; they are tall of stature, and of a stern, vindictive character. To their benefactors they are grateful; to their enemies relentless. If they are insulted, they will risk their life to avenge themselves. If they are asked to help one in distress, they will forget themselves in their haste to render assistance. If they are going to seek revenge, they first give their enemy warning; then, each being armed, they attack each other with lances (*spears*). When one turns to flee, the other pursues him, but they do not kill a man down (*a person who submits*). If a general loses a battle, they do not inflict punishment, but present him with woman's clothes, and so he is driven to seek death for himself. The country provides for a band of champions to the number of several hundred. Each time they are about to engage in conflict they intoxicate themselves with wine, and then one man with lance in hand will meet ten thousand and challenge them in fight. If one of these champions meets a man and kills him, the laws of the country do not punish him. Every time they go forth they beat drums before them. Moreover, they inebriate many hundred heads of elephants, and, taking them out to fight, they themselves first drink their wine, and then rushing forward in mass, they trample everything down, so that no enemy can stand before them.

The king, in consequence of his possessing these men and elephants, treats his neighbours with contempt. He is of the Kshattriya caste, and his name is Pulakêśi (Pu-lo-ki-she). His plans and undertakings are wide-spread, and his beneficent actions are felt over a great distance. His subjects obey him with perfect submission. At the present time Śîlâditya[44] Mahârâja has conquered the nations from east to west, and carried his arms to remote districts, but the people of this country alone have not

[44] That is, Śîlâditya of Kanauj (vol. i. p. 210 ss.)

submitted to him. He has gathered troops from the five Indies, and summoned the best leaders from all countries, and himself gone at the head of his army to punish and subdue these people, but he has not yet conquered their troops.

So much for their habits. The men are fond of learning, and study both heretical and orthodox (*books*). There are about 100 *saṅghârâmas*, with 5000 or so priests. They practise both the Great and Small Vehicle. There are about 100 Dêva temples, in which very many heretics of different persuasions dwell.

Within and without the capital are five *stûpas* to mark the spots where the four past Buddhas walked and sat. They were built by Aśôka-râja. There are, besides these, other *stûpas* made of brick or stone, so many that it would be difficult to name them all.

Not far to the south of the city is a *saṅghârâma* in which is a stone image of Kwan-tsz'-tsai Bôdhisattva. Its spiritual powers extend (*far and wide*), so that many of those who have secretly prayed to it have obtained their wishes.

On the eastern frontier of the country is a great mountain with towering crags and a continuous stretch of piled-up rocks and scarped precipice. In this there is a *saṅghârâma* constructed, in a dark valley. Its lofty halls and deep side-aisles stretch through the (*or* open into the) face of the rocks. Storey above storey they are backed by the crag and face the valley (*watercourse*).[45]

This convent was built by the Arhat Âchâra (O-che-lo).[46] This Arhat was a man of Western India. His

[45] This must refer to the famous Bauddha rock-temples at Ajaṇṭâ, in the Indhyâdri range of hills, cut in the lofty and almost perpendicular rocks that hem in a wild secluded glen. See Fergusson and Burgess, *Cave Temples*, pp. 280–347; *Arch. Sur. West. Ind. Reports*, vol. iv. pp. 43–59.

[46] In the inscription on the Chaitya cave, No. xxvi., at Ajaṇṭâ, we read that "The ascetic Sthavira Achala, who glorified the faith and was grateful, caused to be built a mountain dwelling (*śailagṛha*) for the Teacher, though his desires were fulfilled" (*Arch. Sur. West Ind. Reports*, vol. iv. p. 135). This apparently decides the name of the Arhat mentioned here. But as the

mother having died, he looked to see in what condition she was re-born. He saw that she had received a woman's body in this kingdom. The Arhat accordingly came here with a view to convert her, according to her capabilities of receiving the truth. Having entered a village to beg food, he came to the house where his mother had been born. A young girl came forth with food to give him. At this moment the milk came from her breasts and trickled down. Her friends having seen this considered it an unlucky sign, but the Arhat recounted the history of her birth. The girl thus attained the holy fruit (*of Arhatship*). The Arhat, moved with gratitude[47] for her who had borne and cherished him, and remembering the end of such (*good*) works, from a desire to requite her, built this *saṅghârâma*. The great *vihâra* of the convent is about 100 feet or so in height; in the middle is a stone figure of Buddha about 70 feet or so high. Above it is a stone canopy of seven stages, towering upwards apparently without support. The space between each canopy[48] is about three feet. According to the old report, this is held in its place by the force of the vow of the Arhat. They also say it is by the force of his miraculous powers; others say by the virtue of some magical compound; but no trustworthy account has yet explained the reason of the wonder. On the four sides of the *vihâra*, on the stone walls, are painted[49] different scenes in the life of Tathâgata's preparatory life as a Bôdhisattva: the

Chinese translation of the name is *So hing* (he who does, or, the doer), we retain the equivalent Âchâra.

[47] Compare the words of the inscription given in the preceding note, "who glorified the faith and was grateful."

[48] See the drawings of Cave xix. and of the dâgaba in it, *Buddhist Cave Temples* (*Arch. Sur. W. Ind. Rep.*, vol. iv., pl. xxx., xxxi.; *Cave Temples*, pl. xxxvi., xxxvii. The measurements given "by report" are vastly exaggerated, as such matters very often are in India. But *possibly* there may have been a structural building against the face of the rock, with a dâgaba of larger dimensions, though by no means of the size indicated in the text. It is more probable, however, that the report is only an exaggerated account of the rock-cut chaityas. Hiuen Tsiang does not appear to have visited them personally.

[49] In mosaic, "carved and inlaid" (*teou low*).

wondrous signs of good fortune which attended his acquirement of the holy fruit (*of a Buddha*), and the spiritual manifestations accompanying his *Nirvâṇa*. These scenes have been cut out with the greatest accuracy and fineness.[50] On the outside of the gate of the *saṅghârâma*, on the north and south side, at the right hand and the left, there is a stone elephant.[51] The common report says that sometimes these elephants utter a great cry and the earth shakes throughout. In old days Jina (*or* Channa) Bôdhisattva[52] often stopped in this *saṅghârâma*.

Going from this 1000 li or so to the west,[53] and crossing the Nai-mo-to (Narmadâ) river, we arrive at the kingdom of Po-lu-kie-che-po (Bharukachheva; Barygaza or Bharôch).[54]

PO-LU-KIE-CH'E-P'O (BHARUKACHHA).

This kingdom is 2400 or 2500 li in circuit. Its capital is 20 li round. The soil is impregnated with salt. Trees and shrubs are scarce and scattered. They boil the sea-water to get the salt, and their sole profit is from the sea. The climate is warm. The air is always agitated with gusts of wind. Their ways are cold and indifferent; the disposition of the people crooked and perverse. They do not cultivate study, and are wedded to error and true

[50] This must refer to the famous Ajaṇṭâ frescoes.

[51] This seems to refer to two elephants in *alto rilievo* that were sculptured on the rock in front of Cave xv., but which are now scarcely recognisable. See Fergusson and Burgess, *Cave Temples*, p. 306.

[52] *Jour. R. As. Soc.*, vol. xx. p. 208.

[53] Hwui-lih gives north-west. M. Julien has translated it north-east, by mistake (*Vie*, &c., p. 203).

[54] Bharôch appears in a Pâli inscription at Junnar (*Arch. Sur. West. Ind. Rep.*, vol. iv. p. 96) under the form Bhârukachha; in Sanskrit it is Bharukachchha (*Bṛih. Samh.*, v. 40, xiv. 11, xvi. 6; Vassilief, p. 45) and Bhṛigukachcha (*Bhâg. Pur.*, viii. 18, 21; *As. Res.*, vol. ix. p. 104; inscrip. in *J. Amer. Or. Soc.*, vol. vii. p. 33) or Bhṛigukshêtra—from the locality being the traditional residence of the sage Bhṛigu-ṛishi. The Bhârgava Brâhmaṇs of Bharôch are the representatives of an early colony of the school of Bhṛigu. Bhârukachha is represented by the Greek Βαρύγαζα ἐμπόριον of Ptolemy (lib. vii. c. 1, 62) and of the author of the *Periplus Mar. Eryth.* (s. 42, &c.); Strabo (lib. xv. c. 1, 73) has Βαργόση. See Lassen, *I. A.*, vol. i. pp. 113, 136. It was from Bharôch the Sramaṇa came who burnt himself at Athens.

doctrine alike. There are some ten *saṅghârâmas*, with about 300 believers. They adhere to the Great Vehicle and the Sthavira school. There are also about ten Dêva temples, in which sectaries of various kinds congregate.

Going from this[55] north-west about 2000 li, we come to the country of Mo-la-po (Mâlava).[56]

Mo-la-p'o (Mâlava).

This country is about 6000 li in circuit. The capital is some 30 li round. It is defended (*or* supported) by the Mahî river on the south and east.[57] The soil is rich and fertile, and produces abundant harvests. Shrubs and trees are numerous and flourishing. Flowers and fruit are met with in great quantities. The soil is suitable in an especial manner for winter wheat. They mostly eat biscuits and (*or*, made of) parched corn-flour. The disposition of the men is virtuous and docile, and they are in general of remarkable intelligence. Their language is elegant and clear, and their learning is wide and profound.

Two countries in India, on the borders, are remarkable for the great learning of the people, viz., Mâlava on the south-west, and Magadha on the north-east. In this they esteem virtue and respect politeness (*humanity*). They are of an intelligent mind and exceedingly studious; nevertheless the men of this country are given to heretical

[55] The geography of this part of the pilgrim's route is involved in obscurities. I can only therefore offer some remarks on the text. In Hwui-lih the symbol used is *chi*, not *hing*, from which it might have been gathered that Hiuen Tsiang did not himself visit this country, or at least on this occasion. But in the text the symbol *hing* is used, so that no weight can be given to this supposition.

[56] If this country be Mâlava, it lies north-east from Bharôch. But, on the other hand, it does not follow that the route was a direct one. The pilgrim and his companions from Ceylon may have travelled east towards the head waters of the Mahî river, and then north-west. It is said in a note to be the same as the southern *Lo-lo* (Lâra) country.

[57] The symbol *ku* implies that the capital was "held by" (either defended or supported by) the Mahî river on the south-east, or on the south and east. This would seem to take us to the neighbourhood of Dongarpúr (*Elphinstone's map*). Cunningham considers Dhâranagara to be intended, in which V. de St Martin agrees.

belief as well as the true faith, and so live together. There are about 100 *saṅghârâmas* in which some 2000 priests dwell.[58] They study the Little Vehicle, and belong to the Sammatîya school. There are 100 Dêva temples of different kinds. The heretics are very numerous, but principally the Pâśupatas (*the cinder-covering heretics*).

The records of the country state: Sixty years before this [59] flourished Śîlâditya, a man of eminent wisdom and great learning; his skill in literature was profound. He cherished and protected the four kinds of creatures,[60] and deeply respected the three treasures.[61] From the time of his birth to his last hour, his face never crimsoned with anger, nor did his hands ever injure a living thing. His elephants and horses drank water that had been strained, after which he gave it them, lest any creature living in the water should be injured. Such were his love and humanity. During the fifty years and more of his reign, the wild beasts became familiar with men, and the people did not injure or slay them. By the side of his palace he built a *vihâra*. He exhausted the skill of the artists, and used every kind of ornament in decorating it. In it he put images of the seven Buddhas,[62] Lords of the World. Every year he convoked an assembly called *Môksha mahâparishad*, and summoned the priests of the four quarters. He offered them "the four things" in religious charity; he also gave them sets of three garments used in their religious services, and also bestowed on them the seven precious substances and jewels in wonderful variety. This meri-

[58] This can hardly refer to Ujjain, therefore, because we are told subsequently that the convents there were in ruins, and only about 300 priests in them. It is curious, however, that the circuit of this capital, thirty li (Julien has *twenty* li, by mistake), and that of Ujjain are the same.

[59] See *ante*, book ii. note 91.

[60] Viviparous, oviparous, born from spawn, or by transformation (*fă*) [*water-insects*, and so on].

[61] Buddha, dharma, saṅgha.

[62] For the seven Buddhas consult Eitel, *Handbook*, s. v. *Sapta Buddha*.

torious custom has continued in practice without interruption till now.

To the north-west of the capital about 200 li, we come to the town of the Brâhmaṇs.[63] By the side of it is a hollow ditch; into this the winter and summer streams flow continually, but though through decades of days the water runs into the hollow, yet it never seems to increase in quantity. By the side of it again is a little *stûpa*. The old traditions of the country say: Formerly a Brâhmaṇ of an exceedingly haughty mind [64] fell alive into this pit and went down to hell. In old days there was a Brâhmaṇ born in this town, who was acquainted with all things, and of learning beyond all the eminent men of his time. He had penetrated the secrets and dark sayings of books sacred and profane. He was acquainted with the calculations of astronomy as if they were in his hand; his fame was wide-spread and his behaviour without blemish. The king very highly esteemed him, and the people of the country made much of him. He had some 1000 disciples, who appreciated his doctrine and respected his character. He constantly said of himself, "I am come into the world for the purpose of publishing abroad the holy doctrine and to guide the people. Among the former sages, or those who have arrived at wisdom after them, there is none to compare with me. Mahêśvaradêva, Vâsudêva, Nârâyaṇadêva, Buddha-lôkanâtha, men everywhere worship these, and publish abroad their doctrine, represent them in their effigies, and pay them worship and honour. But now I am greater than they in character, and my fame exceeds that of all living. Why should they then be so notorious, for they have done no wonderful thing."

[63] This may be Brâhmaṇapura; there is a city of the Brâhmaṇs named by Arrian (*Exped. Alex.*, vi. 7) and by Diodorus, called by him Harmatelia (vii. 465). See also Cunningham, *Anc. Geog.*, pp. 267, 268. But the town named in the text cannot be near Harmatelia.

[64] Or it may be a proper name, "the great-proud Brâhmaṇ."

Accordingly, he made out of red sandal-wood figures of Mahêśvaradêva, Vâsudêva, Nârâyaṇadêva, Buddhalôkanâtha, and placed them as feet to his chair, and wherever he went as a rule he took this chair with him, showing his pride and self-conceit.

Now at this time there was in Western India a Bhikshu, Bhadraruchi (Po-to-lo-liu-chi) by name; he had thoroughly exhausted the *Hêtuvidyâ* (*Śâstra*) and deeply investigated the sense of different discourses (*treatises*).[65] He was of excellent repute, and the perfume of his exceeding goodness (*morality*) spread in every direction. He had few desires and was contented with his lot, seeking nothing in the world. Hearing (*of the Brâhmaṇ*) he sighed and said, "Alas! how sad. This age (*time*) has no (*one worthy to be called a*) man; and so it permits that foolish master to dare to act as he does in defiance of virtue."

On this, he took his staff, and travelling afar, he came to this country. Whilst dwelling therein his mind was made up and he acquainted the king with it. The king, seeing his dirty clothes, conceived no reverence for him; but, in consideration of his high purpose, he forced himself to give him honour (*to treat him with respect*), and so he arranged the chair of discussion and called the Brâhmaṇ. The Brâhmaṇ hearing it smiled and said, "What man is this who has dared to conceive such an idea (*to cherish this determination*)."

His disciples having come together, and many (*hundred*) thousands of listeners being arranged before and behind the discussion-arena to attend as hearers, then Bhadraruchi, with his ancient robes and tattered clothes, arranging some grass on the ground, sat down. Then the Brâhmaṇ, sitting on his chair which he carried with him, began to revile the true law and to praise the teaching of the heretical schools.

The Bhikshu, with a clear distinction, like the running

[65] Or, it may possibly be, "different systems."

of water, encircled his arguments in order. Then the Brâhmaṇ after a while yielded, and confessed himself conquered.

The king replying said, "For a long time you have assumed a false reputation; you have deceived the sovereign and affected the multitude with delusion. Our old rescripts say, 'He who is defeated in discussion ought to suffer death.'" Then he prepared to have a heated plate of iron to make him sit thereon; the Brâhmaṇ thereupon, overpowered by fear, fell down to entreat pardon (*deliverance*).

Then Bhadraruchi, pitying the Brâhmaṇ, came and requested the king, saying, "Mahârâja! your virtue extends far and wide; the sound of your praises resounds through the public ways. Then let your goodness extend even to protect this man: give not way to a cruel design. Pass over his want of success and let him go his way." Then the king ordered him to be placed on an ass and to be proclaimed through all the towns and villages (*as an impostor*).

The Brâhmaṇ, nettled by his defeat, was so affected that he vomited blood. The Bhikshu having heard of it, went to condole with him, and said, "Your learning embraces subjects religious and profane; your renown is spread through all parts; in questions of distinction, or the contrary, success or defeat must be borne; but after all, what is there of reality in fame?" The Brâhmaṇ, filled with rage, roundly abused the Bhikshu, calumniated the system of the Great Vehicle, and treated with contumely the holy ones who had gone before; but the sound of his words had scarcely been lost before the earth opened and swallowed him up alive; and this is the origin of the traces still left in the ditch.

Going south-west we come to a bay of the sea,[66] then

[66] Literally, the passage runs, "From this, south-west, we enter a sea-blending, or a confluence of two seas." I have translated it "bay," because it is sometimes used so; it probably refers to the gulf of Kachh. Hwui-lih does not mention this gulf, but takes us away from the

going 2400 or 2500 li north-west we come to the kingdom of 'O-ch'a-li (Aṭali).

'O-CH'A-LI (AṬALI).[67]

This country is about 6000 li in circuit; the capital of the country is about 20 li or so in circnit. The population is dense; the quality of gems and precious substances stored up is very great; the produce of the land is sufficient for all purposes, yet commerce is their principal occupation. The soil is salt and sandy, the fruits and flowers are not plentiful. The country produces the *hu-tsiau* tree. The leaves of this tree are like those of the Sz'chuen pepper (*Shuh tsiau*); it also produces the *hiun-lu* perfume tree, the leaf of which is like the *thang-li*.[68] The climate is warm, windy, and dusty. The disposition of the people is cold and indifferent. They esteem riches and despise virtue. Respecting their letters, language, and the manners and figures of the people, these are much the same as in the conntry of Mâlava. The greater part of the people have no faith in the virtue of religious merit; as to those who do believe, they worship principally the spirits of heaven, and their temples are some thousand in number, in which sectaries of different characters congregate.

Going north-west from the country of Mâlava, after passing over 300 li[69] or so, we come to the country of K'ie-ch'a (Kachha).

"city of the Brâhmaṇs" the same distance as in the text to 'O-ch'a-li.

[67] 'O-ch'a-li appears to be far north of Kachh. May it not have been Uchh or Bâhwalpur? There is a town called Aṭâri in the neighbourhood of Multân (Cunningham, *Anc. Geog.*, p. 228); but it is difficult to know what could have taken the pilgrim there. This place is identified by Cunningham with the city of the Brâhmaṇs, taken by Alexander the Great (*l. c.*)

[68] Can this be the *Sâlai* from which *Kimdura*, Gujarâti *Kindru* or *Sâlainodhûpa*, Indian gum, olibanum, is obtained? This tree (*Boswellia thurifera*, *serrata* and *glabra*) is found in Oudh, Khandês, and Kâthiâwâḍ. *Guggula* (bdellium), the gum resin of *Balsamodenron roxburghii*, *pubescens*, and *mukul*, is also produced in Kachh and Sindh.

[69] In Hwui-lih, the distance is "three days'" journey.

K'IE-CH'A (KACHHA).[70]

This country is 3000 li or so in circuit, the capital about 20 li. The population is dense. The establishments wealthy. There is no king (*great ruler*) amongst them; the country is an appanage of Mâlava, and the climate, products of the soil, and manners of the people are very similar in both countries. There are some ten *saṅghârâmas*, with about 1000 priests, who study alike the Great and the Little Vehicle. There are also several tens of Dêva temples with very many unbelievers (*sectaries*).

From this going north[71] 1000 li or so, we come to Fa-la-pi (Valabhî).

FA-LA-PI (VALABHÎ).

This country is 6000 li or so in circuit, the capital about 30. The character of the soil, the climate, and manners of the people are like those of the kingdom of Mâlava. The population is very dense; the establishments rich. There are some hundred houses (*families*) or so, who possess a hundred lâkhs. The rare and valuable products of distant regions are here stored in great quantities. There are some hundred *saṅghârâmas*, with about 6000 priests. Most of them study the Little Vehicle,[72] according to the Sammatîya school. There

[70] The distance is to be reckoned from the kingdom or country of Mâlava, but the place is not named. General Cunningham proposes to read 1300 li from Dhâr to Khêḍa; this last place is a large town of Gujarât, situated between Ahmadâbâd and Khambay, and would be in its Sanskrit form the same as Kheḍa, which again is the equivalent of the Chinese Kie-ch'a. But Kie-ch'a, although it might be correctly restored to Kheḍa, is the name of a country. The distance, also, being "three days," in Hwui-lih, seems to confirm the 300 li in the text. We must therefore retain the restoration of Kachha.

[71] Although we should expect the direction to be south from Kachh, the reading is north, both in the text and in Hwui-lih; wherever the Valabhî of Hiuen Tsiang was situated, it is said to have been "the kingdom of the Northern Lâra (Lo-lo) people." (Note in the Chinese text).

[72] In a copper-plate deed of Guhasêna of Valabhî, he says, "In order to obtain for my parents and for myself benefits in this life and the next, I have granted, by liba-

are several hundred Dêva temples with very many sectaries of different sorts.

When Tathâgata lived in the world, he often travelled through this country. Hence Aśôka-râja raised monuments or built *stûpas* in all those places where Buddha rested. Scattered among these are spots where the three past Buddhas sat down, or walked, or preached the law. The present king is of the Kshattriya caste, as they all are. He is the nephew of Śilâditya-râja of Mâlava, and son-in-law of the son of Silâditya, the present king of Kanyâkubja. His name is Dhruvapaṭa (T'u-lu-h'o-po-tu).[73] He is of a lively and hasty disposition, his wisdom and statecraft are shallow. Quite recently he has attached himself sincerely to faith in the three "precious ones." Yearly he summons a great assembly, and for seven days gives away most valuable gems, exquisite meats, and on the priests he bestows in charity the three garments and medicaments, or their equivalent in value, and precious articles made of rare and costly gems of the seven sorts. Having given these in charity, he redeems them at twice their price. He esteems virtue (*or the virtuous*) and honours the good; he reverences those who are noted for their wisdom.[74] The great priests

tion of water, to the community of the reverend Śâkya Bhikshus belonging to the eighteen schools (*nikâyâ*) who have come from various directions to the great convent (*Mahâvihâra*) of Duḍḍâ." *Ind. Ant.*, vol. iv. p. 175. This Duḍḍâ was the daughter of Dhruvasêna I's sister (*Ib.*, p. 106), and so a grand-daughter of Bhaṭârka, the founder of the Valabhî dynasty. In another copper-plate of Guhusêna, he makes a grant to "the foreign monks belonging to the eighteen schools, and living in the Abhyantarikâ vihâra built by the venerable Mimmâ, and situated close to the monastery of Bhaṭârka, presented to the Râjasthânîya Śura." *Ind. Ant.*, vol. v. p. 206; conf. Vassilief, *Le Bouddh.*, p. 63. *Arch. Sur. W. Ind. Reports*, vol. iii. p. 94. The "eighteen schools" here mentioned point to the Hînayâna doctrine.

[73] Dr. Buhler argues that this king was the same as Śilâditya VI., surnamed Dhrûbhaṭa, (which he supposes to stand for Dhruvabhata, "the constant warrior"), of whom we have a grant dated "Saṁ. 447" (*Ind. Ant.*, vol. vii. p. 80). General Cunningham adopts the same view (*A. S. Reports*, vol. ix. pp. 16, 18); but Burgess is disposed to regard this king as the Dhruvasêna II. of a Valabhî grant dated "Saṁ. 310" (*Arch. Sur. W. Ind.*, vol. ii. pp. 82, ff.); and Oldenberg, as possibly Dhêrabhata, the cousin of Dhruvasêna II. (*Ind. Ant.*, vol. x. p. 219).

[74] Or, he reverences religion and makes much of wisdom.

who come from distant regions he particularly honours and respects.

Not far from the city is a great *saṅghârâma* which was built by the Arhat Âchâra ('O-che-lo);[75] here the Bôdhisattvas Guṇamati and Sthiramati[76] (Kien-hwui) fixed their residences during their travels and composed treatises which have gained a high renown.

From this going north-west 700 li or so, we come to 'O-nan-to-pu-lo (Ânandapura).

'O-NAN-TO-PU-LO (ANANDAPURA).

This country is about 2000 li in circuit, the capital about 20. The population is dense; the establishments rich. There is no chief ruler, but it is an appanage of Mâlava.[77] The produce, climate, and literature and laws are the same as those of Mâlava. There are some ten *saṅgharamas* with less than 1000 priests; they study the Little Vehicle of the Sammatiya school. There are several tens of Dêva temples, and sectaries of different kinds frequent them.

Going west from Valabhî 500 li or so, we come to the country of Su-la-ch'a (Surâshṭra).

SU-LA-CH'A (SURASHṬRA).[78]

This country is 4000 li or so in circuit, the capital

[75] This is confirmed by a grant of Dharasêna II. of Valabhî, in which the Sanskrit name of the founder is given as Atharya (*Ind. Ant.*, vol. iv. p. 164 n.; vol. vi. p. 9). Julien has Âchâra; the Chinese translation *so-hing* requires this restoration.

[76] Sthiramati Sthavira was one of the famous disciples of Vasubandhu, the twenty-first patriarch, who wrote commentaries on all the works of his master. He is named in a grant of Dharasêna I. as the Âchâryya Bhadanta Sthiramati, who founded the *vihâra* of Śrî Bappapâda at Valabhî (*Ind. Ant.*, vol. vi. p. 9; Vassilief, p. 78; M. Muller's *India*, p. 305; B. Nanjio's *Cat. Budd. Trip.*, c. 372). Guṇamati was also a disciple of Vasubandhu. He had a famous disciple, Vasumitra (Pho-shu-mi), who wrote a commentary on Vasubandhu's *Abhidharmakôshai* (Bunyiu Nanjio's *Cat. Bud. Trip.*, cc. 375, 377; M. Muller, *India*, pp. 305, 309, 310, 632; Burnouf, *Introd.*, p. 505; Vassilief, p. 78).

[77] See *Ind. Ant.*, vol. vii.; *Ar. Sur. W. Ind.*, vol. ii. p. 83.

[78] Surâshṭra, or Surâṭha, or Soraṭh. As this district is in the Gujarât peninsula, it is difficult to under-

about 30 li. On the west the chief town borders on the Mahî river; the population is dense, and the various establishments (*families*) are rich. The country is dependent on Valabhî. The soil is impregnated with salt; flowers and fruit are rare. Although the climate is equable, yet there is no cessation of tempests. The manners of the people are careless and indifferent; their disposition light and frivolous. They do not love learning and are attached both to the true faith and also to heretical doctrine. There are some fifty *saṅghârâmas* in this kingdom, with about 3000 priests; they mostly belong to the Sthavira school of the Great Vehicle. There are a hundred or so Dêva temples, occupied by sectaries of various sorts. As this country is on the western sea route, the men all derive their livelihood from the sea and engage in commerce and exchange of commodities.

Not far from the city is a mountain called Yuh-chen-to (Ujjanta),[79] on the top of which is a *saṅghârâma*. The cells and galleries have mostly been excavated from the mountain-side. The mountain is covered with thick jungle and forest trees, whilst streams flow round its limits. Here saints and sages roam and rest, and Ṛishis endued with spiritual faculties congregate here and stay.

Going north from the country of Valabhî 1800 li or so, we come to the kingdom of Kiu-che-lo (Gurjjara).

KIU-CHE-LO (GURJJARA).

This country[80] is 5000 li or so in circuit, the capital,

stand how its chief town "on the west" borders on the Mahî river; perhaps it should be "on the east." But this part of the pilgrim's narrative seems to be carelessly written. Perhaps, as Fergusson supposes, the original documents had been lost in crossing the Indus at Attok (see Book xii.), and the details supplied from memory or notes. For remarks on localities see V. de St. Martin, *Mémoire*, p. 405; Cunningham, *Anc. Geog.*, p. 325.

[79] The old Prâkṛit name of Girnâra, close to Junâgaḍh in Kâthiâwâḍ; the Sanskrit form is Ujjayanta (*Mahâbh.*, iii. 8347 ff.) Lassen (*Ind. Alt.*, vol. i. p. 686 n.) misplaces it at or near Ajaṇṭâ. It is sacred to Nêminâtha, the twenty-second Jina, and Urjayata (Colebrooke, *Essays*, vol. ii. p. 212; *Arch. Sur. W. Ind. Rep.*, vol. ii. p. 129), and i also called Raivata.

[80] Prof. R. G. Bhâṇḍarkar suggests that Kukura, a district men-

which is called Pi-lo-mo-lo,[81] is 30 li or so round. The produce of the soil and the manners of the people resemble those of Surâshṭra. The population is dense; the establishments are rich and well supplied with materials (*wealth*). They mostly are unbelievers; a few are attached to the law of Buddha. There is one *saṅghârâma*, with about a hundred priests; they are attached to the teaching of the Little Vehicle and the school of the Sarvâstivâdas. There are several tens of Dêva temples, in which sectaries of various denominations dwell. The king is of the Kshattriya caste. He is just twenty years old; he is distinguished for wisdom, and he is courageous. He is a deep believer in the law of Buddha; and highly honours men of distinguished ability.

From this going south-east 2800 li or so, we come to the country of U-she-yen-na (Ujjayanî).

U-SHE-YEN-NA (UJJAYANÎ).

This country[82] is about 6000 li in circuit; the capital is some 30 li round. The produce and manners of the people are like those of the country of Surâshṭra. The population is dense and the establishments wealthy. There are several tens of convents, but they are mostly in ruins; some three or five are preserved. There are some 300 priests; they study the doctrines both of the Great and the Little Vehicle. There are several tens of Dêva temples, occupied by sectaries of various kinds.

tioned in an inscription of Pulumâyi at Nâsik, and in the Rudradâman inscription at Girnâra, might be Kiu-che-lo, but the Chinese syllables are against such an identification (*Trans. Int. Cong. Orient.*, 1874, p. 312; *Arch. Sur. W. Ind. Rep.*, vol. iv. p. 109, and vol. ii. pp. 129, 131. Gurjara is certainly the proper representative, and the district as well as the language extended into the southern parts of modern Râjputâna and Mâlwâ. See Lassen, *Ind. Alt.*, vol. i. p. 136; Colebrooke, *Essays*, vol. ii. p. 31 n.; *Râjatarang.*, v. 144 ff.

[81] Bâlmêr in Râjputâna (lat. 25° 48′ N., long. 71° 16′ E.) From this neighbourhood several of the clans in Kâthiâwâḍ say they originally came.

[82] Ujjayanî or Ujjayinî is properly the capital of Avanti in Mâlava, the capital of Tiastanes (Chashtana), the Ὀζήνη of Ptolemy lib. vii. c. i. 63) and the *Peripl. Mar. Æryth.* (c. xlviii.) Bohlen, *Alte Ind.*, vol. i. p. 94.

The king belongs to the Brâhmaṇ caste. He is well versed in heretical books, and believes not in the true law.

Not far from the city is a *stûpa;* this is the place where Aśôka-râja made the hell (*of punishment*).

Going north-east from this 1000 li or so, we come to the kingdom of Chi-ki-to.

CHI-KI-TO.

This country is about 4000 li in circuit; the capital is some 15 or 16 li round. The soil is celebrated for its fertility; it is regularly cultivated and yields abundant crops; it is specially adapted for beans and barley; it produces abundance of flowers and fruits. The climate is temperate; the people are naturally virtuous and docile; most of them believe in heretical doctrine, a few honour the law of Buddha. There are several tens of *saṅghârâmas* with few priests. There are about ten Dêva temples, which some thousand followers frequent. The king is of the Brâhmaṇ caste. He firmly believes in the (three) precious ones; he honours and rewards those who are distinguished for virtue. Very many learned men from distant countries congregate in this place.

Going from here north 900 li or so, we come to the kingdom of Mo-hi-shi-fa-lo-pu-lo (Mahêśvarapura).

MO-HI-SHI-FA-LO-PU-LO (MAHÊŚVARAPURA).

This kingdom is about 3000 li in circuit; the capital city is some 30 li round. The produce of the soil and the manners of the people are like those of the kingdom of Ujjayanî. They greatly esteem the heretics and do not reverence the law of Buddha. There are several tens of Dêva temples, and the sectaries principally belong to the Pâśupatas. The king is of the Brâhmaṇ caste; he places but little faith in the doctrine of Buddha.

From this, going in a backward direction to the country of Kiu-che-lo (Gurjjara) and then proceeding northward through wild deserts and dangerous defiles about 1900 li, crossing the great river Sin-tu, we come to the kingdom of Sin-tu (Sindh).

SIN-TU (SINDH).

This country is about 7000 li in circuit; the capital city, called P'i-shen-p'o-pu-lo,[88] is about 30 li round. The soil is favourable for the growth of cereals and produces abundance of wheat and millet. It also abounds in gold and silver and native copper. It is suitable for the breeding of oxen, sheep, camels, mules, and other kinds of beasts. The camels are small in size and have only one hump. They find here a great quantity of salt, which is red like cinnabar; also white salt, black salt and rock salt. In different places, both far and near, this salt is used for medicine. The disposition of the men is hard and impulsive; but they are honest and upright, They quarrel and are much given to contradiction. They study without aiming to excel; they have faith in the law of Buddha. There are several hundred *saṅghârâmas*, occupied by about 10,000 priests. They study the Little Vehicle according to the Sammatîya school. As a rule, they are indolent and given to indulgence and debauchery. Those who are very earnest as followers of the virtue of the sages live alone in desert places, dwelling far off in the mountains and the forests. There night and day they exert themselves in aiming after the acquiren ent of the holy fruit (*of Arhatship*). There are about thirty Dêva temples, in which sectaries of various kinds congregate.

The king is of the Śûdra (Shu-t'o-lo) caste. He is by nature honest and sincere, and he reverences the law of Buddha.

When Tathâgata was in the world, he frequently passed through this country, therefore Aśôka-râja has founded several tens of *stûpas* in places where the sacred traces of

[88] Vichavapura—Julien. Reinaud suggests Vasmapura or Balmapura and Minagara. See *Ind. Ant.*, vol. viii. p. 336 f.

his presence were found. Upagupta,[84] the great Arhat, sojourned very frequently in this kingdom, explaining the law and convincing and guiding men. The places where he stopped and the traces he left are all commemorated by the building of *saṅghârâmas* or the erection of *stûpas.* These buildings are seen everywhere; we can only speak of them briefly.

By the side of the river Sindh, along the flat marshy lowlands for some thousand li, there are several hundreds of thousands (*a very great many*) of families settled. They are of an unfeeling and hasty temper, and are given to bloodshed only. They give themselves exclusively to tending cattle, and from this derive their livelihood. They have no masters, and, whether men or women, have neither rich nor poor; they shave their heads and wear the *Kashâya* robes of Bhikshus, whom they resemble outwardly, whilst they engage themselves in the ordinary affairs of lay life. They hold to their narrow (*little*) views and attack the Great Vehicle.

The old reports state that formerly these people were extremely hasty (*impatient*), and only practised violence and cruelty. At this time there was an Arhat, who, pitying their perversity, and desiring to convert them, mounted in the air and came amongst them. He exhibited his miraculous powers and displayed his wonderful capabilities. Thus he led the people to believe and accept the doctrine, and gradually he taught them in words; all of them joyfully accepted his teaching and respectfully prayed him to direct them in their religious life. The Arhat perceiving that the hearts of the people had become submissive, delivered to them the three "Refuges" and restrained their cruel tendencies; they entirely gave up "taking life," they shaved their heads, and assumed the soiled robes of a Bhikshu, and obediently walked according to the doctrine of religion. Since then, generations have passed by and the changed times have weakened

[84] Bk. viii.; Burnouf, *Introd.*, pp. 118, 197, 378 f.

their virtue, but as for the rest, they retain their old customs. But though they wear the robes of religion, they live without any moral rules, and their sons and grandsons continue to live as worldly people, without any regard to their religious profession.

Going from this eastward 900 li or so, crossing the Sindh river and proceeding along the eastern bank, we come to the kingdom of Mu-lo-san-p'u-lu.

MU-LO-SAN-P'U-LU (MÛLASTHÂNAPURA).

This country [85] is about 4000 li in circuit; the capital town is some 30 li round. It is thickly populated. The establishments are wealthy. This country is in dependence on the kingdom of Chêka (Tse-kia). The soil is rich and fertile. The climate is soft and agreeable; the manners of the people are simple and honest; they love learning and honour the virtuous. The greater part sacrifice to the spirits; few believe in the law of Buddha. There are about ten *saṅghârâmas*, mostly in ruins; there are a few priests, who study indeed, but without any wish to excel. There are eight Dêva temples, in which sectaries of various classes dwell. There is a temple dedicated to the sun,[86] very magnificent and profusely decorated. The image of the Sun-dêva is cast in yellow gold and ornamented with rare gems. Its divine insight is mysteriously manifested and its spiritual power made plain to all. Women play their music, light their torches, offer their flowers and perfumes to honour it. This custom has been continued from the very first. The kings and high families of the five Indies never fail to make their offerings of gems and precious stones (*to this Dêva*). They have founded a house of mercy (*happiness*), in which they provide food, and drink, and medicines for the poor and sick, affording succour and sustenance. Men from all

[85] Mûlasthânapur or Multân (see Reinaud, *Mém. s. l. Inde*, p. 98).
[86] Aditya or Sûrya.

countries come here to offer up their prayers; there are always some thousands doing so. On the four sides of the temple are tanks with flowering groves where one can wander about without restraint.

From this going north-east 700 li or so, we come to the country of Po-fa-to.

PO-FA-TO (PARVATA).[87]

This country is 5000 li or so in circuit, its capital is about 20 li. It is thickly populated, and depends on the country of Chêka (Tse-kia). A great deal of dry-ground rice is here grown. The soil is also fit for beans and wheat. The climate is temperate, the disposition of the people honest and upright. They are naturally quick and hasty; their language is low and common. They are well versed in composition and literature. There are heretics and believers in common. There are some ten *saṅghârâmas* with about 1000 priests; they study both the Great and Little Vehicle. There are four *stûpas* built by Aśôka-râja. There are also some twenty Dêva temples frequented by sectaries of different sorts.

By the side of the chief town is a great *saṅghârâma* with about 100 priests in it; they study the teaching of the Great Vehicle. It was here that Jinaputra, a master of *śâstras*,[88] composed the *Yôgâchâryabhûmi Śâstrakârikâ;* here also Bhadraruchi and Guṇaprabha, masters of *śâstras*, embraced the religious life. This great *saṅghârâma* has been destroyed by fire, and is now waste and ruined.

Leaving the Sindh country, and going south-west 1500 or 1600 li, we come to the kingdom of 'O-tin-p'o-chi-lo (Atyanabakêla).

[87] Parvata is given by Pâṇini (iv. 2, 143) as the name of a country in the Panjâb under the group Takshaśilâdi (iv. 3, 93). *Ind. Ant.*, vol. i. p. 22.

[88] Jinaputra, in Chinese Tsui-shing-tszu; his work, the *Yü-chie-sh'-ti-lun-shih*, is a commentary on the *Yôgâchâryabhûmi Śâstra* (*Yü-chie-sh'-ti-lun*) of Maitrêya. Both works were translated into Chinese by Hiuen Tsiang.

'O-TIEN-P'O-CHI-LO.

This country is about 5000 li in circuit. The chief town is called Khie-tsi-shi-fa-lo, and is about 30 li round. It lies on the river Sindh, and borders on the ocean. The houses are richly ornamented, and mostly possess rare and costly substances. Lately there has been no ruler; it is under the protection of Sindh. The soil is low and damp and the ground is impregnated with salt. It is covered with wild shrubs, and is mostly waste land: it is little cultivated, yet it produces some sorts of grain, but principally beans and wheat, of which there is a great quantity. The climate is rather cold and subject to violent storms of wind. It is fit for raising oxen, sheep, camels, asses, and other kinds of beasts. The disposition of the people is violent and hasty. They have no love for learning. Their language differs slightly from that of Mid-India. The people are generally honest and sincere. They deeply reverence the three precious objects of worship. There are about eighty *saṅghârâmas* with some 5000 priests. They mostly study the Little Vehicle according to the Sammatîya school. There are ten Dêva temples, mostly occupied by heretics belonging to the Pâśupatas.

In the capital town is a temple of Ta-tsz'-tsai-tin (Mahêśvara Dêva). The temple is ornamented with rich sculptures, and the image of the Dêva is possessed of great spiritual powers. The Pâśupata heretics dwell in this temple. In old days Tathâgata often travelled through this country to preach the law and convert men, leading the multitude and benefiting the people. On this account Aśôka-râja built *stûpas* on the spots consecrated by the sacred traces, six in number.

Going west from this less than 2000 li, we come to the country of Long-kie-lo (Laṅgala).

LONG-KIE-LO (LAṄGALA).

This country[89] is several thousand li from east to west and from north to south. The capital is about 30 li round. It is named Su-nu-li-chi-fa-lo (Sûnurîśvara?).[90] The soil is rich and fertile, and yields abundant harvests. The climate and the manners of the people are like those of 'O-tin-p'o-chi-lo. The population is dense. It possesses abundance of precious gems and stones. It borders on the ocean. It is on the route to the kingdom of the western women.[91] It has no chief ruler. The people occupy a long valley, and are not dependent on one another. They are under the government of Persia. The letters are much the same as those of India: their language is a little different. There are believers and heretics living together amongst them. There are some hundred *saṅghârâmas*, and perhaps 6000 priests, who study the teaching of both the Little and Great Vehicle. There are several hundred Dêva temples. The heretics called Pâśupatas are exceedingly numerous. In the city is a temple to Mahêśvara-Dêva: it is richly adorned and sculptured. The Pâśupata heretics here offer their religious worship.

From this going north-west, we come to the kingdom of Po-la-sse (Persia).

PO-LA-SSE (PERSIA).

This kingdom[92] is several myriad of lis in circuit. Its chief town, called Su-la-sa-t'ang-na (Surasthâna), is about 40 li in circuit. The valleys are extensive, and so the climate differs in character, but in general it is warm.

[89] General Cunningham thinks this country may represent Lâkoriân or Lakûra, the name of a great ruined city which Masson found between Khozdâr and Kilât, about 2000 li to the north-west of Koṭesar in Kachh (*Anc. Geog. of India*, p. 311). The Chinese symbols might be restored to Longhir.

[90] Cunningham suggests Sambhurisvara as the restoration of this name (*ibid.*, loc. cit.)

[91] See p. 240, *ante*.

[92] This country does not belong to India (*Ch. Ed.*) Hiuen Tsiang did not visit it personally; he writes from report.

They draw the water up to irrigate the fields. The people are rich and affluent. The country produces gold, silver, copper, rock-crystal (*sphâṭika*), rare pearls, and various precious substances. Their artists know how to weave fine brocaded silks, woollen stuffs, carpets, and so on. They have many *shen* horses and camels. In commerce they use large silver pieces. They are by nature violent and impulsive, and in their behaviour they practise neither decorum nor justice. Their writing and their language are different from other countries. They care not for learning, but give themselves entirely to works of art. All that they make the neighbouring countries value very much. Their marriage-customs are merely promiscuous intercourse. When dead their corpses are mostly abandoned. In stature they are tall: they tie up their hair (*arrange their head-dress*) and go uncovered. Their robes are either of skin, or wool, or felt, or figured silk. Each family is subject to a tax of four pieces of silver per man. The Dêva temples are very numerous. Dinava[93] (Ti-na-po) is principally worshipped by the heretics. There are two or three *saṅghârâmas*, with several hundred priests, who principally study the teaching of the Little Vehicle according to the Sarvâstavâdin school. The *pâtra* of Śâkya Buddha is in this (*country*), in the king's palace.[94]

On the eastern frontiers of the country is the town of Ho-mo (Ormus?). The city inside is not great, but the external walls are in circuit about 60 li or so. The people who inhabit it are all very rich. To the north-west this country borders on the kingdom of Fo-lin,[95]

[93] Julien restores this name, doubtfully, to Dinabha. Dinava, or Dinapa, however, may be a contraction for Dinapa(ti), "the lord of the day," or "the sun."

[94] For the wanderings of the *pâtra* of Buddha, see Fa-hian, chap. xxxix. It is interesting to know that there were Buddhist temples and a community of priests in Persia at the time of Hiuen Tsiang. As they belonged to the school of the Little Vehicle, it is probable they had been established there from an early date.

[95] Fo-lin (πόλιν) is generally supposed to represent the Byzantine Empire.

which resembles the kingdom of Persia in point of soil, and manners, and customs; but they differ in point of language and appearance of the inhabitants. These also possess a quantity of valuable gems, and are very rich.

To the south-west of Fo-lin, in an island of the sea, is the kingdom of the western women:[96] here there are only women, with no men; they possess a large quantity of gems and precious stones, which they exchange in Fo-lin. Therefore the king of Fo-lin sends certain men to live with them for a time. If they should have male children, they are not allowed to bring them up.

On leaving the kingdom of O-tin-p'o-chi-lo, and going north 700 li or so, we come to the country of Pi-to-shi-lo.

PI-TO-SHI-LO (PITÂŚILÂ).

This kingdom is about 3000 li round; the capital is some 20 li in circuit. The population is dense. They have no chief ruler, but they depend on the country of Sin-tu. The soil is salt and sandy; the country is subject to a cold tempestuous wind. A great quantity of beans and wheat is grown. Flowers and fruits are scarce. The manners of the people are fierce and rough. Their language slightly differs from that of Mid-India. They do not love learning, but as far as they know they have a sincere faith. There are some fifty *saṅghârâmas* with about 3000 priests; they study the Little Vehicle according to the Sammatîya school. There are twenty Dêva temples, frequented mostly by the heretics called Pâśupatas.

To the north of the city 15 or 16 li, in the middle of a great forest, is a *stûpa* several hundred feet high, built by Aśôka-râja. It contains relics which from time

[96] For some references to the island or kingdom of the western women, see Marco Polo, chap. xxxi., and Colonel Yule's note (vol. ii. p. 339).

to time emit a bright light. It was here that Tathâgata, when in old time he was a Ṛishi, was subjected to the cruelty of the king.

Not far east from this is an old *saṅghârâma*. This was built by the great Arhat, the great Kâtyâyana. By the side of it are traces where the four Buddhas of the past age sat down and walked for exercise. They have erected a *stûpa* to denote the spot.

Going north-east from this 300 li or so, we come to the country of 'O-fan-ch'a.

'O-FAN-CH'A (AVANDA ?).

This kingdom is 2400 or 2500 li in circuit; the capital is about 20 li. There is no chief ruler, but the country is subject to Sin-tu. The soil is fit for the cultivation of grain, and abounds in beans and wheat; it produces but few flowers or fruits; the woods are thin. The climate is windy and cold; the disposition of the men is fierce and impulsive. Their language is simple and uncultivated. They do not value learning, but they are earnest and sincere believers in "the three gems." There are about twenty *saṅghârâmas*, with some 2000 priests; they mostly study the Little Vehicle according to the Sammatîya school. There are some five Dêva temples, frequented by the heretics called Pâśupatas.

To the north-east of the city, not a great distance, in the middle of a great bamboo forest is a *saṅghârâma* mostly in ruins. Here Tathâgata gave permission to the Bhikshus to wear *Kih-fu-to* (*boots*).[97] By the side of it is a *stûpa* built by Aśôka-râja. Although the foundations have sunk into the earth, yet the remains are some hundred feet high. In a *vihâra* by the side of the *stûpa* is a blue-stone standing figure of Buddha. On

[97] There are some remarks made about permission to wear boots or shoes with thick linings in the *Mahâvagga*, varga 13, § 6 (*S. B. E.*, vol. xvii. p. 35). It would seem from these records that this country of Avaṇḍa corresponded with Avanti.

sacred days (*fast-days*) it spreads abroad a divine light.

To the south 800 paces or so, in a forest, is a *stûpa* which was built by Aśôka-râja. Tathâgata, in time gone by, stopping here, finding it cold in the night, covered himself with his three garments: on the morning following he permitted the Bhikshus to wear wadded garments. In this wood is a place where Buddha walked for exercise. There are also a number of *stûpas* placed opposite one another, where the four Buddhas of the past age sat. In this *stûpa* are relics of Buddha's hair and nails. On holy days they emit a miraculous light.

Going from this north-east 900 li or so, we come to the country of Fa-la-na.

FA-LA-NA (VARANA).[98]

This kingdom is about 4000 li in circuit, and the chief town about 20 li. The population is dense. The kingdom is subject to Kapiśa. The chief portion of the country consists of mountains and forests. It is regularly cultivated. The climate is rather cold. The manners of the people are rough and fierce. They are persevering in their habits, but their purposes are low. Their language is somewhat like that of Mid-India. Some of them believe in Buddha, others not. They do not care about literature or the arts. There are some tens of *saṅghârâmas,* but they are in ruins. There are about 300 priests, who study the Great Vehicle. There are about five Dêva temples, frequented mostly by Pâśupata heretics.

Not far to the south of the city is an old *saṅghârâma.* Here Tathâgata in old days preached, exhibiting the profit and delight of his doctrine, and opening the mind

[98] Pâṇini has a country called Varṇu (iv. 2, 103; iv. 3, 93), from a river of the same name, in the group Suvâstavâdi; also in the group Kachchhâdi, in which Gândhâra also is included.

of his hearers. By the side of it are traces where the four past Buddhas sat down or walked for exercise. The common report says on the western frontier of this country is the kingdom of Ki-kiang-na (Kikaṇa?). The people live amid the great mountains and valleys in separate clans. They have no chief ruler. They breed an immense quantity of sheep and horses. The *shen* horses are of a large size, and the countries around breed but few, and therefore they are highly valued.

Leaving this country and going north-west, after traversing great mountains and crossing wide valleys, and passing a succession of smaller towns, and going 2000 li or so, we leave the frontiers of India and come to the kingdom of Tsau-ku-ṭa.

NOTE.—The remainder of the section, noticed on pp. 248, 249, records a mission sent to the same king of Ceylon, Alibunar, by the Emperor of China (Ch'hêng Tsu), under the direction of the eunuch Ch'hing Ho; his object was to offer incense and flowers. Having arrived, he exhorted the king to respect the teaching of Buddha and to expel the heretics. The king being enraged, desired to slay him, but Ch'hing Ho being aware of the plot, escaped. Again the same ambassador was sent to receive the homage of foreign states, and came to Ceylon (Si-lan-shan-kwo, the country of the Seilan mountain). The king rebelliously refused to pay any respect to the embassage, and collected 50,000 soldiers to block the way and to destroy the ships. Ch'hing Ho having learned the purpose of the king, sent secretly by a circuitous way to the ships, and got 3000 soldiers by night to march on the royal city. Being surrounded by the enemy's troops, they defended the city for six days, and then having treated the king with contumely, they opened the gates in the morning, and fought their way for twenty li; when the daylight began to fail, they offered up prayers to the sacred tooth, and suddenly an unusual light shone before them and lighted them on their way. Having reached their ships, they rested in peace, and arrived at the capital in the ninth year of Yung-loh (A.D. 1412), the seventh month, and ninth day.

END OF BOOK XI.

BOOK XII.

Contains an account of twenty-two countries, viz., (1) *Tsu-ku-cha;* (2) *Fo-li-shi-sa-t'ang-na;* (3) *'An-ta-lo-po;* (4) *K'woh-si-to;* (5) *Hwoh;* (6) *Mung-kin;* (7) *O-li-ni;* (8) *Ho-lo-hu;* (9) *Ki-li-seh-mo;* (10) *Po-li-ho;* (11) *Hi-mo-ta-lo;* (12) *Po-to-chang-na;* (13) *In-po-kin;* (14) *Kiu-lang-na;* (15) *Ta-mo-si-tie-ti;* (16) *Shi-k'i-ni;* (17) *Shang-mi;* (18) *K'ie-p'an-to;* (19) *U-sha;* (20) *Kie-sha;* (21) *Cho-kiu-kia;* (22) *K'iu-sa-ta-na*

TSU-KU-CHA (TSAUKÛṬA).

THIS country[1] is about 7000 li in circuit, the capital, which is called Ho-si-na (Ghazna), is about 30 li round. There is another capital, Ho-sa-la,[2] which is about 30 li round. Both of them are naturally strong and also fortified.[3] Mountains and valleys succeed each other, with plains intervening, fit for cultivation. The land is sown and reaped in due season. Winter wheat is grown in great abundance; shrubs and trees grow in rich variety, and there are flowers and fruits in abundance. The soil is favourable for the *yo-kin* plant (*turmeric*) and for the *hing-kiu;*[4] this last grows in the valley Lo-ma-in-tu.[5]

In the city Ho-sa-lo is a fountain, of which the water

[1] For some reference to the country Tsaukûṭa, see *ante*, vol. i. p. 62, n. 218. Cunningham identifies it with the Arachosia of classical writers (*Anc. Geog. of India*, p. 40).

[2] The identification of Ho-si-na with Ghazni was first made by M. V. de St. Martin; he also proposed to restore Ho-sa-la to Hazâra, but General Cunningham remarks that this name, as applied to the district in question, is not older than the time of Chinghiz Khan; he, therefore, proposes Guzaristan, on the Helmand, the Ozola of Ptolemy, as the equivalent of the Chinese symbols (*ibid.*, loc. cit.)

[3] For the strength of Ghazni see Cunningham (*op. cit.*, pp. 41, 42).

[4] *Hiṅgu*, assafœtida (Julien).

[5] Râmêndu? (Julien).

divides itself into many branches, and which the people utilise for the purposes of irrigation. The climate is cold; there are frequent hail and snow storms. The people are naturally light-hearted and impulsive; they are crafty and deceitful. They love learning and the arts, and show considerable skill in magical sentences, but they have no good aim in view.

They daily repeat several myriads of words; their writing and language differ from those of other countries. They are very specious in vain talk, but there is little body or truth in what they say. Although they worship a hundred (*many*) spirits, yet they also greatly reverence the three precious ones. There are several hundred *saṅghârâmas*, with 1000 or so priests. They all study the Great Vehicle. The reigning sovereign is sincere and honest in his faith, and is the successor of a long line of kings. He applies himself assiduously to religious work (*merit*) and is well instructed and fond of learning. There are some ten *stûpas* built by Aśôka-râja, and several tens of Dêva temples, in which sectaries of various denominations dwell together.

The Tîrthaka[6] heretics are very numerous; they worship principally the Dêva Kshuna (T'seu-na). This Dêva spirit formerly came from Mount Aruṇa ('O-lu-nao) in Kapiśa, and took up his abode here in the southern districts of this kingdom, in the Mount Sunagir.[7] He is severe or good, causing misfortune or exercising violence. Those who invoke him with faith obtain their wishes; those who despise him reap misfortune. Therefore people both far off and near show for him deep reverence; high and low alike are filled with religious awe of him. The princes, nobles, and people of this as well as of foreign

[6] The symbols *Wai-tao* may denote the Tîrthakas, as Julien seems to suppose; or they may be simply equal to "only the greater part are *Wai-tao*," the symbols *wai-tao* are generally applied to the Tîrthakas, for which see Eitel, *Handbook*, sub voc.

[7] For this mountain see *ante*, vol. i. p. 62. It may be restored to Kshuna Hilo or Hila.

countries assemble every year at a season of rejoicing which is not fixed, and offer gold and silver and precious objects of rare value (*choice trifles*), with sheep, and horses, and domestic animals; all which they present in simple and confiding trust, so that though the earth is covered with silver and gold, and the sheep and horses fill the valleys, yet no one would dare to covet them: they consider them as things set apart for sacred purposes. The heretics (Tîrthakas), by subduing their minds and mortifying their flesh, get from the spirits of heaven sacred formulæ. By the use of these they are frequently able to control diseases and recover the sick.

Going from this northwards 500 li or so, we come to the kingdom of Fo-li-shi-sa-t'ang-na.

FO-LI-SHI-SA-T'ANG-NA (PARŚUSTHÂNA, *or* VARDASTHÂNA ?)

This kingdom[8] is about 2000 li from east to west and 1000 li from north to south. The capital is called U-pi-na (Hupiân),[9] and is 20 li round. As regards the soil and the manners of the people, these are the same as in Tsu-ku-cha; the language, however, is different. The climate is icy cold; the men are naturally fierce and impetuous. The king is a Turk (Tu-kieuh). They have (*or* he has) profound faith for the three precious objects of worship; he esteems learning and honours virtue (*or*, the virtuous, *i.e.*, the priests).

Going to the north-east of this kingdom, traversing mountains and crossing rivers, and passing several tens of little towns situated on the frontier of the country of Kapiśa, we come to a great mountain pass called Po-lo-

[8] Panini mentions Parśusthâna, 'the country of the Parśus, a warlike tribe, in this direction (v. 3, 117; *Brih. Sam.*, xiv. 18). Baber (*Mem.*, p. 140) mentions the Parâchis among the tribes of Afghanistan. Ptolemy has two places, Parsiana (lib. vi c. 18, s. 4) and Parsia (*ib.*, s. 5), and also the tribes Parsioi and Parsuêtai (*ib.*, s. 3), somewhere in this vicinity.

[9] Hupiân or Opian, a little to the north of Charikar, in lat. 35° 2′ N., long. 69° 1′ E., at the entrance of a pass over the north-east end of the Paınghân range.

si-na (Varasêna),[10] which forms part of the great snowy mountains. This mountain pass is very high; the precipices are wild and dangerous; the path is tortuous, and the caverns and hollows wind and intertwine together. At one time the traveller enters a deep valley, at another he mounts a high peak, which in full summer is blocked with frozen ice. By cutting steps up the ice the traveller passes on, and after three days he comes to the highest point of the pass. There the icy wind, intensely cold, blows with fury; the piled snow fills the valleys. Travellers pushing their way through, dare not pause on their route. The very birds that fly in their wheeling flight[11] cannot mount alone this point, but go afoot across the height and then fly downwards. Looking at the mountains round, they seem as little hillocks. This is the highest peak of all Jambudvîpa. No trees are seen upon it, but only a mass of rocks, crowded one by the side of the other, like a wild forest.

Going on for three days more, we descend the pass and come to 'An-ta-lo-po (Andar-âb).[12]

'AN-TA-LO-PO (ANDAR-ÂB).

This is the old land of the Tu-ho-lo country.[13] It is about 3000 li round; the capital is 14 or 15 li round. They have no chief ruler; it is dependent on the Turks (Tuh-kiueh).[14] Mountains and hills follow in chains, with valleys intersecting them. The arable land is very contracted. The climate is very severe. The wind and the snow are intensely cold and violent; yet the country is regularly cultivated and productive: it is suitable also for flowers and fruits. The men are naturally fierce and

[10] This pass over the Hindu Kush (the Paropamisus or Indian Caucasus) is probably the same as the Khawak Pass described by Wood (*Oxus*, p. 274). He found it to be 13,000 feet in height.

[11] *Ngo ts'ung*, soaring birds.

[12] See Book i., n. 146

[13] That is, of the Tokhâri people. See Book i., n. 121.

[14] That is, on the Turkish tribe from the borders of China that had overrun this district (see note, *loc. cit.*)

violent. The common people are unrestrained in their ways, and know neither wrong nor right. They do not care about learning, and give themselves only to the worship of spirits. Few of them believe in the religion of Buddha. There are three *saṅghârâmas* and some tens of priests. They follow the teaching of the Mahâsaṅghika (Ta-chong-pu) school. There is one *stûpa* built by Aśôka-râja.

Going north-west from this we enter a valley, skirt along a mountain pass, traverse several little towns, and after going about 400 li we arrive at K'woh-si-to.

K'WOH-SI-TO (KHOST).[15]

This also is the old land of the Tu-ho-lo country. It is about 3000 li in circuit; the capital is about 10 li round. It has no chief ruler, but is dependent on the Turks. It is mountainous, with many contracted valleys; hence it is subject to icy-cold winds. It produces much grain, and it abounds with flowers and fruits. The disposition of the men is fierce and violent; they live without laws. There are three *saṅghârâmas*, with very few priests.

Going from this north-west, skirting the mountains and crossing the valleys, and passing by several towns, after about 300 li we come to the country called Hwoh.

HWOH (KUNDUZ).[16]

This country is also the old land of the Tuh-ho-lo country. It is about 3000 li in circuit; the chief town is about 10 li. There is no chief ruler, but the country depends on the Turks. The land is level and plain. It is regularly cultivated, and produces cereals in abundance. Trees and shrubs grow plentifully, and flowers and fruits (*of various kinds*) are wonderfully abundant. The climate is soft and agreeable; the manners of the people simple

[15] See Book i., n. 145.

[16] See Book i., n. 35.

and honest. The men are naturally quick and impulsive; they clothe themselves with woollen garments. Many believe in the three precious objects (*of worship*), and a few pay their adoration to the spirits. There are ten *saṅghârâmas* with several hundred followers (*priests*). They study both the Great and the Little Vehicle, and practise the discipline of both. The king is of the Turkish clan; he governs all the little kingdoms to the south of the Iron Gates.[17] He constantly shifts his dwelling, like a bird (*his bird-dwelling*), not constantly occupying this town.

Going east from this, we enter the T'sung-ling mountains.[18] These mountains are situated in the middle of Jambuduvîpa. On the south they border on the great snowy mountains; on the north they reach to the hot sea (*Lake Temurtu*), and to the "Thousand Springs;" on the west they extend to the kingdom of Hwoh; on the east to the kingdom of U-cha (Och). From east to west and from north to south they run equally for several thousand li, and abound in many hundreds of steep peaks and dark valleys. The mountain heights are rendered dangerous by the glaciers and frozen snow. The cold winds blow with fury. As the land produces a great quantity of onions therefore it is called T'sung-ling; or because the crags of these mountains have a greenish-blue tint, hence also the name.

Going east 100 li or so, we come to the kingdom of Mung-kin.

MUNG-KIN (MUNJAN).

This country [19] is an old territory of the Tu-ho-li country. It is about 400 li in circuit. The chief city is about 15 or 16 li round. The soil and manners of the people resemble to a great extent the Hwoh country. There is no chief ruler, but they depend on the Turks. Going north we come to the country of 'O-li-ni.

[17] For the "iron gates" see Book i., n. 119.

[18] For the T'sung-ling Mountains see Book i., n. 77.

[19] For Mung-kin see Book i., n. 144.

O-LI-NI (AHRENG).

This country[20] is an old territory of Tu-ho-lo. It borders both sides of the river Oxus.[21] It is about 300 li in circuit; the chief city is 14 or 15 li round. In character of its soil and manners of the people it greatly resembles the Hwoh country.

Going east, we come to Ho-lo-hu.[22]

HO-LO-HU (RAGH).

This country[23] is an old territory of Tu-ho-lo. On the north it borders on the Oxus (Fo-ts'u, Vakshu). It is about 200 li in circuit. The chief town is about 14 or 15 li round. The products of the soil and the manners of the people greatly resemble the Hwoh country.

Going eastward from the Mung-kin country, skirting along high mountain passes, and penetrating deep valleys, and passing in succession various districts and towns, after a journey of 300 li or so we arrive at the country of Ki-li-si-mo.

KI-LI-SI-MO (KHRISHMA or KISHM).

This country[24] is an old territory of Tu-ho-lo. From east to west it is 1000 li or so; from north to south it is 300 li. The capital is 15 or 16 li round. The soil and the manners of the people are just like those of Mung-kin, except that these men are naturally hot-tempered and violent.

Going north-east we come to the kingdom of Po-li-ho (Bolor).

PO-LI-HO (BOLOR).

This country[25] is an old territory of Tu-ho-lo From

[20] For this country see Book i., n. 143.

[21] The Po-t'su (Vakshu).

[22] The Japanese gives Ka-ra-ko. After Julien it represents Roh or Roshan (V. St. Martin, p. 421).

[23] See Book i., n. 142.

[24] See Book i., n. 141.

[25] See Book i., n. 140.

east to west it is about 100 li, and from north to south about 300 li. The chief town is some 20 li or so in circuit. The produce of the soil and the manners of the people are like those of Ki-li-si-mo.

Going east from Ki-li-si-mo, after traversing mountains and crossing valleys for about 300 li, we come to the country of Hi-mo-ta-lo.

HI-MO-TA-LO (HIMATALA).

This country[26] is an old territory of the country of Tu-ho-lo. It is about 300 li in circuit. It is cut up by mountains and valleys. The soil is rich and fertile, and fit for cereals. It produces much winter wheat. Every kind of plant flourishes, and fruits of all sorts grow in abundance. The climate is cold; the disposition of the men violent and hasty. They do not distinguish between wrong and right. Their appearance is vulgar and ignoble. In respect of their modes of behaviour and forms of etiquette, their clothes of wool, and skin, and felt, they are like the Turks. Their wives wear upon their head-dress a wooden horn about three feet or so in length. It has two branches (*a double branch*) in front, which signify father and mother of the husband. The upper horn denotes the father, the lower one the mother. Whichever of these two dies first, they remove one horn, but when both are dead, they give up this style of headdress.

The first king of this country was a Śâkya,[27] fearless and bold. To the west of the T'sung-ling mountains most of the people were subdued to his power. The frontiers were close to the Turks, and so they adopted their low customs, and suffering from their attacks they protected their frontier. And thus the people of this kingdom were dispersed into different districts, and had many tens of fortified cities, over each of which a separate chief was

[26] See Book i., n. 139.

[27] Referring, as I suppose, to the history of the champions who were banished from Kapilavastu.

placed. The people live in tents made of felt, and lead the life of nomads.

On the west side this kingdom touches the country of Ki-li-si-mo. Going from this 200 odd li, we arrive at the country of Po-to-chang-na (Badakshân).

PO-TO-CHANG-NA (BADAKSHÂN).

This kingdom[28] is an old territory of the Tu-ho-lo country; it is about 2000 li in circuit, and the capital, which is placed on the side of a mountain precipice, is some 6 or 7 li in circuit. It is intersected with mountains and valleys, a vast expanse of sand and stone stretches over it; the soil is fit for the growth of beans and wheat; it produces an abundance of grapes, the khamil peach, and plums, &c. The climate is very cold. The men are naturally fierce and hasty; their customs are ill-regulated; they have no knowledge of letters or the arts; their appearance is low and ignoble; they wear mostly garments of wool. There are three or four *saṅghârâmas*, with very few followers. The king is of an honest and sincere disposition. He has a deep faith in the three precious objects of worship.

Going from this south-east, passing across mountains and valleys, after 200 li or so we come to the country of In-po-kin (Yamgân).

IN-PO-KIN (YAMGÂN).

This country[29] is an old territory of the Tu-ho-lo country. It is about 1000 li or so in circuit. The capital is about 10 li round. There is a connected line of hills and valleys through the country, with narrow strips of arable land. With respect to the produce of the soil, the climate, and the character of the people, these differ little from the kingdom of Po-to-chang-na, only the character of the language differs slightly. The king's nature is

[28] See Book i., n. 136.

[29] See Book i., n. 137.

violent and impulsive, and he does not know clearly the difference between right and wrong.

Going from this south-east, skirting the mountains and crossing the valleys, traversing thus by narrow and difficult ways a distance of 300 li or so, we arrive at the country of Kiu-lang-na.

KIU-LANG-NA (KURÂN).

This country[30] is an old territory of Tu-ho-lo; it is about 2000 li round. As regards the character of the soil, the mountains and the valleys, the climate and the seasons, it resembles the kingdom of In-po-kien (Invakan). The customs of the people are without rule, their disposition is rough (*common*) and violent; the greater portion do not attend to religion; a few believe in the law of Buddha. The appearance of the people is displeasing and ungainly. They wear principally woollen garments. There is a mountain cavern from which much pure gold is procured (*dug out*). They break the stones and afterwards procure the gold. There are few *saṅghârâmas*, and scarcely any priests. The king is honest and simple-minded. He deeply reverences the three precious objects of worship.

Going north-east from this, after climbing the mountains and penetrating valleys, and going along a precipitous and dangerous road for 500 li or so, we come to the kingdom of Ta-mo-si-tie-ti.

TA-MO-SI-TIE-TI (TAMASTHITI ?).

This country[31] is situated between two mountains. It is an old territory of Tu-ho-lo. From east to west it extends about 1500 or 1600 li; from north to south its width is only 4 or 5 li, and in its narrowest part not more than one li. It lies upon the Oxus (Fo-t'su) river, which it follows along its winding course. It is broken up with

[30] See Book i., n. 138.

[31] See Book i., n. 135.

hills of different heights, whilst sand and stones lie scattered over the surface of the soil. The wind is icy cold and blows fiercely. Though they sow the ground, it produces but a little wheat and pulse. There are few trees (*forest trees*), but plenty of flowers and fruits. Here the *shen* horse is bred. The horse, though small in size, yet easily travels a long distance. The manners of the people have no regard to propriety. The men are rough and violent; their appearance low and ignoble. They wear woollen garments. Their eyes are mostly of a blue colour,[32] and in this respect they differ from people of other countries. There are some ten *saṅghârâmas*, with very few priests (*religious followers*).

The capital of the country is called Hwăn-t'o-to. In the middle of it is a *saṅghârâma* built by a former king of this country. In its construction[33] he excavated the side of the hill and filled up the valley. The early kings of this country were not believers in Buddha, but sacrificed only to the spirits worshipped by unbelievers; but for some centuries the converting power of the true law has been diffused. At the beginning, the son of the king of this country, who was much loved by him, fell sick of a serious disease; he employed the utmost skill of the medicine art, but it brought no benefit. Then the king went personally to the Dêva temple to worship and ask for some means of recovering his child. On this the chief of the temple, speaking in the name of the spirit, said, "Your son will certainly recover; let your mind rest in peace." The king having heard it, was greatly pleased, and returned homewards. On his way he met a Shaman, his demeanour staid and remarkable. Astonished at his appearance and dress, the king asked him whence he came and whither he was going. The Shaman having already reached the holy fruit (*of an Arhat*), desired to spread the law of Buddha, and therefore he had

[32] *Pih*, either blue or green, like the deep sea.

[33] In constructing and shaping its courts and halls.

assumed this deportment and appearance; so replying he said, "I am a disciple of Tathâgata, and am called a Bhikshu." The king, who was in great anxiety, at once asked him, "My son is grievously afflicted; I scarcely know whether he is living or dead. (*Will he recover?*") The Shaman said, "You might raise (*from the dead*) the spirits of your ancestors, but your loved son it is difficult to deliver." The king replied, "A spirit of heaven has assured me he will not die, and the Shaman says he will die; it is difficult to know what to believe, coming from these masters of religion."[34] Coming to his palace, he found that his loved son was already dead. Hiding the corpse and making no funeral preparations, he again asked the priest of the Dêva temple respecting him. In reply he said, "He will not die; he will certainly recover." The king in a rage seized the priest and held him fast, and then upbraiding him he said, "You and your accomplices are monstrous cheats; you pretend to be religious, but you practise lying. My son is dead, and yet you say he will certainly recover. Such lying cannot be endured; the priest (*master*) of the temple shall die and the building be destroyed." On this he killed the priest and took the image and flung it into the Oxus. On his return, he once more met the Shaman; on seeing him he was glad, and respectfully prostrated himself before him, as he gratefully said, "Hitherto I have ignorantly followed (*my guide*), and trod the path of false teaching. Although I have for a long time followed the windings of error, now the change has come from this.[35] I pray you condescend to come with me to my dwelling." The Shaman accepted the invitation and went to the palace. The funeral ceremonies being over, (*the king*) addressed the Shaman and said, "The world of men is in confusion, birth and death flow on ceaselessly; my son was sick, and I asked whether he would remain with me or depart, and the lying spirit said he would surely re-

[34] *Kwei tsuh che jin*, men who reprove the world.
[35] *I.e.*, from this interview.

cover; but the first words of indication you gave were true and not false. Therefore the system of religion you teach is to be reverenced. Deign to receive me, deceived as I have been, as a disciple." He, moreover, begged the Shaman to plan and measure out a *saṅghârâma;* then, according to the right dimensions, he constructed this building, and from that time till now the law of Buddha has been in a flourishing condition.

In the middle of the old *saṅghârâma* is the *vihâra* built by this Arhat. In the *vihâra* is a statue of Buddha in stone above the statue is a circular cover of gilded copper, and ornamented with gems; when men walk round the statue in worship, the cover also turns; when they stop, the cover stops. The miracle cannot be explained. According to the account given by the old people, it is said that the force of a prayer of a holy man effects the miracle. Others say there is some secret mechanism in the matter; but when looking at the solid stone walls of the hall, and inquiring from the people as to their knowledge (*of such mechanism*), it is difficult to arrive at any satisfaction about the matter.

Leaving this country, and traversing a great mountain northward, we arrive at the country of Shi-k'i-ni (Shikhnân).

SHI-K'I-NI (SHIKHNÂN).

This country[36] is about 2000 li in circuit, the chief city is 5 or 6 li. Mountains and valleys follow each other in a connected succession; sand and stones lie scattered over the waste lands. Much wheat and beans are grown, but little rice. The trees are thin, flowers and fruits not abundant. The climate is icy-cold; the men are fierce and intrepid. They think nothing of murder and robbery; they are ignorant of good manners or justice, and cannot distinguish between right and wrong. They are deceived as to the happiness and misery of the future,

[36] See Book i., n. 133

and only fear present calamities. Their figure and appearance are poor and ignoble; their garments are made of wool or skin; their writing is the same as that of the Turks, but the spoken language is different.

Passing along a great mountain to the south of the kingdom of Ta-mo-si-tie-ti (Tamasthiti?[37]), we come to the country of Shang-mi.

SHANG-MI (ŚÂMBHÎ ?).

This country[38] is about 2500 or 2600 li in circuit. It is intersected with mountains and valleys; with hills of various heights. Every kind of grain is cultivated; beans and wheat are abundant. Grapes are plentiful. The country produces yellow arsenic. They bore into the cliffs and break the stones, and so obtain it. The mountain spirits are cruel and wicked; they frequently cause calamities to befall the kindgom.

On entering the country, sacrifice is offered up to them, after which good success attends the persons in coming and going. If no sacrifice is offered them, the wind and the hail attack the travellers. The climate is very cold; the ways of the people are quick, their disposition is honest and simple. They have no rules of propriety or justice in their behaviour; their wisdom is small, and in the arts they have very little ability. Their writing is the same as that of the kingdom of Tu-ho-lo, but the spoken language is somewhat different. Their clothes are mostly made of woollen stuff. Their king is of the race of Śâkya.[39] He greatly esteems the law of Buddha.

[37] Tamasthiti, according to Eitel (*Handbook*, s. v.), was "an ancient province of Tukhâra, noted for the ferocious character of its inhabitants." But this is probably derived from Julien's restoration in the text, which he gives doubtfully.

[38] This is the country over which one of the banished Sâkya youths reigned (see *ante*, p. 21). It is restored by Julien to Sâmbhî in the passage before us, but to Sâmbî, vol. ii. p. 318. Eitel (*op. cit.*, s. v.) speaks of this kingdom as founded by refugees of the Sâkya family, and situated near Chitral, lat. 35° 35′ N., and long. 72° 27′ E.

[39] See previous note.

The people follow his example, and are all animated by a sincere faith. There are two *saṅghârâmas*, with very few followers.

On the north-east of the frontier of the country, skirting the mountains and crossing the valleys, advancing along a dangerous and precipitous road, after going 700 li or so, we come to the valley of Po-mi-lo (Pâmir).[40] It stretches 1000 li or so east and west, and 100 li or so from north to south; in the narrowest part it is not more than 10 li. It is situated among the snowy mountains; on this account the climate is cold, and the winds blow constantly. The snow falls both in summer and spring-time. Night and day the wind rages violently. The soil is impregnated with salt and covered with quantities of gravel and sand. The grain which is sown does not ripen, shrubs and trees are rare; there is but a succession of desert without any inhabitants.

In the middle of the Pâmir valley is a great dragon lake (Nâgahrada); from east to west it is 300 li or so, from north to south 50 li. It is situated in the midst of the great T'sung ling mountains, and is the central point of Jambudvîpa.[41] The land is very high; the water is pure and clear as a mirror; it cannot be fathomed; the colour of the lake is a dark blue; the taste of the water sweet and soft: in the water hide the *kau-ki* fish (*shark-spider*), dragons, crocodiles, tortoises; floating on its surface[42] are ducks, wild geese, cranes,

[40] Pâmir, according to Sir T. D. Forsyth (*Report of Mission to Yarkand*, p. 231, n.) is a Khokandi Turki word signifying "desert." For a description of this district and its watersheds, see Forsyth (*op. cit.*, p. 231), also Wood's *Oxus*, chap. xxi.

[41] This no doubt refers to the Sarik-kul lake, otherwise called Kul-i-Pâmir-kulân, the lake of the Great Pâmir; see *ante*, vol. i. p. 12, n. 33. The great Nâga lake is sometimes called the Râvaṇa-hrada; Râvaṇa also dwelt on Laṅka-giri (Potaraka ?), and possibly from him is derived the Arabic name for Adam's Peak, Mount Rahwan. The remark in the text "that it cannot be fathomed" is a mistake. Wood found soundings at 9 fathoms (*Oxus*, p. 237.

[42] Hiuen Tsiang's visit was during the summer months (probably of A.D. 642); in the winter, the lake is frozen to a thickness of two feet and a half (Wood's

and so on; large eggs are found concealed in the wild desert wastes, or among the marshy shrubs, or on the sandy islets.

To the west of the lake there is a large stream, which, going west, reaches so far as the eastern borders of the kingdom of Ta-mo-si-tie-ti (? Tamasthiti), and there joins the river Oxus (Fo-t'su) and flows still to the west. So on this side of the lake all the streams flow westward.

On the east of the lake is a great stream,[43] which, flowing north-east, reaches to the western frontiers of the country of Kie-sha (? Kashgâr), and there joins the Si-to (Śîtâ) river[44] and flows eastward, and so all streams on the left side of the lake flow eastward.

Passing over a mountain to the south of the Pâmir valley, we find the country of Po-lo-lo (Bolor);[45] here is found much gold and silver; the gold is as red as fire.

On leaving the midst of this valley and going south-east, along the route there is no inhabited place (*no men or village*). Ascending the mountains, traversing the side of precipices, encountering nothing but ice and snow, and thus going 500 li we arrive at the kingdom of K'ie-p'an-to.

K'IE-P'AN-TO.

This country[46] is about 2000 li in circuit; the capital

Oxus, p. 236). But in the summer the ice on the lake is broken up, and the hills in its neighbourhood clear of snow; this (according to the statement of the Khirghiz who accompanied Wood) takes place as early as the end of June, "at which time the water swarms with aquatic birds" (*op. cit.*, p. 239); this confirms the remark in the text. For the other remarks, see Marco Polo, book i. chap. xxxii., and Yule's notes.

[43] "The story of an eastern outflow from the lake is no doubt a legend connected with an ancient Hindu belief (see *Cathay*, p. 347), but Burnes in modern times heard much the same story" (Yule, *Marco Polo*, vol. i. p. 166).

[44] For some remarks on the Sîtâ river see *ante*, vol. i. n. 34. Julien, in a note found on p. 572, vol. iii., corrects the name to Śîtâ, meaning "cold;" his authority is the Chinese Dictionary, *I-tsi-king-in-i*.

[45] Perhaps the same as Balti, a Tibetan kingdom. See Cunningham (quoted by Yule, *M. P.*, vol. i. p. 168).

[46] Julien restores the symbols K'ie-p'an-to to Khavandha doubtfully. V. de St. Martin in his *Mémoire* (p. 426) restores it to Kar-

rests on a great rocky crag of the mountain, and is backed by the river Śîtâ. It is about 20 li in circuit. The mountain chains run in continuous succession, the valleys and plains are very contracted. There is very little rice cultivated, but beans and corn grow in abundance. Trees grŏw thinly, there are only few fruits and flowers. The plateaux are soppy, the hills are waste, the towns are deserted; the manners of the people are without any rules of propriety. There are very few of the people who give themselves to study. They are naturally uncouth and impetuous, but yet they are bold and courageous. Their appearance is common and revolting; their clothes are made of woollen stuffs. Their letters are much like those of the Kie-sha (? Kashgar) country. They know how to express themselves sincerely, and they greatly reverence the law of Buddha. There are some ten *saṅghârâmas* with about 500 followers. They study the Little Vehicle according to the school of the Sarvâstivâdas.

The reigning king is of an upright and honest character; he greatly honours the three treasures; his external

chu, and in *Fa-hian* (p. 9, n. 6). I have adopted this restoration. Col. Yule, however (Wood's *Oxus*, xlviii. n. 1), speaks of Karchu as "a will-o'-the wisp, which never had any existence." On the other hand, he says, "We know this state (*i.e.*, Kabandha, the *K'ie-p'an-to* of the text) to be identical with the modern territory of Sarikol, otherwise called Tush Kurghan from its chief town" (*op. cit.*, p. xlviii.); and again, "As for Karchu, which in so many maps occupies a position on the waters of the Yarkand river, it was an erroneous transliteration of the name Hatchût or Ketchût, which appeared in the (Chinese) tables of the later Jesuit surveyors to the south of Sarikol and was by them apparently intended as a loose approximation to the position of the frontier of the Dard state of Kanjût or Hunza" (*op. cit.*, p. lv.) It would appear from the above extracts that K'ie-pa'n-to must be identified with Sarikol and Tush Kurghan (stone-tower), and not with the Kie-cha of Fa-hian. I am unable, however, to trace Fa-hian's route to "Kie-cha or Ladak," as stated by Yule (*op. cit.*, xl.), and Cunningham (*Ladak*, quoted by Yule, *ibid.*); for if *Kie-cha* be Ladak, how can the pilgrim describe it as in the middle of the T'sung-ling mountains (chap. v.), or say that a journey of one month westward across the T'sung-ling mountains brought him to North India (chap. vi.)? Dr. Eitel identifies the K'ie-cha of Fa-hian with the Kasioi of Ptolemy (*Handbook*, s. v. *Khaśa*); M. V. de St. Martin observes (*Mémoire*, p. 427) that Kashgâr and its territory correspond with the *Casia regio Scythiæ* of Ptolemy.

manner is quiet and unassuming; he is of a vigorous mind and loves learning.

Since the establishment of the kingdom many successive ages have passed. Sometimes the people speak of themselves as deriving their name from the Chi-na-ti-po-k'iu-ta-lo (China-dêva-gôtra). Formerly this country was a desert valley in the midst of the T'sung-ling mountains. At this time a king of the kingdom of Persia (Po-la-sse) took a wife from the Han country. She had been met by an escort on her progress so far as this, when the roads east and west were stopped by military operations. On this they placed the king's daughter on a solitary mountain peak, very high and dangerous, which could only be approached by ladders, up and down; moreover, they surrounded it with guards both night and day for protection. After three months the disturbances were quelled (*they put down the robbers*). Quiet being restored, they were about to resume their homeward journey. But now the lady was found to be enceinte. Then the minister in charge of the mission was filled with fear and he addressed his colleagues thus: "The king's commands were that I should go to meet his bride. Our company, in expectation of a cessation of the troubles that endangered the roads, at one time encamped in the wilds, at another in the deserts; in the morning we knew not what would happen before the evening. At length the influence of our king having quieted the country, I was resuming the progress homeward when I found that the bride was enceinte. This has caused me great grief, and I know not the place of my death. We must inquire about the villain who has done this (*secretly*), with a view to punish him hereafter. If we talk about it and noise it abroad, we shall never get at the truth." Then his servant, addressing the envoy, said, "Let there be no inquiry; it is a spirit that has had knowledge of her; every day at noon there was a chief-master who came from the sun's disc, and, mounted on horseback, came to meet her." The envoy said, "If this be so, how can I clear myself from fault? If I go back I shall certainly be put to death; if I delay here they will send to have me punished. What is the best thing to do?" He answered, "This is not so complicated a matter; who is there to make inquiries about matters or to exact punishment outside the frontiers? Put it off a few days *from morning to evening*)."

On this he built, on the top of a rocky peak, a palace with its surrounding apartments;[47] then having erected an enclosure round the palace of some 300 paces, he located the princess there as chief. She established rules of government and enacted laws. Her time having come, she bore a son of extraordinary beauty and perfect parts. The mother directed the affairs of state; the son received his honourable title;[48] he was able to fly through the air and control the winds and snow. He extended his power far and wide, and the renown of his laws was everywhere known. The neighbouring countries and those at a distance subscribed themselves his subjects.

The king having died from age, they buried him in a stone chamber concealed with a great mountain cavern about 100 li to the south-east of this city. His body, being dried, has escaped corruption down to the present time. The form of his body is shrivelled up and thin: he looks as if he were asleep. From time to time they change his clothes, and regularly place incense and flowers by his side. From that time till now his descendants have ever recollected their origin, that their mother (*or*, on their mother's side), they were descended from the king of Han, and on their father's side from the race of the Sun-dêva, and therefore they style themselves "descendants of the Han and Sun-god."[49]

[47] This may be the origin of the term *Tash Kurghan*, stone tower.

[48] That is, the son of the Sun-god.

[49] There is in this story a sort of resemblance to the tale about Syáwush the Persian and Afrâsyab the Turanian. The latter gave to the royal refugee his daughter Farangis, with the provinces of Khutan and

The members of the royal family in appearance resemble the people of the Middle Country (China). They wear on their heads a square cap, and their clothes are like those of the Hu people (Uïghurs). In after-ages these people fell under the power of the barbarians, who kept their country in their power.

When Aśôka-râja was in the world he built in this palace a *stûpa*. Afterwards, when the king changed his residence to the north-east angle of the royal precinct, he built in this old palace a *saṅghârâma* for the sake of Kumâralabdha (T'ong-shiu). The towers of this building are high (*and its halls*) wide. There is in it a figure of Buddha of majestic appearance. The venerable Kumâralabdha was a native of Takshaśilâ. From his childhood he showed a rare intelligence, and in early life gave up the world. He allowed his mind to wander through the sacred texts, and let his spirit indulge itself in profound reveries. Daily he recited 32,000 words and wrote 32,000 letters. In this way he was able to surpass all his contemporaries, and to establish his renown beyond the age in which he lived. He settled the true law, and overcame false doctrine, and distinguished himself by the brilliancy of his discussion. There was no difficulty which he could not overcome. All the men of the five Indies came to see him, and assigned him the highest rank. He composed many tens of *śâstras*. These were much renowned and studied by all. He was the founder of the Sautrântika (King-pu) school.

At this time in the east was Aśvaghôsha, in the south Dêva, in the west Nâgârjuna, in the north Kumâralabdha. These four were called the four sons that illu-

Chín or Mâchín (Mahâchín?). They settled at Kung, some distance north-east of Khutan. See Bellew, *History of Kashgar* (chap. iii., Forsyth's *Report*). The fame of Kaikhusro (Cyrus) as a hero-child of the sun seems to agree with the miraculous birth and conquests of the child whose birth is narrated in the text. I may add that a consideration of the circumstances connected with the history of the Persian (Iranian) and Turanian tribes confirms me in the opinion that the Tu-ho-lu of Hiuen Tsiang refers to the Turanian people, and not to the Turks (so-called).

mined the world. The king of this country, therefore, having heard of the honourable one (*Kumâralabdha*) and his great qualities, raised an army to attack Takshaśila, and carried him off by force. He then built this *sanghârâma*.

Going south-east 300 li or so from the city, we come to a great rocky scarp in which two chambers are excavated, in each of which is an Arhat plunged in complete ecstasy. They are sitting upright, and they could be moved but with difficulty. Their appearance is shrivelled, but their skin and bones still survive. Though 700 years have elapsed, their hair still grows, and because of this the priests cut their hair every year and change their clothes.

To the north-east of the great crag after going 200 li or so along the mountain-side and the precipices, we come to a *Punyaśâlâ* (*a hospice*).

In the midst of four mountains belonging to the eastern chain of the T'sung-ling mountains there is a space comprising some hundred *k'ing* (*thousand acres*). In this, both during summer and winter, there fall down piles of snow; the cold winds and icy storms rage. The ground, impregnated with salt, produces no crops; there are no trees and nothing but scrubby underwood. Even at the time of great heat the wind and the snow continue. Scarcely have travellers entered this region when they find themselves surrounded by vapour from the snow. Merchant bands, caravans, in coming and going suffer severely in these difficult and dangerous spots.

The old story says: "Formerly there was a troop of merchants, who, with their followers, amounted to 10,000 or so, with many thousand camels. They were occupied in transporting their goods and getting profit. They were assailed by wind and snow, and both men and beasts perished.

As this time there was a great Arhat who belonged to the kingdom of Kie-p'an-to, who, taking a wide look, saw them in their danger, and being moved by pity, desired to exert his spiritual power for their rescue; but when he arrived they were already dead. On this he collected the precious objects that lay scattered about and constructed a house, and gathering in this all the wealth he could, he bought the neighbouring land and built houses in the bordering cities for the accommodation of travellers, and now merchantmen and travellers enjoy the benefit of his beneficence.

Going north-east from this, descending the T'sung-ling mountains to the eastward, after passing dangerous defiles and deep valleys, and traversing steep and dangerous roads, assailed at every step by snow and wind, after going 100 li or so, we emerge from the T'sung-ling mountains and come to the kingdom of U-sha.

U-SHA (OCH).

This kingdom is about 1000 li in circuit; the chief town is about 10 li round. On the south it borders on the river Śîtâ. The soil is rich and productive; it is regularly cultivated and yields abundant harvests. The trees and forests spread their foliage afar, and flowers and fruits abound. This country produces jade of different sorts in great quantities; white jade, black, and green. The climate is soft and agreeable; the winds and rain follow in their season; the manners of the people are not much in keeping with the principles of politeness. The men are naturally hard and uncivilised; they are greatly given to falsehood, and few of them have any feeling of shame. Their language and writing are nearly the same as those of Kie-sha. Their personal appearance is low and repulsive. Their clothes are made of skins and woollen stuffs. However, they have a firm faith in the law of Buddha and greatly honour him. There are some ten *saṅghârâmas*, with somewhat less than 1000 priests. They study the Little Vehicle according to the school of the Sarvâstivâdas. For some centuries the royal line has been extinct. They have no ruler of their own, but are in dependence on the country of K'ie-p'an-to.

Two hundred li or so to the west of the city we come to a great mountain. This mountain is covered with brooding vapours, which hang like clouds above the rocks. The crags rise one above another, and seem as if about to fall where they are suspended. On the mountain top is erected a *stûpa* of a wonderful and mysterious character. This is the old story:—Many centuries ago this mountain suddenly opened; in the middle was seen a Bhikshu, with closed eyes, sitting; his body was of gigantic stature and his form was dried up; his hair descended low on his shoulders and enshrouded his face. A hunter having caught sight of him, told the king. The king in person went to see him and to pay him homage. All the men of the town came spontaneously to burn incense and offer flowers as religious tribute to him. Then the king said, "What man is this of such great stature?" Then there was a Bhikshu who said in reply, "This man with his hair descending over his shoulders and clad in a *kashâya* garment is an Arhat who has entered the *samâdhi* which produces extinction of mind. Those who enter this kind of *samâdhi* have to await a certain signal (*or period*); some say that if they hear the sound of the *ghaṇṭâ* they awake; others, if they see the shining of the sun, then this is a signal for them to arouse themselves from their ecstasy; in the absence of such signal, they rest unmoved and quiet, whilst the power of their ecstasy keeps their bodies from destruction. When they come from their trance after their long fast, the body ought to be well rubbed with oil and the limbs made supple with soft applications; after this the *ghaṇṭâ* may be sounded to restore the mind plunged in *samâdhi*." The king said, "Let it be done," and then he sounded the gong.

Scarcely had the sound died away, but the Arhat, recognising the signal, looking down on them from on high for a long time, at length said, "What creatures are you with forms so small and mean, clothed with brown robes?" They answered, "We are Bhikshus!" He said, "And where now dwells my master, Kâśyapa Tathâgata?" They replied, "He has entered the great *nirvâṇa* for a long time past." Having heard this, he shut his eyes, as a man disappointed and ready to die. Then suddenly he asked again, "Has Śâkya Tathâgata come into the world?" "He has been born, and having guided the world spiritually, he has also entered *nirvâṇa*." Hearing this, he bowed his head, and so remained for a long time. Then rising up into the air, he exhibited spiritual transformations, and at last he was consumed by fire and his bones fell to the ground. The king having collected them, raised over them this *stûpa*.

Going north from this country, and traversing the rocky mountains and desert plains for 500 li or so, we come to the country of Kie-sha.[50]

KIE-SHA (KASHGÂR).

The country of Kie-sha is about 5000 li in circuit. It has much sandy and stony soil, and very little loam. It is regularly cultivated and is productive. Flowers and fruits are abundant. Its manufactures are a fine kind of twilled haircloth, and carpets of a fine texture and skilfully woven. The climate is soft and agreeable; the winds and rain regularly succeed each other. The disposition of the men is fierce and impetuous, and they are mostly false and deceitful. They make light of decorum and politeness, and esteem learning but little. Their custom is when a child is born to compress his head with a board of wood.[51] Their appearance is common and ignoble. They paint (*mark*) their

[50] Anciently called Su-li: this also is the name of its chief city; the full name is Shi-li-ki-li-to-ti (Śrîkrîtati). The sound Su-li is corrupt.—*Ch. Ed.*

[51] See vol. i. p. 19, n. 60.

bodies and around their eyelids.[52] For their writing (*written characters*) they take their model from India, and although they (*i.e., the forms of the letters*) are somewhat mutilated, yet they are essentially the same in form.[53] Their language and pronunciation are different from that of other countries. They have a sincere faith in the religion of Buddha, and give themselves earnestly to the practice of it. There are several hundreds of *saṅghârâmas*, with some 10,000 followers; they study the Little Vehicle and belong to the Sarvâstivâda school. Without understanding the principles, they recite many religious chants; therefore there are many who can say throughout the three *Piṭakas* and the *Vibhâshâ* (*Pi-p'o-sha*).

Going from this south-east 500 li or so, passing the river Śîtâ and crossing a great stony precipice, we come to the kingdom of Cho-kiu-kia.[54]

CHO-KIU-KIA (CHAKUKA? YARKIANG).

This kingdom[55] is some 1000 li or so round; the capital is about 10 li in circuit. It is hemmed in by crags and mountain fastnesses. The residences are numerous. Mountains and hills succeed each other in a continuous line. Stony districts[56] spread in every direction. This kingdom borders on two rivers;[57] the cultivation of grain and of fruit-trees is successful, principally figs, pears, and plums. Cold and winds prevail

[52] This is the only translation I can give. Julien renders it, "They have green eyeballs;" but his text must differ from mine.

[53] This passage, too, is very obscure; Julien has omitted it. As an alternative translation of the whole passage, this may be offered: "They paint their bodies and their eyelids; for their models in these figures (painted letters) they take (those of) India; although they thus disfigure themselves, yet they retain great vigour of form (or body)."

[54] Anciently called Tsie-ku.

[55] V. de St. Martin identifies Cho-kiu-kia with Yarkiang, but he gives no authority. Dr. Eitel (Handbook, *s. v. T'chakuka*) states that "it is an ancient kingdom in Little Bukharia, probably the modern Yarkiang." The distance and bearing from Kashgâr would point to Yarkand.

[56] Compare W. H. Bellew's account of this neighbourhood. *Kashmir and Kashgir*, p. 365.

[57] Probably the Yarkand and Khotan rivers.

throughout the year. The men are passionate and cruel; they are false and treacherous, and in open day practise robbery. The letters are the same as those of K'iu-sa-ta-na (Khotan), but the spoken language is different. Their politeness is very scant, and their knowledge of literature and the arts equally so. They have an honest faith, however, in the three precious objects of worship, and love the practice of religion. There are several tens of *saṅghârâmas*, but mostly in a ruinous condition; there are some hundred followers, who study the Great Vehicle.

On the southern frontier of the country is a great mountain, with lofty defiles and peaks piled up one on the other, and covered with matted underwood and jungle. In winter and all through the year the mountain streams and torrents rush down on every side. There are niches and stone chambers in the outside; they occur in regular order between the rocks and woods. The Arhats from India, displaying their spiritual power, coming from far, abide here at rest. As many Arhats have here arrived at *nirvâṇa*, so there are many *stûpas* here erected. At present there are three Arhats dwelling in these mountain passes in deep recesses, who have entered the *samâdhi* of "extinction of mind." Their bodies are withered away; their hair continues to grow, so that Shamans from time to time go to shave them. In this kingdom, the writings of the Great Vehicle are very abundant. There is no place where the law of Buddha is more flourishing than this. There is a collection here[58] of ten myriads of verses, divided into ten parts. From the time of its introduction till now it has wonderfully spread.

Going east from this, skirting along the high mountain passes and traversing valleys, after going about 800 li, we come to the kingdom of K'iu-sa-ta-na (Kustana—Khotan).

[58] Series of sacred books

K'IU-SA-TA-NA (KHOTAN).

This country is about 4000 li in circuit; the greater part is nothing but sand and gravel (*a sandy waste*); the arable portion of the land is very contracted. What land there is, is suitable for regular cultivation, and produces abundance of fruits. The manufactures are carpets, haircloth of a fine quality, and fine-woven silken fabrics. Moreover, it produces white and green jade. The climate is soft and agreeable, but there are tornados which bring with them clouds of flying gravel (*dust*). They have a knowledge of politeness and justice. The men are naturally quiet and respectful. They love to study literature and the arts, in which they make considerable advance. The people live in easy circumstances, and are contented with their lot.

This country is renowned for its music;[59] the men love the song and the dance. Few of them wear garments of skin (*felt*) and wool; most wear taffetas and white linen. Their external behaviour is full of urbanity; their customs are properly regulated. Their written characters and their mode of forming their sentences resemble the Indian model; the forms of the letters differ somewhat; the differences, however, are slight. The spoken language also differs from that of other countries. They greatly esteem the law of Buddha. There are about a hundred *saṅghârâmas* with some 5000 followers, who all study the doctrine of the Great Vehicle.

The king is extremely courageous and warlike; he greatly venerates the law of Buddha. He says that he is of the race of Pi-shi-men (Vaiśravaṇa) Dêva. In old times this country was waste and desert, and without inhabitants. The Dêva Pi-shi-men came to fix his dwelling here. The eldest son of Aśôka-râja, when dwelling in Takshaśilâ

[59] Compare the remark of Fa-hian (chap. iii.), "They love religious music." For the products and general abundance of the district round Khotan consult *Marco Polo*, Yule's notes, vol. i. pp. 174, 175.

having had his eyes put out, the King Aśôka was very angry, and sent deputies to order the chief of the tribes dwelling there to be transported to the north of the snowy mountains, and to establish themselves in the midst of a desert valley. Accordingly, the men so banished, having arrived at this western frontier (*of the kingdom*), put at their head a chief of their tribe and made him king. It was just at this time a son of the king of the eastern region (*China*) having been expelled from his country, was dwelling in this eastern region. The people who dwelt here urged him also to accept the position of king. Years and months having elapsed, and their laws not yet being settled,[60] because each party used to meet by chance in the hunting-ground, they came to mutual recriminations, and, having questioned each other as to their family and so on, they resolved to resort to armed force. There was then one present who used remonstrances and said, "Why do you urge each other thus to-day? It is no good fighting on the hunting-ground; better return and train your soldiers and then return and fight." Then each returned to his own kingdom and practised their cavalry and encouraged their warriors for the fray. At length, being arrayed one against the other, with drums and trumpets, at dawn of the day, the western army (*lord*) was defeated. They pursued him to the north and beheaded him. The eastern king, profiting by his victory, reunited the broken parts of his kingdom (*consolidated his power*), changed his capital to the middle land,[61] and fortified it with walls; but, because he had no (*surveyed*) territory, he was filled with fear lest he should be unable to complete his scheme, and so he proclaimed far and near, "Who knows how to survey a dominion?" At this time there was a heretic covered with cinders who carried on his shoulder a great calabash full of water, and, advancing to the king, said,

[60] *I.e.*, the mutual relations of the two. The passage respecting the "western frontier" refers to the frontier of the "western kingdom."

[61] That is, according to Julien (note, p. 225), "the land between the eastern and western states."

"I understand a method" (*a territory*), and so he began to walk round with the water of his calabash running out, and thus completed an immense circle. After this he fled quickly and disappeared.

Following the traces of the water, the king laid the foundation of his capital city; and having retained its distinction, it is here the actual king reigns. The city, having no heights near it, cannot be easily taken by assault. From ancient times until now no one has been able to conquer it. The king having changed his capital to this spot, and built towns and settled the country, and acquired much religious merit, now had arrived at extreme old age and had no successor to the throne. Fearing lest his house should become extinct, he repaired to the temple of Vaiśravaṇa, and prayed him to grant his desire. Forthwith the head of the image (*idol*) opened at the top, and there came forth a young child. Taking it, he returned to his palace. The whole country addressed congratulations to him, but as the child would not drink milk, he feared he would not live. He then returned to the temple and again asked (*the god*) for means to nourish him. The earth in front of the divinity then suddenly opened and offered an appearance like a pap. The divine child drank from it eagerly. Having reached supreme power in due course, he shed glory on his ancestors by his wisdom and courage, and extended far and wide the influence of his laws. Forthwith he raised to the god (*Vaiśravaṇa*) a temple in honour of his ancestors. From that time till now the succession of kings has been in regular order, and the power has been lineally transmitted. And for this reason also the present temple of the Dêva is richly adorned with rare gems and worship is punctually offered in it. From the first king having been nourished from milk coming from the earth the country was called by its name (*pap of the earth*—Kustana).

About 10 li south of the capital is a large *saṅghârâma*,

built by a former king of the country in honour of Vairôchana[62] (Pi-lu-che-na) Arhat.

In old days, when the law of Buddha had not yet extended to this country, that Arhat came from the country of Kaśmîr to this place. He sat down in the middle of a wood and gave himself to meditation. At this time certain persons beheld him, and, astonished at his appearance and dress, they came and told the king. The king forthwith went to see him for himself. Beholding his appearance, he asked him, saying, "What man are you, dwelling alone in this dark forest?" The Arhat replied, "I am a disciple of Tathâgata; I am dwelling here to practise meditation. Your majesty ought to establish religious merit by extolling the doctrine of Buddha, building a convent, and providing a body of priests." The king said, "What virtue has Tathâgata, what spiritual power, that you should be hiding here as a bird practising his doctrine (*or* rules)?" He replied, "Tathâgata is full of love and compassion for all that lives; he has come to guide living things throughout the three worlds; he reveals himself by birth or he hides himself; he comes and goes. Those who follow his law avoid the necessity of birth and death; all those ignorant of his doctrine are still kept in the net of worldly desire." The king said, "Truly what you say is a matter of high importance." Then, after deliberation, he said with a loud voice, "Let the great saint appear for my sake and show himself; having seen his appearance, then I will build a monastery, and believe in him, and advance his cause." The Arhat replied, "Let the king build the convent, then, on account of his accomplished merit, he may gain his desire."

The temple having been finished, there was a great assembly of priests from far and near; but as yet there was no *ghaṇṭâ* to call together the congregation; on

[62] In Chinese *Pin-chiu*, "he who shines in every place," or, "the everywhere glorious."

which the king said, "The convent is finished, but where is the appearance of Buddha?" The Arhat said, "Let the king exercise true faith and the spiritual appearance will not be far off!" Suddenly in mid-air appeared a figure of Buddha descending from heaven, and gave to the king a *ghaṇṭâ* (*kien-ti*), on which his faith was confirmed, and he spread abroad the doctrine of Buddha.

To the south-west of the royal city about 20 li or so is Mount Gôśṛiṅga (K'iu-shi-ling-kia); there are two peaks to this mountain, and around these peaks there are on each side a connected line of hills. In one of the valleys there has been built a *saṅghârâma;* in this is placed a figure of Buddha, which from time to time emits rays of glory; in this place Tathâgata formerly delivered a concise digest of the law for the benefit of the Dêvas. He prophesied also that in this place there would be founded a kingdom, and that in it the principles of the bequeathed law would be extended and the Great Vehicle be largely practised.

In the caverns of Mount Gôśṛiṅga is a great rock-dwelling where there is an Arhat plunged in the ecstasy called "destroying the mind;" he awaits the coming of Maitrêya Buddha. During several centuries constant homage has been paid to him. During the last few years the mountain tops have fallen and obstructed the way (*to the cavern*). The king of the country wished to remove the fallen rocks by means of his soldiers, but they were attacked by swarms of black bees, who poisoned the men, and so to this day the gate of the cavern is blocked up.

To the south-west of the chief city about 10 li there is a monastery called Ti-kia-p'o-fo-na (Dîrghabhâvana?), in which is a standing figure of Buddha of Kiu-chi.[63] Originally this figure came from Kiu-chi (Kuchê), and stayed here.

[63] This is restored by Julien to Kuchê (text *in loco*); a Chinese note tells us it was in the "icy mountains," and is now called Tu-sha (? Tush kurghan).

In old time there was a minister who was banished from this country to Kiu-chi; whilst there he paid worship only to this image, and afterwards, when he returned to his own country, his mind still was moved with reverence towards it. After midnight the figure suddenly came of itself to the place, on which the man left his home and built this convent.

Going west from the capital 300 li or so, we come to the town of Po-kia-i (Bhagai?); in this town is a sitting figure of Buddha about seven feet high, and marked with all the distinguishing signs of beauty. Its appearance is imposing and dignified. On its head is a precious gem-ornament, which ever spreads abroad a brilliant light. The general tradition is to this effect:—this statue formerly belonged to the country of Kaśmîr; by the influence of prayer (*being requested*), it removed itself here. In old days there was an Arhat who had a disciple, a Śrâmaṇêra, on the point of death. He desired to have a cake of sown rice (*ts'hu mai*); the Arhat by his divine sight seeing there was rice of this sort in Kustana, transported himself thither by his miraculous power to procure some. The Śrâmaṇêra having eaten it, prayed that he might be re-born in this country, and in consequence of his previous destiny he was born there as a king's son. When he had succeeded to the throne, he subdued all the neighbouring territory, and passing the snowy mountains, he attacked Kaśmîr. The king of Kaśmîr assembled his troops with a view to resist the invaders. On this the Arhat warned the king against the use of force, and said, "I am able to restrain him."

Then going to meet the king of Kustana (K'iu-sa-ta-na), began to recite choice selections of scripture (*the law*).

The king at first, having no faith, determined to go on with his military preparations. On this the Arhat, taking the robes which were worn by the king in his former condition as a Śrâmaṇêra, showed them to him. Having seen them, the king reached to the knowledge of his previous lives, and he went to the king of Kaśmîr and made profession of his joy and attachment. He then dispersed his troops and returned. The image which he had honoured when a Sha-mi he now respectfully took in front of the army, and came to this kingdom at his request. But having arrived at this spot, he could not get further, and so built this *saṅghârâma;* and calling the priests together, he gave his jewelled headdress for the image, and this is the one now belonging to the figure, the gift of the former king.

To the west of the capital city 150 or 160 li, in the midst of the straight road across a great sandy desert, there are a succession of small hills, formed by the burrowing of rats. I heard the following as the common story:—"In this desert there are rats as big as hedgehogs, their hair of a gold and silver colour. There is a head rat to the company. Every day he comes out of his hole and walks about; when he has finished the other rats follow him. In old days a general of the Hiung-nu came to ravage the border of this country with several tens of myriads of followers. When he had arrived thus far at the rat-mounds, he encamped his soldiers. Then the king of Kustana, who commanded only some few myriads of men, feared that his force was not sufficient to take the offensive. He knew of the wonderful character of these desert rats, and that he had not yet made any religious offering to them; but now he was at a loss where to look for succour. His ministers, too, were all in alarm, and could think of no expedient. At last he determined to offer a religious offering to the rats and request their aid, if by these means his army might be strengthened a little. That night the king of Kustana in a dream[64] saw a great

[64] For these desert rats, which are probably the same as the "golden ants" of Herodotos and Nearkhos, see Mrs. Spiers' *Ancient India*, p. 216. For "the dream" and the destruction of the Assyrian army in Egypt by mice, see Herodotus, Bk. ii. chap. 141.

rat, who said to him, "I wish respectfully to assist you. To-morrow morning put your troops in movement; attack the enemy, and you will conquer."

The king of Kustana, recognising the miraculous character of this intervention, forthwith arrayed his cavalry and ordered his captains to set out before dawn, and at their head, after a rapid march, he fell unexpectedly on the enemy. The Hiung-nu, hearing their approach, were overcome by fear. They hastened to harness their horses and equip their chariots, but they found that the leather of their armour, and their horses' gear, and their bow strings, and all the fastenings of their clothes, had been gnawed by the rats. And now their enemies had arrived, and they were taken in disorder. Thereupon their chief was killed and the principal soldiers made prisoners. The Hiung-nu were terrified on perceiving a divine interposition on behalf of their enemies. The king of Kustana, in gratitude to the rats, built a temple and offered sacrifices; and ever since they have continued to receive homage and reverence, and they have offered to them rare and precious things. Hence, from the highest to the lowest of the people, they pay these rats constant reverence and seek to propitiate them by sacrifices. On passing the mounds they descend from their chariots and pay their respects as they pass on, praying for success as they worship. Others offer clothes, and bows, and arrows; others scents, and flowers, and costly meats. Most of those who practise these religious rites obtain their wishes; but if they neglect them, then misfortune is sure to occur.

To the west of the royal city 5 or 6 li[65] is a convent called Sa-mo-joh (*Samajña*). In the middle of it is a *stûpa* about 100 feet high, which exhibits many miraculous indications (*signs*). Formerly there was an Arhat, who, coming from a distance, took up his abode in this forest, and by his spiritual power shed abroad a miraculous light. Then the king at night-time, being in a tower of

[65] Julien has "fifty or sixty li."

his palace,[66] saw at a distance, in the middle of the wood, brilliant light shining. Asking a number of persons in succession what their opinion was, they all said, "There is a Śramaṇa who has come from far, and is sitting alone in this wood. By the exercise of his supernatural power he spreads abroad this light." The king then ordered his chariot to be equipped, and went in person to the spot. Having seen the illustrious sage, his heart was filled with reverence, and after having offered him every respect, he invited him to come to the palace. The Śramaṇa said, "Living things have their place, and the mind has its place. For me the sombre woods and the desert marshes have attraction. The storeyed halls of a palace and its extensive courts are not suitable for my tastes."

The king hearing this felt redoubled reverence for him, and paid him increased respect. He constructed for him a *saṅghârâma* and raised a *stûpa*. The Śramaṇa, having been invited to do so, took up his abode there.

The king having procured some hundred particles of relics, was filled with joy and thought with himself, "These relics have come late; if they had come before, I could have placed them under this *stûpa*, and then what a miracle of merit it would have been." Going then to the *saṅghârâma*, he asked the Śramaṇa. The Arhat said, "Let not the king be distressed. In order to place them in their proper place you ought to prepare a gold, silver, copper, iron, and stone receptacle, and place them one in the other, in order to contain the relics. The king then gave orders to workmen to do this, and it was finished in a day. Then carrying the relics on an ornamented car (*or*, stand), they brought them to the *saṅghârâma*. At this time the king, at the head of a hundred officers, left the palace (*to witness the procession of the relics*), whilst the beholders amounted to several myriads. Then the Arhat with his right hand raised the *stûpa*, and holding it in his palms, he addressed the king and said, "You can now conceal the relics underneath." Accordingly he dug

[66] *Or*, a double tower; a belvedere.

a place for the chest, and all being done, the Arhat lowered the *stûpa* without hurt or inconvenience.

The beholders, exulting at the miracle, placed their faith in Buddha, and felt increased reverence for his law. Then the king, addressing his ministers, said, "I have heard it said that the power of Buddha is difficult to calculate, and his spiritual abilities difficult to measure. At one time he divided his body into ten million parts; at other times he appeared among Dêvas and men, holding the world in the palm of his hand without disturbing any one, explaining the law and its character in ordinary words, so that men and others, according to their kind, understood it, exhibiting the nature of the law in one uniform way, drawing all men (*things*) to a knowledge of it according to their minds. Thus his spiritual power was peculiarly his own; his wisdom was beyond the power of words to describe. His spirit has passed away, but his teaching remains. Those who are nourished by the sweetness of his doctrine and partake of (*drink*) his instruction; who follow his directions and aim at his spiritual enlightenment, how great their happiness, how deep their insight. You hundred officers ought to honour and respect Buddha; the mysteries of his law will then become clear to you."

To the south-east of the royal city 5 or 6 li is a convent called Lu-shi,[67] which was founded by a queen of a former ruler of the country. In old time this country knew nothing about mulberry trees or silkworms. Hearing that the eastern country had them, they sent an embassy to seek for them. At this time the prince of the eastern kingdom kept the secret and would not give the possession of it to any. He kept guard over his territory and would not permit either the seeds of the mulberry or the silkworms' eggs to be carried off.

The king of Kustana sent off to seek a marriage union

[67] *Lu-shi* means "stag-pierced;" but it is probably a phonetic form in this passage, and is the name of the daughter of the prince of the eastern kingdom.

with a princess of the eastern kingdom (China), in token of his allegiance and submission. The king being well-affected to the neighbouring states acceded to his wish. Then the king of Kustana dispatched a messenger to escort the royal princess and gave the following direction: "Speak thus to the eastern princess,—Our country has neither silk or silken stuffs. You had better bring with you some mulberry seeds and silkworms, then you can make robes for yourself."

The princess, hearing these words, secretly procured the seed of the mulberry and silkworms' eggs and concealed them in her head-dress. Having arrived at the barrier, the guard searched everywhere, but he did not dare to remove the princess's head-dress. Arriving then in the kingdom of Kustana, they stopped on the site afterwards occupied by the Lu-shi *saṅghârâma;* thence they conducted her in great pomp to the royal palace. Here then they left the silkworms and mulberry seeds.

In the spring-time they set the seeds, and when the time for the silkworms had come they gathered leaves for their food; but from their first arrival it was necessary to feed them on different kinds of leaves, but afterwards the mulberry trees began to flourish. Then the queen wrote on a stone the following decree, "It is not permitted to kill the silkworm! After the butterfly has gone, then the silk may be twined off (*the cocoon*). Whoever offends against this rule may he be deprived of divine protection." Then she founded this *saṅghârâma* on the spot where the first silkworms were bred; and there are about here many old mulberry tree trunks which they say are the remains of the old trees first planted. From old time till now this kingdom has possessed silkworms, which nobody is allowed to kill, with a view to take away the silk stealthily. Those who do so are not allowed to rear the worms for a succession of years.

To the south-east of the capital about 200 li or so is a

great river[68] flowing north-west. The people take advantage of it to irrigate their lands. After a time this stream ceased to flow. The king, greatly astonished at the strange event, ordered his carriage to be equipped and went to an Arhat and asked him, "The waters of the great river, which have been so beneficial to man, have suddenly ceased. Is not my rule a just one? are not my benefits (*virtues*) widely distributed through the world? If it be not so, what is my fault, or why is this calamity permitted?"

The Arhat said, "Your majesty governs his kingdom well, and the influence of your rule is for the well-being and peace of your people. The arrest in the flow of the river is on account of the dragon dwelling therein. You should offer sacrifices and address your prayers to him; you will then recover your former benefits (*from the river*)."

Then the king returned and offered sacrifice to the river dragon. Suddenly a woman emerged from the stream, and advancing said to him, "My lord is just dead, and there is no one to issue orders; and this is the reason why the current of the stream is arrested and the husbandmen have lost their usual profits. If your majesty will choose from your kingdom a minister of state of noble family and give him to me as a husband, then he may order the stream to flow as before."

The king said, "I will attend with respect to your request and meet your wishes." The Nâga (*woman*) was rejoiced (*to have obtained the promise of*) a great minister of the country (*as a husband*).

The king having returned, addressed his dependents thus, "A great minister is the stronghold of the state. The pursuit of agriculture is the secret of men's life. Without a strong support, then, there is ruin to the state;

[68] Probably the Karakash river. Its sandy and dry bed is still marked with a dotted line on Shaw's map (High Tartary and Yarkand). Or it may be the Khotan-dâria.

without food there is death to the people. In the presence of such calamities what is to be done?"

A great minister, leaving his seat, prostrated himself and said, "For a long time I have led a useless life, and held an important post without profit to others. Although I have desired to benefit my country, no occasion has offered. Now, then, I pray you choose me, and I will do my best to meet your wishes. In view of the good of the entire people what is the life of one minister? A minister is the support of the country; the people the substance. I beg your majesty not to hesitate. I only ask that, for the purpose of securing merit, I may found a convent."

The king having consented, the thing was done forthwith, and his request complied with. On this the minister asked to be allowed to enter at once the dragon-palace. Then all the chief men of the kingdom made a feast, with music and rejoicing, whilst the minister, clad in white garments and riding a white horse, took leave of the king and respectfully parted with the people of the country. So, pressing on his horse, he entered the river; advancing in the stream, he sank not, till at length, when in the middle of it, he whipped the stream with his lash, and forthwith the water opened in the midst and he disappeared. A short time afterwards the white horse came up and floated on the water, carrying on his back a great sandalwood drum, in which was a letter, the contents of which were briefly these: "Your majesty has not made the least error in selecting me for this office in connection with the spirit (*Nâga*). May you enjoy much happiness and your kingdom be prosperous! Your minister sends you this drum to suspend at the south-east of the city; if an enemy approaches, it will sound first of all."

The river began then to flow, and down to the present time has caused continued advantage to the people.

Many years and months have elapsed since then, and the place where the dragon-drum was hung has long since disappeared, but the ruined convent by the side of the drum-lake still remains, but it has no priests and is deserted.

Three hundred li or so to the east of the royal city is a great desert marsh, upwards of several thousands acres in extent, without any verdure whatever. Its surface is a reddish-black. The old people explain the matter thus: This is the place where an army was defeated. In old days an army of the eastern country numbering a hundred myriads of men invaded the western kingdom. The king of Kustana, on his side, equipped a body of cavalry to the number of ten myriads, and advanced to the east to offer the enemy battle. Coming to this spot, an engagement took place. The troops of the west being defeated, they were cut to pieces and their king was taken prisoner and all their officers killed without leaving one to escape. The ground was dyed with blood, and the traces of it still remain (*in the colour of the earth*).

After going east 30 li or so from the field of battle we come to the town of Pimâ (Pi-mo). Here there is a figure of Buddha in a standing position made of sandalwood. The figure is about twenty feet high. It works many miracles and reflects constantly a bright light. Those who have any disease, according to the part affected, cover the corresponding place on the statue with gold-leaf, and forthwith they are healed. People who address prayers to it with a sincere heart mostly obtain their wishes. This is what the natives say: This image in old days when Buddha was alive was made by Udâyana (U-to-yen-na), king of Kauśâmbî (Kiao-shang-mi). When Buddha left the world, it mounted of its own accord into the air and came to the north of this kingdom, to the town of Ho-lo-lo-kia.[69] The men of this city were rich and prosperous,

[69] Râgha or Raghan, or perhaps Ourgha.

and deeply attached to heretical teaching, with no respect for any other form of religion. From the time the image came there it showed its divine character, but no one paid it respect.

Afterwards there was an Arhat who bowed down and saluted the image; the people of the country were alarmed at his strange appearance and dress, and they hastened to tell the king. The king issued a decree that the stranger should be covered over with sand and earth. At this time the Arhat's body being covered with sand, he sought in vain for food as nourishment.[70] There was a man whose heart was indignant at such treatment; he had himself always respected the image and honoured it with worship, and now seeing the Arhat in this condition, he secretly gave him food. The Arhat being on the point of departure, addressed this man and said, "Seven days hence there will be a rain of sand and earth which will fill this city full, and there will in a brief space be none left alive. You ought to take measures for escape in knowledge of this. They have covered me with earth, and this is the consequence to them." Having said this he departed, disappearing in a moment.

The man, entering the city, told the tidings to his relatives, but they did nothing but mock at him. The second day a great wind suddenly arose, which carried before it all the dirty soil, whilst there fell various precious substances.[71] Then the men continued to revile the man who had told them (*about the sand and earth*).

But this man, knowing in his heart what must certainly happen, excavated for himself an underground passage leading outside the city, and there lay concealed. On the seventh day, in the evening, just after the division of the

[70] It would seem that his body was buried up to his neck.

[71] Stas. Julien prefers substituting *Sha-tu* in the text for *Tsah-pao*. In that case it would be "sand and earth;" but, if this be so, why did the people still find fault with the prophet?

night, it rained sand and earth, and filled the city.[72] This man escaped through his tunnel and went to the east, and, arriving in this country, he took his abode in Pima. Scarcely had the man arrived when the statue also appeared there. He forthwith paid it worship in this place and dared not go farther (*change his abode*). According to the old account it is said, "When the law of Śâkya is extinct then this image will enter the dragon-palace."

The town of Ho-lo-lo-kia is now a great sand mound. The kings of the neighbouring countries and persons in power from distant spots have many times wished to excavate the mound and take away the precious things buried there; but as soon as they have arrived at the borders of the place, a furious wind has sprung up, dark clouds have gathered together from the four quarters of heaven, and they have become lost to find their way.

To the east of the valley of Pima[73] we enter a sandy desert, and after going 200 li or so, we come to the town of Ni-jang. This city is about 3 or 4 li in circuit; it stands in a great marsh; the soil of the marsh is warm and soft, so that it is difficult to walk on it. It is covered with rushes and tangled herbage, and there are no roads or pathways; there is only the path that leads to the city, through which one can pass with difficulty, so that every one coming and going must pass by this town. The king of Kustana makes this the guard of his eastern frontier.

Going east from this, we enter a great drifting sand desert. These sands extend like a drifting flood for a great distance, piled up or scattered according to the wind. There is no trace left behind by travellers, and

[72] For an account of sand-buried cities, and particularly of Kaṭak, see Bellew, *Kashmir and Kashgar*, pp. 370, 371. Also for Pimâ, probably near Keria, see Yule, *Marco Polo*, vol. ii., Appendix M.; and also vol. i. chap. xxxvii. and *note* 1. It is probably the *Han-mo* of Sung Yun.

[73] Pimâ was probably the Pein of Marco Polo. See Yule, *ut supra*.

oftentimes the way is lost, and so they wander hither and thither quite bewildered, without any guide or direction. So travellers pile up the bones of animals as beacons. There is neither water nor herbage to be found, and hot winds frequently blow. When these winds rise, then both men and beasts become confused and forgetful, and then they remain perfectly disabled (*sick*). At times sad and plaintive notes are heard and piteous cries, so that between the sights and sounds of this desert men get confused and know not whither they go. Hence there are so many who perish in the journey. But it is all the work of demons and evil spirits.

Going on 400 li or so, we arrive at the old kingdom of Tu-ho-lo (Tukhâra).[74] This country has long been deserted and wild. All the towns are ruined and uninhabited.

From this going east 600 li or so, we come to the ancient kingdom of Che-mo-t'o-na,[75] which is the same as the country called Ni-mo. The city walls still stand loftily, but the inhabitants are dispersed and scattered.

From this going north-east a thousand li or so, we come to the old country of Navapa (Na-fo-po), which is the same as Leu-lan.[76] We need not speak of the mountains and valleys and soil of this neighbouring country. The habits of the people are wild and unpolished, their manners not uniform; their preferences and dislikes are not always the same. There are some things difficult to verify to the utmost, and it is not always easy to recollect all that has occurred.

[74] This was probably the extreme limit of the old kingdom of Tu-ho-lo towards the east. When the Yue-chi spread eastwards they dispossessed the old Turanian population.

[75] This is the Tso-moh of Sung-yun. It must have been near Sorghák of Prejevalsky's map. For some interesting notes on this place see Kingsmill, *China Review*, vol. viii. No. 3, p. 163.

[76] Also called Shen-shen; see *China Review*, loc. cit. Kingsmill makes Navapa equal to Navapura, *i.e.*, Neapolis.

But the traveller has written a brief summary of all he witnessed or heard. All were desirous to be instructed, and wherever he went his virtuous conduct drew the admiration of those who beheld it. And why not? in the case of one who had gone alone and afoot from Ku, and had completed such a mission by stages of myriads of li! [77]

[77] M. Julien renders this passage: "How could he be compared simply to such men as have gone on a mission with a single car, and who have traversed by post a space of a thousand li?" But if the symbol *Ku* be for *Ku-sse*, *i.e.*, "the ancient land of the Uigurs" (see vol. i. p. 17, n. 51), then I think the translation I have given is the right one. Respecting this land of Kau-chang, we are told it was called Ming-fo-chau in the Han period, and Ku-sse-ti (the land of Ku-sse) during the Tang period (*vid.* the map called *Yu-ti-tsun-t'si*).

END OF BOOK XII.

INDEX.

References to the Introduction are indicated by black figures.

D.

E.

F.

O.

P.

R.

W.